Plateaus of Freedom

Plateaus of Freedom

Nationality, Culture, and State Security in Canada, 1940–1960

Mark Kristmanson

OXFORD
UNIVERSITY PRESS

UNIVERSITY PRESS

70 Wynford Drive, Don Mills, Ontario M3C 1J9
www.oup.com/ca

Oxford University Press is a department of the University of Oxford.
It furthers the University's objective of excellence in research, scholarship,
and education by publishing worldwide in

Oxford New York
Auckland Bangkok Buenos Aires Cape Town Chennai
Dar es Salaam Delhi Hong Kong Istanbul Karachi Kolkata
Kuala Lumpur Madrid Melbourne Mexico City Mumbai Nairobi
São Paulo Shanghai Taipei Tokyo Toronto

Oxford is a trade mark of Oxford University Press
in the UK and in certain other countries

Published in Canada
by Oxford University Press

Copyright © Oxford University Press Canada 2003

The moral rights of the author have been asserted

Database right Oxford University Press (maker)

First published 2003

All rights reserved. No part of this publication may be reproduced,
stored in a retrieval system, or transmitted, in any form or by any means,
without the prior permission in writing of Oxford University Press,
or as expressly permitted by law, or under terms agreed with the appropriate
reprographics rights organization. Enquiries concerning reproduction
outside the scope of the above should be sent to the Rights Department,
Oxford University Press, at the address above.

You must not circulate this book in any other binding or cover
and you must impose this same condition on any acquirer.

National Library of Canada Cataloguing in Publication
Kristmanson, Mark, 1960–
Plateaus of freedom: nationality, culture and state security in Canada,
1940–1960 / Mark Kristmanson

(Canadian social history series)
Includes bibliographical references and index.
ISBN 0–19–541866–2

1. Internal security—Canada—History—20th century.   2. Intelligence service—Canada—
History—20th century.   3. Canada—Cultural policy—History—20th century.
I. Title.   II. Series.

FC95.4.K75 2002   971.063   C2002–905384–6   F1021.2.K75 2002

1 2 3 4 – 06 05 04 03

Cover Design: Brett Miller

This book is printed on permanent (acid-free) paper ∞.
Printed in Canada

Contents

Acknowledgements   vi

Abbreviations   vii

Introduction   ix

1   Characterizations of Tracy Philipps   1

2   Love Your Neighbour:
The RCMP and the National Film Board, 1948–1953   49

3   Remembering to Forget   86

4   State Security and Cultural Administration:
The Case of Peter Dwyer   95

5   Pulp History: Repossessing the Gouzenko Myth   137

6   I Came to Sing: Paul Robeson on the Border   181

Conclusion   228

Notes   234

Index   289

Acknowledgements

The author gratefully acknowledges the attentive critical support of Léa Deschamps, Graham Carr, Sherry Simon, Mary Vipond, Stanley French, and Ian McKay. Dorian and Kyrie provided their uncritical support all along. The manuscript benefited from discussions with friends, colleagues, specialists, and family members, including Robert McMillan, Michael McLoughlin, Nicholas Cull, Myron Momryk, Andrew Bartlett, Ernest Bauer, Paul Eprile, and David Kristmanson, as well as from written comments by Richard Tallman and two anonymous readers. Elizabeth Harrison explained the significance of her painting and kindly agreed to its reproduction. Daniel J. Leab edited Chapter 2, 'Love Your Neighbour', for *Film History*. New Theatre of Ottawa produced the documentary play *Blue Panopticon* based on this work. Thanks are extended to those who granted the author interviews, to the archivists, librarians, and Access to Information officers who assisted the research, and to the National Library of Canada for providing a congenial research environment over a number of years. Encouragement came unexpectedly at a crucial juncture from Gregory Kealey and Laura Macleod, who guided the project to completion.

Abbreviations

AMTORG	Soviet Purchasing Mission in North America
ATIP	Access to Information and Privacy (Canada)
BBC	British Broadcasting Corporation
BSC	British Security Co-ordination
BUP	British United Press
CBC	Canadian Broadcasting Corporation
CBNRC	Communications Branch, National Research Council (Canada)
CCA	Canadian Conference of the Arts
CCCC	Committee on Co-operation in Canadian Citizenship
CCF	Co-operative Commonwealth Federation (Canada)
CFI	Canadian Film Insititute
CIA	Central Intelligence Agency (US)
CNE	Canadian National Exhibition
FO	Foreign Office (UK)
CSE	Canadian Security Establishment
CSIS	Canadian Security Intelligence Service
DEA	Department of External Affairs (Canada)
DL(2)	Defence Liaison Two (Canada)
DND	Department of National Defence (Canada)
DNWS	Department of National War Services (Canada)
FBI	Federal Bureau of Investigation (US)
FLQ	Front de libération du Québec
GRU	main intelligence directorate (USSR)
HUAC	House Un-American Activities Committee
IMF	International Monetary Fund
IUMMSW	International Union of Mine, Mill and Smelter Workers
LPP	Labour Progressive Party (Canada)
MI5	British domestic security service
MI6	British foreign intelligence service
NAC	National Archives of Canada
NATO	North Atlantic Treaty Organization

NDP	New Democratic Party of Canada
NFB	National Film Board of Canada
NKVD	Soviet political intelligence directorate
NRC	National Research Council of Canada
NSA	National Security Agency (US)
OUDS	Oxford University Dramatic Society
OSS	Office of Strategic Services (US)
PCO	Privy Council Office (Canada)
PID	Political Intelligence Directorate (UK)
PRO	Public Record Office (UK)
RCMP	Royal Canadian Mounted Police
SIGINT	signals intelligence
SIS	Secret Intelligence Service, MI6 (UK)
SOE	Special Operations Executive (UK)
TUC	Trades Union Council (UK)
UAW-CIO	United Auto Workers-Congress of Industrial Organizations
UCC	Ukrainian Canadian Committee
UNESCO	United Nations Educational, Scientific and Cultural Organization
UNRRA	United Nations Relief and Rehabilitation Agency
WO	War Office (UK)

Introduction

There was a cultural logic to this cultural struggle . . . and the powers-that-be realized it before I did.

Paul Robeson, 1958

Ottawa, 1993

In a small, wood-panelled dining room in the Ottawa Press Club a dwindling group of retired security intelligence officials, along with some of their counterparts who once served in branches of Canada's federal cultural agencies, meet weekly for lunch, as they have since the 1950s. Invited to sit in, I hear them reminisce, exchange opinions on current affairs, and turn over a few well-chewed enigmas. One former External Affairs man explains the exact status of the Saarland in 1938–9; another marvels at the lax security in the present Privy Council Office. Despite long familiarity there is an air of formality. An occasional flash of steel in the repartee serves as a reminder that these men (they are all men) once wielded considerable power.

My interest lies in one of the founders of this lunch group, Peter Dwyer, who died in 1973, and for a moment their eyes turn to me as I wonder aloud about his dual role in Canada's national culture and state security, and how far each realm may have extended into the other. I mention a coincidence that had caught my attention a few years earlier when I studied the founding of the Canada Council and the Arts Council of Great Britain: i.e., before Peter Dwyer came to Canada in 1950 and became a key architect of the Canada Council for the Arts, drafting its enacting legislation and eventually becoming its Director, he had been Britain's highest-ranking secret service officer in North America. Might his dual career in state security and cultural administration signal some deeper Cold War undercurrent flowing beneath my own career in Canadian theatre and arts administration?

A pause settles around the lunch table until, finally, someone says, 'Well, Dwyer was a remarkable fellow', and another mumbles, 'Cultural attachés? No, no . . . passport officers', and the conversation moves on.

Afterwards, as the party rises to disperse, a man who once directed the Security Service of the Royal Canadian Mounted Police shakes my hand. Fixing his steely eyes on me, he says, '*Kristmanson* . . . that's Icelandic.'

'No,' I reply, 'it's Canadian.'

'Well,' he smiles, 'we watched your traffic.'

He meant that while he headed the Intelligence section of Canada's Department of External Affairs he had read Icelandic diplomatic transmissions intercepted by the top-secret Communications Branch of the National Research Council (CBNRC). And though he offered his remark lightly, it stayed with me. I understood then that my name marks me as 'already-different' in the gaze of Canada's state security apparatus. It is a style of thinking—indeed, a political rationality or a cultural logic—of which I had either been innocent, or else chose not to remember. It is only a slight exaggeration to say that this prompted me to look closely at intelligence and national security in what was slated to be a more conventional treatment of culture and citizenship in twentieth-century Canada.

Five years later, as I approached the end of this project, I happened to see the same man again, aged but still dapper. I observed him turning a corner on to Sparks Street, making his way to the weekly lunch party. The spring in his step reflected his status in the secret world: it was the step of 'the man who knows' and for whom the restricted realm of secret knowledge is both sufficient and satisfactory. It was the step of a man whose adversaries have been laid so low as to be almost beyond remembering.

There were others inside this magic circle for whom the confinement of secrecy was uncomfortable, who regretted the intellectual constraints induced by the Cold War, who felt disgust at the silent civil struggle that purified the state's departments and agencies of internal dissent. They watched their little 'secret society' turn itself inside out to create a society of secrets. The evident rudderlessness of Canada's flagship cultural institutions during their first post-Cold War decade seemed to justify that sense of uneasiness. For my part, I have come to know more about these men and their shadowy world than I thought one could, certainly more than most people want to.

Censorship, Intelligence, and Propaganda

Canadians are not accustomed to thinking of censorship, secret intelligence, and propaganda as a single entity. Much less do they consider that these covertly militaristic activities have anything to do with culture. Even the cautious arcana of security and intelligence studies treat these three basic branches of state security separately, and rarely associate them with culture. The result of persistent archival digging, this book sets out to unearth connections among intelligence, censorship, and propaganda, and more specifically between national culture and state security in mid-twentieth-century Canada.

What will be illuminated? For one thing, the extent to which a security imperative conditioned cultural policies in Canada during and after World War II. Who remembers today, for example, how official multiculturalism evolved hand in hand with the security apparat during World War II? Or that a substantial corps of cultural experts—from translators and interpreters to information-gatherers and analysts— accumulated within the Royal Canadian Mounted Police, the Canadian Security Intelligence Service, and the Canadian Security Establishment, not to mention the Department of External Affairs, the Department of National Defence, and the Immigration Department? Moreover, the parallel latticework of cultural institutions, including the Canadian Broadcasting Corporation, the National Film Board, and the National Arts Centre and National Museums, shaped national culture in conformance with fairly rigid Cold War protocols. This book questions to what extent this great policy canopy was indeed a police canopy that suffocated intellectual and cultural alternatives with officially blessed mediocrity. And if cultural policy *was* commandeered by national security during the Cold War, what is to be done about it now?

In cultural studies the term 'security' might best be described as an 'absent presence'. The influential post-war critic Raymond Williams did not mention it explicitly in his well-known book *Keywords* (1983). On the other hand, his 'vocabulary of culture and society' explores adjacent terms such as 'bureaucracy', 'communication', 'hegemony', 'nationalism', and 'psychological'. He helped launch British cultural studies with *Culture and Society* (1958), a book that culminates in a strained appreciation of George Orwell: lapsed socialist, wartime radio propagandist, and ambivalent harbinger of Cold War culture. In *Problems in Materialism and Culture* (1980) Williams opens with 'A Hundred Years of *Culture and Anarchy*', an essay connecting Matthew Arnold's peevish sense of insecurity in the late nineteenth century with the authoritarian tendencies of the New Right a century later. Even if he did not use the term directly, one suspects that Williams was aware enough of Cold War culture's 'security' consciousness. (Of his fellow Arts Council trustees he once quipped that you only have to 'shift the accent a little, to "trusties", to name the obvious danger.')[1]

In suggesting that 'security' is a neglected dimension in cultural studies, I, too, propose to shift the accent a little. Setting aside questions about ethnicity, sexualities, and youth subcultures that preoccupy contemporary cultural studies, I have combed the archive to see how national culture *sensed for and managed* what is alien, marginal, or unfamiliar. By bringing 'security' to bear on Williams's central notion of a culture acting as a 'signifying system' I want to shift the emphasis away from 'signification' towards sensing, from 'identity' towards identification and the systematic ways cultures attune themselves to apprehend and regulate human differences.[2]

Masts, Totems, and Antennas

'Secure' or 'security': the Latin root is *cura*, or care. Pre-modern usage of 'security' meant being cared for, protected from, or not exposed to danger. In its modern usage, security is attached to 'nation' to form 'national security', and this limits the term in space and time, locating it in narratives of state development and technological advance. I will return to what this might mean for the field of arts policy and for Canadian Studies, but for now it is enough to say that during and after World

Haida poles, Masset, Queen Charlotte Islands, ca *1881.* Photo: Edward Dossetter. Courtesy British Columbia Provincial Archives, B-03588, detail.

War II Canada's censorship, intelligence, and propaganda components clustered in an institutional array that drew as much from Canada's diverse cultural resources as it did from the revolution in distance communications.

To analyze a culture as a collective sensing system means locating the points where it is seized with the problem of its own security. A culture of security is a necessary feature of any successful inhabitation of a landscape. Yi-Fu Tuan's global historical catalogue of territorial insecurity among human groups suggests that anywhere the sign 'culture' is invoked, a latent reference is made to a concern for security. 'In a sense,' he writes, 'every human construction is a component in a landscape of fear because it exists to contain chaos.'[3] Cultures thus not only permit the assertion of unique group identities as clans, tribes, or nations, but they also set up regimes of identification in order to sense out and manage the alien, the marginal, the Other.

Prehistoric Aboriginal peoples maintained their cultural presence on the northwest coast of North America through a non-scientific knowledge of nature: the sensorial acuity of sentinels and trackers, messengers' fleetness of foot, a feeling

Installations at Camperdown, NS, 1949. NRC Collection, National Archives of Canada (NAC), PA 198296.

for the tides, weather, animal behaviour, and the interpretation of shamans' visions. According to a Haida proverb, life is as sharp as a knife, as precarious as walking on a razor-thin blade. They vested their individual and collective security in the body, in manual implements, in the shaman's vision and their totems.

The art of the Haida people is pertinent in this regard. In the 1881 photo of the village of Masset on the Queen Charlotte Islands, one finds totem poles crested with sentinel figures the Haida called 'watchmen'. In a cultural sense, one can imagine these great poles operating as *paleo-radar*, establishing each house and the shore-line village itself as an immediate zone of protection.

I cite this example because, in the 1940s, these magnificent poles quite literally were superseded by electronic interception antennas—exactly like the five-point Adcock array seen above—installed at the Canadian military's signals intelligence station located just above old Masset village.[4]

The counter-intelligence expert Peter Dwyer once referred in jest to these inter-cept arrays as 'quinqueremes of the senses', and indeed, the masts of modern Canada's electromagnetic sensorium distantly echo the spars of its early colonizing vessels. Juxtaposing totems with antennas evokes a way of thinking about culture and security, about dwelling versus occupying, and a migration of human sensory capacities from the body into a technological realm. It evokes the *sentience* of culture and links this to the circulation of information (and disinformation) through the nation's censorship-propaganda-intelligence complex during the Cold War.

The 'State' within the State

The National Archives reveal the interstices of national culture and state security to be the site of a neurotic 'state' within the modern technocratic state, one that liberal political theorists and nationalist historians have hesitated to acknowledge. What unites national culture and state security is an illiberal element of mistrust that underscores the citizen's bond with the liberal state, a 'forced choice' that inducts each individual subject into the grid of nationalities. If one does not wish to remain the citizen of one nation it may be possible to emigrate and 'choose' to be naturalized as the citizen of another. Yet Herbert Spencer surely was prescient when he wrote 150 years ago that 'a long time will pass before the right to *ignore* the state will be generally admitted, even in theory.'[5] To decline the attribution of citizenship and nationality would be to decline one's essential participation in a culture of security.

'Denizens' may or may not have forgone various rights that citizens enjoy on what liberal theorists call the 'plateau of equality'. But ineluctably, as the archive shows, any hesitation or inability to participate in a culture of security invited repressive consequences such as surveillance, detention, and expulsion. On the other hand, for 'hyphenated' Canadians, ascension to the liberal state's plateau of equality sometimes came at the price of becoming a police informant.

This intercultural tension suffused the censorship-intelligence-propaganda complex that took shape in Canada during World War II and persisted through the Cold War. 'Nationality', taken as a geopolitical social system, is, to some extent, a coercive prerequisite to liberal conceptions of individual freedom.[6] This underlying coercion induces recognizable symptoms, and in the following chapters Canada's Cold War culture of security is explored through manifestations of this nervous 'state' within the state as an institutional instrumentality and also as a pathological 'complex'.

The National Library of Canada, through whose good auspices much of this research was conducted, is an easy place to locate this 'state' within the state. It requires no more than sitting at a reference terminal and checking the holdings of periodicals published in minority languages. One finds an astonishingly rich collection that spans much of the twentieth century. Casual browsers must be impressed with a multicultural ethos so even-handed that an almost complete set of minority-language publications exists in its National Library alongside the majority-language collections.

The National Archives' internal records correct this impression. The story begins in 1926 when RCMP Commissioner Courtland Starnes wrote to the Dominion Archivist, Arthur Doughty:

> I have among my records . . . a certain number of newspapers, most, though not all, of a more or less subversive nature. They are pressing upon my accommodation and it has occurred to me that you might like to take charge of them.[7]

Another load arrived in 1928, and yet another in 1933. Deputy Commissioner J.W. Spalding advised Doughty that he 'had the honour to send by police truck, as of ultimate interest to yourself, a number of bundles of more or less seditious publications . . . . It has occurred to me that it would be advisable to preserve them for the future.'

In November 1951, the National Archivist received another RCMP communication marked 'secret':

> During approximately the last ten years, this Force has been in receipt of a large number of foreign language newspapers published in Canada. They are comprised of Communist and Nationalist publications, in the latter case, the majority being in the Ukrainian language. The communist papers are in the languages of various prominent ethnic groups in Canada.
>
> . . . For the years up to 1950, we have practically a complete set of duplicate issues.
>
> . . . We have a considerable amount of Italian material in the forms of books, periodicals and newspapers of a Fascist nature.[8]

Such a rich resource for cultural history research exists *only* because ethnocultural communities were the objects of the liberal state's distrust and surveillance, and this presents one face of the culture-security paradox. The xenophobic and suspicious mounted policemen were, equally, the sensitive custodians of materials for a plural, multilingual, and non-cultural-nationalist history.

Multiculturalism in Canada is popularly thought to have begun in the Trudeau era but its true origins lie early in the century, when immigration brought Southern and Eastern Europeans to North America in vast numbers; its first official expression occurred during World War II. By 1940 the allegiance of the so-called 'nationalities' groups to the British war effort was of sufficient concern to prompt a new type of policy initiative, and on the scene to 'do the actual building' was Tracy Philipps, imperial intelligence veteran, eccentric minor aristocrat, former member of Lawrence of Arabia's immortal company.

Philipps's Canadian story, the matter of Chapter 1, has an eerie echo in the novel *The Man Who Knew* (1927), a story of colonial espionage that thinly disguises Philipps as its hero, 'Phillip Tracey'. Before being hustled out of Canadian service in 1944, Philipps evolved a strange and intricate network that illuminates the murky workings of wartime censorship, intelligence, and propaganda. He remains a stubborn paradox: still revered in some quarters for championing the cause of ethnocultural minorities in Ottawa, and yet ridiculed by historians as a crank who impeded the development of a rationalized multicultural policy.

One of the National Film Board's first wartime propaganda successes was a feature called *Peoples of Canada* that extolled the virtues of a multicultural society. NFB founder John Grierson was quick to exploit this theme and he made Canadian Icelanders, Poles, and Ukrainians the subjects of other NFB films. Moreover, he openly championed cinema as a means of conditioning people to the duties and obligations of citizenship.

The origins of the Film Board as a propaganda agency are known but over-shadowed by accounts of a post-war 'security scare' that shook the Board to its foundations. The RCMP undertook what it called a 'full scale clean-out' of supposed subversives after the Soviet defector Igor Gouzenko named NFB employees as spies, including Grierson's secretary. Chapter 2 examines recently released RCMP files documenting a witch hunt that led to many more firings and forced resignations (more than 40) than have ever been revealed (just three). In the midst of this purge, the animator Norman McLaren made his Oscar-winning film *Love Your Neighbour*, obliquely criticizing not just the RCMP Security Service but the Griersonian vision of nationalized cinema spectators. Despite McLaren's left-wing inclinations, the Security Service did not press for the dismissal of this perennial prize winner. Instead, two of his young assistants were targeted. McLaren's direct and indirect resistance to these actions helps reveal a hidden continuity of purpose between the two neighbours on the Rideau, the NFB and the RCMP.

Ignoring the Sky

The remaining chapters engage with Canada's post-war culture of secrecy, reopening the question of how the space for intellectual political freedom contracted after 1945, and the way emerging post-colonial cognitive models were, as one vigilante Canadian historian puts it, 'thrown forcibly into the dustbin'. To introduce this manoeuvre in cultural policy I will take as an example CBC Chairman Arnold Davidson Dunton's 1954 convocation address at the University of Saskatchewan.[9]

Ten years earlier the newspaperman Dunton had been John Grierson's protégé and he succeeded Grierson as head of the Wartime Information Board. With some discomfort, Dunton adapted himself to the post-progressive era, taking over the CBC as Wartime Information staff were absorbed into the various information-related government departments. In this 1954 address, 'Freedom for Whom?', Dunton laid out the liberal dilemma: how to defend the West's cherished freedoms while still reining in Canadian Communists, who exploited such freedoms in the hope of wrecking liberal democracy. 'Right within our own borders communism works to beset and bedevil the cause of freedom', beguiling people with falsehoods and tainting worthy causes by infiltrating legitimate organizations:

> What do we do? . . . If we tried to ban expression of even just the fundamental doctrines of communism we still could not escape the fact that we would be putting a restraint on thought and discussion. Once a society starts banning mere discussion it can hardly call itself free.

At the same time, 'we know the communists are actually partners in a long range plot' to destroy freedom. 'This', Dunton claimed, 'is the dilemma of our kind of democracy.'

Dunton cautioned that capitalism and technological progress have their dangers, too. The rise of mass communications, he acknowledged, had concentrated the means of information into just a few hands. No one can avoid the fact that broadcasting 'is monopolistic by nature' and that its commercial imperative tends towards censorship: 'you might as well try and ignore the sky', he said. Therein lay the importance of the CBC as a safeguard to free expression, 'free from any government control'. He added that 'we in it are very conscious of our responsibility.'

Dunton did not burden his audience with details concerning how he discharged this responsibility, despite an edge of anguish underscoring his words. He did not mention his suppression of a program about the Russian defector Gouzenko in the winter of 1946, nor his regular policing of program content in order to 'avoid distortion'. (In one instance, he ordered the Citizens' Forum 'Have We Freedom of Expression in the Press?' changed to 'How Could Canadian Radio Better Serve the Public Interest?') His acquiescence in the purging of Sally Solomon, Stuart Griffiths, and others from the CBC's International Service on ideological grounds in 1948 passed without remark. He was silent about his cancellation of a live broadcast of Rimsky-Korsakov's opera, *May Night*, in 1952 at the behest of RCMP Inspector John Leopold, and he did not alert the University of Saskatchewan students to the CBC's internal ban preventing the singer and activist Paul Robeson from appearing on its programs.[10]

Equally, he avoided mention of any risk he may have run by defending a suspect person or program. Instead, Dunton called for greater 'public understanding and interest', granting the CBC the widest mandate possible under the circumstances, and for Canadians to trust CBC executives to represent fairly the spectrum of opinion. 'The first safeguard for free movement of ideas to people by mass means', he intoned, 'should come from the sense of responsibility of those who control the means.' This circular formulation was the best he could offer the students, but he did warn them, unflinchingly, that 'at the university you have known a freedom of the mind that you may not quite know again.'

By the time Dunton presented a convocation address on the same theme at the University of New Brunswick in Fredericton three years later, the device of cultural nationalism had resolved the internal tensions that marked the earlier speech.[11] Gone were the direct references to communism. The word was not mentioned at all. Rather, Dunton was concerned to give the word 'freedom' a new inflection, and he answered his previous question 'Freedom for Whom?' in the title of the new speech: 'Freedom for Minds'. With the official launch of the Canada Council just three months away, Dunton let the students in on the new line of thinking.

He introduced it by stages. First, he allowed that the universities were islands of free thought, but ones that were greatly affected 'by the surrounding mental climate'. He drew a metaphor from fluid dynamics: 'ideas flow in the society around [universities] as well as within their own confines.' The rise of mass communications was viewed by Dunton as a part of human progress that cannot be undone; to suggest such a possibility 'is like saying the flow of the St Lawrence River should be reversed.' Between 1952 and 1957, 60 per cent of Canadians had invested close to a billion dollars outfitting themselves with television sets, and they 'appear to be spending well over twenty hours a week watching them.' The danger of concentrating media ownership in a few hands ought to be obvious, he said, and he stressed the importance of public broadcasting as the bastion against the possibility of 'thought control'.

Dunton had cleared the stage for his new concept of 'freedom', which he defined as 'the opportunity for Canadians effectively to communicate among themselves through the airwaves'. There must be the freedom, he said, for 'the output of Canadian minds to circulate among Canadians'. It was a credo that would occupy cultural politics in Canada for the next three decades, painting over the rich mural of dissent left over from the progressive era.

The Conspiratorial Text

Parachuted into the middle distance of a historical vista, the interdisciplinary historian ventures outward in concentric rings, eschewing the comfortable spatial orientation of the Quattrocento perspective that foregrounds objects against a unified background and historically scheduled time. Aurally, a kind of textual 'echolocation' gives some sense of the surrounding environment. Restricted to what one can know immediately, the terrain easily can seem like a landscape of conspiracy, a fearful and suspicious space in the political unconscious. Merely taking the jump into a restricted zone of information betrays one's desire for some alternative solidarity.

Yet, the embarrassment of transgression can be productive in unexpected ways. As Fredric Jameson writes:

> the 'conspiratorial text' . . . whatever other messages it emits or implies, may also be taken to constitute an unconscious, collective effort of where we are and what landscapes and forces confront us in a later twentieth century whose abominations are heightened by their concealment and their bureaucratic impersonality.[12]

With the conspiracy genre, Jameson continues, 'it is the gesture that counts.' Definitive proof of any conspiratorial hypothesis is less important than 'the intent to hypothesize, in the desire called cognitive mapping—therein lies the beginning of wisdom.' At some 'deeper level of our collective fantasy . . . we think about the social system all the time, a deeper level that also allows us to slip our political thoughts past a liberal and anti-political censorship.'[13]

The purpose of this study is not to unearth a grand conspiracy but rather to render in narrative how culture and security were caught up in a *self-organizing* intensification of 'nationality' as a global system in the middle decades of the twentieth century. The resolution of World War II in something new called the Cold War accelerated Canada's transition from British to American tutelage—and no doubt numerous conspiracies were hatched by various interested parties. But underlying the giant swells of national interest, and to some extent irrespective of them, one discerns a tidal rise of nationality as a system. This system discreetly regulated cultural differences throughout the era of decolonization, rapid population movements, accelerating informatics, and mass communications.

For this reason, the distinction of nationalism from nationality is germane to what follows; it provides a way of seeing through the publicity and propaganda promoting cultural nationalism into the endemic and systemic secrecy imposed by nationality as a global system. Chapter 3 reflects on the primacy of official secrecy over freedom of information, arguing that secrecy and even 'forgetting' are national civic obligations that prefigure the citizen's so-called 'right to know'. By mid-century, one finds a rich paradox of the new Anglo-Canadian nationalism loudly proclaiming its sovereign uniqueness even as the silent isomorphism of nationality enmeshed its citizens in the post-colonial international grid of security states. The immense intellectual concentration on the 'problem' of nationalism after the fall of the Berlin Wall in 1989 is a fascinating indicator of a severe disturbance that slowly, almost imperceptibly, is repoliticizing the notion of nationality, a regime that passed unchallenged through the Cold War.

The approach I have taken seeks to reauthorize memories and states of affairs that never 'made it', historically. These data never were integrated in Canada's processing of its own history. For the most part, the narratives that follow are composed of documentary debris, but debris still encoded with historical potential. This potential depends on readers. It trusts that borne along in history's dispersed freight are disused, outmoded, perhaps even censored ways of thinking. It assumes that in their solitary wanderings readers carry not just maps to convey them through unfamiliar landscapes, but also, rattling loose in the bottom of their packs, what Michel de Certeau calls 'the seeds of alternative traces'.[14] Such retro-potential is not directly 'activist'—historical writing only rarely can be—but nonetheless these seeds may yet have the potential to *reactivate*, and this will be necessary to the invention of new socio-cultural realities adapted finely to their time and their place. The three chapters comprising the second half of this study concern such potentialities.

It seems far-fetched to suggest that the redesign of Canada's Cold War government security measures and the task of fashioning the new national arts council proposed by the Massey Commission should have been assigned to a single official. Yet that is exactly what happened. In the early 1950s a former senior British Intelligence officer, Peter Dwyer, juggled both culture and security briefs within the Privy Council Office.

Who was this self-effacing man who had such influence in Canadian institutions and Canadian national identity? Chapter 4 follows him from his recruitment to theatre and to espionage at Oxford, through active war service as an intelligence officer, to his participation in the Gouzenko affair, his exposure of nuclear spy Klaus Fuchs, his shadowy role in Canadian security intelligence, and his directorship of the Canada Council. Dwyer was a wit and an allegorist, and a steely proponent of a top-down Eurocentric cultural policy. He was a veritable impresario of secrecy. But on the opening night of his play, *Hoodman-Blind*, in 1953 his net of secrets was about to unravel. That the Peter Dwyer story is not legendary is a testament to Canada's culture of secrecy.

Dwyer's privy information still retains its charge in part because it is tied to his involvement in the Gouzenko affair. Close study of a wartime painting by Elizabeth Harrison in Chapter 5 hypothesizes a revision of the received history of the

Gouzenko case. The defector's autobiography, *This Was My Choice*, a masterful combination of Gouzenko's own prose with ghost-written propaganda, puts forward the basic misinformation used to such devastating effect: namely, that in September 1945 he fled the Soviet embassy in Ottawa of his own volition. After more than 50 years, this account of the defection has achieved almost architectural solidity in Canadian historiography. Yet no available primary documents conclusively support it. Indeed, the available evidence points a different way. Interdisciplinary techniques and fresh sources strip away the 'papier mâché' history layered upon it during the Cold War decades. These findings support better the hypothesis that a 'friendly' secret service engineered the defection behind the backs of the Canadian authorities as part of a wider reorientation vis-à-vis the Soviet Union at the end of World War II.

How can one be certain that vibrant cultural alternatives were curtailed by the events introduced above? Is it not possible that the post-war national culture simply took its natural course by favouring the strongest contenders? The Canadian journeys of Paul Robeson provide a case study of the rise and decline of an alternative cultural formation that is now largely discredited or forgotten. Robeson was made the object of Western censorship, intelligence, and propaganda so intensively that the final chapter reconsiders the 'threat' he presented, his triumphs, and his ultimate demise. While it is true that his unwavering pro-Soviet stance left him vulnerable to criticism, his RCMP file (running to more than 1,200 pages) reveals a more complex subject, one bound up with songs, languages, and the dissemination of an intercultural project that far exceeded his characterization as a Soviet stooge. His 1952 concert at the Peace Arch border crossing south of Vancouver brings into sharp focus the contours of the 'national security state' and its uses of cultural nationalism. The Robeson concert opens up a forgotten space within 'nationality' wherein an emergent left-wing discourse was effectively blocked half a century ago.

My approach in examining the influence on security and culture of such figures as Phillipps, McLaren, Dwyer, Gouzenko, and Robeson draws upon various fields of inquiry. The historical characters who emerged from the archive into this text were themselves, with one or two exceptions, *interdisciplinary actors* of one kind or another. The epistemological foundations thus shift in accordance with their at times flagrantly anti-systematic concatenations of specialized knowledge. To some extent the disciplinary grip of Canadian history is held together only by cultural nationalist policies, and I propose these be relaxed in order to restore a wider play of lived subjectivity. As a result, 'culture' is not understood here as a stable platform for national identity but rather as a complex and unstable process of (self-)identification at the margins.

During the Cold War, 'Canada' *presenced* itself restlessly against its Others along a continuum of remote and intimate sensing systems, from the DEW Line to the Canada Council's jury rooms. What follows is a gesture, at least, towards counteracting the climate of tension and silence inherited from the Cold War that remains unabated in the current trade-dominated phase of international relations and indeed has intensified following the September 2001 terrorist attacks in the United States.

Launching a post-Massey Report era of cultural policy north of the 49th parallel may well require readings of Canadian history that reconsider questions of security and nationality. Perhaps the 'freedom' that could define a truly sovereign cultural future—one that has not already internalized the discipline of the censor, the market, or the border post—is spectacular precisely in ways that pass undetected by the Janus-faced radar of the contemporary nation-state and the global corporation.

1

Characterizations of Tracy Philipps

*It is maintained, on the whole, that the English are in Canada either to
avoid military service . . . or to 'sit out the war' in 'cushy jobs'. . . .
British Officers will, according to these stories, simply 'idle away' the war
in Canada. Even the Royal Family is said to prefer life in Canada . . . .
The authorities in Montreal conveniently provide 'Blackouts' so that those
hordes of Englishmen may disembark under the cover of darkness. . . . [We]
Canadians will (like fools) accept all classes and conditions of Englishmen
. . . . The English always put Canadian troops in the front line . . . . French
Canadians, it is charged, will be used as suicide troops . . . . [R]umors
assert that [Mackenzie] King and Churchill are planning an invasion . . .
with Canadian troops taking the lead. But at the same time, Churchill is
plotting to achieve the defeat of Soviet Russia, or else he is scheming for a
separate peace. No matter how you look at it, we Canadians lose out.*

Committee on Morale, *Rumour Summary, 1942*

The Managing Director, Scott's, 1 Old Bond Street, W1:

*In summer, I do not wear a hat. It is therefore only to wear in very
windy, wet and snowy weather. It is therefore a heavy-weight turn-down,
medium-wide brim, hat which I need, plenty large enough, and with all
the details set out on my card. The initials T.P. should be stencilled inside
and it should be well ventilated and 'insulated' against hair grease or
sweat penetrating back and showing upon (very dark coloured) inside
leather band.*

*If there is any doubt please enquire by airmail rather than despatch in
error. Thank you for your unfailing courtesy and care over a long series
of years.*

Tracy Philipps
On War Service in Canada, 1942

1

Disturbances manifested as rumours, and passed by word of mouth from citizen to citizen, trace a spectral double of the triumphalist nationalism with which the anti-Fascist world war has been historicized. One wartime rumour pattern of particular concern to the Canadian government's Committee on Morale was widespread distrust of British war aims and the use of Canada to further them. The Committee's professional psychologists took such rumours seriously, regarding them not as idle 'fantasies' but rather 'as important indices of the state of the "public mind" '. In their opinion:

> They are dramatizations of attitudes, beliefs, or values, or they are attempts to fill in the gaps left by the sources of authentic information.
> . . . They express both the state of the public mind and they are one of the ways in which it is molded.[1]

In retrospect, public anxiety concerning Canada's embryonic national sovereignty is patterned in the rumours. Ignorant of radar development, for example, Canadians worried about their nation's territorial security, propagating rumours of easy enemy penetration both by sea and by air. Concern that their fragile bicultural society was breaking down under the stress of war surfaced in English Canada with rumours that some *Québécoises* freely consorted with German U-boat crews on the St Lawrence. In Quebec it was said that the 'zombies'—conscientious objectors— were forced to board troop convoys at bayonet point and that some were tortured to death in the internment camps. Again, these bear some fantasmic relation to suppressed information concerning the internees' camp mutiny in Terrace, BC, in 1944, and of other war resisters hiding out in the bush. Widespread anti-Semitic rumours occupied a yawning chasm in public information regarding the Holocaust before its harrowing truth was accepted. It is true that Axis short-wave propaganda planted rumours to foster dissent in ethnocultural minorities, but tales also circulated among Canadians of East European descent intimating that a massive Allied censorship eavesdropped on all their personal communications.

The 1942 *Rumour Summary* cited above does not signal any public uneasiness with the Soviet Union and its international activities, although it credits the anti-Communist Tracy Philipps, European adviser to the Nationalities Branch of the Department of War Services, with supplying various rumours to the Committee. The officers of the Special Branch of the RCMP were the most regular collectors and their sensitivity to patterns of anxiety was a natural consequence of information-gathering networks directed primarily at left-wing organizations; indeed, occasionally they would plant a rumour to test the efficiency of their dispersed host of informants.[2]

The idiosyncratic Philipps was perhaps too much the object of innuendo to have so enthusiastically collected rumours. But the pattern of disturbance he created in wartime Ottawa matches up with the anxieties such rumours expressed. He was fully assimilable neither to Canadians' residual affiliations to the British Empire nor to their emerging cultural nationalism. Shocks, static, surges, and short circuits punctuate his four-year sojourn as a self-described 'electrical engineer of culture'.

Cloud-Cuckoo-Town

A British ethnologist, linguist, naturalist, explorer, Intelligence officer, and relief co-ordinator, Tracy Philipps was characterized with controlled disdain by one of his numerous enemies as a 'minor British aristocrat who arrived in Ottawa in 1940 as a typical soldier adventurer'. This might be misconstrued as a compliment, particularly if one is attracted by the purple splash painted by the 50-year-old Philipps on the dour wartime capital. In private communications with his protégé Vladimir Kysilewsky, Philipps referred to Ottawa as 'cloud-cuckoo-town', inhabited by officials he dubbed 'the tweed people'. Flitting through the recesses of Mackenzie King's administrative labyrinth were shadowy adversaries: 'the Armenian', 'the Hindu Kush', and someone he referred to only as 'Dynamite'.[3]

Despite the intermittent flow of his private income Philipps lived in the style of a gentleman. Disembarked at Montreal in June 1940 with his striking young wife, Ukrainian concert pianist Lubka Kolessa Philipps, he was incensed with Thomas Cook agents for having assigned them a second-class cabin.[4] For a year he travelled across the country on a self-appointed mission, first assuring Canadians that Britain would remain supreme in the Mediterranean and afterwards inspecting the 'foreign-born' labour force.[5] In a letter to Judge T.C. Davis, Deputy Minister of the Department of National War Services, Philipps likened his work in Canada to 'Muhammed's coffin, in mid-air with no visible means of support'.[6] After deluging Davis with unsolicited reports and memoranda, Philipps would at last secure paid government service under the Judge's watchful eye as 'European adviser' to a newly formed bureau, the Nationalities Branch.

As the war intensified, Philipps's flow of personal supplies from London reduced to a trickle and his luck seemed to run out. Letters arrived from London shops, in one case regretting 'our inability to be of service on this occasion as the casts for your shoes were destroyed when we were blitzed'.[7] Philipps's closely guarded supply of 'serum' dried up, as did hope for replacement spectacles.[8] At his lowest point, facing real and imagined enemies on every front, he was struck down on his way to work by children riding a toboggan and suffered a painful back injury. The single bright spot was his unshakable friendship with Vladimir Kysilewsky, his confidant in the Nationalities Branch.

In his work, Philipps observed few bureaucratic protocols. Cabinet ministers such as Louis St Laurent and Colin Gibson, fellow residents of the Roxborough Apartments, were ambushed in the corridors by the peripatetic expert on European nationalities. To Philipps's dismay such informal access to ministers ended in 1942 with the departures of Judge Davis and his own minister, Icelandic-Canadian Joseph Thorson, neither of whom had seriously objected to his unorthodox style. The incoming Minister of National War Services, General Léo R. LaFlèche, barred Philipps from his office and forbade any meetings with high officials. LaFleche instructed his timid deputy, Chester Payne, to reel in the roving Englishman and ground him to Ottawa.

Even worse things were afoot. Philipps's fractious separation from his wife soon after their arrival in the capital raised eyebrows in the strait-laced upper echelons of the bureaucracy and provided salacious ammunition to his detractors. She took refuge first in a convent and then with a family friend, Ladislaus Biberovich, chief translator in the Press Censorship division. A scandal ensued, with charges hurled back and forth between the parties. Press reports smeared Philipps, branding him as an appeaser with Fascist inclinations who used his government position to promote right-wing ethnic elements while secretly attacking legitimate left-wing individuals and organizations. For his part, Philipps whispered about a private piano recital his wife gave for Hitler, suggesting that she might be a German spy.

As Philipps's star set both publicly and privately in the eyes of Ottawa's bureaucratic elite, natural predators began to close in. When left-leaning John Grierson took over as Manager of the Wartime Information Board in February 1943, he discussed the complaints against Philipps with Norman Robertson, the Undersecretary of State for External Affairs. It was only a matter of time before means were found to force Phillips's exit. Terrorized by his 'incomprehensible' European adviser, Deputy Minister Chester Payne expressed deep gratitude when educationist Robert England agreed to write a consultant's report that resulted in Philipps's departure from Canadian government service in 1944.

Despite Tracy Philipps's failure to stabilize his position in cloud-cuckoo-town, many so-called 'new' Canadians regarded him as their champion. He was received 'almost as a Messiah', as he put it, in parts of Canada where immigrant communities went entirely ignored by government except as security risks to be monitored by the RCMP. He compared his reception in remote areas to his experiences with T.E. Lawrence in the Near East. Philipps lobbied vociferously on behalf of ethnic minorities even as he used their trust to glean information to improve his standing with the Special Branch of the RCMP. As both an early exponent of official multiculturalism and a police informant, Philipps personified multiculturalism's ambivalent relationship to state security.

The traces of Philipps's Canadian story are retained mainly by the good graces of his friend Vladimir Julian Kysilewsky, or 'Kaye', who stored the Englishman's wartime papers for many years.[9] As an unofficial fixture at the National Archives in Ottawa during his retirement, Kysilewsky prepared and deposited Philipps's manuscripts perhaps to settle some old scores. In his mild way, while protecting his friend from the revelation of adverse personal information, Kysilewsky nonetheless made a gesture against the climate of official secrecy and suspicion towards minorities he had endured during his public service career. He must have known that these documents included details of RCMP and government activities otherwise unavailable in open records, including documents with some bearing on the Gouzenko case.

In their rush to characterize Philipps as antithetical to Canadian cultural nationalism, scholars have overlooked the fascinating security dimension of his activities. For example, Leslie Pal writes, reprovingly:

Philipps was British, had little experience of Canada, and approached the ethnic question not from a Canadian vantage point but from a European one. This had led him to propose positions . . . at odds with Canadian Government and Allied

Edmonton Journal
20¼ Nov. 40

Edmonton

EDMONTON, ALBERTA,

Distinguished Soldier Is Sure Britain Will Remain Supreme in Mediterranean

T. Phillips Says Moham-medans Call Hitler "Father of Lies"

IS VISITOR IN CITY

The 200,000,000 members of the Mohammedan world stretching from Morocco eastward to the Dutch East Indies have their own name for Hitler. It's Abu Kabbass; it means "Father of Lies."

Tracy Phillips, distinguished British soldier, administrator, scientist and journalist, said this in an interview in Edmonton Wednesday in explaining why Britain will remain supreme in the Mediterranean and Near East, whether Turkey topples or is able to resist increasing pressure of the combined Russian-Nazi "squeeze."

Descendant of a family whose members have been servants of the crown and empire builders since 1155 when one of their number was knighted for saving the life of Richard Coeur de Lion in battle, Mr. Philipps has had a story-book career approaching in adventure that of his late friend and colleague, "Lawrence of Arabia."

Abandoned Retirement

The war caused him to abandon a retirement earned by nearly three decades of exciting life as a soldier, foreign office agent and London Times correspondent in southeast Europe and Africa.

He came to Canada at the invitation of the National Council of Education and will remain in Edmonton for a week addressing Ukrainian meetings at several points and gatherings of the men's Canadian club and the Edmonton branch of the Institute of International Affairs. He is addressing the Canadian club at a luncheon meeting in the Macdonald on Nov. 27.

Accompanied by Dr. V. J. Kl—

TRACY PHILLIPS

—ewsky, Ottawa, one of Canada's outstanding Ukrainian citizens, Mr. Philipps will tell Ukrainian audiences about conditions causing unrest in their homeland, and of the desire of Canada and Britain that they should enjoy all the privileges and advantages of their adopted land.

A graduate of Oxford and holder of an honorary doctor of laws degree from Durham university awarded for "public work at home and abroad, in colonial science and in international relations toward the betterment of British and foreign understanding," Mr. Philipps won the military cross while fighting in Africa in the last war.

Following the war he directed Red sea patrols fighting slave-running in Arabia, was administrator of the mountain district on the frontier of mandated Belgian East Africa, crossed Africa on foot along the equator on a scientific expedition,

*Thinks British to Hold Near East Whatever Turkey's Fate

STORY-BOOK CAREER

served as a British relief commissioner in south Russia, filled other foreign office posts and was correspondent for the Times during the Greco-Turkish war.

Discussing the war, he said he believes:

Superior sea power and friendship of the Mohammedan world means victory for Britain in the battle of the Mediterranean and Africa.

Russia is suffering from serious internal weaknesses due to unrest in the Ukraine and other republics in the Soviet empire seeking independence. By bowing before Germany, Russia is "putting off the evil day of reckoning." A religious revival is under way in Russia, weakening Stalin's hold on the masses.

Sees Turkey Fighting

Turkey will fight before letting German troops cross the country, but is mindful of the republic's tradition that it must "never be on the opposite side of the fence to Russia."

The French colonies in Africa have been duped by belief in the "independence" of Vichy and there is a possibility General Weygand might re-organize resistance, although the French armies in Africa have been systematically disarmed by the German-Italian armistice commission. (Mr. Philipps is a personal friend of the French generals commanding the African colonies.)

Hitler turned the entire Mohammedan world unswervingly against him forever when he wrote in "Mein Kampf" that when Germany ruled supreme over the world, all dark races would be wood carriers and servants for their "blond masters."

policy. With [Prof. George W.] Simpson's resignation and the Cabinet's failure to appoint a deputy minister, Philipps effectively took over the administration of the branch. A British soldier and adventurer was thus in charge of a Canadian branch of government responsible for non-English and non-French nationalities.[10]

Philipps's unfettered circulation among Canadian ethnocultural minorities in 1940–1 is rendered as counterproductive; indeed, it was *embarrassing* to the emergent rhetoric of the 'society of immigrants' that was so seamlessly articulated in Paul Martin's Citizenship Act just a few years later, in 1947.

Yet, Philipps is a unique incandescent flare illuminating the murky cultural workings of Ottawa during the war years. Perhaps only an upper-class British eccentric could so have insinuated himself into the propaganda, censorship, and intelligence components of Canada's nascent culture/security apparatuses. At once a multiculturalist, RCMP informant, recipient of censored communications, propagandist, and voracious consumer of secret security intelligence data, the dervish-like Philipps left many traces.

Characterization and Historical Truth

Wittgenstein somewhat obscurely locates 'character' in such qualities as *tempo, colour, intonation, and the major or the minor key*, that is, in an ensemble of ineffable attributes that can pass through a lens of talent, he says, and sometimes produce genius.[11] This is how newness enters and renews wonderment in human societies. It is possible to have talent without genius, he believes, but never genius without 'character', and *having character* as opposed to simply being identified by a name is crucial to the 'truth' of any historical characterization of genius. The case of Tracy Philipps suggests that historical characterization may be baffled by a genius already outmoded in its own time and, indeed, may ascribe it to madness.

That Tracy Philipps was out of his element in Canada, operating uncomfortably in a changing communicative context, placed his very rationality in question. Whereas Wittgenstein suggests that madness can 'be seen as a more or less sudden change of character', the mental instability attributed to Tracy Philipps is more plausibly the inverse of this relation.[12] That is, Philipps's 'character' *did not change enough*, and such a figure partially left behind by a society's changing tenets of rationality only rarely gives his or her name to the time. In characterizing Philipps I will not filter out traces of his out-of-step strangeness, for this friction leads into Canada's emerging culture-security complex.

N.F. Dreisziger is the only historian to have written in any detail about Tracy Philipps, placing him at the outset of Canadian multicultural policy during World War II.[13] In September of 1939 Canada was prepared to fight a war in Europe in neither military nor psychological terms, writes Dreisziger, 'in particular, the country did not possess the administrative machinery to involve in the war effort the portion of the population that was neither of British nor of French background.' The formation of the Nationalities Branch was one solution to this problem; it resulted from the efforts of 'several members of the country's elite' who recognized that masses of unassimilated immigrants impeded war mobilization. Despite early set-backs, '[t]he beginnings of this bureaucratic apparatus were a small but telling and vital aspect of the general process whereby ethnic minorities in Canada have acquired a higher profile and greater influence in the country's affairs.' The result of this governmental effort was an 'increased integration of newcomers into the Canadian economy as well as into social and cultural life'.

Tracy Philipps enters the picture in June 1940, in the crisis that prevailed during the sweep of Hitler's armies across Northern Europe towards the English Channel. Philipps emerged by default because 'old hands' considered more capable of dealing with European minorities, such as Robert England and Watson Kirkconnell, had declined the Nationalities brief. It happened that Philipps was on the scene to 'do the actual building of the bureaucratic infrastructure'.[14]

Philipps descended from 'an upper-class family, many of whose members had served Britain and the Empire with distinction', Dreisziger writes, noting Philipps's Oxford degree and his soldiering in Africa, 'after which he had been in the service of the British government on various diplomatic and intelligence-gathering assignments.' Author of published papers in scientific and anthropological journals, Philipps 'also prided himself on his linguistic skills. He spoke French, German and Italian, and claimed knowledge of Turkish as well as thirteen African languages.' Dreisziger describes Philipps as 'a man of determination, boundless energy, and a great deal of ambition', who won admiration and provoked hostility as he addressed audiences across the country with inspired oratory.

Philipps's 'bombardment' of Judge Davis and other government contacts in Ottawa with unsolicited memoranda and his frenetic itinerary of public speaking and factory inspections in 1940–1 are rendered by Dreisziger as a gradual erosion of the Englishman's credibility. Although he was tranferred to work directly under Davis, he was disliked by Norman Robertson of the Department of External Affairs, deliberately overlooked as a candidate in the search for a Director of the Nationalities Branch, and eventually 'grounded to Ottawa'. The Branch remained mired in controversy and inactivity until Robert England reorganized it in 1944. Philipps progressively alienated himself from influential officials, leading to calls from 'just about every senior bureaucrat in External Affairs, as well as John Grierson of the Wartime Information Board . . . for the resignation of the controversial Englishman'. Robert England's reorganization 'avoided some of the deficiencies of the Nationalities Branch', Dreisziger writes, 'notably it eased Philipps out of Canadian government service.'[15]

In his most recent offering, Dreisziger relegates Philipps to a footnote, and instead crafts his tale around senior bureaucrat Norman Robertson, characterizing him as Ottawa's enlightened benefactor of European immigrant groups.[16] He focuses on 7 December 1941, a date of special significance to the subsequent treatment of ethnic minorities in Canada. In the first place, Canada declared war that day on Axis allies such as Finland, Hungary, and Romania. Robertson pressed the cabinet to exempt Canadian Finns, Hungarians, and Romanians from internment provisions in the Defence of Canada Regulations. The second event of that day was Japan's bombing of Pearl Harbor, leading to the forced resettlement of Japanese

Canadians. Although Robertson did not forestall the latter process, Dreisziger credits him both with preventing further internments and with aiding ethnic minorities in general by helping to create the Nationalities Branch and its steering committee.

As historical characterization, Dreisziger's 'Norman Robertson' performs stalwart ideological work: modern liberal Canada stands out against the reactionary background personified by Mackenzie King's close adviser, Ernest Lapointe.[17] Indeed, when Lapointe 'passes on' Robertson is ready to fulfill his destiny: 'Fate had prepared Robertson for an important role by giving him a humanistic upbringing and a pivotal position in wartime Ottawa.' By conviction a civil libertarian and a humanist, 'a gentle man who operated in the world of power', the character 'Norman Robertson' is cut to fit Canada's future posture, as written in its official histories: intelligent, moderate, humanistic, gentle, and compassionate:

> From the time of Lapointe's illness and death, Robertson played a key role in the efforts to improve the treatment of Canada's enemy ethnic population . . . Robertson and other moderates failed only in their desire to avert the implementation of harsh measures against Canadians of Japanese background. . . . But . . . [t]hey had helped make a virtual non-event—the Canadian declaration of war on Finland, Hungary and Romania—a turning point. . . . Canadians can regard that date as an occasion when their country came a step closer to being a tolerant society.[18]

By foregrounding Robertson and his preventing the internment of former nationals of minor Axis powers, the fact of *actual* internments, not just of the Japanese but of Italian, German, and French Canadians, as well as others, recedes from view.[19] Moreover, institutionalized anti-Semitism and the steep restrictions placed on Asian immigration pass without mention.[20] Dreisziger fails to discuss the extent of security operations against ethnic minorities during the war, the way these blended into a latent anti-Communism in government circles, or how ethnic intermediaries within the security services shaped official opinion regarding their respective communities.

Without disputing the liberal virtues of Norman Robertson, or how far the tentacles of his characterization extend into various corridors of Canada's national history, is it clear enough how he is deployed here as a character type. Underlying Dreisziger's characterization of Robertson is a legitimation of the actually existing Canadian state in relation to cultural minorities, and the very criterion of Robertson's visibility is his contribution to multiculturalism's socially integrating force.

Conversely, his characterizations of Tracy Philipps in these two accounts verge on embarrassment, as if Dreisziger does not quite know how to handle Philipps's contradictory qualities. It is thus striking that the third of Dreisziger's characterizations of Philipps is *unembarrassed* and keyed closely to the Englishman's dissonance.[21] This account dispenses with an omniscient narrator who charts the nation's steady progress towards multicultural equilibrium. Crucially, Ukrainian Canadians are brought into historical visibility here not by the interests of state but rather by Tracy Philipps's wayward circulation in the autumn of 1940 among the

Ukrainian diaspora in Canada. As such, Dreisziger repositions the reader in a more contested dialogue with the state's official history.

This detachment can be specified, for example, in the stated obscurity of the Canadian government's intentions towards Ukrainian Canadians at the outset of the war. Despite Judge Davis's 'ex-post-facto claim' that the Department of National War Services achieved the unification of rival Ukrainian-Canadian groups during the autumn of 1940, Dreisziger's central argument is that the government had nothing to do with the creation of the Ukrainian Canadian Committee (UCC). Unification resulted primarily from Tracy Philipps's 'personal mission' to create an independent anti-Communist Ukraine as an eastern bulwark of British influence against Bolshevism. Philipps is characterized by Dreisziger in this instance as acting above the call of duty, solely on the strength of his own convictions, and out of step even with the British Foreign Office. To revise the false impression left by Davis, Dreisziger characterizes Tracy Philipps as a 'real character', in Wittgenstein's sense, one with at least a modicum of genius.

Philipps helped secure the unification of Ukrainian-Canadian elements against the odds during two days of high-pressure meetings in Winnipeg. He and Professor George Simpson presided over negotiations between various factions to create the solidly anti-Communist UCC. Not least, this unification officially established the term 'Ukrainian' as designating a single nationality group in Canada, formerly referred to severally as 'Austrians', 'Bukowinians', 'Galicians', 'Ruthenians', and 'Little Russians'.[22]

As it turned out, Philipps's shotgun marriage of disparate factions did not please all parties for long. After Hitler turned on the Soviet Union in 1941, the UCC's squabbles with the Ukrainian Communists who had been shut out of the Winnipeg negotiations turned it into a destabilizing force in Canada-Soviet relations. Furthermore, Hitler's invasion obviated Philipps's estimates of British interests in Eastern Europe. Despite these turns of fortune, Dreisziger insists that Philipps be credited as the peculiar external catalyst without whom nationalist and conservative Ukrainian Canadians could not have combined their efforts as a single ethnic lobby in Ottawa; that achievement, such as it was, cannot be claimed for the Canadian government.

Details of Philipps's role are known because of a car ride he took with Bill Burianyk after the Winnipeg meeting concluded. The Englishman welcomed a lift to Saskatoon, and in the beguiling intimacy of Burianyk's automobile, passing across the flat and sparsely populated autumn prairie, Philipps confided frankly his views and motives regarding the Ukrainians and the Canadian government. Alas for Philipps, Burianyk was a regular informant of Manitoba provincial authorities, and a report of the conversation was soon on the desk of Norman Robertson in Ottawa.[23] Philipps's incautious statements deriding 'old fogeys' in the British Foreign Office, who were not 'big enough' to aggressively support an independent Ukraine, could not have impressed Robertson. Moreover, he learned that Philipps viewed his mission primarily as furthering the *imperial* interest through his actions in Canada.

Philipps may never have learned of Burianyk's duplicity, but he noticed the change in his rapport with Robertson, whom he had praised to Kysilewsky as 'unusually capable and charming'.[24] Given Philipps's own addiction to secret information, his previous Intelligence service, and the alacrity with which he reported to the RCMP Commissioner any leftish stirrings during his travels around the country, it is surprising and perhaps fitting that he should have unburdened himself to an unreliable stranger. Philipps's hard-earned moment of success thus foreshadowed his eventual undoing, and it provides an entry point to the aspect of his historical characterization suppressed in accounts such as Dreisziger's, that is, his relations with the various branches of state security.

Colonial Panic

In 1927, British writer F.A.M. Webster published a novel of colonial espionage, *The Man Who Knew*. Like Tracy Philipps, Webster served British Military Intelligence in Asia and Africa during World War I. His novels and journalism specialized in athletics, elite education, military history, and colonial espionage fiction. In the latter category he wrote more than a dozen novels, including *The Black Shadow* (1922), *M'Sengo, The Witch Doctor* (1927), *The White Nigger* (1937), *Son of Abdan* (1936), and *East of Kashgar* (1940), this one subtitled 'a secret service story [set] in little-known parts of Asia [and based on] the author's peculiar knowledge of out-of-the-way corners of the world and the men who work there'.[25] Although it has hitherto passed unremarked, *The Man Who Knew* is cited prominently in Tracy Philipps's *curriculum vitae* as a fictionalized treatment of his own career as an Intelligence officer in Africa and the Near East after World War I.[26] Webster's indomitable imperialist hero serves as a foil for the 'real' Tracy Philipps and his peculiar moments of helplessness in Canada.

In many ways Webster's 'Phillip Tracey' does resemble the Tracy Philipps the researcher encounters through his papers in the National Archives. Philipps's claim that Webster's novel was written 'without consultation' seems doubtful.[27] Much of its ethnological detail derives directly from Philipps's accounts of African secret societies opposed to European rule.[28] Furthermore, despite Kysilewsky's judicious weeding of the Philipps papers (snipping off dates and names and adding his own marginal comments), it is obvious that Philipps had a habit of supplying 'off-the-record' information to writers and journalists.

The Man Who Knew is consistent with the genre of espionage fiction that first emerged as anti-German propaganda in Britain during World War I, though it has little to say about Germany.[29] Post-war Weimar is rendered as corrupt and under the sway of a Jewish conspiracy whose influence is considered to be global. The novel's gung-ho anti-Semitism is a depressing reminder to post-Holocaust readers of the robustness of that prejudice in interwar Britain and its colonies. Webster's Germany is an errant but thoroughly chastised brother in the European fraternity, and his geographical focus for British espionage activity will not be Europe itself but rather its colonies in Africa and Asia.

Phillip Tracey, Deputy Director of African Intelligence, receives secret information imparting nothing less than an impending global uprising against European imperial rule. Manipulated from Moscow by ruthless 'Jewish Bolsheviks', the

CHARACTERIZATIONS OF TRACY PHILIPPS   11

'Coloured League' is poised to launch a concerted, global anti-colonial insurgency leading to 'a world conquered by coloured peoples, but ruled by the Russian Terrorists of Leningrad'. A leader named Kosdrewski is 'to be the biggest kind of noise in the coming trouble':

> He it was, who was neither black nor white—that piece puzzled us badly—who was going to overcome all those religious and racial scruples which, so far, held the innumerable warring factions in Africa, Asia and India apart. (70–1)

According to Tracey's source, the insurgents' intended program was: 'USA negroes return [to] West Indies and Africa; Africa for Africans; Australia for China and Aborigines; America for Japan ((possible revival of North American Indians)).'[30] It enrages Tracey's friend Jim Carruthers to think of his Africa delivered from the beneficent, ordering effects of white rule:

> nor did it make me feel any better to read that tosh about Red Indian power in North America. When I thought of those jolly looking Canadian lads I had last seen going up at Ypres, just before the Huns launched the first gas attack against them, my blood fairly boiled.

Carruthers believes that only Phillip Tracey—'among the first half-dozen of Great Britain's secret service agents'—stands any chance of foiling this great conspiracy (129).

F.A.M. Webster hails readers as white, male gentiles 'in the club'. The book's dedication signals that the novel 'deals with some things that are known and some that are within the realm of possibility.' This cue to subtext is not simply the prudent self-censorship that J.M. Coetzee diagnoses in racist theorist Geoffrey Cronjé's veiled justifications for South African apartheid.[31] Cronjé's extremism set out *en clair* could have been turned against him by his opponents. On the contrary, *The Man Who Knew* is disarmingly overt in its racism, as if intensifying a racialized consciousness helped resist any relaxation of colonial authority or of anti-Semitism, generally.

As an index of imperial neuroses—what one might isolate as a 'colonial panic' underscoring Anglo-imperial occupation—the novel delineates themes that are elided from more discreet accounts. The 'real' Tracy Philipps, despite his penchant for secrecy, intrigue, and encrypted communication, also was notoriously and uncontrollably indiscreet about European colonialism. For him it remained an alert and vibrant formation, even if this distressed some of his Canadian hosts during the early 1940s. In this context *The Man Who Knew*, like the records of its real-life hero in Canadian archives, is an embarrassing text because it exposes with unintended precision the cultural, political, and sexual contours of colonial panic.

Black Shadows

As war churned across Europe cultural policies in Canada attempted, albeit tentatively, to integrate recent Eastern, Central, and Southern European immigrants in a pan-Canadian civic consciousness. That the 'foreign-born element', so defined, came to Canada from Europe, and not yet from any of the Asian or African colonies, is a demographic fact that helped sustain the erasure of imperialism from Canadian multiculturalist discourse. How much easier it was to erect a rhetorical 'nation of immigrants' when this mass of immigrants arrived relatively unmarked by former colonial associations. The figure of Tracy Philipps reconnects this phase of European immigration to Canada with the broader trajectory of Northern European colonial expansion, routing attention back neither to the imperial centre, Britain, nor even to Europe, but to Africa, and specifically South Africa, Canada's fellow Dominion in the Commonwealth.

Phillip Tracey's friend and colleague, Afrikaner Peter Pirow, is the anchor of a white supremacist rationality in *The Man Who Knew* and also a foil to Tracey's 'advanced' English ambivalence towards 'race consciousness'. Pirow's repulsion/attraction to black masculinity and the novel's reversals of the master-slave relation in various projective fantasies are connected to a repulsion/attraction to 'Africa' itself, personified by turns as a compliant feminine entity, erotically attracted to Carruthers's 'six feet of brawn', and as a sorceress or succubus with powers to entrance Phillip Tracey, deceiving his senses with illusions and controlling his will. These homoerotic and heterosexual configurations of colonial desire periodically crack Peter Pirow's calm to reveal a berserker. Whereas the animus of Pirow's racist personality is a patriarchal claim to what Carole Pateman calls male sex right to women and to a precious racial purity of blood, Phillip Tracey is content that 'not one in a hundred fallen women in East are of British extraction'.[32] Appreciative of their 'usefulness to the Secret Service', Tracey says simply, 'they are jolly good news gatherers' (305).

This connection of imperialism with a zone of male 'protection' of women in *The Man Who Knew* resonates with non-fictional traces of Tracy Philipps in Canada. While the exact reasons for Philipps's departure from England remain obscure (the evidence hints at a complex blend of private and public pressures during the year prior to his departure), one of his appointed or self-appointed tasks in Canada was to report regularly to his mentor, Edward Wood, Lord Halifax, on various matters, including the reception in Canada of British war evacuees and, by extension, the possible further reception of an evacuated British Establishment should German invasion send them hither.[33]

In his third report to Halifax, dated 25 June 1940, Philipps mentioned assisting his cousin, Mrs Marcus Dimsdale, with her plan to evacuate British children to Canada. On 7 July, writing from the Hotel Saskatchewan in Regina, Philipps warned Halifax that 'grave misunderstandings' will arise from the 'settling English children in Canadian homes':

> Very few of the hosts . . . have any full realisation of the full implications of their hastily and generously assumed responsibilities. When I was with Nansen, the same thing was foreseeable when Serbs took in children of their fellow-Slavs from RUSSIA. Here the very future of the race lies in this experimental migration.[34]

Philipps vehemently denied the charge made a year later that he had been, along with Halifax, a member of a group of upper-class appeasers known as the Cliveden Set, but it hovers uneasily over this correspondence.[35] During the summer of 1940, as Hitler's armies poised to cross the Channel and invade Britain, the British upper classes rushed to exercise privilege in securing scarce evacuation berths for wives, children, and servants.[36] Tracy Philipps's 'personal mission' to Canada on behalf of Halifax cannot be dissociated from emergency planning in the matter of Anglo-Saxon blood, or as he put it, 'the very future of the race'.[37]

A combination of flattery, imprecation, and cryptic intimation in Philipps's letters to his patron calls upon a discreet rationality that informed their class fraction. 'To Anglosaxon America, the British Government IS just two men, Winston and yourself', goes the flattery; 'for them you represent the great amalgam of the Mind and the Spirit combined in action.' Imprecations crept into asides such as, 'I shall continue to carry on this work without pay so long as I can get my income from England . . . this is now being blocked at source.' Cryptic intimations about the 'future of the race' were conveyed in a diagnosis of Anglo-Canadian envy of European culture. Such envy was manifested in 'an almost ferocious fumbling after Things of the Spirit . . . they therefore go in fear of being fooled.'[38]

He warned Halifax of Canadians' 'uncomprehending criticism of England doing things on the cheap' and that 'North American channels of information (radio, magazine, contacts) predominate over British.' This triggered a further interjection on the theme of race and racism in Canada. Philipps noted that 'it is a bad sign that the Jews are beginning, by precaution, to cease to speak about Nazism in public.' On the theme of propaganda he advised Halifax that 'Canadians seem to be the best interpreters of Britain to the States. Englishmen can provide the raw material . . . it is unwise for us to go further.'[39]

The common thread in these erratic reports is Philipps's testing for the persistence of imperial rationality in Canada. Clearly, he was confused at the fluctuating hot and cold receptions he encountered, depending on the residual strength of the imperial bond in any given situation, and he remained blind to the fact that what he called 'Britishthinking' [sic] among Canadians had entered a contested and transitory phase during the war years.[40] On the one hand, he was accepted without question by the business elite at Empire Club dinners, by military men, and even by a few younger journalists such as Blair Fraser, who responded warmly to Philipps's 'Boys'-Own-Fiction' qualities. On the other hand, the Canadian nationalists he encountered, especially John Grierson's young helpers in the Wartime Information Board, were put off by Philipps's air of imperial pacification.

For Philipps, imperialism was entirely consistent with liberal principles. As he wrote from Ottawa in September 1940 to a correspondent in New York:

There is a great illusion about 'democracy' which is confused with liberalism, and it suffices for half a dozen unfortified mud-villages in half a dozen African countries to be evacuated for it to be imagined a colonial empire is breaking into collapse.

Here Philipps expressed what Lord Milner, his erstwhile superior in British Intelligence during World War I, had long maintained, that the Empire comprised two distinct political spheres.[41] One was 'democratic' because white majorities in Canada, Australia, and New Zealand ensured an overarching political rationality isomorphic with that of Britain. In the other cases non-white majorities had special recourse to native political cultures, unintelligible to British thinking, and so could not similarly be eligible for democracy. As a newcomer to North America, Philipps was keen to know if there was a 'a real reason why to think North American should be incompatible with thinking Anglosaxon or with thinking British.'[42] That something so simple and commonsensical to Anglo-Canadians puzzled him shows how complex the gradual retraction of imperial authority from Canada was, viewed from the outside. It cautions against the temptation to render 'Philipps the Imperialist' as a kind of quixotic jungle fighter battling on after the Empire was doomed. The substantial residue of imperialism persisting in Canada ensured that, perhaps half the time, Philipps went among fully like-minded people; traversing the rising cultural nationalism was rougher going. In these circles his 'Britishthinking' increasingly was a source of discomfort.

F.A.M. Webster's arch villain in *The Man Who Knew*, 'Kosdrewski', combined all of imperial Whitehall's deepest fears, and elicits Webster's most eviscerating racist and anti-Communist slurs. Having established with mechanical repetition the towering black male figure as an object of fear/desire, he surprises readers by casting the villain Kosdrewski as 'the White Nigger . . . a white-skinned man with the features of a Negro', a combination that fascinates Phillip Tracey. In the smoking room of the Sports Club in London, he explains to his fellow agents that the fact Kosdrewski is 'neither white nor black' is of special 'allegorical' significance, for his indeterminate racial status threatens to undo carefully cultivated internal divisions among those opposed to European colonial rule. Peter Pirow remarks, 'I am glad that Phillip Tracey is back in England. We shall have a better chance of dealing with these black devils. I have a sort of longing to see that white nigger, in particular, dangling at the end of a long rope over a short drop.'

Webster's inspiration for Pirow may well have come in part from Colonel Richard Meinertzhagen, Webster's and Tracy Philipps's elder comrade in the King's African Rifles. T.E. Lawrence counted Meinertzhagen the outstanding intelligence officer in the British campaign against Turkey in World War I, a man who went 'beyond negative precautions . . . to give the enemy specific (and speciously wrong) information'. Lawrence rhapsodized on 'Meiner's' prowess:

> Meinertzhagen knew no half measures. He was logical, an idealist of the deepest, and so possessed by his convictions that he was willing to harness evil to the chariot of good. He was a strategist, a geographer, and a silent laughing masterful man; who took as blithe a pleasure in deceiving his enemy (or his friend) by some unscrupulous jest, as in spattering the brains of a cornered mob of Germans one by one with his African knob-kerri.[43]

Anyone unconvinced of the necessity of pursuing the concept of the 'postcolonial' in literary and historical studies ought to glance through Meinertzhagen's diaries. Take, for instance, the orgy of killing when this imperialist berserker first went to Kenya as a young officer in 1902. Irritated by the practice of 'savages . . . entering our camp as a soon as we leave . . . digging up the dead, and mutilating them[,] I decided to teach them a lesson.' His company ambushed a party of 49 warriors of the Tetu people:

> None got past me. I was surprised at the ease with which a bayonet goes into a man's body. One scarcely feels it unless it goes in to the hilt. But one frequently has to make a desperate tug to pull it out.[44]

If the character Peter Pirow echoes Meinertzhagen's real-life bloodthirstiness, Tracy Philipps, like Phillip Tracey, was a tamer sort. It is true that in the novel Phillip Tracey is ferried back to Britain on a navy submarine, carrying with him the severed head of an insurgent warrior as a phrenological exhibit for the British Museum. Thus Webster shows that the British imperial power could operate as murderously and covertly as it pleased. The real Tracy Philipps, on the other hand, arrived in Canada in 1940 in a second-class cabin. On his personal mission among 'the jungle of the foreign-born' in Canada, he had no access to submarines, much less his fictional alter ego's invitation to cabinet-level deliberations.

The Man Who Knew might be left in deserved literary oblivion had not its real-life model brought his notion of 'Britishthinking' to bear on early Canadian multi-cultural policy. As a self-described 'applied anthropologist' and cultural expert, Philipps found race politics of perennial concern. Writing to Lord Halifax he observed that the foreign-born in Canada had not yet affiliated themselves to 'shrewd and correctly-dressed British citizenship'.[45] In Regina he was startled when 'a non-Anglosaxon asked me, whom he thought to be Swedish-Canadian, whether I was "for the British."' Nationality groups, he advised Halifax, must be 're-nationalized'. At the moment, their diasporic associations were cast widely across the entire western hemisphere, irrespective of national boundaries. On 25 June 1941, he wrote urgently, at '2 a.m.', from his Toronto hotel room to RCMP Commissioner Wood: 'The very high proportion of Italian blood in Argentina, the whitest state in South America, is not without a contagious significance when it comes to hemispheric defence.' Eight months later, disconsolate that the government had ignored his pleas for a concerted policy regarding the foreign-born labour force, he wrote in self-pity to the RCMP Commissioner:

> In a time of war and total 'state-of emergency', a trained navigating officer is sent out with his ship to embark foreign-born WHITE CARGO. The only things which are withheld from him are Orders, his course, a Compass, a crew or a port of destination. It therefore only remains for him to be court-martialed for saving dagoes.[46]

W.E.B. Du Bois and the 'Coloured Peril'

Desperate as it may seem, Philipps's view of himself as a man who knew all about colonial race relations was not unfounded. Indeed, he had studied the subject and was personally acquainted with the black American radical intellectual, Dr W.E.B. Du Bois. He first met Du Bois in 1921 when Halifax, then Britain's Colonial Secretary, assigned him to monitor Du Bois's second Pan-African Congress conducted in London, Brussels, and Paris. Du Bois later recalled that these congresses were memorable chiefly 'for the excitement and opposition which they caused among the colonial imperialists . . . a warning for colonial governments to clamp down on unrest'.[47]

Du Bois's second novel, *Dark Princess*, published in 1928, just a year after *The Man Who Knew*, takes up the identical theme of a worldwide anti-colonial uprising but from the insurgents' perspective. Though tough enough in its social realism, Du Bois's *Dark Princess* is also romantic, intellectually curious, and well-informed by comparison to the brutality, masochism, sexual repression, and closed-mindedness of *The Man Who Knew*. Despite their anti-European aims Du Bois's principal characters are fully conversant with European modernity and modernist aesthetics. They recharge the double consciousness of black modernity in a positive way, operating deftly within modernist codes while insisting upon examining Euro-America's repressed ethical debt to slavery and colonialism. Where Webster shored up the male imperialists' nerve, Du Bois breathed confidence into anti-colonial critique. Webster's secret agents consider women at best weak links in the imperial cause; by contrast, Du Bois's female characters propel *Dark Princess* towards its messianic conclusion.

These parallel yet diametrically opposed texts serve as a reminder that the political rationality of what Paul Gilroy calls 'the Black Atlantic', forged among chains in the holds of slavers and disseminated throughout the colonial world, was the object of a neurotic fixation above decks.[48] It is a reminder that the traffic of European imperialism produced *colonizers* as diasporic communities, too, and that black double consciousness is not geographically differentiated from these white colonial mappings. The cultural histories of the Black Atlantic and the White Atlantic are irretrievably intertwined.[49]

F.A.M. Webster was concerned that this parallel formation should be monitored with all vigilance by British imperial intelligence and believed that immigration of coloured persons to Britain should be prevented. Even though the intellectual output of the Black Atlantic had virtually no *popular* currency in the dominant white culture (Du Bois reports that readership for *Dark Princess* was tiny), its texts were read with interest by intelligence agencies, searching for keys to understanding its oppositionality.[50] Gilroy argues that the Black Atlantic's internal coherence derived from ineffable, non-discursive qualities such as music and gesture, precisely because such vernaculars remained inscrutable to colonial administration.[51]

What happens when the Intelligence officer acknowledges 'double consciousness'? Both 'Phillip Tracey' and the actual Tracy Philipps walked that line of peril, stopping just short of 'going native'. To disguise oneself as the member of a different race, explains Tracey, an agent must rely not on costume or makeup but rather on *internalizing the other's identity*: 'A clever man looks the same and *is* different.' He passes by allowing himself to be what he pretends to be. But this willed entry into double consciousness, he warns, also jeopardizes the predominance of the agent's own rationality, a deeper fealty he must protect at all costs.

From time to time the real Tracy Philipps ruminated on his own desire to become the Other. Knowing that one's own civilization has betrayed one, he wrote, can 'gnaw deep into a man's morale and sap his ability and self-confidence in his work.'[52] In T.E. Lawrence's 'Seven Pillars and the pathetic inscription to his translation of Homer', Philipps found 'the same heartbreaking conviction':

> He too, in the most publicly useful stage of his career, used to tell us that he was sometimes tempted to believe the great illusion that the 'foreign'-folk underdogs to whom he gave his life often understand more of the needs and depths of the human heart than do one's own, more comfortable, kind. It is the Great Illusion. But how it illudes [sic] at times![53]

The fictional Phillip Tracey's crisis of identity occurs during a confrontation with Kosdrewski, the leader of the Coloured League:

> Major Tracey, . . . we are fully aware of your sympathetic feelings towards and plans for the eventual emancipation of the coloured peoples of the world. In your own mind you have granted us race consciousness. . . . We aim to raise the coloured peoples not debase them. . . . It is necessary that we have allied to us one who is of the white races and yet in full sympathy with the coloured peoples. . . . I am here to ask you, Phillip Tracey if you will take up that great destiny. (171)

Phillip Tracey 'looked for a long time at our strange visitor' and answered, finally: 'I must stand by the men of my own race until the end.'

Just a few pages later he is captured again and placed under hypnosis. Peter Pirow is dismayed 'by the sight of a fearless English gentleman, crawling on his hands and knees and fawning at the feet of a filthy African witch-woman'. But the gibbering Tracey is playing Hamlet, engineering yet another escape from Kosdrewski's clutches. Webster's plot construction, at each stage, places imperial rationality at risk and then ratchets it up to an even tighter pitch to overcome the Coloured Peril. The trouble for Phillip Tracey is that his superiors lack his finely developed sensitivity to anti-colonial threats. Called to a cabinet meeting to explain the emergency presented by the Coloured League, Tracey salutes them ruefully: 'When I spoke feelingly of Ba Sezzi cannibalism just before the War I was scoffed at as a visionary.' He goes on, in his longest uninterrupted statement in the novel, to describe Gilroy's 'Black Atlantic' from the imperialist's perspective, as a secret movement dedicated to terrorizing and 'expelling' Europeans from Africa.[54]

Imperialist security intelligence, he argues, must above all else sniff for non-compliance with the imperial power's political rationality, especially for any erosion of its own capacity to terrorize colonial subjects. Unfortunately for Tracey, the Coloured League has infiltrated the highest levels of British government. Not only was one of their agents present during the cabinet briefing, but this man dissuades the committee from responding swiftly to the crisis.

In June 1940, Tracy Philipps wrote from Montreal to philanthropist Anson Phelps Stokes in Massachusetts proposing an American lecture tour and requesting information on W.E.B. Du Bois's whereabouts. He added that he had met Dr Thomas 'Jesse' Jones, Director of the Phelps-Stokes Foundation, 'on the steamer *Energic* in the Congo in 1921'. Stokes supplied detailed information on the 'Negro Universities' but offered no financial support:

> Dr. Du Bois is still alive and active. . . . He would I am sure be glad to hear from you. He has been somewhat critical of the British, especially in Kenya and South Africa, and in matters of Native policy, but he has greatly broadened his point of view in recent years and is a man of great force.[55]

Philipps pursued his lecture tour proposal with Jesse Jones, describing his topic in a characteristic flight of tortuous imagery:

> I have not felt it necessary to put forward any British point of view . . . rather a picture of conditions . . . seen through the chinks in the 'blinds' of the kitchen windows of Italy's and Germany's tradesmen's Entrances and Back Doors. The view may be as 'through a glass, darkly.' But the silhouette stands out all the more clear-cut . . . . It is in short an attempt at interpretation not only of the transitory oligarchies of this apocalypse which are wrenching the world out of the true, but also an appreciation, seen from beneath, of the deep-seated sentiments of the great masses of the Peoples who, the more that anarchy seems to threaten, will thrust up from below and make felt their elemental human will. It is a tour-of-the-horizon of the Shape of Things to Come wherever the sombre outline of the swelling cloud-the-size-of-a-man's-clenched-hand can already dimly be discerned.[56]

Replying on behalf of the Foundation, Jones refrained from commenting on the proposed lecture theme but he encouraged Philipps to attend Dr Du Bois's First Phylon Conference to be held at Atlanta's Fisk University in April 1941.[57]

In response to Philipps's overture, Du Bois saluted 'My dear Mr. Philipps' and challenged the Englishman to provide 'a frank verbal statement before representatives of some forty American Negro Institutions of learning', responding directly to the following question:

> 'After the present war and in case the British Commonwealth of Nations survives, how far are the British people willing to regard their colored subjects in Africa and Asia as existing for their own good, capable of education to develop their own abilities and organize to produce goods and furnish services for their own best development and not for the profit or convenience of England and the white world?'
> I hope you can prepare such a statement and later let us publish it.[58]

Du Bois already had a general idea of Philipps's views from having published the latter's October 1938 address to the Italian Royal Academy in Rome. *Phylon*'s

'Chronicle of Race Relations' served as Du Bois's human rights watch and as a barometer of global race relations. Among its more provocative selections was a speech given by Adolf Hitler on 10 December 1941, otherwise suppressed by Allied censorship.[59] In that case, Du Bois pointed out that Hitler 'did not touch at all on his favorite race theories' and instead 'struck England, France and America in their vulnerable parts.' Hitler cited statistics of imperialism: 'Forty-six million English rule and govern a total territory of roughly 40,000,000 square kilometres in this world . . . gained by force and robbery.' In order to sustain the 'band of several hundred people who possess immeasurable fortunes', he added, '100,000,000 colonial workers must work in India under a miserable standard of living.' But even such massive colonial exploitation did not produce uniform wealth for everyone in Britain or America. On the contrary, Hitler concluded, the extremes of wealth and poverty inside these countries 'baffle description'. Du Bois's coda to Hitler's speech posed the same question he addressed to Philipps:

> It is, of course, not to be doubted that in the redistribution of world ownership which Hitler has in mind, the suppressed races and masses could look for no further share in the ownership themselves . . . but that does not keep the man in the street, particularly if he is colored, from asking the Anglo-Saxon frankly 'Suppose you do overcome Hitler and obtain power, where do we come in?'[60]

Du Bois introduced Philipps to *Phylon* readers as 'a distinguished Englishman who has spent much time in the colonies'.[61] Philipps defined three principles of decolonization: 'a) to give in good time; b) to give from strength [and] c) to ensure that the European language and culture can take root and produce sympathy long after the colony becomes independent.' Just as Macaulay's famous Minute had prescribed the British acculturation of higher castes in Indian society, so Philipps promoted the 'quiet building-in' of a certain European political understanding in the colonies.

'Official censorship of liberal thought', warned Philipps, was 'among the chief causes of the loss to Europe of the South American colonies.' And colonial administrators in Africa and Asia were careless censors, too apt to fear using the press to teach colonized peoples '*positive* and satisfying doctrine'. These administrators acted like 'Tritons among the minnows', heedless of the aspirations of their colonial subjects. Crucially, they prepared neither themselves nor these subjects for the inevitably explosive confluence of liberal thought with local nationalisms. Insipid rhetorical commitments to liberal democratic principles were 'dangerous and illogical' when 'democracy is tacitly withheld by those same democrats.'[62]

On the other hand, what Philipps considered 'positive and satisfying doctrine' did not necessarily advance the cause of democratic suffrage. On the contrary, he said, what promises to be preparatory to full liberal democracy presents the greatest *danger*. In strains that resonate with Phillip Tracey's statements in *The Man Who Knew*, Philipps described to his Italian audience a combined European 'Colonial Power' preoccupied on every front with excessive local demands for political sovereignty that ignored 'the European cry of "Safety First" '.

Speaking in Mussolini's Rome of 1938, it is not surprising that Philipps's intimated colonial policy for Africa frankly rejected British parliamentary democracy as unsuitable. Instead, colonial authority ought to be refined through increased sensitivity to 'the unwritten, delicate and deep democracy within the totemic clan'. He advocated the immediate cessation of colonial instruction in 'unsuitable European philosophies'. Already, these had spread through the colonial arena in 'virulent and haphazard patches'. Rather, a new and unspecified—but traditionally authoritarian and patriarchal—political culture must emerge to stem Africans' 'loss of faith in the simple and suitable religions of their own'.

Dr Du Bois left it to readers to sort out the address's ambivalent implications for colonial emancipation. Behind the scenes, though, he sent Philipps a further note about the upcoming conference. 'We are counting on your presence', he emphasized:

> Your speech will take place in a fairly small room before an audience of two or three hundred persons about half of whom will be special trained persons in sociology and economics from Negro colleges throughout the South.[63]

In the event, Philipps shared the platform with two presidents of southern colleges in a plenary session entitled 'Economic Security for the Darker Races'. Their exchanges were not transcribed, but Philipps reported to Sir Gerald Campbell, his contact in the British embassy to Washington, that his talk prompted 'numerous questions, which I invited'.[64] The audience 'showed some bitterness, and considerable prejudice,' he wrote, 'based on misrepresentations made to them, probably from Communist sources, and on inadequate and outdated information.'

While attending Du Bois's Phylon Conference Philipps once again became a civil servant, receiving the long-awaited offer of Canadian government employment. It came not from Judge Davis but from the RCMP.[65] Philipps bewailed Commissioner S.T. Wood's strict remunerative terms, but he left Atlanta no longer a 'dollar-a-year man' but a civilian Mountie assigned to monitor and analyze the activities of ethnic groups. Back in Ottawa, he renewed his *Phylon* subscription and he would soon write once more to Du Bois.

Neither Du Bois's published correspondence nor his autobiography mentions Tracy Philipps. Admittedly, he was a minor character in that civil rights crusader's long and busy life. Philipps, on the other hand, clearly was in awe of Du Bois, seeking his recognition (while also betraying him); he was drawn to Du Bois's unswerving commitment to emancipate black America and colonized peoples everywhere, and yet fearful of its success.

Propaganda

First steps towards a propaganda initiative directed specifically at minority 'nationalities' were taken at an interdepartmental meeting in the East Block in October 1941. In Room 123 of the Department of External Affairs, representatives of both culture- and security-related departments gathered around Chairman T.C. Davis to initiate a 'committee on cultural-group cooperation'. Of the 16 men in attendance only press censor Ladislaus Biberovich was a member of a minority nationality group, yet his presence did not reflect 'affirmative action' but rather the negative spectre of minorities as security risks.[66]

Tracy Philipps's reserve during this meeting is not surprising since his role as European adviser to the new committee was not expected to be central. His marginal comment 'WHY?' penciled next to Biberovich's name on his agenda suggests that he was preoccupied with his bitter personal dispute with the latter. Philipps's estranged wife and son were staying with the Biberoviches, a domestic situation that eventually led to vilification on both sides; but on this day the two listened in silence to deliberations on how best to 'Canadianize' the nationality groups.

From an intelligence perspective, 'various ways of maintaining close contact with these communities were considered from the point of view of integrating the individuals composing such communities into the national war effort.'[67] Representing the Department of External Affairs, Norman Robertson expressed concern that the Defence of Canada Regulations cast too wide a net and hoped the committee might supply information to justify certain exemptions. The RCMP's Inspector Saul sought feedback on variations in the treatment minorities received at the hands of local and provincial authorities. With respect to free movements and foreign forces, Robertson felt 'the new section would be extremely useful in providing reports of the trends . . . among the various foreign-language groups.' Such information would become part of the inter-Allied exchange of intelligence, and as such the new committee would be expected to co-operate closely with his department.

Censorship representative Wilfred Eggleston agreed that his unit could step up its monitoring of foreign-language presses and supply translations of such material to the new committee. It was agreed that the committee might also care to make recommendations regarding the future of the Ukrainian Labour-Farmer Temple Association. Their halls were seized by the Custodian of Enemy Property at the outset of the war to forestall Communist subversion. Tracy Philipps had already proposed that they be turned over quietly to non-Communist elements within the Ukrainian communities across Canada, but he refrained from any comment at this gathering.

On the propaganda side, the NFB's John Grierson represented the Department of Wartime Information. The recent film *Peoples of Canada* featured immigrant groups, he said, and the Film Board's growing non-theatrical film distribution system brought such films to even the most remote communities. The CBC's Peter Aylen promised to provide translations of foreign-language broadcasts carried on commercial stations monitored by the CBC's radio censorship authority. He cautioned that any foreign-language broadcasts planned by the committee would have to be delivered through local commercial stations 'rather than the CBC national network'. At the close of the meeting 'the representatives present were wholly agreed that the Committee did not have as its object the preservation of group differences, but should seek to encourage individuals from these foreign-language groups to identify themselves as closely as possible with the rest of the Canadian community.'[68]

The new Committee on Co-operation in Canadian Citizenship (CCCC), a name suggested by Norman Robertson, was not exactly what Philipps had lobbied for, but its autonomy from the Department of Wartime Information came as a relief. He had written beforehand to a confidante: 'between ourselves, I am not at all happy about . . . any European Section . . . [forming] part of the Dept. of Information. The Department of Information is designed to deal with Anglosaxon and Francophone Canadians whose countries and near kindred are not hostages or tools in foreign and enemy hands.'

Assigning him to this department would be like 'putting an electrical engineer under home consumption publicity men'. For Philipps, the task of 'Canadianizing' the foreign-born paralleled electrification: 'This new kind of foreign-European work, in the long and delicate process of transmuting over 2½ million souls to a Canadian current, is as technical and complicated as the work of an electrical engineer.' The general direction of the work, he believed, 'can only be guided by the Department of External Affairs.'[69]

As it turned out, the Committee quickly drifted away from the guidance of External Affairs and Philipps developed his own network of contacts. Norman Robertson's distant attitude perplexed Philipps, as did the coolness he encountered in exchanges with Intelligence chief T.A. 'Tommy' Stone and his newly appointed deputy, George Glazebrook. After illness removed CCCC Chairman George Simpson from the scene, Philipps gravitated towards his RCMP contacts, with whom he carried on a lively exchange of correspondence. He turned, too, towards the United States, where he cultivated counterparts in the FBI, the Office of Strategic Services, and the State Department.[70] He nurtured contacts with British officials in Ottawa, New York, Washington, and Detroit, although notably he failed to win the confidence of Malcolm MacDonald, Britain's High Commissioner to Canada and formerly his superior in the British Foreign Office.

Returning from Du Bois's 1941 Phylon Conference in Atlanta the previous spring, Philipps stopped in New York to meet fellow Briton Michael Huxley at the Inter-Allied Information Committee on the fifth floor of the Rockefeller Center. Huxley directed this 'high grade' or 'white' propaganda outlet launched in the autumn of 1940 to help win US support for Britain against the Axis. Specifically, the Committee sought to cast British war aims in the light of a new 'internationalism', a message intended to counteract Americans' suspicions that Britain's true war aim was to preserve its empire.[71] Huxley regarded his visitor with caution: clearly Philipps had sniffed 'black' propaganda on the wind, and he wanted to know more.

Unaware that 30 storeys above and two below Huxley's office British Security Co-ordination was already planning deceptions behind enemy lines and in neutral countries, not least the United States, Philipps sought Huxley's views on a request by Count Vladislav Radziwill 'to have selected Poles trained in Canada for eventual work between the Prussians and the Russians along the eastern margin of Europe'.[72] Personally, he felt enemy intelligence services would have 'Radziwill pretty closely taped'. Huxley replied crisply that he was 'not competent to respond' and whatever suggestions Philipps had ought to be directed to Malcolm MacDonald in Ottawa.[73]

MacDonald's brief and patronizing replies to Philipps's unsolicited estimates— on matters ranging from anti-English resentment in Quebec to the outlook for striking miners in Cape Breton—reminded him not to extend his activities beyond monitoring and reporting on the condition of the foreign-born labour force in Canada.[74] Apparently this was the field where it was calculated Philipps could do the least damage, and, noisily, he obeyed. In New York, Michael Huxley either knew or had been warned to keep the former imperial intelligence officer in the dark, so Philipps left the Inter-Allied Information offices knowing nothing about BSC, the SOE training centre 'Camp X' near Oshawa, or the 'black' propaganda and sabotage activities it supported. More importantly, he left without a true appreciation of the orientation of British 'white' propaganda vis-à-vis the United States. He failed to grasp that his explicit valorization of the old British Empire was completely unsynchronized to the rhetoric of 'new internationalism', soon to find formal expression in the Atlantic Charter and the creation of the United Nations and other world institutions.

In Ottawa, Philipps's propaganda efforts through the CBC met a similar pattern of resistance. At first, the CBC had seemed co-operative; indeed, the Committee received word from Dr J.S. Thomson, the Director-designate of the CBC, expressing 'his fullest sympathy with the aims of our Committee'.[75] Philipps explained that 'recent-Europeans . . . form almost one body in the Western Hemisphere from Arctic Canada to Antarctic Argentine.' Following the Americans' lead, domestic foreign-language radio ought to be used to 're-nationalize' these diaspora. Robert England agreed, stressing 'the great importance in the first generation of broadcasting (to people who cannot yet think in French or English) in their mother-tongues.' Philipps's contacts reported that daily Axis short-wave propaganda broadcasts successfully promoted disaffection among foreign-born listeners in Canada.[76] Philipps had urged the CBC to recruit and train foreign-born broadcasters, people fully conversant with the cultural vernaculars and political niceties of each cultural minority, to produce short but routine broadcasts first in Italian, with other languages to follow.

It was an exaggeration to say Dr James Thomson had 'fullest sympathy' for Philipps's proposal. As Thomson wrote to John Grierson, Philipps's 'belief that such broadcasting might have a useful effect upon such groups in giving them a sense of solidarity with the Canadian people' raised what was probably an 'inevitable' question as a result of American foreign-language broadcasting. He continued, without enthusiasm:

> The question is a somewhat difficult one in which the Canadian Broadcasting Corporation would not wish to take any isolated responsibility. We should be ready to undertake a strictly limited amount of such broadcasting, but only if it were considered by responsible authorities to be in the national interest.
>
> Mr. Philipps tells me that the groups . . . of primary importance at the present time . . . are the Italian speaking communities both in Toronto and in Montreal. He believes it might have considerable usefulness if on certain festival occasions a short programme of combined music and talk were provided for these particular groups.[77]

CBC broadcasts set the pace both in radio censorship and in domestic radio propaganda directed at English and French elements of the population. The CBC censored itself and it policed the self-censorship policy devolved on private broad-casters under the 1939 Defence of Canada Regulations. Cognizant of the acute alienation felt by linguistic minority groups, Philipps believed that the mood of censorship preventing their inclusion in national broadcasting only perpetuated negative effects of guardianship by repressive apparatuses. Ultimately, his inces-sant lobbying induced the CBC to produce one 15-minute broadcast in Italian, for which Philipps received warm personal thanks from Italian Canadians. Then Thomson reaffirmed Peter Aylen's initial position with finality: henceforth foreign tongues would not interrupt CBC's streams of English and French programming.[78]

Once again, Philipps misapprehended Canada's emerging national culture. When he observed to Sir Gerald Campbell in Washington that national minority groups were 'compartments of Canada that are States in miniature' he intended that they be treated as a multiplicity, pending a gradual coalescence of group identity as Canadians. But segmenting this audience to narrow-cast propaganda messages to ethnocultural communities ran counter to the CBC's understanding of its mandate. To the contrary, it seemed to Thomson and his associates that the value of linguis-tic and cultural *continuity* in disseminating a pan-Canadian official consciousness outweighed any possible negative effects of leaving minority-language groups exposed to unopposed enemy short-wave propaganda.[79]

The Hour Strikes

Unlike his friend Watson Kirkconnell, the university professor, translator, and liter-ary critic, Tracy Philipps had little affinity for artistic and literary expressions of Canadian cultural nationalism. True, he once noted on his desk pad that 'authors of REO [recent European origin] writing of Canada with their inherited genius [are] contributing to Canadian unity in the air and atmosphere Canada is giving them.' But this was an isolated jotting. Philipps appears to have read no Canadian or neo-Canadian writer or poet, nor to have examined the work of its painters or musi-cians. Appointed to the Committee on Co-operation in Canadian Citizenship, Watson Kirkconnell failed to interest Philipps or the Committee with his proposal to launch a War Writers Board similar to the American initiative of that name.[80]

Kirkconnell was nonetheless an influential friend during Philipps's years in Ottawa. As lead author of a seminal 1944 report on *The Humanities in Canada* he called for a massive invigoration of Canadian universities after the war: 'Higher edu-cation', wrote Kirkconnell, 'shall liberalize or humanize the modern student, so as to educate the whole man and make him completely human, a representative of the uni-versally human spirit.'[81] In the tradition of nineteenth-century educational reformers Matthew Arnold and Cardinal Newman, Kirkconnell's university of the humanities was to define the intellectual profile of national culture. It required the establishment of expensive new federal cultural institutions such as a National Library, but in return Canadians would benefit from a thriving national literature and drama, an enriched understanding of 'Canadian society', and enhanced international stature.

Kirkconnell's humanities report should be read in conjunction with his June 1941 propaganda booklet, *Canadians All*, written for and published by the Director of Information in Ottawa.[82] With the theme 'Unity, Not Uniformity', Kirkconnell sought to derive the national population along new lines. Setting aside 'the few Indian survivors, a few Asiatic immigrants and some negroes brought from Africa', he emphasized that the vast majority of Canadians shared a common European heritage. His discussion of physical types touches on eugenics, arguing that there 'is no such thing as a French race, an Italian race, an Anglo-Saxon race or a German race—or, for that matter, a Ukrainian race, or a Russian race.' All these were variants of Europe's diverse civilization.[83]

Thus Kirkconnell's booklet grouped 'Canadians All' under a European race umbrella, providing each with a capsule description and statistical profile. English Canadians and French Canadians were absorbed into the alphabetical sequence of 25 nationalities groups, which was illustrated by stills taken from the NFB's *Peoples of Canada*. Each of these cultural groups, Kirkconnell warned, was vulnerable to sinister infiltration by the 'World Conspiracies' of Fascism and Communism. The least acculturated groups, he wrote, were primary targets for a 'Propaganda for Disunity' that sought the destruction of Canada and the British Empire. Internment of German and Italian Canadians was necessary to suppress the agents of world conspiracies pursuing this aim. These, he wrote, 'are no better than rats gnawing fatal holes through the bottom of a vessel as it passes through stormy seas.'[84]

Kirkconnell was the most strident anti-Communist academic of his generation. That he was tasked with writing *Canadians All* and *The Humanities in Canada* leaves no doubt about the official ideological orientation of the emerging national culture, even prior to the Cold War.[85] Anti-Communism was an outlook he shared with Tracy Philipps, although the latter was not so attuned to what this meant in the shifting sands of Canadian higher education. For his part, Philipps had a keener sense that fears regarding Communist fifth columns augured a rapid expansion and refinement of the state security apparatuses.

When the Hitler-Stalin Pact collapsed in June 1941, Kirkconnell observed to Philipps that 'Hitler has given the kaleidoscope a real twirl as far as the various European groups are concerned.'[86] They now met stiffened resistance to their anti-Communist propagandizing. Indeed, they and their Committee became the object of hostile propaganda emanating from Communist circles. Where initially 'Quisling Kirkconnell' bore the brunt of the criticism, Philipps and Kysilewsky soon became targets as well.

In September 1942 a blistering attack in *The Hour*, a mimeographed New York news sheet, was received in Ottawa. It struck directly at the character of Tracy Philipps:[87]

MR. PHILLIPS GOES TO WASHINGTON
Within the past fortnight a dapper gentleman by the name of Tracy Phillips [*sic*] has visited Washington . . . 'advising' State Department officials regarding the European situation and problems of the foreign born in this country. Those State Department officials are doubtless unaware of certain of this gentleman's past associations and of some of the more interesting aspects of his career.

A former member of the British Colonial Office, Tracy Phillips was known to be in close touch with 'appeasement circles' in England before the war. Lady Astor and Lord Halifax, whose names were then associated with the so-called Cliveden Set, were among Phillips' intimate friends. Phillips was also said to be a great admirer of Benito Mussolini. He was a frequent visitor to fascist Italy. In October, 1938, Phillips attended the Congress of the International Colonial Institute in Rome. With him at the time was the Viscountess Dorothy Downe, well known in England for her pro-Nazi sympathies and as an intimate friend of Sir Oswald Mosely, the leader of the British Fascists, who is now in jail.

The Fascist Government of Italy displayed considerable warmth towards Phillips who, as late as March, 1940, publicly expressed his admiration for the brutal Fascist colonial policy in Africa. He informed the English public: 'the Italian technique of overseas settlement offers us much to learn.'

Interesting Connections

U.S. State Department officials might find of greatest interest the relations that have existed between Phillips and certain fascist-Ukrainians in North America who have been connected with the German War Office and the German ministry of Propaganda.

Tracy Phillips arrived in Canada from England on June 10th, 1940, and was promptly contacted by Luke Myshuha, editor of the pro-Nazi Ukrainian American newspaper, SVOBODA. This paper was banned by the Canadian Government subsequent to exposures of its pro-Nazi character appearing originally in the THE HOUR. . . . Only a short time before this Myshuha had returned from Nazi Germany where he had been a guest speaker on one of Dr. Goebbel's radio programs.

Phillips' visit to Canada had been preceded by that of a fascist-Ukrainian, W. Kissilevsky [sic], who spread the word that Phillips was coming as a 'special emissary of Lord Halifax'. From the day he set foot on Canadian soil, Phillips was enthusiastically hailed by fascist-Ukrainian organizations set up by representatives of the German Intelligence Service. The very friendly reception accorded to Tracy Phillips by these persons at a time when Germany and England were at war seemed rather strange, to say the least.

As a matter of fact, Phillips association with the fascist-Ukrainians dates back some years. In the summer of 1939 Phillips visited the town of Alassio, Italy, and spent a week at the Villa Romana, home of Jacob Macohin, a meeting place for Nazi-Ukrainian agents from all parts of the world. . . . According to the London DAILY EXPRESS of December 5th, 1938, Macohin was then proclaiming his intention to lead a fascist-Ukrainian army of 600,000 men, trained and equipped by Nazi Germany, against Soviet Russia. Interestingly, W. Kisselevsky, who now serves as Tracy Phillips' private secretary, formerly worked as a propaganda agent for Macohin.

Aid to War Effort?

Tracy Phillips has been in Canada for two years. His influential friends in England were doubtless useful to him in securing his present position with the Canadian Department of War Services. Phillips now works with a section of this Department called the Committee on Canadian Citizenship which has the function of organizing the foreign born behind the war effort of the United Nations.

It would appear to THE HOUR that, in view of his strange connections and expressed opinion, Tracy Phillips is hardly the man to organize effective support of the war effort or to give 'advice' to the United States State Department.

With the publication of this article, the propagandist Philipps became a victim of his own genre. Moreover, as if the anonymous *Hour* article was not scalding enough, it was reprinted in the respectable and widely circulated *New Republic* in 1942.[88] For the most part the allegations were true, if exaggerated. Philipps's papers contain superficial references at least to Myshuha, Dorothy Downe, Macohin, and Fascist Italy. Kysilewsky did work for Macohin during the 1930s and among his photographs is a beach shot he took at Alassio in June 1938 of Macohin and his American wife, Lee, standing on the beach with 'General Rossi' in blackshirt and riding boots. On at least one occasion Philipps passed a request for money through Kysilewsky to a group he described only as the 'M's'—Kysilewsky was to convey it surreptitiously through 'the brother' in New York. On the whole, though, the *Hour*'s characterization of Philipps as a rabid agent of Fascism was a distortion.

The article's content and tone convinced Philipps that the information emanated from a Canadian source; indeed, he deduced it could only have been the work of his arch rival, censor Ladislaus Biberovich.[89] But he had no proof. For the time being, Philipps's immediate superior, T.C. Davis, stood by him, but the Judge's departure for Australia was imminent. Minister Thorson had already been elevated to the bench, and his successor, General LaFlèche, was as yet an unknown quantity. Truth or slander, the Ottawa mandarinate buzzed with the news of *The Hour*.

R.B. Bryce, Treasury official and future Clerk of the Privy Council, received a copy of the article from 'a friend in New York' and circulated it to Clare Moyer, Secretary of the Wartime Information Board.[90] Lester Pearson mentioned the article at the Board's meeting, and Moyer had it distributed to Board members. Both Arnold Heeney and Brooke Claxton read the clippings, and when the articles reached General LaFlèche he wrote to Norman Robertson asking if there 'was any grounds for the adverse comments'.[91] George Glazebrook was assigned to trace the origins and development of the Committee and Philipps's role in its activities. Furthermore, Philipps sensed a new threat moving up the chessboard in the person of the Film Board chief, John Grierson, soon to take over as the Director of Wartime Information. As a result of the negative publicity, Philipps became a focus of attention for Grierson's cadre of capable deputies: Donald W. Buchanan, Malcolm Ross, and Arnold Davidson Dunton.

John Grierson, January 1943. NFB Archives.

Philipps accurately identified the youthful Dunton as the rising star of this group, and he exerted his considerable charm on the younger man.[92] On a personal and confidential basis Philipps began sending him RCMP intelligence reports and often passed by his office to share confidences. On 13 November he sent him a secret report concerning a prominent Hungarian Canadian, but Dunton was out of the office that day. In fact, he was with Judge Davis, George Glazebrook, and Saul Rae discussing the future of Philipps and the Nationalities Branch.

In Judge Davis's mind, Philipps and Kysilewsky already had resigned 'on account of the attacks in American publications'. As Dunton recorded:

This means the disbanding of the Committee on Nationalities (with all its aliases). Davis said he was going to recommend to General LaFleche that . . . work on foreign-language press in Canada be transferred to WIB. He, Glaze-brook and Rae said they would like . . . WIB to work closely on this with External Affairs which would formulate policy and consider in particular the question of direct contacts with foreign language groups other than through their press.

The way Glazebrook expressed it was: the Simpson Committee is disbanded and its paid employees set at large. Some can be rehired if wanted. He, Davis and Rae are all doubtful about Kaye . . . they feel he is so tarred with the Philipps brush that his usefulness is questionable . . . he might be considered for straight reading and reporting work. Glazebrook and Rae know a young man of Russian extraction named [Leo] Malania whom they regard very highly.[93]

Clearly, Judge Davis did not expect Philipps to cling to his post, nor was the Judge mindful of General LaFlèche's glacial progress in taking charge of the Ministry of National War Services. Philipps railed at LaFlèche's inactivity, telling Simpson that he was as 'suspicious as a peasant-come-to-town'.[94] But it was only the General's disinclination to be rushed that stood between the European adviser and outright dismissal. Through the winter of 1942–3, with Grierson at the helm of wartime information, the Philipps case percolated among External Affairs officers and Grierson's staff, leading to Donald Buchanan's definitive brief on the 'Ukrainian Question'.

Through consultations with Glazebrook and Malcolm Ross, Buchanan determined that 'no continuity of policy in regard to war information and Canadian groups of Ukrainian origin has ever been established' despite the efforts of agencies concerned with this question. His list of these agencies nicely captures the security dimension of the nascent multiculturalism infrastructure:[95]

(1) Committee on Cooperation in Canadian Citizenship, in which the work of Tracy Philips [*sic*] is centralized. (NWS)
(2) Press Censorship under W. Eggleston and H.W. Baldwin. (NWS)
(3) Censorship of Incoming Publications (Foreign) exercised in practice by Dr. Biberovich, working in co-operation with H.W. Baldwin.[96] He also prepares a resume of Ukrainian Press Comment (Canadian) for W.I.B. reports division. Biberovich is a well-educated Ukrainian, held in high regard by Press Censorship and by External Affairs. (Department of National Revenue)
(4) Custodian of Enemy Property . . . E.H. Coleman. . . . This bureau is in charge of the seized Ukrainian Labour Halls. (Department of Secretary of State)
(5) RCMP . . . they investigate subversive activities. (Department of Justice)
(6) . . . External Affairs takes an extra-curricular interest in what other departments do in regard to Ukrainian groups in Canada.

In red ink, Buchanan bolded the heading: WHY THE QUESTION OF UNIFORM POLICY IS URGENT. He explained that anti-Russian articles in the right-wing ethnic press and the activities of the Ukrainian Canadian Committee had drawn protests from the Soviet ambassador. The UCC's petition for Ukrainian self-determination particularly rankled the Soviets. Furthermore, committees on civil liberties passed resolutions protesting the action of the government in continuing to hold Ukrainian Labour-Farmer halls that were seized at the outset of the war.

Both External Affairs and the Press Censorship agreed with Buchanan's action plan. He foresaw a standing interdepartmental committee with a permanent secretary appointed from the WIB to co-ordinate policy regarding foreign-language groups. The Committee would begin with press sources and then move into radio and film as alternative propaganda outlets:

Glazebrook feels that [the Department of National] War Service[s] must, if approached, consent to what is suggested above. There is no suggestion of doing away at once with the Committee on Cooperation in Canadian Citizenship, but if Tracy Philipps began to deviate from the uniform policy laid down by the inter-departmental committee, then of course his position would become untenable and he would have to resign.[97]

Buchanan's dossier included 'further confidential information about T. Philipps' received by Malcolm Ross from Glazebrook. The latter also confirmed 'that the order in council for Simpson's Committee never passed, but that the Committee was called together by the Minister of National War Services.'[98] It met just twice in 1942 and 'the minutes do not show anything beyond vague general discussion. Philipps's activities are impossible to define as he never sent to External Affairs copies of the material which he sent out to the Foreign Language Press in Canada.' That Malcolm Ross was prominent in the National Council for Soviet Friendship may explain why he attached a fresh copy of the *Hour* article to Buchanan's report and not Philipps's published rebuttals. Ross confirmed that Philipps's 1941 book review in *The Manchester Guardian* did state that '[w]e have a great deal to learn from the way the Italian Fascists have colonized Libya.'[99]

Armed with Buchanan's report, Grierson paid a visit to the Canadian Prairies where he collected anti-Philipps testimony from a deputation of the Canadian Unity Council. They did not view Philipps as any kind of messiah. His branch 'was political', they told Grierson, 'coloured from the outset. Instead of getting the whole thing together on a healthy basis, it announced guardianship over helpless divided Ukrainians.' Philipps, Grierson jotted, 'is associated with sanitizing the country', and this sanitization was itself a disease that needed treatment: 'The Communists regard T.P. as Fascist and his presence was interpreted right away as divisive. He created resentment.' Even the title of the Committee was considered to be insulting. 'After fifty years they don't want T.P. a newcomer to say they are Ukrainians or Poles or . . . to have the impertinence to say where their Canadianism lies.' Danes, Norwegians, Jews, Ukrainians, and Poles, wrote Grierson, were 'against setting up an Anglo-Saxon Committee of guardianship'.

Upon his return Grierson wrote to General LaFlèche to report the views of these 'English-speaking, French-speaking, Ukrainian, Armenian and Polish groups':

[A] positive policy was wanted, promoting a greater inter-acquaintance between the various ethnic groups. . . . The delegation expressed strong views in the matter of Mr. Tracy Philipps. They said that under his direction the Nationalities Branch . . . had been divisive rather than unifying [and] a co-operative understanding in the matter of information could not be implemented while he remains a negative force in the set-up.[100]

Censorship

A month after the initial meeting in October 1941 that created the Nationalities Branch, Tracy Philipps and George Simpson began receiving translations of foreign-language press articles from the press censors. Norman Robertson monitored these reports and occasionally forwarded his comments to Simpson. The machinery of censorship now open to him, Philipps exploited it to full advantage. In addition to receiving the routine translation of foreign press articles, he read locally intercepted mail on a selective basis and eventually had access to mail and cables intercepted by the centralized Allied censorship.[101]

Philipps had pressed his friend Vladimir Kysilewsky to join him when the branch finally came into being. 'I would not care to come to Ottawa,' Kaye answered, 'however well paid, to work among strangers in some office where there were a political or parochial atmosphere. . . . You know how I fear intrigue and mistrust "politics".' He left an opening, though, writing that 'if what were contemplated were to work closely with you, whose ways I know, and to work on the larger aspect . . . I know I could render real service and therefore be happy, and therefore would be inclined to accept.'[102] Against his better judgement he joined Philipps in Ottawa, where his small editorial section monitored the foreign-language press and supplied its editors with government information written in their own languages.

Philipps befriended the Director of Censorship, Col. O.M. Biggar, whose pro-Empire and staunch anti-Communist outlook he found congenial. 'Your new Division of co-ordinated censorship of all communications could help us with the most valuable material of all,' he wrote to Biggar, 'communications, including photostats of letters, concerning peoples, matters and persons of recent continental European origin whether in Europe, the Far East or the Americas.' In an annex he explained that 'an essential feature of the enemy's campaigns of rumour and of poison' was the 'whisper' used to 'discredit public or private insinuations, and thus to undermine the people's confidence.' The Communists, specifically, were 'organizing attacks on the Canadian Government' and, in a surprising turn, he added that they wished to privately discredit 'and thus to eliminate (in their own phrase) "Coldwell of the C.C.F., and Mosher, Millard and Moore of the Trade Unions." Such people's political aims and their private lives have been the subject of shameless misrepresentation.'[103]

Philipps dropped in Biggar's ear the name of his cousin, Charles des Graz, Director of the Imperial Censorship at Bermuda, where mails were censored and transatlantic cable communications intercepted. Philipps told Biggar, 'I am already getting the information from Bermuda. . . . I should like a chance to chat . . . we may be able to furnish certain information.'[104] Although his Ottawa manuscript collection contains only Canadian censorship circulars, cover slips and letters indicate that he did receive and judiciously distribute a certain number of illicitly procured intercepts. When des Graz encountered Philipps during a visit to Ottawa in June 1942, he outlined 'the new coordinated censorship set-up in Washington' and instructed his cousin on how henceforth he might obtain material through the proper channels.[105]

Des Graz visited Ottawa twice after the war to offer advice on Canada's peacetime censorship organization.[106] On 6 September 1946, the newly created interdepartmental Security Panel gave des Graz the floor. Arnold Heeney, George Glazebrook, and Norman Robertson listened as he sketched the development of imperial censorship during the war and announced Britain's decision to maintain a peacetime 'shadow' censorship organization. Returning to meet the Security Panel in July 1951, des Graz explained how Britain had silently recruited the core group of censors. Networking behind the scenes through its own veterans, British officials had signed up and trained 2,400 censors with not a breath of publicity. Approximately two-thirds of the total Censorship staff would be women, he said, as was the case during the war.[107]

Censorship is often thought to be primarily *withholding* information to prevent the transmission of knowledge, ideas, images, or objects perceived to be inimical to state interests. True, des Graz affirmed, this was one of its functions; indeed, effective censorship required the complete 'control of all channels of communication likely to be used for the transmission of such information'. This ran the gamut from telecommunications and wireless to postal services, from newspapers and publishing to broadcasting and films. Each medium required a different type of censorship organization and he went on to explain how these might be grouped.

The more important half of censorship, he emphasized, was less well known. This was as a supplier of intelligence. As Commander G.R. Tottenham reported to the Director of Naval Intelligence after the meeting, des Graz 'seemed to feel that Intelligence was the main purpose of Censorship and that Security was quite secondary.'[108] Here the censor's faculty for sensing deviance was crucial. During the war the actual tasks of covert listening, opening mail, and transcribing telegraphic messages were performed almost exclusively by women. In the male-dominated security and intelligence organizations it was assumed that women were better fitted for such tasks, and not merely because this freed men for combat-related work. It was believed that women had a special alertness to the subtleties of interpersonal communication and, if properly supervised, discretion. The gendering of electromagnetic communications was not lost on censorship and intelligence chiefs. Naval intelligence considered its women censors such a valuable resource that their identities were jealously guarded for fear of inter-agency poaching.[109]

The senior-ranking woman within the Canadian security establishment at the end of World War II was Mary Oliver. As administrator of the top-secret signals intelligence branch she participated in the rapid post-war expansion of Canada's SIGINT capability. She was also sister to Norman Robertson. To what extent their careers were interdependent is unknown; it is said by former insiders that his protection helped her rise to a position of authority in the male-dominated signals intelligence establishment. Having helped start up the signals intelligence work in Canada, she accrued influence beyond the purely administrative role of her office.[110]

On the other hand, security screenings eliminated women, too. In May 1943, when Muriel Chapin of Montreal applied for temporary editorial work in the Nationalities Branch, Philipps requested an RCMP security check. John Leopold replied that Chapin was once 'a member of a Montreal Committee of the Spanish Children's Relief Campaign' and she was suspected of subscribing to the *Canadian Tribune*. Chapin's application was rejected, and a week later Leopold added, 'it has now been learned . . . [she] is secretary of the Montreal Branch of the Writers, Artists and Broadcasters War Council. . . . Our observations show that the

Communists are taking some interest in this organization.' 'Thank you', replied Philipps. 'It is exceedingly lucky that we asked you.'[111]

By Christmas of 1942 Tracy Philipps verged on despair.[112] The brave face he put on rebutting the *Hour*'s character assassination masked an intense crisis. A legal opinion had discouraged any court action, and his shrill protests elicited few words of support. A pro forma offer of resignation had not been refused, and he stayed on beyond a self-imposed deadline without receiving any fresh endorsement. Kysilewsky retreated to his farm, nursing a stress-aggravated health condition. Philipps himself was in pain, strapped into a back brace after being 'run into on ice by children on a sledge-out-of-control'. He was astonished and further disheartened to learn that despite the minister's edict grounding him to his desk, LaFleche hardly seemed to know who he was:

> Master has not yet learned my name. When I meet him in the street, for I don't have a chance to see him elsewhere, he answers my 'Good morning, General' with a 'Good morning, Mr. Tracy.' I do not therefore flatter myself that I am ever in his mind or an object of any hostility![113]

Norman Robertson's resounding silence Philipps believed was the product of Ladislaus Biberovich's influence with George Glazebrook.[114] Indeed, discreet raids on LaFlèche's file cabinets confirmed to Philipps that machinations behind the scenes were working towards his dismissal, possibly even the closure of the Nationalities Branch. His belief that 'poison gas' was being spread by Biberovich prompted him to denounce the censor to the RCMP, naming him as a crypto-Communist and the anonymous slanderer both of his good name and that of the Simpson Committee. The RCMP received Philipps's anti-Biberovich blast with caution, but nonetheless within a few days the chief censor, A.W. Merriam, brought up with Biberovich an anti-Philipps article in *Narodna Wolya*.

Biberovich admitted to Merriam that indeed he had been Ottawa correspondent for *Narodna Wolya*, 'one of the very few independent, truly democratic Ukrainian publications'. It was true that he had criticized the Ukrainian Canadian Committee as ineffective. Indeed, he still felt that the Committee 'showed its complete incompetence in connection with the plebiscite on the conscription issue when, even in Winnipeg, Ukrainian polling divisions returned negative majorities.' Yes, Sydney Roe, his former chief, had received an anonymous letter questioning his right as a civil servant to write for a newspaper, and he was asked 'to discontinue my journalistic work which I immediately did.'[115]

After that, he said, '<u>my wife</u> started to supply *Narodna Wolya* with a weekly news letter, which fact I reported to Mr. Roe. Mrs. Biberovich is a native Canadian, a university graduate [and] a competent free-lance writer both in Ukrainian and in English.' Biberovich was outraged by Philipps's insinuations: 'I have not written the said anonymous letter', he insisted. 'I challenge Mr. Philipps . . . to prove my authorship of the letter in question, or suffer the consequences.' The true reason for Philipps's enmity, he asserted, was his help to Philipps's estranged wife: '<u>This is the back ground of Mr. Philipps['s] antagonism toward me.</u>' Yet Biberovich did not stop there:

Mr. Philipps['s] affiliation with the Canadian Ukrainian Committee goes back to
the year of his arrival in Canada in 1940. Originally there existed two Ukrainian
committees . . . on Mr. Philipps' insistence were these two committees
merged. . . . He is thus [its] spiritual father. . . . He needed the committee to get
a permanent position in Ottawa, which he finally achieved. . . . Mr. Philipps
seems to be a typical soldier of fortune, with a rather shady past. . . . Being a
pathological liar, Mr. Tracy Philipps is likely to create much additional troubles
and confusion owing to his unbalanced mind. Personally I wonder if a man
occupying a government position should be permitted to launch a police hunt
against another civil servant, instead of acting through the proper channels.[116]

Biberovich may have been unaware that Philipps also had attacked him through
Watson Kirkconnell, a friend of the English-language press censor, Wilfred Eggleston. Kirkconnell wrote to Eggleston that 'postal intercepts I have seen' proved
Biberovich's authorship of the *Narodna Wolya* letter. Supposedly, Biberovich had
written that Professor Glazebrook 'is interested in the foreign-language press and
on his initiative there will soon appear reviews of that press in the English
language.'[117] Kirkconnell warned:

If Biberovich persuades the ingenuous Glazebrook to let him prepare the reviews,
there may be interesting complications. The Communist group in Toronto also
seems to be getting advance confidential information from some source in
Ottawa, but the complicity of Biberovich in this is not so clearly proven.

Kirkconnell's letter puzzled Eggleston, who knew Biberovich to be politically
conservative. Kirkconnell wrote again: 'I seriously feel that the Philipps-Kolessa-
Biberovich feud has been a red herring across the trail, and that Biberovich has
been duping your Department and External Affairs. I . . . urge you, confidentially,
to be on your guard.'[118] Eggleston expressed confusion and feared 'that you have
been misinformed' by Tracy Philipps:

Please don't misunderstand my attitude about your drive on the Communist
Press. Why should I object to that? Do you suppose it would have been possible
for me to have held my post for three years without developing utter contempt
for the whole pack of them? . . . If you can prove he is a Red you have really
shown up cruelly a bunch of fairly bright people who have been almost daily
contact with him . . . I wish I understood your reference to . . . placing of cre-
dence of Biberovich above the RCMP translators. Do you believe the sheets you
mentioned in your speech . . . are being . . . 'whitewashed' by Biberovich . . . ?
It's news to me. We banned the originals—mainly on Biberovich's reports. He
tipped us off when the spiritual successors came on the scene. . . . We've been
watching them suspiciously ever since. . . . In all this Biberovich has been
invaluable. Where is the 'whitewash'?

Biberovich was engaged by Sydney Roe . . . a good old English boy, a former
Press Gallery man for the Conservative press, a cautious civil servant. Syd had

been excluding Red literature for a good many years. . . . He would have a pretty good nose for a Communist. He praised B. in the highest terms. . . . B.'s present chief is Arthur W. Merriam, an active Conservative . . . private secretary to R.B. Bennett for five years, and I think a good Catholic. Arthur values B. as highly as Syd did [and as do] Charpentier, and Baldwin and Girouard, our deputies. They have had constant discussion with B. . . . Until you made the suggestion, I had never entertained the slightest suspicion about him.[119]

Reading Eggleston's frank but nervous endorsement of his bureau's anti-Communist bona fides, Kirkconnell was 'mystified' in turn:

My problem is this: since its formation fifteen months ago, our Committee has been under fire from the Left . . . the Ottawa correspondent of *Narodna Volya* has played a part. . . . In conversation with Norman Robertson, I found that his department had been somehow influenced against the Committee and was in favour of sacking Kaye and Philipps. The known intimacy of Glazebrooke [*sic*] and the <u>assumed</u> correspondent of *Narodna Volya* led me to leap to a conclusion, perhaps unwarranted.[120]

Suspicions of Biberovich lingered, and may or may not have contributed to his summary dismissal from his censorship post in 1946 for unexplained 'special reasons'. Knowing the background, Eggleston took up his case with various cabinet ministers and officials in an attempt to undo what both he and Biberovich believed was Tracy Philipps's treachery. For his part, Kirkconnell reserved judgement even when he learned through Eggleston that one of Philipps's Ukrainian contacts confessed on his deathbed to slandering Biberovich to the RCMP at Philipps's behest.[121]

Indeed, when eventually Eggleston received a report about Biberovich's file it included none of the denunciations mentioned. Biberovich's dismissal had some deeper cause. After five years of fruitless lobbying for an explanation to this mystery, Eggleston was invited by Intelligence chief George Glazebrook to visit his office for an off-the-record chat.[122] 'I have looked into the case', he said, and he explained the true reason for Biberovich's dismissal. Whatever it was, Eggleston kept it to himself, and he took his distance from Biberovich, who never obtained another government post. That Biberovich's dismissal occurred during the period of the Gouzenko disclosures raises the possibility that he was somehow implicated with the Gouzenko espionage cases. More likely, it was involvement in the movement for a free Ukraine that put him out of favour. Or perhaps Philipps had even craftier means to damage his adversary's reputation. Whatever the case, by interpolating his feud through the censorship-intelligence-propaganda complex Philipps did nothing to improve his own chances.

Intelligence

The frequent and close interactions between Censorship, the Department of External Affairs, and the Wartime Information Board, as seen through the Philipps case, did not extend so freely into the headquarters of the RCMP. The Mounties kept to themselves, and they were not implicated in the efforts to get rid of Philipps. To the contrary, when it became obvious that the Englishman's claim to be under attack had substance, Assistant Commissioner Mead's suspicion fell not on Philipps but on his opponents. If Philipps was, as he described it himself, 'tolerated with amused curiosity' in his own department, he was taken seriously by the Mounties almost until the end.

Philipps recalled that during intelligence service in World War I, Lord Milner had called him his 'live wire', and electrification was Philipps's favoured metaphor for disseminating 'Britishthinking' to ethnocultural minorities. Philipps's former connection to British Imperial Intelligence carried weight with the RCMP. The federal police responded collegially to Philipps's disdain for 'weak-liberal assimilators' with no first-hand knowledge of handling ethnocultural minorities. Only experienced 'reintegrators' such as himself, an 'electrical engineer' in the field of culture, knew how to combine intelligence, censorship, and propaganda in order to bring minorities around safely to 'Britishthinking'.[123]

During his three-month contract as an RCMP irregular in 1941 he travelled about Canada interviewing foreign-born workers and conveying his impressions to S.T. Wood. But the 'almost messianic' reception he met reverted to suspicion as his foreign-born contacts realized that Philipps had nothing concrete to offer on behalf of the government. Their 'innate resistance to Ministry of Information style propaganda', Philipps wrote to Wood, was part of a fear of the 'clever cousins of wolfish Political Police' familiar to them in their own countries. Not unreasonably, they began to suspect Philipps of ferreting for information rather than genuinely seeking their co-operation.[124] S.T. Wood, too, began to wonder about the motives of this clever British cousin.

For example, Philipps's claims to a colonel's pay, expense claims for first-class rail travel, not to mention valet services, generous tips, and use of taxis, triggered alarm bells in the frugal RCMP.[125] Commissioner Wood took a dim view of such extravagances and ordered Philipps in no uncertain terms to adapt his lifestyle to the spartan regime expected of an RCMP officer. For his part, Philipps chided the RCMP for operating reactively and not as a truly anticipatory and event-shaping intelligence agency should. He suggested that the RCMP should secretly institute foreign-language newspapers to strengthen and control moderate opinion in the ethnic communities, and that the force should produce and disseminate foreign-language radio broadcasts on the same basis. Wood demurred, receiving advice that there were already sufficient 'friendly' papers through which to convey the Mounties' point of view. On the other hand, he approved of Philipps's ideas for radio broadcasts, although these fell outside the scope of the RCMP.[126]

S.T. Wood was not about to let Philipps or any other civilian know the full extent of the Mounties' intelligence capabilities. Yet Philipps's raids on his superiors' file cabinets yielded indications of how the Mounties did on occasion shape events in advance. Through the activities of Constable Michael Petrowsky, Philipps glimpsed an interaction of intelligence and propaganda components at this early stage of their development in the months before Igor Gouzenko's defection radically accelerated their development.

During the 1930s Petrowsky became well known in the Ukrainian community in southern Ontario as a writer, translator, and playwright, as well as a staunchly anti-Communist journalist. In 1939, after various attempts to find steady work, he became an RCMP translator and interpreter, and within a year or two he was working undercover monitoring nationality groups of Slavic origin. As an active participant in Ukrainian organizations he identified their Communist and Fascist elements and assessed the strength and intentions of 'Free Ukraine' movements. Petrowsky in fact became a key RCMP operative whose centrality in the Gouzenko affair will be discussed in Chapter 5.[127]

For now, Philipps learned that a difficulty had emerged with Professor George Simpson's appointment as Chairman of the Committee on Co-operation in Canadian Citizenship. Judge Davis wanted Simpson to have the benefit of RCMP intelligence reports, but this raised an awkward problem. The RCMP Commissioner advised Davis:

> Professor Simpson's name is prominently linked with the [Ukrainian] Convention. . . . Under the circumstances, and in order to avoid embarrassment or ill-feeling, it might be good policy to treat [Petrowsky's] report as strictly confidential.[128]

Indeed, Petrowsky had overheard 'a highly confidential conversation with a member of the executive who revealed plans for forming a Free Ukrainian Movement in London.' This was 'regarded as top secret'. Petrowsky believed that even if Simpson was not directly involved, he was at least aware of and 'favoured this decision'. Davis agreed with the RCMP Commissioner that Simpson 'would note immediately that someone was in attendance at these gatherings on behalf of the RCMP and making reports [and] might rather resent this.'[129] Little could be revealed to Simpson since even severed versions of the reports would signal the presence of a police informer in his closest counsels. Eventually, it was determined that a careful briefing by Inspector Saul might convey certain important points without attracting Simpson's attention to the source of the information.[130] Knowing all this, Tracy Philipps allowed nothing to Simpson, but other than sending Petrowsky a jolly Christmas card he seems to have given the talented special constable a wide berth.

Philipps's reports were received and read by Assistant Commissioner F.J. Mead, Director of Criminal Intelligence. When the RCMP passed Philipps over to Judge Davis at the end of his initial three-month employment, Mead became his primary police contact, and to some extent Philipps sensitized him to the reality of life for cultural minorities. One report explained that 'we are not applying at home the principles for which we are inviting them to fight abroad', and Mead highlighted the following paragraph:

> They are being told [by hostile propaganda sources] that 'Canadian citizenship purports on paper to offer equality and security. But when that equality and security is inconvenient to the Anglosaxons, they invalidate its value . . . so, when a citizen needs it most, it only lets him down. Therefore those who try to become

good Canadians, and who rely on Canada's citizenship, need not expect anything in the future but to be betrayed. When "they" in effect regard you as aliens and enemies, how can you feel they are your fellow citizens and your friends?' It is pressing that we should . . . counter the effect of this poisonous propaganda.

A strong case can be made for denaturalization of individual unworthy citizens, however rich. This action would clear the way . . . to rehabilitate the full value to our citizenship to any generation or Canadian community as a whole without weakening the powers of the Federal Police.[131]

Philipps concluded by calling for co-ordinated resistance 'to disintegrating unCanadian propaganda by extremists'. The solution was at once punitive and positive, selectively targeting troublesome immigrants for denaturalization while using counter-propaganda to 'lead men by their hearts where one cannot drive them with sticks, or even by regulations.'

Mead wrote to Inspector Saul: 'There is a lot to this. I should like to discuss it with you.' In reply to Philipps, he allowed that although the Defence of Canada Regulations had been necessary as a precautionary measure, now they provided a target for provocateurs operating among the immigrant groups. He agreed the government should exploit the ceremonial value of naturalization (and punitive denaturalization) rather than simply using it to register aliens as potential security risks 'as our enemies claim'. It was regrettable that 'minor police officials' in some cases 'exercise officiousness' towards people who 'desire nothing more than to be assimilated as Canadians'. Indeed, Mead believed that:

on the whole the behaviour of the 'New Canadians' of enemy origin during this war has been as good as any other section of the community. If the government were to now tell them, in effect by lifting the impugnment of their loyalty of having to register in the manner prescribed for enemy aliens, this would be received as a striking manifestation on how Democracy works in war time and would make these people appreciate more than ever before the advantages of British citizenship.[132]

In expressing these personal views, Mead signalled his awareness that Canada had transgressed its own purported norms of civility with respect to its minorities during the wartime crisis. Philipps seized the opening to champion the cause of Doukhobor and Italian internees, the provision of chaplain services in minority languages in the Armed Forces, and foreign-language broadcasts on the CBC.

Philipps's incessant lobbying for minority rights attenuated only as he came under personal attack in the press in the autumn of 1942. From then on, his requests for security checks on individuals grew in proportion with public criticisms. Mead responded to dozens of Philipps's queries that invariably drew attention to one or another individual's rumoured Communist tendencies.[133]

When the defamatory *Hour* article came to John Leopold's attention in September 1942, he judged that Philipps must already have learned of it and reported to Mead that it 'is a bombastic statement and although based on certain known facts the attack is unwarranted.' Leopold was unmoved when Philipps wrote to

S.T. Wood denouncing Ladislaus Biberovich as the *Hour*'s anonymous source. He advised the Commissioner that 'there is nothing we can do about it nor do I think it advisable to take any part in the controversy.' He examined postal intercepts forwarded by Philipps but concluded that 'if there is a certain communist tendency . . . it cannot be described as prejudicial' and noted that Philipps's 'personal grievances [are] really of no interest to us as a police organization.'[134]

Philipps adapted his tactics accordingly and instead of attacking Biberovich directly, he cast doubt on his more immediate enemies: John Grierson and his associates. Recalling the RCMP's genuine interest in his ideas about foreign-language CBC broadcasts, he supplied the RCMP with correspondence showing how the initiative was being blocked by Grierson. Philipps brought the issue to a head by pointing out to Grierson that his plan had RCMP support. When the General Manager of Wartime Information flatly refused to co-operate, Philipps sought out Dunton, Grierson's deputy, encouraging him to break ranks with his chief. 'If you were in agreement,' he wrote, 'the [directive] could issue from this office.' Dunton replied immediately: 'the General Manager is opposed . . . therefore it is impossible to say we are in agreement.'[135]

The Mounties studied these exchanges, supplied by Philipps. Mead noted to Leopold: 'There appears to be a concerted lack of support to this Branch—can you suggest why?' No doubt Leopold had suggestions to offer. Philipps may not have known it, but the RCMP already doubted Grierson's reliability and kept a file on him. On the other hand, Philipps's escalating hysteria undermined his own credibility. His latest plea asked for RCMP backing in responding to the criticisms of Arthur Raymond Davies of Toronto. Philipps wrote to Wood complaining that 'the odds are overwhelmingly in favour of the libeller', so he urged him 'to trace the motives and source of these attacks'.

'It is difficult to say what the writer is driving at', Leopold noted laconically:

Mr. Philipps apparently thinks he has become the victim of public and political sabotage and it will be noted he requests help tracing the motives and sources. . . . [He] appears to be unduly sensitive, or perhaps he likes to play the role of a political martyr. In either case it is a private matter. . . . If every public servant or figure would be so sensitive, the courts of Canada would be devoting most of their time to hearing libel actions.[136]

Inspector Saul instructed that no reply be made pending further inquiries; after consulting with Leopold, Mead drew the matter to Commissioner Wood's attention. Thereafter, Philipps's two-way traffic with Mead and Wood ended. Despite the Englishman's redoubled flow of reports, tips, and emphatic statements of record, the Mounties elected to stand back and let matters take their course.

Contagion

From the outset F.A.M. Webster emphasized the heightened sensory capacities of the British agents in *The Man Who Knew*. They have learned from Africans how to track 'the spore of a man' even through a modern city, and to hear or smell the earliest signs of trouble. The Coloured League's undetectable airship, made of some transparent material and armed with a fantastic weapon, was immune to the usual air route surveillance maintained at British posts from Afghanistan to Egypt. Only Phillip Tracey had the savvy to spot it and shoot it down. But defeat of the Coloured League cannot be achieved solely through early warning systems and superior intelligence. Rather, through its diffused, medicalized consciousness, the Empire will tamper with 'coloured blood' in a way that prefigures mid-century developments in bacteriological weapons.

The novel's climax occurs in underground Calcutta. Wearing ammonia-soaked white shrouds, Peter Pirow and Jim Carruthers are led beneath the city to attend the Grand Council of the Coloured League. Phillip Tracey has engineered their presence to witness the terrible end of the leading insurgents, part of a plan he executed through the mysterious Agent #4. Travelling across Eastern Europe, Asia, and Africa, Agent #4 had met with each dissident group preparing for the great rebellion and infected them with a plague. Thus, within moments of the arrival of Carruthers and Pirow at the council chamber—not a grand hall, as they expected, but a 'mean little apartment, hung with rugs'—the leaders of the Coloured League will be stricken with the illness:

> We saw a shrouded figure which reclined upon a low divan. In a semi-circle before this strange figure . . . squatted maybe twenty men of various nationalities. The majority of them were Hindus and Mohammedans of India, there was, however, at least one well known Arab chief . . . two frock-coated Turks wearing the fez, a couple of Egyptians . . . a very famous West African king . . . and other men from various coloured races . . . some Russian Bolshevik emissaries, a bearded Afghan, a yellow-faced Lama from Tibet and a sprinkling of overdressed American negroes. (312)

They witness the assembly fall into chaos and the victims writhe in death agonies. The two agents, protected by their Ku Klux Klan-like medicated sheets, close in on the divan, where the shrouded figure is revealed to be Agent #4:

> I am the so-called Polish Jew peddlar who gave you certain papers and instructions. . . . You have helped to save the world from a colour war [and] saved white women and children . . . from degradation . . . .
> I went to China . . . there I found a disease . . . from which there is no reprieve. I took that plague myself and I have carried it to the uttermost ends of the earth. Wherever sedition has been talked or a rising planned, there have I gone. Every hand that has clasped mine is palsied already and soon will be cold in death. . . . You must segregate the natives where I have passed. Phillip Tracey will receive instructions. . . . Thus the disease I have spread may be stamped out—but let it run its course in Russia. (314–15)

'Thus passed the Man Who Knew', Carruthers mused; 'we never learned his name, nor even knew his nationality . . . the greatest secret service agent the world has ever seen.'

Compare this to the final pages of W.E.B. Du Bois's *Dark Princess*: the emissaries of the anti-colonial movement gather at Matthew Towns's mother's humble cottage in rural Virginia to bless the birth of Matthew's and Kautilya's African-American-Indian child. Princess Kautilya sends an aircraft to fetch Matthew, labouring far away, digging Chicago sewers:

> Last night, twenty-five messengers had a preliminary conference in this room, with ancient ceremony of wine and blood and fire. I and my Buddhist priest, a Mohammedan Mullah, and a Hindu leader of Swaraj, were India; Japan was represented by an artisan and the blood of the Shoguns, young China was there and a Lama of Thibet; Persia, Arabia, and Afghanistan; black men from the Sudan, East, West, and South Africa; Indians from Central and South America, brown men from the West Indies, and—yes, Matthew, Black America was there, too. . . . We came as laborers, as cotton pickers, as peddlars, as fortune tellers, as travelers and tourists, as merchants, as servants. . . . The Day has dawned Matthew—the Great Plan is on its way. (297)

In the period of their fiercest combat at the end of 1943, Tracy Philipps and John Grierson entered into an odd interlude of co-operation. It came courtesy of Dr Du Bois, through the communicative circuits of the Black Atlantic. In May 1943, a rumour coursed through a war munitions plant in Verdun, Quebec, intended to dissuade employees from donating blood. Rumour had it that the blood would be sent overseas 'to save lives of Chinese and Negroes' and as a result the workers shunned the blood campaign. In a plea to change their attitude, the editor of the plant newsletter wrote an article assuring the workers that the blood of white Canadians would never be used to treat non-whites. Alerted somehow to this newsletter, Du Bois reprinted the item in *Phylon*'s 'Chronicle of Race Relations' under the ironic heading: 'Canada has come forward to reassure Asia and Africa', and with the afterword: 'Attitudes like that here indicated are of sinister import.'[137]

Philipps brought the matter to Grierson's attention, vouched for Du Bois's credentials, and raised concerns that the story might be used 'to the detriment of the reputation for fair-dealing of the sister-nations of the British Commonwealth'. In effect, he wrote, 'the quotation tends to give an impression that, in Canada's war industry plants, the racial myth and racial discrimination are practiced by a "master race."'[138] A report requested by Grierson from labour liaison officer David Petegorsky supported Philipps: 'Unfortunately the quotation from "PHYLON" is all too true', he confirmed, and 'it was most embarrassing. The Editor was fired . . . and authorization for the issuance of a house organ was withdrawn from Canadian Car Munitions.' Worse than that:

> copies got into the hands of the local Negro and Chinese communities who naturally raised quite a fuss about it. The Editor actually appeared before the Congregation of the Negro United Church and apologized. Someone else sent a copy to Diefenbaker, who raised the question in the House and the pot boiled over.[139]

It happened that Grierson had just received further ammunition to use against Philipps from Arnold Heeney, George Glazebrook, and Brooke Claxton, but in forwarding Petegorsky's report he thanked Philipps for bringing the matter to his attention and added, 'it is unlikely that the same sort of thing will occur again.' Unsatisfied with this result, Philipps cautioned him that:

PHYLON is apt to collect and publish a 'picture gallery' of the English-speaking nations' attitude towards Jews and colour. We might, I think, be able to circumvent any follow-up detrimental to Canada in any subsequent issues. [W]ould you care to let me have a brief text, either for them to publish or as part of a personal and confidential letter to Dr. Du Bois 'not for publication'? I shall take no action unless I hear from you.[140]

After consulting Dunton, Grierson asked Philipps to reply 'unofficially' to Du Bois, explaining all the circumstances but avoiding any mention of Hansard, since Diefenbaker 'did not bring the whole issue out into public view . . . apparently careful not to raise a storm of publicity.' Because Philipps knew Du Bois personally:

it would be better for you to do this than for either you or me to send an official statement intended for publication. . . . Published denials or letters of explanation are, as you know, not usually as effective as a friendly word with the editor.

Aside from the prickle in the last sentence, Grierson's tone was not hostile; indeed, he 'very much appreciated' Philipps's willingness to follow the matter up, and his letter would be of 'considerable service'.[141]

The munitions plant rumour drew attention to underlying fears of contagion and purity of blood in Canadian racism, connecting it to the 'white consciousness' prevailing in various degrees from Cape Town to Toronto. Through *Phylon*, Du Bois reflected this back on Canada, and in Philipps's struggle with the Scot Grierson the health metonym was transfigured into another set of meanings about purification and sanitization. In Canada's nascent cultural bureaucracy the mark of impurity and contagion had settled on Philipps himself. Philipps was 'unhealthy', 'divisive', 'a negative force', promoting an 'Anglo-guardianship' that was by turns 'mischievous', 'incomprehensible', 'pathological', and 'mentally unbalanced'. Even as Grierson wrote warmly to thank Philipps, a press censorship report arrived on his desk prepared by Biberovich's section underlining a denunciation of Philipps, Kysilewsky, and Kirkconnell published in Toronto's *La Vittoria* the previous week. It diagnosed Philipps and his Branch as a diseased limb of government that had to be severed if the purity of national culture was to be preserved. All that was required was a physician to perform the amputation.

The England Report

Robert England arrived in Ottawa on 6 April 1944 to prepare his report on the reorganization of the Nationalities Branch. Already he had a rather stale account of activities from Philipps, 'done for the General himself' when LaFleche took over from Thorson 14 months earlier. 'Rest well', Philipps wrote to England, 'It's nice to have you here.'[142] In fact, despite his upbeat tone Philipps had been the sole occupant of the Nationalities Branch since the last remaining stenographer took sick leave. He wrote to Kysilewsky, still convalescing at his farm, that 'the Hindu Kush is hanging around Ottawa with the Armenian, & bodes no good. It was the latter who has taken him to Ext. Affs. and to LaFleche. *Usque quo, in Domine.*'[143]

Deputy Minister Chester Payne had the effrontery to tell Philipps that a new director, a 'Canadian', would soon be appointed for the Nationalities Branch. Obviously passed over, the implication for Philipps was clear. The man who once trekked from eastern to western equatorial Africa via Lake Kivu, the discoverer of the otter species *Lutra Paraonyx Philippsi*, member of Lawrence of Arabia's company, and descendant of Richard Philipps, governor of Nova Scotia when *les Acadiens* famously refused to swear allegiance to the King, was reduced to suffering indignities from the most timid and procedural of Ottawa bureaucrats. Haughtily, Philipps pointed out that there was a type of official who, just to pad his own position, would punish the subordinate who broke with procedure *in order to save lives*. He assured Payne that it was precisely this type of attitude that had ruined a once-great civil service.[144]

When not terrorizing the Deputy Minister, Philipps lobbied friends and acquaintances for support, signing his letters 's.o.s.', searching for an escape hatch in advance of Robert England's descending hatchet. His former military intelligence compatriot living in London, Meinertzhagen, could offer no help. 'Meiner' replied to Philipps that he 'did not know you had transferred your dynamo efforts to Canada where from what you say you seem to have done well.' Meinertzhagen had retired from Military Intelligence two years before:

> The modern army has no use for my age nor my experience which is out of date and perhaps almost senile. . . . The present DMI is no friend of mine and I have no influence. . . . If you are after UNRRA, there should be no difficulty. . . . They send you to a school to learn what you learned 40 years ago, guarantee nothing and then place you under a man who knows less about administration than you do. . . . Such an upheaval as this is bound to leave its mark on humanity . . . and all the worst side of human nature will manifest itself. That is what you want to get mixed up in. If I were twenty years younger, I should also want to lend a hand, but at 67 I should only burn my fingers.[145]

With no prospects in England, Philipps pursued the United Nations Resettlement and Rehabilitation Administration (UNRRA), lobbying hard both for himself and for Kysilewsky. Overtures there showed promise, although, unknown to Philipps, Chester Payne scuttled Kysilewsky's chances by providing a negative health report.[146] On the other hand, Payne and Robert England nurtured Philipps's application in order to avoid, if possible, the adverse publicity sure to follow his outright dismissal. In London, Norman Robertson tested out Sir Eric Machtig, Permanent Undersecretary of State for Dominion Affairs, who let it be known in no uncertain terms that the British would neither take Philipps back nor recommend him to anyone else.[147] That left just the UNRRA and the delicate matter of supplying a sufficiently positive character reference. Gambling that the UNRRA would not consult the British Foreign Office separately, a carefully worded letter went out over Payne's signature to Joseph P. Harris, the UNRRA's personnel director in Washington: 'I send you, herewith, our estimate as requested of [Tracy Philipps's] loyalty, character and suitability, together with details of his present work, experience and proficiency.' Philipps, the reference letter attested, was employed by the Canadian government for three years; 'he is a loyal servant and colleague . . . his linguistic gifts are notable, and he has considerable literary talent as well as a gift of presentation of viewpoints in public speech.' Relief work 'would give him a greater sphere of usefulness because of his special competence and experience in this field.'[148] With this judicious characterization the fate of Tracy Philipps passed into the hands of the UNRRA's Joseph Harris.

Hume Wrong's pessimism at External Affairs 'that UNRRA would appoint Philipps to a post without checking with the United Kingdom authorities' proved unfounded.[149] On the day of what otherwise would have been his final showdown with Robert England, Philipps was already on the train to Washington: 'I am so sorry not to see you again', he jotted to England. 'Things had to be arranged after Sat. office hours in order to fall in with the wishes of those who for some time have been calling. Good luck to you.'[150] RCMP Commissioner Wood received Philipps's cheerful note, with an extract from Martin Dies's testimony on 'communist smear activities against public servants' and a reprint from the journal *Nineteenth Century*: 'Climate and the Arctic Route'.[151]

On 19 May, the Washington *Colonist* reported Philipps's appointment as 'chief of planning' for the UNRRA. In Ottawa, Labour Progressive Party member Fred Rose and fellow-traveller Dorise Neilson attacked General LaFlèche in Parliament for his department's association with Philipps and Kirkconnell.[152] In view of Philipps's departure, England advised the minister not to reply. Instead, he wrote a speech for LaFlèche announcing a new era in minority relations. Without mentioning Philipps, he corrected the impression that he was 'Dr' England: 'I am neither professor nor Dr. nor have a title of any kind.' He tabled his report, and then set Kysilewsky to work on uncontroversial tasks. Finally, at the end of June 1944, his reorganization took effect when Frank Foulds was appointed Director of the Nationalities Branch, to be relaunched as the Citizenship Division of the Secretary of State.

After two years of criticism regarding his Englishness and evident unfamiliarity with Canadian minority groups it must have astonished Tracy Philipps to learn that the man cultivated as his replacement was the Acting Chief of Inspection Services for Plant Products in the Department of Agriculture. Indeed, when Frank Foulds presented his credentials at External Affairs, Léon Mayrand wrote in consternation to Hume Wrong that:

> Mr. Fouldes [*sic*] has as yet a rather hazy conception of the problems involved. . . . He seems to divide foreign language groups into a good lot (respectable, loyal, solid, substantial) and a bad lot (leftists, Communists). . . .

I would suggest that Mr. Fouldes be asked to come in at the earliest opportunity and that the Under-Secretary or a senior officer should have a long chat with him.[153]

What quality did Foulds have that Philipps lacked, particularly if he shared the latter's anti-Communist outlook? Perhaps it was a matter of 'character'. As an average Anglo-Canadian, Foulds was not expected to have special insight into the affairs of minority groups; indeed, precisely someone so utterly normal and unexceptional would be the most reliable node for their interaction with official Ottawa.

Homesick

Both F.A.M. Webster's *The Man Who Knew* and the records of Tracy Philipps share a remarkable disinterest in *place*. Like Webster's fiction, Philipps's copious writings—frequently typed adjacent to the window of a train compartment rumbling across the Canadian landscape—are utterly insensitive to topographic variety, qualities of light, sound, or variations in flora or fauna. If landscape is mentioned at all, it is merely by reference to place names. *Geographical space*, by contrast, is stressed continuously. That is, a specifically colonial space constitutes the scene of utterance for both Webster and Philipps, and each utterance refers back to the European metropolis. In this sense, Tracy Philipps was a character who moved through Canada as a series of imagined locales produced solely with reference to the colonial centre, thus disturbing Canadians' fragile sense of being at home in their territory. His overt anti-Communism was perhaps 'premature' in Cold War terms, but this alone was insufficient to justify his removal. Rather, I suggest, his anachronistic presence kept reminding Canadians of their colonial antecedents.

It did not take long for Philipps's fingers to get burned at the UNRRA. Just seven weeks after his departure from Ottawa, Nationalities Branch secretary Gwen Baxter reported to Robert England in Victoria, 'I ran into Capt. Cameron yesterday and had a little chat with him. He gave me a very private bit of news for you which was quite in line with your predictions—T.P. has left UNRRA and gone to Turkey but no details are forthcoming.'[154]

In Ottawa, surrounded by his closest friend's enemies and tormentors, Vladimir Kysilewsky lost heart for his work. His premonitions of 'politics and intrigue' had more than materialized, and his single purpose in being in Ottawa—to work closely with Philipps—lay in ruins. Yet he stayed with the Citizenship Branch for nearly two decades. He shuttled between various cultural minorities, conveying their views and supplying articles in their languages for their presses. The RCMP tapped him for information on Communist elements, and he watched the unveiling of the new citizenship apparatus following the passage of Paul Martin's Citizenship Act in 1946–7.

Just how anachronistic and displaced he felt is captured in his Christmas letter to Tracy Philipps in 1957, just two years before the latter's death:

Vladimir Kysilewsky playing a toy xylophone at the Nationalities Branch Christmas party, 22 December 1944, room 156, New Supreme Court Building. NAC, PA 195826.

Is it fifteen years since you gave the Christmas party for children at the Rox-borough? Do you remember? . . . The war was on, London was bombed, friends were killed. In Ottawa, too, we had our tribulations, although of another kind. I think—it is better to forget it.

When I have the 'blues', I feel 'homesick'. I miss the bygone days. I miss the old pictures on the walls. I even miss the rather sedate atmosphere of the Edwardian times, if you remember. It was unthinkable to raise one's voice.[155]

If national culture was to provide a degree of cognitive stability to a whole continent of persons suffering various states or stages of colonial displacement, it did little for Tracy Philipps's strange genius:

Like Nansen, under whom I had the honour to work in east Europe, Lawrence of Arabia made clear . . . the bitter lot and final disillusionment of those of us who give our lives to work for men of other blood and less mechanised minds in the uphill struggle towards [a] better understanding among mankind. . . .

In the services of the Crown, which has been the second religion around which my ideals have resolved, I have spent a lifetime far from the men and women of my race. . . . But today, for deep reasons, <u>some</u> of which you happen by chance to know, I have had almost enough. I have been both humiliated and disillusioned . . . suffered both the public kiss of Judas and the private betrayal of Delilah. I begin to feel the nostalgia and the need of sight and sound, of the slow shy touch, of those of my own kindred and of my own kind in my own home. [156]

With Foulds's arrival on the scene, Canadian characterizations of Tracy Philipps lapsed, but his restless and ambivalent legacy persists in the National Archives. The man who lobbied for Canadian minorities' cultural rights during World War II was, at the same time, an emissary of a reactionary colonial ideology fading like the disintegrating Union Jacks and imperial insignia decking Ottawa's Anglican Cathedral. Freud once diagnosed the 'state' within the state as a trauma, expressed in the form of deferred obedience to the vanquished 'double' of a prevailing authority figure. Philipps's and Kaye's homesickness was symptomatic of a 'passionate and traumatized' element in Canada's colonial past that, to borrow from Jacqueline Rose, 'runs backwards and forwards, never completely in the grasp of its subjects, through psychic time.'[157]

Cultures and Translation

Was Tracy Philipps an anti-Semite and Fascist fellow-traveller, as his enemies maintained? Colonel Meinertzhagen's 1937 diary railed at British ambivalence towards Zionism, and he was particularly incensed with Philipps, who had the temerity:

> to question the practicability of a Jewish Home in Palestine and could not see its purpose and suggested we should scuttle out of Palestine and leave the Jews to go to the Devil in their own way.[158]

While in Canada Philipps denied emphatically that he ever had been an appeaser or an anti-Semite, professing dismay 'when one is such a straight liberal show'. Perhaps characterizing Philipps as prejudiced, or even as a 'typical soldier-adventurer', is to take him out of context. He is better assigned to the occupational category he so frequently cited himself: the technician of minority nationalities, or the 'electrical engineer of culture'. That is, he is best understood as among that erudite-but-slippery, proud-but-shadowy cohort of translators and special constables who acted as intermediaries between ethnocultural minorities and state security agencies.

The reflex one may feel to criticize these people as stool pigeons and informants is not altogether misplaced. Indeed, their status with the RCMP appears to have been directly dependent on their performance in pointing the police towards supposed subversive elements within their communities. But because many such translators and interpreters served their respective groups in highly complex if not contradictory ways, any assessment necessitates looking closely at each case to see how he or she exercised the responsibility.

Setting aside personal feuds, Philipps and Kysilewsky group naturally with the censor Biberovich, the RCMP's Yiddish language specialist and chief translator, Moïse Hassan Arnoni, and his staff, including the Finn H. Sorvari, the Lithuanian M. Krupka, the Russian-born Mervyn Black, the Estonian E.W. Elfengren, George Steffen, Georges Cliche, and even the Special Branch's most famous undercover agent, John Leopold. It is doubtful that any other sector within the Canadian security agencies had better intellectual credentials. Biberovich had a Ph.D., and Kaye had one each from Vienna and London. Mervyn Black and Michael Petrowsky both were accomplished writers, and the latter was also a playwright, an executive in the Canadian Authors' Association, and a consultant to the National Film Board.[159] To some extent the actions of Petrowsky, Philipps, and Kysilewsky perhaps did help prevent further mass detentions during the war, particularly of Ukrainian Canadians. One might weigh this against the cultural damage caused by the closing of the Labour-Farmer temples and the ideological polarization of these communities.

Yet, the more interesting question concerning these cultural intermediaries is larger than their individual responsibilities vis-à-vis repressive and illiberal actions of the state, important as these might be. It rather concerns secrecy, and the way this cultural component of the state has been so thoroughly camouflaged in Canadian history. One reason for this, I suggest, is that if these cultural intermediaries are exposed to public scrutiny and discussion it would be understood directly how multicultural states are, intrinsically, *security states*.

The index of difference that attracts consideration for special *cultural rights* is precisely the one that attracts the state's mistrust and, hence, the interest of its security components. That cultural rights and state security coexist uneasily in the 'tolerant' society is demonstrated again and again in the available archival records of state security. Viewed through the wartime case of Tracy Philipps, 'liberal tolerance' prevailed in direct proportion to the efficacy of the censorship-intelligence-propaganda complex in its various and mysterious interactions with Canada's ethnocultural minorities.

2

Love Your Neighbour:
The RCMP and the National Film Board,
1948–1953

Interviewer: This was at the same time as Neighbours . . . *a period where the Film Board was under great attack. It was felt there were communists at the Film Board; in fact, three people were fired. Do you recall if you were ever on a list or under suspicion, since you had been in China?*
Norman McLaren: No, I don't think so. I don't consider Neighbours *a political film.*
Interviewer: Could you tell me about the technique used?
Norman McLaren: Very simply . . . treat a human being as animatable material.

Has Anyone Here Seen Canada?
A History of Canadian Movies, 1939–53,
dir. John Kramer (1978)

The Eye of Canada

In January 1945 John Grierson stated in his radio address, 'The Changing Face of Propaganda', that 'there is a paradoxical point where a national information service must become international to fulfill itself. [Nation-states] have at many points sublimated their national interests to international ones.' With the end of the war approaching it was now the 'logic of the national information services' to turn to think of the 'cooperative world to which their nations are pledged'.[1] To some extent this meant inviting motion pictures to treat questions related to international development. But for Grierson the more important question was not so much the content of films but rather how cinema could 'direct men's vision and determine their loyalties', in the Kantian sense of a 'structuring structure'. One should be 'concerned not only with the conscious processes of the mind', he said, 'but with the subconscious ones which insensibly govern the pattern of men's attention and the manner of their action.' Semantics were less important than the widest possible dissemination of a certain gaze and the construction of a specific type of filmic observer: an 'audio-visual citizen'.

'Documentary', Grierson once declared, 'was from the beginning an anti-aesthetic movement.' The history of that movement is confused because:

> we always had the good sense to use the aesthetes . . . we liked them and needed them. We were concerned not with the category of 'purposiveness without pur-pose' but with that other category beyond which used to be called teleological. [R]eformers . . . concerned—to use the old jargon—with 'bringing alive the new materials of citizenship,' 'crystallising sentiments' and creating those 'new loy-alties from which a progressive civic might well derive.'[2]

Audiovisual citizenship necessitated new protocols of reception whose lines of development were not easy to predict. He cited 'the disintegration of the image in Cézanne and the abandonment of perspective in abstract painting' as a precedent for his view that 'the deeper needs of mankind will not always be the apparent ones.' For this reason, abstraction was 'an important directive to modern thought and appreciation', one that overruled all question of representation: 'Such manifes-tations I account as new forces . . . of appreciation which attend changes in techno-logical pattern and therefore of the pattern of human relationship in society.'[3]

Artists, or 'aesthetes' as he called them, were invaluable sensorial interpreters of these 'changes in technological pattern'. Modern artists were not to be thought of as individual geniuses endowed with gifts of 'personal expression' but rather as early intimators of social patterning 'within the technological economy'. Film-making was not art for art's sake but a means of saturating the field of filmic com-munication with a generalized audiovisual rationality suitable for national government. For this reason, Grierson gave film distribution special emphasis in the early development of the NFB.

The distribution of non-theatrical motion pictures in rural Canada was pio-neered by Donald Buchanan, who founded the National Film Society in 1935.[4] Grierson charged Buchanan with putting this initiative on a wartime footing. Cred-iting Grierson with encouraging 'films that relate familiar scenes to wider concepts of citizenship and statehood', Buchanan celebrated the NFB's expanding non-theatrical distribution network, then consisting of 70 mobile film units, each serv-ing a circuit of 20 villages, most 'populated by citizens of foreign origin'.

Buchanan explained that these rural film circuits were becoming more inter-active:

> Here the real test of the documentary movie comes. Will these people respond to its stimulus? . . . [A]t first they seem to be merely passive spectators. A new movie technique, however, is proving effective in encouraging these and other audiences to come forth with their own opinions.[5]

Three-minute 'discussion movies' tagged at the end of the main feature showed panels debating the film's themes and guiding the verbal responses of the rural audiences. 'In such ways,' Buchanan wrote, 'the motion picture becomes a gadfly to social discussion. It can relate one part of the nation to the other.'[6]

Buchanan's article 'Canadian Movies Promote Citizenship' reported that projectionists 'are being trained to gather and make reports on these opinions so that there may be a two-way transmission of ideas.'[7] One projectionist reported that it was 'a revelation to see the morale improvement' as a result of the films and the interactive discussions. Buchanan's enthusiasm echoed Grierson's, as he described the rural circuits as an 'experimental venture in the use of modern means of communication in the service of citizenship'.[8]

Accounts of these early rural circuits record the wonderment occasioned by the arrival of cinema in remote places where electrification remained a dream. Stories are told of generators and film projectors hauled on dogsleds to isolated villages in winter, and of projectionists sleeping with their equipment to prevent it from freezing. One projectionist arrived at a village hall to find the audience turned around expectantly to face the film projector. In another case, viewers tumbled backwards off a bench when a train appeared to sweep over them.[9] These anecdotes signal the marginal integration of as-yet unformed filmic observers to new protocols of reception.

For Grierson and his wartime NFB team it was 'common sense' and not analyses of film spectatorship and human perception that guided the development of a distinctly 'Canadian' film diegesis, or national audiovisual narrative. Ordering the spatio-temporal limits of national territory and population within a consistent audiovisual representational field helped mobilize a polyglot people for war. It was a question of establishing the minimal communicative rationality through which the 'call' of authority could be disseminated. Early NFB films such as *Peoples of Canada*, *Iceland on the Prairies*, *Ukrainian Winter Holiday*, and *Poland on the Prairies* were the Film Board's earliest attempts to establish a nationalized film diegesis among hundreds of thousands of foreign-born Canadians. This initiative combined the pen of Tracy Philipps's ally, Watson Kirkconnell, with the film units of his nemesis, Grierson, in a common project to fashion 'Canadians All' from the mosaic of nationalities.

Circuit audiences introduced to the 'Discussion Quiz' accompanying Gordon Sparling's *Peoples of Canada* in 1941 were told that this 'film carries an impressive measure of understanding and tolerance at a time when jungle-born fears and hatreds on which Nazi-Germany was nourished are again clouding men's minds.'[10] In no other country 'are inter-racial relations better than here.' This was credited to 'the fact of the original division of the land into two tongues and nationalities', whose 'unusual degree of tolerance . . . has been expanded to cover all the later arrivals.' Discussion points focused on the benefits to Canada of large-scale immigration and the best means of assimilating immigrants to Canadian citizenship.[11]

Soon after taking up the film commissionership in 1939 Grierson engaged the Canadian filmmaker Evelyn Spice, a veteran of his General Post Office film unit in Britain, to write a treatment for *Peoples of Canada*.[12] From rural Saskatchewan, Spice indulged Grierson's cartographic fetish by supplying a script that began with an unfurling chart and the commentary: 'Up the river went the first people of Canada to unroll the map of the third largest country of the world.'[13] As the map opened on Quebec, Grierson's busy editorial pencil deleted Spice's mention of the Pope, and he toned down her references to the 'guidance of the church' in French-

Canadian life. He retained her emphasis on the North and the use of aerial shots, including the film's penultimate image of a vertical zoom-in to a tight close-up on the Parliament buildings in Ottawa, ending with 'a resumé of faces and environments . . . prominently featured in the film'.

Screening the first cut of *Peoples of Canada* in November 1940, Grierson judged Gordon Sparling's direction too literal, lacking the 'inside life' and 'depth of feeling' that ought to have been found on location among ethnic minority groups.[14] 'The film was shot too stiff to script', Grierson complained, and 'there is a tendency to pile on the trimmings: elaborate and complicated opticals.' He railed that these 'don't make up for "inside" lacks; they will, if anything exaggerate them', and he vetoed Sparling's 'fancy parchment' background for the main titles.[15]

Sparling's restaging of the Hutterites' first arrival at the Regina train station left Grierson and producer Stuart Legg unmoved. Responding to Legg's criticism that the prairie sequences 'lacked a smell of truth and authenticity', Sparling wrote that the problem was not that his subjects were 'wooden actors' but that they were utterly uncomprehending of their relation to the camera. With 'the appearance of the big out-fit', Sparling reported, they became 'very shy and suspicious', their gestures 'self-conscious and hesitant'.[16] There was neither mirror identification with the camera nor complicity with its gaze. The new citizens as yet not only lacked audiovisual competence as observers able to identify with that gaze, but also remained innocent of a voyeuristic capacity to imagine themselves behaving as its objects.

Sparling also reminded Legg that Evelyn Spice's portrait of mutual tolerance was at best proto-factual:

> We have been getting a bit of criticism about the characters we are chasing, particularly the Doukobors and other 'communities'. People out here say they do nothing for Canada, demand exemption from military services, flout our laws continually and do not put their profits back into circulation in Canada. No authority can be found for our statement that the Chinaman is the unofficial banker of the prairies, nor that the Mennonites were <u>invited</u> to come over because of advanced farming methods. The former, by and large, are anti-social and send all their profits out of the country. The Japs are the same. The Mennonites wrote over asking what conditions and treatment they could expect here. It was purely an escape mechanism. Their methods are primitive—not advanced. One man asked me 'Aren't you admitting there are a few "white" people in the West?'[17]

Grierson's damnation of the film during production was undone by the picture's success when released in the winter of 1941. One letter of congratulation from Regina praised 'the true atmosphere created in Peoples of Canada by taking pictures on the spot'.[18] In rather quaint and pre-Cold War terminology the writer told Grierson, 'if anything, it surpasses your previous "propaganda" films, all of which struck me as interesting presentations.' A newsreel version of the film was granted international distribution under the 'Canada Carries On' series and a three-reel French version including extra footage shot in Quebec was released for screenings in that province.

In 1943, the Psychological Warfare Executive in London cited *Peoples of Canada* as a model for future propaganda films. The NFB should be:

> putting across the concept of the United Nations as an international new order . . . the breakdown of natural barriers, racial barriers . . . showing the triumph of organisation within Canada itself. . . . The possession within Canada of a large number of racial minorities, many of whom still speak their native languages but have adopted a specifically Canadian culture and viewpoint is a very important propaganda contact with Europe.[19]

In 1944, Britain's Political Intelligence Directorate rated the film as 'excellent' for use in re-educating Nazi POWs, thus fulfilling Grierson's ambitions in every direction.[20]

José Arroyo points perceptively to the would-be 'propaganda General' in Grierson's personality. Grierson viewed Hollywood in 1939 as 'one of the greatest potential munitions factories on earth', and its theatre of war was 'spread across the earth with an audience of a hundred million a week.' If, by comparison, Ottawa presented modest possibilities, at least the Canadian government was receptive to his idea that film could help shape 'the pattern of civic appreciation, civic faith, and civic duty which goes with them'. Grierson wanted film spectators who responded to the film's call to order:

> They mean nothing—literacy, knowledge or skill, the whole lot of them—if they do not make for order in the world . . . we have failed [to realize] the implications of the change which the technological revolution has brought upon us . . . we have become more and more citizens of a community we do not adequately see. Under our feet go wires. . . . A simple weather forecast is a daily drama of complicated observation. . . . We do not see [that] this is the fact of modern society . . . we are slow to adopt the habits of thought which must necessarily go with interdependency, if we are to control the forces which we ourselves have released. We have given ourselves a new kind of society, but we have not yet given ourselves the kind of imagination or the new conception of citizenship which makes it tolerable. . . . I think it is no wonder that we are full of frustrations and neuroses of one kind or another.[21]

That the NFB was to be shattered by the Cold War, truncating the careers of Grierson and many others, would have shocked many who shared his statist, not to say authoritarian, outlook on the form and function of documentary cinema during the war.

Grierson directed the NFB for less than five years, but he left an indelible mark on the organization and its personnel. One of his early recruits was animator Norman McLaren, who arrived in Ottawa from New York in 1941 and who stayed with the NFB for the rest of his career. For Grierson, the fact that he and McLaren hailed from the Scottish town of Stirling licensed him to treat the latter as a slightly daft younger brother for whose way in the world he assumed responsibility. Yet, the 'aesthete' McLaren did not necessarily share Grierson's outlook, perhaps least his views about cinema and citizenship. Grierson may have coined the NFB's motto 'The Eye of Canada', but McLaren liked to trick that eye with his animations, most forcefully with his 1952 animated short, *Love Your Neighbour,* or *Neighbours.*

Grierson disparaged *Neighbours* with more than his usual acerbity, calling it 'a very naive film' and doubting McLaren's intellectual merit:

> I wouldn't trust Norman round the corner as a political thinker. I wouldn't trust him round the corner as a philosophic thinker. That's not what Norman is for. Norman is for 'Hen Hop.' 'Hen Hop.' That's wonderful! And so many other things. That is his basic gift. He's got joy in his movement. He's got loveliness in his movement. He's got fancy in his changes. That's enough.[22]

Why did the documentary film master so discount what McLaren himself considered to be his greatest work? Created during the nightmare of the NFB's 'security scare', *Neighbours* was amazingly successful. Against all the odds it won an Academy Award. In a mere eight minutes, McLaren delivered an enigmatic but devastating image of the 'state' within the state, the very 'frustrations and neuroses' suppressed by Grierson's model for civic film spectatorship.

The Censor as Painter

Norman McLaren hunched over his table at the National Film Board for year upon year, laboriously filtering the passage of light through film, a miniaturist hand-painting images on each frame. Assuming the same posture, the Access to Information censor in the Canadian Security Intelligence Service patiently filters the passage of historical signs through page after page of text, shading and cross-hatching the state's self-projection into historiography. As an animator, McLaren understood censorship's principle of invertibility: he made images appear to move on the screen by releasing light through scraped openings on black, exposed film, while on clear stock he blocked light with ink. With the same gestures, the censor patterns the release of data into historiography by blocking out words and phrases, or, where rules require it, inverting the process to reveal a few fragments here and there on otherwise blank pages. Both animator and censor route the spectator's attention through plays of obscuration and revelation, deferral and release.

The censor's upstream filtration of historical signs forces historians to reveal how our authority as narrators depends upon a fetish, just as McLaren's animations at times reminded audiences that 'motion' in cinema is illusory. Although historians quietly disavow the past's appalling absence by employing rhetorical effects, conjuring up illusions of plenitude, censorship makes such disavowal unsustainable. Professionalism dictates that readers be told when such-and-such is only likely to have been so, was apparently the case, or that '_____' almost certainly was so-and-so. Indeed, unless narrative 'suturing' is traded up to outright embroidery, qualifiers flock into accounts based on censored sources to menace their claim to empiricity.

South African critic J.M. Coetzee describes the writer internalizing the censor to form a 'mirror couple' whose 'vicissitudes of blockage and deflection [are] inherently incompatible with political practice.' Any political discourse about the censor 'is a discourse of control: either of taking control of the censor or evading his control.'[23] Confronting 'the censor in the genre of polemic', he writes, inevitably follows 'a course of accelerating violence and loss of difference', finally bending the writer in one way or another to the censoring authority.

The secret files concerning the RCMP Security Service's purge of suspected Communists from the National Film Board have been released piecemeal through Canada's Access to Information apparatus over the past decade. They are typical of the intentionally shattered security intelligence records that weaken rather than strengthen narrative accounts. Of 810 pages of material accumulated by the RCMP between June 1948 and June 1953, for example, 253 pages have been blanked out entirely and the remaining pages are pockmarked with excisions.

Yet, this is hardly a catastrophe. Taken in this sense of invertibility, as a play of presence and absence, the censor's gesture in fact adds the contemporary signature of the state to traces left by its Security Service's investigations of yesteryear. The removal of names, file numbers, references to 'police techniques', and exchanges with other governments may taint the empirical authority of my narrative, but these patterns of withholding may also enhance my rendering of the state's modes of envisioning information and its interest in fostering a certain kind of national history. This is germane to the somewhat counterintuitive question posed here in reading these secret files: to what extent was the National Film Board continuous with the state's internal security apparatus in patterning Canadian citizenship during the Cold War?

Neighbours

The metaphor of 'neighbours' is not intended as an ironic play on the RCMP's muscular handling of the Film Board, but rather is meant to expose a spatial logic of neighbourliness encoded in the records of the investigation. Suburban neighbours occupy bounded, individuated plots, but the ongoing division of property depends on the constant reproduction of shared beliefs. As a result, property lines are never as stable as site surveys might suggest; privacy and discretion are flexed by gossip and rumour; provisional solidarities formed during summer barbecues may recede into winter aloofness; imprecise parking habits may be tolerable for just so long. In sum, the aspect of neighbourliness that concerns us here is not the presumed fixity between these socially defined spaces but rather neighbours' constant sensing for any alteration in their bilateral conditions of existence.

Canada's capital city was situated prudently, a hundred miles north of the giant American neighbour, where the Rideau River drops to meet the Ottawa. Just south of the city at a rock formation known as 'Hog's Back' the Rideau Canal diverts from the river's natural bed, running in straight reaches to descend a flight of locks between the Chateau Laurier and the Parliament. The shallow bed of the Rideau River follows a different course, describing slow arcs and passing just behind the RCMP's austere Overbrook headquarters, housed in a former monastery. This

Opening tableau of Norman McLaren's Neighbours, *Jean-Paul Ladouceur and Grant Munro.* NFB.

building was the epicentre of a security chill that settled over 'progressive' employees of the federal civil service after Gouzenko's defection became public knowledge in February 1946. Half a mile further on, National Film Board studios once flanked the curtain falls where the Rideau cascades into the Ottawa. Grierson built the National Film Board there in a disused sawmill.

Given the spatial proximity of the RCMP to the Film Board, it is not surprising that space-time routines intersect even at the level of individual employees. Take, for example, Mark McClung, the Mounties' specialist in political philosophy. Son of the pre-eminent Canadian feminist and social reformer, Nellie McClung, Mark took the opposite tack from her political activism to work for the RCMP's anti-subversive squad. From his office in the Overbrook headquarters he wrote and edited briefs on suspect individuals and organizations throughout the Cold War.

In 1952, McClung wrote a memo to Superintendent George B. McClellan, his superior in the Special Branch, that described one neighbour held apart from another by what they have in common, the very motif Norman McLaren was at that moment exploring not far downstream, shooting his film *Neighbours*. 'I must go back some months', McClung wrote, 'to explain the oddness' of a recent encounter. Soon after moving into a western suburb of Ottawa in 1951 he and his wife had struck up a friendship with their neighbours, who, as it turned out, were NFB employees under investigation as suspected Communists:

2. We moved into our house last May and I think in the same month met the _____. From that time on there have been occasions when the _____ would

invite us over for a beer usually on Sunday noons and these invitations were reciprocated by us but at no time did I feel that _____ was taking a particular interest in me, although he knew from the beginning that I work for the RCMP.

3. During the fall, I happened to mention this connection to Sgt. McLaren and then read our file on _____. Since that time I have continued, as before, neither seeking nor particularly avoiding _____ company. Until last Tuesday, I suppose we have been in their home four or five times and they in ours as often.

4. That afternoon my wife phoned me to say that _____ not his wife, had phoned and rather abruptly invited us for supper the same evening. The short notice and the manner of the invitation seemed odd to us but we accepted. The other guests were: _____ (phonetic spelling) whose husband is a Film board man but absent from the dinner at work; _____ the orchestra man, I believe; _____, a BBC man who has just arrived in Canada for a 6-months visit having to do with television.

5. Throughout the evening, the bulk of the conversation was on movies, theatre, Eskimos, _____ trip to Karachi, and other fairly safe subjects. Occasionally however it took turns that made me feel I was expected to react. For example _____ denounced _____ condemnation some months ago of her _____'s organization as Communist-inspired. Again, _____ claimed the plan to move the NFB to Montreal is a secret political deal between Duplessis and the Cabinet. These themes were not pressed and the talk moved on to more neutral subjects. We left at about 11:45 but the others showed no signs of moving.

6. This is the first time we have been invited for a meal at the _____ and it actually was mentioned that two other people, not named as far as I can remember, were to have come but at the last moment fell ill. One interpretation therefore is that we were invited to fill in. On the other hand _____ may have been instructed to invite us and, perhaps being reluctant to do so, displayed the abruptness my wife detected over the phone.

7. It hardly seems credible to me that this was a serious attempt to feel me out as a possible weak link in our chain because of the rather crude and abrupt approach used but, after discussion with Cpl. McEwan, the incident seemed worth describing for the file.

8. May I ask for your advice for future occasions? According to _____, the _____ now owe the _____ a meal with at least beer and an atrocious wine called 'Manoir St. David.'[24]

As a witness to the Mounties' surveillance and manipulation of NFB suspects over the previous three years, McClung wrote with well-founded circumspection. His suggestion of a parity in these domestic transactions with his neighbours subtly emphasized the boundary line in their association. Perhaps as intended, George

Mark McClung, 1945. NAC, PA 187759, detail.

McClellan's attention lighted on his reference to wine: 'I think there is no harm in Mr. McClung letting this thing develop, if it will', he wrote. 'It may be a feeler. At any rate—anyone who serves Manoir St. David deserves rigorous scrutiny.'

McClellan had recruited McClung, a former Rhodes Scholar and naval intelligence veteran, after the Gouzenko affair as a civilian expert to help the Security Service differentiate subversive activities from loyal dissent. 'Policemen don't read books on politics, this is a political kind of thing and we want guys with your kind of education to come in and research for us', he told McClung.

It was not an unqualified success. Thirty years later McClellan implied to the NFB documentarian Donald Brittain that civilian employees hired during the Cold War for their putative intellectual abilities proved indeed to be 'weak links' in the chain: 'I don't know that a man who has taken a course in political science is necessarily better than a man who has lived with a subversive party for 10 years of his life.'[25] For his part, McClung, a forerunner of such recruitment, told Brittain the Security Service was 'blinkered', and described the 'epitome of the true mounted policeman' in less than flattering terms:

In his own mind he is an omni-competent human being. He can go anywhere and do anything any time. He can govern the North, he can catch murderers, he can catch dope traffickers, he can do everything. And he does this because of his very special training. Now that's one trait in him. The other trait is profound anti-intellectualism, they distrust the thought process and any person who thinks in any deviant way at all is suspect.[26]

The purging of Film Board staff has been derided as a McCarthyist episode of police excess and official cynicism urged on by aggressive private film interests, yet reading the police files suggests that a neighbourly sensitivity towards deviation forms a neglected part of the explanation.[27] Canadian historiography portrays John Grierson's NFB as a candle of enlightenment snuffed out by reactionary philistines, a poignant 'might-have-been' in the history of Canadian cinema.[28] I will argue rather that a continuity of purpose in the two organizations, not a vast disparity, defined the pattern of the 'security scare'.

A Punch in the Eye

Norman McLaren once showed a British documentary crew how *Neighbours* was born in 1951 from dissecting the trajectory of a punch.[29] 'A punch accelerates quickly', he said, his right fist moving delicately in lengthening increments towards his actor's left cheek. He counted out the 'click . . . click . . . click' of the animation camera to demonstrate how increasing each segment of the gesture created the illusion of acceleration when projected at normal speed. Actor Grant Munro grinned at the gentle arrival of McLaren's fist and turned his cheek away as if from the force of the blow. By using this step technique, McLaren found that even gentle gestures, when replayed at normal speed, acquire the appearance of violence.

If five years of investigative activity into the Film Board were accelerated into a single gesture, the records of the RCMP Security Service would share this profile of the punch—a wind-up of surveillance and data collection preceding a sharp blow of dismissals and trauma, leaving a lingering bruise of censorship. The following sequence of 10 six-month-long 'exposures' renders that gesture in the form of a 'damaged' narrative, digesting the police records in their shattered state without explicit interpretation. I have attempted to leave intact traces of internal dialogues among the investigators, the fluctuating intensity of their inquiries, and also the extent to which CSIS has withheld words, passages, and many entire pages.

This RCMP activity during the NFB 'security scare' forms the unseen backdrop to McLaren's *Neighbours*, his first animation using live actors. To be sure, Cold War hysteria escalated after the Chinese Revolution and the outbreak of the Korean War, and these events were cited at the time as the fearful referents of McLaren's allegory. But the most immediate manifestation of Cold War tensions so far as he was concerned was right inside the NFB's ramshackle John Street labs. If the security scare was successfully minimized by its managers as a 'non-event' that impinged on a small handful of NFB employees, the records of police activity and McLaren's resistance to it reveal its wider scope and its lasting impact.[30]

Norman McLaren shooting Neighbours, *1952*. Photo by Evelyn Lambart. NFB.

July to December 1948 (240 pages; 108 pages removed)

On 24 June 1948, Superintendent George McClellan advised his investigators that James J. McCann, Minister of National Revenue, was 'somewhat concerned about the possibility of Communist activity among the [NFB] employees'. The substance of the minister's request for an investigation of six of the almost 600 Film Board employees is excised, but a decision not to take Film Commissioner Ross McLean into his confidence necessitated an 'indirect' approach. By early July, surveillance and research suggested, as McClellan reported to Commissioner S.T. Wood, that at least two of the six suspects had 'strong Communist Party connections'.

In spite of the investigators' discretion, employees instantly went on the defensive:

> Unfortunately, hearsay information is making the rounds and these various sto-
> ries are exaggerated as they are carried from person to person. Numerous inci-
> dents have been related to brand this person or that one a Communist and it has
> often occurred that in an effort to trace the story to its origin we have found our-
> selves stalled right in the middle of the procedure.[31]

The 'term "Communist" itself', Constable Miller continued, had become 'an obstacle' as a result of the 'general international situation'. 'Well-meaning and well-educated persons will brand any person a Communist who shows signs of being critical of one or several of our government's institutions . . . assisted by ensuing rumour, a good citizen can often be victimized.'

Spurred to a 'concerted effort to pry further into the activities of certain members who are in the employ of the Film Board', investigators duly produced new information. Commissioner Wood advised Minister McCann on 15 July that 'persons other than those mentioned by you . . . may be Communists.' He asked the minister 'without creating comment' to obtain a nominal roll of all NFB employees, adding that 'it would also be preferable if [it] contained the full Christian names . . . in order that we can make an accurate check against our indices.'[32]

While issuing security clearances to two NFB administrative employees who agreed to swear to secrecy, Superintendent O. Larivière wrote to Commissioner Wood on 21 July wondering if, 'in view of the information obtained . . . you may consider the possibility of having steps taken to preclude _____'s appointment to the position mentioned.' An unnamed officer proposed that 'something should be done to prevent _____ from taking up a position with the United Nations', and that '_____ is suspicious because he is too clean.'

At the end of July the investigators found names of three NFB employees on mailing lists seized on 28 May from the Victory Book Shop in Montreal, described as 'a centre for distribution of Communist literature . . . shut down by police action'. The briefs accumulated new references drawn from Sergeant D.E. McLaren's historical name-searches through files on organizations. One informant put '_____' under suspicion because he was 'not considered personally financially able to' pay for a planned trip. All new information was to be kept from informants 'for fear of drying up sources'.

Corporal McLaren's research found NFB Distribution Director Jack Ralph (whose name accidentally passed the censor's hand) on the Canadian-Soviet Friendship Council in 1945, as well as the Quebec Committee for Allied Victory. Moreover, Ralph had publicly opposed Quebec's anti-Communist 'Padlock Laws'. A four-page brief described these and other associations, but only a few references have been released, such as a neighbour's comment to investigators that Mrs Ralph had been heard to utter 'left-wing views'.

In August, a general reticence in one case turned to outright revocation. This employee 'stood out conspicuously during his last days in the Film Board . . . critici[zing] anything and everything pertaining to Communism and it is calculated someone must have spoken to him about his former attitude.' Several suspects convinced investigators they were 'loyal and trusted citizens' while others remained under suspicion. One man 'would be an active Communist were it not for the fact that he was scared', and a further name resurfaced from 'the Espionage enquiries in 1945–46'.[33]

A heavily censored page dated 17 September 1948 allows only that new NFB employees were being 'carded', that is, entered on the card indexes; an investigator reported 'a strong tendency to be cautious on the part of all those who formerly expressed sympathies towards Russia or those who were critical of our governmental policies. [T]here is general suspicion in the ranks of the National Film Board that their organization is under investigation.' He questioned the appropriateness of conducting such a strenuous investigation in the case of the Film Board, citing at length an informant who claimed the rumour of 'communistic or radical activities was an injustice to the organization':

From Norman McLaren's Neighbours.

_____ was of the opinion that while there are certainly some individuals who bear watching, the great majority are loyal to Canada, although critical of several of our government's policies. _____ opined that the youth of Canada is taking a keener interest in politics today than ever before; many of these are men and women who served during the last war who not only fought for the . . . democracies but are continuing in their efforts to make Canada better and more prosperous. . . . The contention was advanced that a conglomeration of such people thrown together, most of whom are still imbued with their college-day 'Academic Freedom', causes discussions to take place where people often argue for the sake of argument and the more precocious of these are often misunderstood, particularly by those who adhere to the traditional 'old party' lines. _____ thought that with so many rumours going around about the 'Red' Film Board it was gratifying to know that various suspects are being concentrated on as this would certainly eliminate many over whom these rumours cast a shadow and would, at least, give a clearer picture of the Film Board to authorities, all of which would be in the Film Board's favor.

January to June 1949 (102 pages; 45 pages removed)

In January, dossiers had been created for each of apparently 28 suspect individuals. A new name was cross-referenced from the subscription list of the Canadian Seamen's Union paper, *Searchlight*. Inspector John Leopold traced 56 persons who signed a protest under the auspices of the Civil Service Association. Fifteen proved to be current NFB employees, so he attached adverse slips to their files adding 'suitable comment against each'. Inspector R.A.S. MacNeil complained that it 'is unfortunate that we have no background information on many of these employees . . . and that it is therefore essential to approach this security problem in such an indirect manner.' On 25 February the *Toronto Telegram* reported that G.J. Fraser, MP, 'calls for an inquiry and suggests communist infiltration.' The Premier of New Zealand was 'asking for an investigation of that country's Film Board. They have Communists in there', warned Fraser. 'I am not saying whether we have them or not.' On the same day, Inspector MacNeil reviewed records from the NFB's film library, noting a film 'twice drawn from storage under very suspicious circumstances', the second time by 'a woman . . . described as being one of the well-known Communists'.

G.G. 'Bill' Crean, of Defence Liaison II, the intelligence division of the Department of External Affairs, questioned the appropriateness of Film Board employees participating in 'The World Union of Documentary' in Warsaw. An estimate of the Warsaw organization's status was requested of 'Mr. Dwyer' (the North American liaison for Britain's MI6 was Peter Dwyer). Responses from Dwyer and Canada's Warsaw legation, though withheld in the released material, were sufficiently negative for Crean to conclude that 'on the basis of this information we should suggest that the National Film Board of Canada should gracefully decline.'

Increased correspondence with foreign intelligence agencies regarding the movements of NFB employees abroad included a report on _____'s visit to Moscow in 1935, _____'s work in England with _____ in 1948–9, and information from British or American sources concerning _____ in Toronto, who was with British Security Co-ordination in New York in 1944. 'She was romantically involved with one of the Gouzenko suspects and considered to be a "parlour pink." ' The RCMP provided the _____ with briefs on NFB suspects who were either in or likely to visit the US.

Inspector Leopold's inquiries through government channels concerning one 'employee of high standing in the Film Board' followed up informants' reports that a spider-like John Grierson ran the NFB by 'remote-control' through a web of former deputies. Adverse information on Grierson and fellow Briton Stuart Legg, exhumed from the early 1940s, judged Legg to have been an 'appeaser' and 'defeatist' based on informant reports of his original script for *The Tools of War* (1941).[34] On 10 October 1949, Corporal D.E. McLaren extracted information from a 1943 report on Grierson stating that:

> _____ was recently appointed _____ of the Wartime Information Board and that in addition to these duties he will continue to act as _____. From the information at hand it would appear that _____ is a Communist sympathizer and as such any press releases or films prepared under his direction might reflect his sympathies. . . . It is significant that he described 'We' (Canadians) as 'a peasant and proletarian people.'

Six years on, the Mounties remained suspicious. Corporal McLaren noted for the file Grierson's admission to the Kellock-Taschereau Commission that 'he knew and liked PAVLOV . . . the NKVD head',[35] and he concluded that Grierson's 'association with The World Today Inc. in New York City after leaving the Film Board does not lessen the suspicion attached to him.'[36]

July to December 1949 (136 pages; 38 pages removed)

Suspicion cascaded over Grierson's remaining Film Board associates. Ross McLean and James Beveridge were believed to be closest to the source and their relationships to Grierson were explored in detail. Informants told Constable Miller that McLean 'showed signs of weakness' and possibly was 'being blackmailed'. The informant recounted that McLean spotted Grierson in the 1930s 'when he was on the staff of our Canadian Legation in London.' McLean was 'quite a brilliant young man and thought to be a _____.' Miller reasoned that McLean owed his

commissionership to Grierson and felt a 'sense of obligation' to favour the Griersonian 'group' within the NFB. This explained his presence at 'the gay private parties' of this 'clique', his toleration of 'shady financial angles' and 'wastage', and
supported the view that he was susceptible to Grierson's continuing influence.

Corporal McLaren also assembled a detailed personal history of an employee
whom McLean had permitted to travel to Russia that autumn. An informant
described 'the conduct of these Canadians, being filled up with Vodka by their
hosts and fawning over them', as presenting a 'very repulsive scene particularly
when one considered the positions of trust and confidence they hold in the Canadian Government.'

On 16 November, Constable Miller assembled further information received
from a female informant that the Grierson 'clique' was blackmailing Ross McLean.
She recalled that McLean 'became involved in some difficulty 'at the High Commission in London in the late 1930s' and Grierson 'took him under his wing and
made him the Deputy Film Commissioner.'[37] In a highlighted passage, Miller
explained that Grierson felt an obligation since without McLean 'providing the
liaison . . . plus the influence . . . he would not have accomplished what he did.' On
the other hand, 'having made a fizzle of his job in the Canadian Legation', McLean
had 'little hope for a good position'. The informant called him 'backward and suffering from a complex of inferiority . . . he was saved by Grierson's call at the critical moment and . . . he has always felt a keen sense of indebtedness.'

Although the dynamic Grierson was prone to impatience with McLean, he recommended that McLean succeed him as Film Commissioner.[38] The fact that
McLean knew 'little or nothing about the Film Industry' did not matter, and the
'combine of close associates' remained intact. McLean depended on Grierson's
four 'old reliables' to run the Board, knowing 'all too well that the "big four" are
carrying him and he knows, too, that the "big four" know it.' These four were 'allied
more closely than any union could bind them' and McLean accepted their direction
rather than be met with a 'wholesale "walkout"' and thereby cut his own throat'.

_____ reported on McLean's performance at a recent conference in Halifax,
where 'as the highest ranking Government official [he] had the most marvelous
opportunity to build up the prestige of the Film Board' and 'failed completely'. He
'did no lobbying, no entertaining—worst of all, failed miserably on the platform . . . in fact, was continually trying to hide . . . his complete lack of gumption.'
Bearing Constable Miller's conclusion that Grierson 'is still running the Board by
remote control', the brief on McLean was forwarded to Commissioner Wood,
whose reaction is blanked out in the released documents.

Through their clippings service the investigators watched an anti-NFB media
campaign waged by its enemies gather momentum in late October and crescendo
on 17 November when a front-page exposé in the *Financial Post* revealed the
Defence Department had suspended its use of NFB services due to security concerns.[39] Documents relating the decision to allow Ross McLean's term as Film
Commissioner to expire without renewal in January 1950 are removed.

Remarkably, the damaging *Financial Post* article is not among released file clippings, but investigators kept follow-up articles in the *Toronto Star* and the *Ottawa*

Journal stating that Prime Minister St Laurent was 'visibly embarrassed' by the leak.[40] Minimizing the scale of the investigation, St Laurent allowed that the 'very few' policemen assigned to the investigation found the task so distasteful that they were 'reluctant even to go about securing the information'. The Labour Progressive Party paper, the *Canadian Tribune*, implied that F.R. 'Budge' Crawley, a pioneer Canadian documentarist whose private Ottawa film company had grown up entwined with the NFB, was behind it. The *Tribune* accused Crawley of helping to orchestrate a campaign against the NFB monopoly on government film contracts and of personally confronting Ross McLean with a 'secret blacklist supplied by the RCMP to Crawley Films' naming '50 Film Board workers who should be fired as "reds."' [41]

The *Tribune* article sparked a two-page report by Inspector MacNeil, the contents of which have been blocked out. But a document remains to shed at least some light upon the *Tribune*'s claims. On 22 November, three days after the *Financial Post* article, R.W. Wonnacott, in charge of the RCMP's Identification Branch, received a call from Crawley reporting a threatening call received by his firm's switchboard operator. The anonymous caller said, 'I would suggest that [Crawley] lay off talking to the Press, as they are just looking for trouble. The Minister wants you to know that he doesn't like this.' Crawley requested police protection 'against any possible willful and malicious damage to his premises [because] some of the officials of the Film Board cannot be considered as friendly towards him.'

The RCMP used the unwanted publicity surrounding the NFB investigation to measure reaction among leading Communist Party members. Inspector MacNeil wrote to the officer commanding 'O' Division's Special Branch in Toronto, Ken Shakespeare, noting that the screening 'has been discussed in the House of Commons and the Press generally . . . it is essential that we obtain as much information as possible concerning repercussions, particularly within Communist circles.' The technical nature of the 'urgent attention' given this request is deleted.

Shakespeare responded that 'there have been no repercussions to speak of within Communist circles as a result of the publicity.' Party members were 'apathetic', leading Corporal McLaren to comment that 'the most significant feature is the lack of reaction among those who might have been expected to show concern.' In the NFB's Toronto bureau, also under surveillance, Constable J.T. Halward reported 'a decided lack of talk around the office', that a general 'bad feeling exists', and that 'leftist employees such as _____ and _____ have become very cautious in discussing controversial issues such as the present one.' John Leopold's attention turned to Montreal, where he monitored _____ on a temporary assignment with _____, a private film interest awarded military contracts. He learned that she was making an 'innocuous' children's film and was not exposed to the Defence Department projects.

Press clippings reported Opposition leader George Drew's virulent attack in Parliament on the Film Board's reliability, as well as Minister of Reconstruction and Supply Robert Winters's response that no NFB films were currently withdrawn from circulation due to leftist content. The Liberal member for Toronto-Spadina, David A. Croll, pleaded for 'a little understanding':

These people are a little different from the average civil servant. They are artistic people, imaginative people. They are wrapped up in their work. They are zealous. They don't press their pants, nor comb their hair as often as some people would like them to do.

Corporal McLaren assembled four pages of (excised) material on _____, 'who will likely become second in command after [Ralph] Foster leaves.' An additional page concerns a former employee in Quebec City, who had called _____ to offer any 'under cover' help she could give, allowing that she was 'lying low until the Film Board affair is cleared up'.

On the ground, Sergeant Keeler and Constable J.H. Korntoff stalked NFB suspects through Ottawa neighbourhoods 'without arousing suspicion', in one case noting visitors 'engaging in what appeared to be serious conversations'. An informant attended a 'beer session' among NFB employees in Toronto in early November but his report of insider talk and office gossip is largely eliminated from the released document. The reports mention Norman McLaren, who was known to be temporarily in China with UNESCO. Due to 'the bust-up' with Ross McLean and other reasons excised from the file, he postponed his imminent return to Ottawa.

January to June 1950 (140 pages; 29 pages removed)

The *Canadian Tribune* pricked the Mounties' ire by stridently accusing the government of subjecting the NFB to 'a witchhunt' and calling for the Board's removal from direct 'political control of the government'. The *Globe and Mail*'s headline— 'Film Board Shakeup Pending'—more accurately predicted the impending sequence of events. Protests from organizations such as the Canadian Association for Adult Education and the Ontario Association of Film Councils (OAFC), and from individuals such as lawyer Frank Park, earned them renewed police scrutiny. E.L. Gibson, secretary of the OAFC, wrote to the *Ottawa Citizen* calling for a letter campaign: 'As a self-governing nation in the British Commonwealth, Canada cannot afford to weaken one of her most effective tools for use in forging and strengthening her status.'[42]

Gibson's letter coincided with the national distribution of a 'special edition' of the *Ottawa Citizen* containing a series of editorials defending the NFB. In an attempt to provoke public response to what they believed was a 'calculated plan to destroy the Film Board', a group of employees distributed tens of thousands of copies to individuals and organizations across the country. The RCMP traced the distribution of these papers to the Besserer Street postal station but could not identify who had mailed them. In the case of the National Council of Women of Canada, which received 30 copies, the RCMP stymied further distribution. 'Needless to say,' O. Lariviere reported to the Commissioner, '_____ is not mailing them and will advise her co-workers accordingly.' On the other hand, the Ottawa Special Branch reported to Headquarters that they 'could find no visible connection' between any of the NFB suspects and the Labour Progressive Party.

Constable Korntoff's suspicion lighted upon individuals within the NFB who once retrieved from storage a secret British Admiralty film, *Spotting Fall of Shot*, 'when no one of due authority had granted them that privilege.' Korntoff received similar information (excised) relating to *Exercise Adonis* and concluded his report with information that 'an animator is now claimed to be a protégé of _____ which may speak for itself.'

Ross McLean departed for UNESCO in January 1950, accompanied by his deputy, Ralph Foster, which coincided with reports that a 'majority of employees have an insecure feeling in regard to their job, there is no liaison whatsoever between offices; and working under these conditions is understood to be most difficult.'[43] An investigator noted 'the clique will fight and buck the new Commissioner at every turn', and a sour joke circulated that the first film made under Arthur Irwin's regime was to be titled 'You Can Get Ulcers Too'. The clique's attempt to raise enough money to buy Ross McLean a Buick car as a going away gift was to 'show the Government that a mistake was made in changing Commissioners.' When the subscription fell short amid acrimony, 'they settled for a cheaper one' and their intended message 'did not materialize'. Corporal McLaren wrote out the names of the 'Big Four' and eight names forming the next tier, assigning them with letter grades 'x', 'y', and 'z'. He suggested to McClellan that due to 'the clique's reported attitude towards _____ perhaps more dismissals will be necessary.'

Corporal Darrell McLaren's study of the *Citizen* articles yielded a thoughtful report.[44] 'From our point of view,' he wrote, 'these articles and [the] editorial might be boiled down to two main points.' Without commenting on the editorialist's claims regarding the NFB's 'vitality to the development of Canadian culture, no less than to its unity as a nation', McLaren focused on 'the voluble and studious effort . . . to trace the recent attack on the Film Board back to private interests and the huge powers of Hollywood'. This was 'dealt with so thoroughly', he wrote, 'that the average reader would very likely come away with the impression that the "security angle" of the Film Board situation is only incidental to, and perhaps only a part of, the greater plan of private industry to cripple this great public institution.' Inspector MacNeil found this 'very interesting', as he did McLaren's second point, drawing attention to:

> the 250 film councils and the 5,000 other urban organizations, as well as some 3,300 rural outlets, which have been integrated by the Film Board into a vast co-operative organization throughout the country.[45] Should the government intend to whittle away the Film Board . . . such a move could meet with widespread resistance from the public.

While incoming Film Commissioner Arthur Irwin was guided through securing forced resignations from the three designated employees, new RCMP inquiries concentrated on Jack Ralph's Distribution Department. The Mounties found evidence of extensive use of NFB films by ethnic and labour organizations, and one letter that met with their approval. An executive of United Steelworkers, Local __, wrote to a Film Board employee in Toronto to complain about the 'well-known Communists that somehow by chance appear in the film—for instance _____.'

[O]f course, you and I have deplored this aspect on many occasions. The new change in leadership . . . I imagine, will assure the elimination of this kind of subtle propaganda, which will in turn make their films more acceptable to labour.

(Forgetting to remove a sticky note, the censor here for once added rather than removed an indication. In shaky, elderly characters he wrote that 'this letter is probably not releasable but it gives the perspective from which labour viewed the NFB in 1950.') Shortly following receipt of this letter, _____ of the Toronto Branch of the NFB 'received notice of his dismissal . . . along with several others on the dismissal list.' This occurred despite protests from a deputation from the Ontario Association of Film Councils, whom MacNeil doubted were 'people of any significance'. To be safe, he requested that Corporal McLaren acquire 'some background which would reflect [their] reputation and political tendencies.'

Fragments of text show the Mounties investigating NFB film distribution in Guelph, Ontario, and placing surveillance on a couple newly arrived in Ottawa to work at the Film Board. Informants 'heard them condemn racial discrimination, particularly with regard to Jews and Negros', and reported that they seemed prepared 'to argue this question. . . . The above will illustrate the ease with which Communists, like _____, are able to obtain employment in the Government service, more especially the National Film Board.'

The *Montreal Gazette* 'learned on reliable authority' on 28 March that just 'three minor officials have left their jobs as a result of the security screening.' For its part, the *Canadian Tribune* tallied up four more NFB dismissals pursuant to the RCMP's investigation of the *Citizen* special edition. The *Tribune* pointed to the coincidence that four dismissed employees had also signed the Civil Service Association petition. Corporal McLaren noted for the file that Inspector MacNeil's interrogations of these four were conclusive, and he suspended a fingerprint search then underway. After being 'told very pointedly by _____ that he was to leave . . . and that security considerations were not involved', one of the employees finally took responsibility for 'the preparation of the questionable articles . . . and for the arrangements to . . . distribute one hundred thousand copies . . . throughout the country'.

Further disciplinary actions were afoot, McLaren noted, citing Irwin's instruction to the Toronto office to have '_____ discharged', that '_____ is to go in the near future', and if _____ 'does not resign then she will be discharged.' The terminations were in effect by the end of March, but investigations of all these individuals continued on new files.

The music director, Eugene Kash, 'great friend of _____', attracted renewed police interest for his vociferous objection to his friend's dismissal. Kash called it 'a dirty deal, most unfair kicking a fellow out without an explanation'. In another case, the RCMP accepted a reinstatement because the original termination was in error: 'it can safely be assumed she is not one of the "clique", _____ claim her to be on the right side.' A letter clipped from the *Montreal Gazette* prompted a long investigator's comment, excised from released copies. The letter accused the government of using the public dismissals of three employees as a screen: 'after a month's lull there will be more', it was charged, 'thus hacking away at guarded intervals.'

Corporal McLaren compared lists of invitees to NFB parties to lists for social events held at Soviet bloc embassies, patiently tracing out connections between Film Board employees and diplomats and government officials, noting with interest that his cross-references had yielded _____ of the Canada Foundation and _____, the Assistant Undersecretary of State for External Affairs. Assistant Commissioner Nicholson advised British counterparts on 27 May that _____ was preparing to leave for England, noting his separation from another NFB filmmaker, _____, who was living in New York, and asking the British to advise them regarding his associations and activities while serving as the NFB's London liaison.[46] Further research produced names of individuals who had vouched for the passports of suspect NFB employees.

In June, Film Commissioner Irwin advised reporters that the security screening was complete and that the NFB was again cleared to meet all film and still photography requirements of the Department of National Defence. On a *Citizen* clipping reporting MP Allistair Stewart's charge that a 'smear campaign' had forced these workers out, Inspector MacNeil noted coolly that 'I understand this will include, among others, _____.' Constable Korntoff reported that one employee, who 'prior to the Espionage trials in 1946 [was] a strong follower of the Party', had now 'confessed to be most sorrowful to have had anything to do with the Reds and as far as can be ascertained is now leading a more rational life.' He noted that 'a most uneasy atmosphere exists at the NFB. No one appears to be sure of their ground and seem to be jockeying for positions . . . careful whom they talk to and what they talk about.'

Irony was neither intended nor taken when one informant denounced a colleague writing the script for a Labour Board film, *Teamwork Yesterday and Today*. This 'Leftist' writer was incensed at having to revise his script to conform with Irwin's new regime. The informant predicted that in addition to the three employees forced to resign publicly 'there are 50 more—30 who will be asked to do the same and 20 that are a headache.' Superintendent McClellan remarked, 'Close Estimate!'

July to December 1950 (55 pages; 9 pages removed)

In July 1950, the Mounties took note of Norman McLaren's return to Ottawa from China during a flurry of employee departures. Constable P. Isber noted that McLaren 'is described as a genius in his field of work, one phase of which is to draw soundtrack on film.' He also reported the 'general atmosphere of wariness and expectancy' and the 'keen awareness' of Arthur Irwin's 'intention of stabilizing the status of the Board by operating it in much the same way as a business venture.' Irwin's managerial style 'and also the International situation, has caused all members, especially those who have shown Communistic or radical tendencies to become most reticent.'

According to Isber's informants, Norman McLaren himself was non-communicative, and 'attempts to secure _____'s views and learn of his activities' encountered difficulties because he was such a 'quiet, reserved person'. Isber noted that 'it might take a little time to adduce his views and theories' but that efforts would continue to be exerted 'with the ultimate submission of forms 215 in mind, should they be warranted.'[47] The animator dropped out of sight until December, when a press clipping caught him adjudicating a children's art contest. The investigation produced little of significance—two employees were known to be 'at a cottage together'—and Superintendent Larivière admitted that 'exhaustive inquiries have failed to bring anything to the surface which would indicate sentiments of a subversive nature', and 'numerous individuals against whom suspicion was reflected [are] cautious even in their conversations with intimates.' [48]

January to June 1951 (17 pages; 3 pages removed)

Through the winter further inquiries into the distribution system showed that 'while not an integral part of the Board, persons affiliated with [Film] Councils feel that their affiliation is more than that of a "consumer."' Information was gathered on various individuals involved in these councils. The following summer a story clipped from the *Citizen* reported Arthur Irwin's initiative to move the Film Board to Montreal. Irwin also announced 'a new international information film program to be known as "Freedom Speaks"'. He went on to say that:

> this program will present the everyday pursuits of Canadians in their work and worship, in their social and political relationships. . . . [T]he drama of ordinary Canadian people in a democracy and its approach will be realistic and honest. It will reflect for the peoples of other countries something of the values which Canadians, as a free people, believe to be basic in a democratic society.[49]

July to December 1951 (37 pages; 9 pages removed)

In the fall, renewed complaints from a disgruntled former Film Board employee in Vancouver jolted the RCMP investigation.[50] In a telegram to the Prime Minister, he reiterated earlier accusations that Grierson continued to direct the Board from abroad; he accused the NFB of ridiculing the Canadian Navy and Canadian prisons, and of distributing films 'to be used against the Canadian people by Soviet sympathizers'. He also accused the NFB of harbouring 'perverts', including one convicted pedophile. 'Is it true', he asked, 'that the RCMP has a large file on the NFB? If the above questions are true while Canadian boys are shedding their blood in Korea should not something be done about such a vile situation? And who is protecting the NFB? I would like to know if these questions can be answered. Will be in Ottawa this afternoon.'

The informant detailed his objections to Corporal McLaren during two hours of meetings. In a five-page memorandum McLaren reminded McClellan of a previous Vancouver report of 3 May 3 1949, based on the remarks of the same individual, who was described as 'earnest, sincere and devoid of personal antagonism'. McLaren considered it 'advisable to go a step farther', and noted 'unnatural detachment' and 'eccentricity, to say the least'. But with increasing coherence and reliability, McLaren believed, his informant went on to assert that it was principally Jim Beveridge, the NFB's London representative, who was the conduit for Grierson's influence, 'despite the efforts' of Arthur Irwin.

Darrell McLaren's internal inquiries to the Criminal Investigation Branch refuted the claim that _____ had once been charged for pedophilia, but the informant reaffirmed that 'the staff at the John and Sussex Street establishment contains a considerable number of "queers."' His main complaints were against Grierson and the 'clique', whose 'unscrupulous' activities had included the ousting of various employees with 'anti-communist attitudes'. He cited various cases of the Distribution Department pursuing outright the Soviet cause, naming various films and organizations. He remained in Ottawa overnight in order to inform McLaren of one final item: since 1947 the NFB had circulated still photographs 'showing the RCMP in a ridiculous light'.[51]

This telegram to Prime Minister St Laurent reactivated security concerns over the NFB in the Defence Research Board and the National Research Council. A typewriter 'stolen' from the NRC's Chalk River nuclear facility was reportedly somewhere on Film Board premises. Constable Isber cautioned that intensifying inquiries as a result of these new allegations might rekindle publicity and he recommended stepping up the investigation only 'after the lapse of a reasonable period'.

Isber also broached the issue of homosexuality with a delicacy appropriate to the force's male homosocial culture:

> Enquiries have also been conducted concerning immorality at the Film Board . . . although no tangible indication of it is available, rumours are prevalent that several members of the John Street Branch are so afflicted. I hasten to add, however, that such rumours are related by individuals who depend on appearance and mannerisms . . . it would be unfair to credit such allegations without some more substantial evidence. _____ mentioned in the telegram of _____ is one of the persons whose appearance and mannerisms create such an impression. The 'artistic' personnel of the Film Board are, to a large extent, individualistic to the point of being considered 'queer' but whether this feature is sufficiently conclusive to confirm suspicions is very questionable, Nonetheless, it will be a little difficult to quell such rumours as long as people associate peculiar modes of dress and peculiar mannerisms with 'queer' individuals.

At 'A' Division headquarters in Ottawa, Inspector J.D. McCombe emphasized this paragraph, noting that 'rumours have been circulating for some time about several members of the "Artistic" group at the John St. Branch.' But on 5 December 1951, Inspector MacNeil 'informed Mr. Irwin verbally . . . that the investigations had failed to reveal any evidence to back up the allegations.'

January to June 1952 (38 pages; 11 pages removed)

During the winter of 1952 the NFB staff provided little of interest to the Security Service. In the week of Mark McClung's dinner with his neighbours at the end of March, news clippings reported renewed interest in the security problem and the formation of a special Parliamentary Committee to review the operations of the Film Board. In April outgoing Security Panel Secretary Eric Gaskell visited Arthur Irwin to present his successor, the British intelligence expert Peter Dwyer. By June, the press clippings record Arthur Irwin actively rebuilding the Board's image before the Parliamentary Committee, announcing the Board's general theme of 'Canada—A Developing Nation', and the distribution through NFB circuits of a 'very excellent' Crawley industrial film. Further police inquiries followed Irwin's comment to the *Citizen* that 'the Board has two men taking shots in Korea.' A directors' group meeting for informal discussions in various homes had faded away.

July to December 1952 (40 pages; 2 pages removed)

NFB staff members continued to be exceedingly cautious until December, when a few suspect employees organized a Korean War benefit concert at the University of Ottawa's Academic Hall. Informants sprang to life to report various activities and eavesdrop on conversations. Mark McClung renewed his interest in the filmmaker Robert Anderson, writing, 'this is more derogatory to Anderson than any other item I have seen. Do you think it would be possible to ask "A" [Ottawa Division headquarters] if perhaps _____ could find out?'[52]

Constable Parsons learned of a party in the 'home of _____ to raise funds for Korean children'. He added that 'most of the invitations were sent to people employed at the NFB . . . meaning they would have to be Communist or Communist sympathizers', prompting Superintendent McClellan's epithet, '*opinion!*' Only broken phrases from the report of an informant attending the party passed the hand of the censor: 'she is a "pro-active" thinker'; '_____ shows considerable interest in the distribution service'; '_____'s wife is an English girl, and appears to be a "progressive type."' On the night of the concert, police took plate numbers from cars around Academic Hall while informants inside eavesdropped on their colleagues. One suspect startled an informant with the direct question: 'What's the matter, do you think it's subversive?'

January to June 1953 (5 pages; 2 pages removed)

Although it was suspected that $25 from the benefit's proceeds were handed secretly to the Labour Progressive Party, an extended diary date was set for the next NFB report. On 1 May, Constable Parsons noted without comment the January announcement of Arthur Irwin's appointment as Canadian High Commissioner to Australia. With greater interest, he wrote that on 19 March '_____ was given wide publicity when his picture _____ commonly called 'Neighbours', won the Motion Picture Academy Award ("Oscar") for the best short documentary film.' Parsons continued:

> [T]he 21-3-53 Ottawa Evening Citizen [carried an article by] JOHN BIRD of the Southam News Service, [who] describes the movie adequately: 'Love thy neighbour' depicts two men who acquire neighbouring houses in a typical development on the outskirts of any city. They begin by being good friends and sharing the lawn in common, without a barrier. Shortly, a marigold pops to bloom amid the grass. Each admires it and takes pleasure in its fragrance and color. Then some question arises as whose side it is on of the undrawn property line. . . . Rival fences go up, and are torn down . . . the story of human greed is told in

From Norman McLaren's Neighbours.

simple brutality . . . wives and children are slain almost incidentally . . . turning faces of friendliness into faces of primal savagery. This is the story of the destruction and disintegration of human character under greed's urge. It ends with the neighbours, killed by each other, lying in adjacent newly dug graves. Two marigolds pop out and bloom, one upon each gravepit.

Here a bemused Superintendent McClellan interjected, 'OH NO!' but Parsons concluded the summary evenly, noting that the film 'provokes fierce controversy, some seeing it as "pacifist propaganda" others as a leftist onslaught upon the sacredness of property rights.' The award of an Oscar to McLaren was surprising 'because of Hollywood's dread of political controversy'. Parsons recorded that 'The above newspaper article is being kept on _____'s file', noting that the animator 'is still with UNESCO in India.'

Aftermath

Over the next several years, surveillance continued and the dismissal list grew shorter. In 1954, a story appeared in the *Ottawa Journal* based on unnamed RCMP sources, announcing the appointment of the NFB's Michael Spencer as 'a special security officer for close liaison with the Justice Department and the RCMP's anti-subversive squad'. An intensive new screening system weeded out 'unreliable' applicants to the Board. A new application form asked for 'Country from which paternal ancestor emigrated to Canada', fingerprints, addresses for the previous 10 years with dates, a full list of relatives, including in-laws, their addresses, and employers. Although there were 'no questions which require a direct assertion of loyalty . . . it is understood that risks should be avoided at all costs, regardless of the professional qualifications of the applicant, or even his or her lack of personal subversive leanings.'

In 1955 the new Film Commissioner, Albert Trueman, crossed the country advising audiences to be wary because, although he had seen no indication of it personally, 'it is perfectly possible to use [the Film Board] for propaganda purposes.' Behind the scenes Constable A.M. Barr, reported that '_____ has now managed to oust all of the former circuit men in South-western Ontario.' In 1958, Darrell McLaren, by then an Inspector, advised the RCMP Commissioner that a search had been undertaken on the 'MacBee Keysort Punch Card System' to produce 'a complete list of all known subversives actually in the employ of the National Film Board'. The advent of automated data retrieval on 'punch cards' also permitted group searches of cultural agencies such as the NFB, the CBC's Domestic and International Services, and the Canada Council. Although there were 'still a few employees of interest to our Directorate', he wrote, the '*full scale clean-out after 1949*' resulted in the removal of '*some 40 employees*' and effectively cleared the Film Board of suspicion (emphasis added).

Screenings

If passing on to readers the censor's textual damage brings historiography to the brink of incoherence, 'repairing' the preceding narrative would have obscured the way the Access to Information procedure reinforces and deepens suspicion surrounding the (blank) name. The intended removal of all names other than those of the investigators shows that the patience of the secret policemen as genealogists is equal to that of the censor screening the files for release. Hundreds of names entered on these files were excised before the pages were released, leaving only a tendentious pall of imputed treacherous relationships.

As a sensing system, the Security Service and its myriad informants worked primarily at the level of the name by testing its connections to other suspect individuals or organizations. Their removal denies the pleasure of reading the name as a link in a narrative; the blanks contribute nothing to characterization, making the files difficult for historians to use. More importantly, the centrality of the name, accentuated by its removal, perpetuates a 'centre-periphery model' of leftist activities wherein the Communist Party was placed at the centre. This generated strict criteria for data selection and the 'surface of visibility' upon which a certain image of Canada was projected.

Cultural historian Michael Denning believes that Cold War cultural studies have too frequently complied with this 'fetishization of Party membership' and overemphasize 'the narrative of affiliation and disaffiliation'.[53] He suggests that the centre-periphery model has misrepresented a much broader social formation within which 'Party membership was not that central' even for many people who described themselves, generically, as 'communists'. This view is borne out here by the RCMP's evident failure to demonstrate any direct Party influence whatsoever among the NFB employees.

If we accept Denning's point and set the Security Service's favoured model to one side, different sorts of questions emerge. Why, for example, during five years of 'screening' NFB employees, was it not considered necessary to screen a single NFB film? Why was the domestic and international reception of films produced by the Board never studied? Why did it go unremarked that a significant number of the Board's films were made by women, many of whom were on the list of suspects?[54] What impact did the ongoing security scare have on the films themselves? The absence of these lines of inquiry suggests that the Security Service, habitually focused on (male) labour agitators and leaders of immigrant groups, was patently unequipped to 'screen' the Film Board.

Indeed, the Security Service's sensing system was so attuned to patterns of names that it remained oblivious to the production of audiovisual consciousness so central to the Film Board's role. This lacuna suggests that the NFB's legitimacy as the promoter of 'audiovisual citizenship' was already taken for granted in the common sense of the investigators. Mark McClung's description of the security police as 'blinkered' can thus be extrapolated to include this very special blindness that Norman McLaren made the object of oppositional practice in *Neighbours*. To specify this practice I will turn briefly to what John Grierson sought to achieve through the Film Board.

Audiovisual Citizenship

At this stage in its development the Security Service had little critical understanding of the audiovisual apparatus itself. Generally, the investigators shared the 'myopic' vision that permits spectators to be drawn into unconscious identification with an audiovisual diegesis, or narrative structure. In particular, they overlooked how persuasive propaganda triggers emulative desire in film spectators by presenting them with a model who desires some object, some person, or even a state of affairs. To operate a triangulation between the spectator, the model, and the desired object, mimetic desire as an effect of cinema requires that the audiovisual apparatus itself recede behind the head of the spectator, so to speak. That is, the technological mediation of the film camera and the projector must remain tacit in order to produce a certain kind of viewing subject.

As a propagandist, John Grierson sought to minimize the cognitive intrusion of film technology in the audiovisual consciousness he promoted through Film Board productions. This is why he insisted on standardizing the diegesis, something that came up frequently in his exchanges with NFB directors during the war. His basic insight was that the masses must see *themselves* represented on the screen realistically, and without obvious mediation, before they would emulate cinematic images as models of civic conduct.

'This all-seeing eye of the motion picture is a very prescient power', he stated in a 1940 CBC broadcast:

> [T]he film can give us the scene as a living whole . . . a sense of the communion that exists in spite of the apparent distance in our daily lives. . . . It is, and who does not want it, a way of national self-realization.[55]

'National self-realization' was to be Janus-faced: integrating citizens domestically within a national population even as their image was projected externally to integrate the nation within the international community of nations. His formula still provides the NFB with its corporate motto: 'why can't we say and be done with it, the National Film Board will be the *eyes of Canada*. It will . . . see Canada . . . whole, its people and its purposes.'[56]

The catch-phrase 'eyes of Canada' described a surveillant and disciplinary 'panoptic' apparatus, but moreover it suggested that the Film Board was to be just one node in a cross-national regime of audiovisual production and reception. Envisaging film boards for all nation-states was Grierson's theme from the 1930s through to his comment to James Beveridge in 1970 that 'the greatest export of the Film Board' was 'the Canadian Film Act itself'.

> It's been translated into many languages, . . . the model of serious intention by the cinema in the service of government, all over the world. . . . [W]hat has been good is the Film Board's service to the government with its initial intention of reflecting the country to itself and to the world. . . . The Film Board has been important in saying to countries of very different kinds, all over the world, that *the film is an instrument of very great importance in establishing the patterns of national imagination.*[57]

Grierson's global filmic apparatus was to be an 'interlocking web' patterning each national 'imagination' as an independent entity but also ensuring its isomorphism with all the others. The isomorphism was not just institutional, facilitating the international exchange of films, nor purely technical, establishing common standards. Pre-eminently it was *cognitive*, a shared diegesis to be projected evenly all around the globe at 24 frames per second. Organizing and intensifying the pattern of cultural nationalisms was to be cinema's great educational contribution to 'teleology':

> You may find [Americans] a little extravagant in their need to pronounce themselves one-hundred percent hygienically pure Americans, but damn it, it really is, I think, that way. . . . you've got to use the imaginative media, like television or radio or films, to the hilt.[58]

Peter Morris has shown that in the years immediately following Grierson's departure the Film Board continued to pattern and frame the nation's population and territory as a 'generalized reality' that denied 'the events any specificity of their own'.[59] His description is succinct:

> [I]ts ideology is clearly characteristically postwar Canadian. Social change is possible and desirable but should be gradual. Everyone has a place in Canadian society and everyone should be in his/her place. Canada is a well-managed society and problems only arise when people do not trust the managers to manipulate the levers on their behalf.[60]

That the success of the Film Board in disseminating audiovisual citizenship extended even to the Security Service is demonstrated by Corporal Darrell McLaren's respectful description of the NFB as 'that great public institution'. Darrell McLaren steps forward here as Norman McLaren's security alter ego, another 'mirror couple' whose vicissitudes mark a boundary. When the Mountie Darrell traced animator Norman's background and associations, his films passed unexamined. When Norman affronted audiovisual citizens with *Neighbours* he disrupted that taken-for-granted transparency of film spectatorship that Darrell never questioned, and its jarring effect reveals the continuity in purpose between the Security Service and the Film Board.

Palindrome

As photographic representation *Neighbours* is wholly unsatisfying, bordering on the grotesque. Its props are bland: two deck chairs, bungalows painted on two simple flats, a white picket fence, a weedy marigold. Even the neighbours' white shirts, slacks, and pipes appear identical. The overall effect is not exactly a 'doubling' but something more complex: expressing in visual symbols the palindrome blazing in the headlines of the newspapers they read in the opening sequence of the film. 'Peace . . . War/War . . . Peace' is a pivot point that supplies the key to the film's rationality. Read simultaneously from beginning to the end, and from the centre outwards, pleasure in palindromic reading is yielded by the tension between the serial rationale of a sentence and the radial rationale of the palindrome. A solely linear reading of *Neighbours* as a simplistic allegory of war yields little pleasure.

In a palindromic reading, the marigold serves as the focal point of mimetic desire between the two men and the source of escalating violence. One neighbour observes the other's deep desire for the flower and his desire is drawn in turn. Yet the very equivalence of the neighbours in relation to that point neutralizes viewer identification with either of them as a potential model. McLaren's hermetic scheme denies the film the necessary imbalance or internal difference to ignite mimetic desire and elicit mimetic action from its viewers.[61] When one neighbour places the fence 'one inch to the left' in order to claim the flower as his own (recalling Grierson's claim to be at any time 'one inch to the left' of the government in power), the other imitates the action and moves the fence one inch to the right. By blocking our identification with either neighbour, McLaren's *mise en scène* was implicitly anti-Griersonian and well outside the NFB tradition discussed above.

The BBC's documentary on McLaren, *The Eye Hears, The Ear Sees*, echoed Grierson's criticisms, judging *Neighbours* to be 'unsatisfying', an 'uneasy . . . mixture of over-simple philosophy and surprising violence'. The commentator deemed McLaren's application of an animation technique to human actors 'occasionally whimsical rather than playful', and he intoned with relief that McLaren 'never returned to the theme of *Neighbours*'. McLaren himself remained unswayed: 'if all my films were burning in a fire I think I'd prefer *Neighbours* to be saved.'[62]

Exactly what is meant by 'over-simple philosophy'? Read in a linear way, McLaren's insistence on equivalence in the two neighbour's comportment and beliefs implied, preposterously, that there was no difference between rival ideologies in the Cold War. It was this calculated oversimplicity, I suggest, that vaulted the film over the hurdles of censorship raised by Arthur Irwin's new NFB regime. As the police files show, the film was dismissed as sentimental by George McClellan at Overbrook RCMP Headquarters. It is as if McLaren supplied the authorities with a feeble linear allegory in order to deflect attention from his direct transgression of film spectatorship itself.

My reaction to the film as a schoolboy in the late 1960s was memorable enough for it to become embedded in my own NFB-influenced audiovisual consciousness. I do not recall mapping the warring neighbours' conflict on to an East-West partition of the world; I associated it immediately with the neurotic (in)security of suburban life, where one norm-enforcing neighbour might cross the property line and mow another's lawn if it grew an inch or two too high. I recall, too, a reaction of what Eve Sedgewick calls 'homosexual panic' at the sight of the two men's violent embraces, near kisses, and torn clothing, imagining the intimacy experienced by the two actors making the film. As McLaren intended, perhaps, I was forced to consider my own relation to the filmic apparatus and desire.[63]

A Damaged Ballet

McLaren acknowledged his debt to the pioneering *trucage* films of Georges Méliès in France at the turn of the century, and subsequent ad hoc experimentations by Hans Richter, Len Lye, Richard Massingham, and others. A deeper genealogy of *Neighbours* might be traced to the 1880s and Gilles de la Tourette's close studies of the human gait and erratic mannerisms, and Eadward Muybridge's experiments in step-photography at the University of Pennsylvania. Rigorous segmentation and analysis of human gesture at this historical juncture, as Giorgio Agamben has noticed, prophesied both the advent of motion pictures and also the crisis in the realm of human gesture that resulted from the very widespread mechanization that made such pictures possible. 'In the cinema,' Agamben writes, 'a society that has lost its gestures seeks to re-appropriate what it has lost while simultaneously recording that loss.'[64] In ceasing to resist that paradox, *Neighbours* transgressed cinema's fetishistic protocols of reception.

Reaction to McLaren's use of the pixillation technique emerged in reports of the film's reception when it was released in the summer of 1952. Although critics at the Edinburgh Film Festival were ecstatic (the *New Statesman* called it 'the best abstract I have seen by Norman McLaren for a long time'; the *Daily Mail* named it 'the film of the festival . . . a ferocious eight-minute parable of war and peace . . . that wears a freezing smile on its face. . . . It is brilliantly good.'), *The Manchester Guardian* warned readers that 'the audience is led laughing uproariously into a nasty little corner where Mr. McLaren, without warning, kicks it in the teeth.'[65]

In North America, too, distributors were uneasy with the film. Maurice Crompton, co-ordinating distribution for the NFB, reported that 'all the major distributors including Fox, Loew's, M.G.M., Warner Brothers, (Paramount refused to look at it) . . . turned [it] down for a variety of reasons: principally poor technical quality, and "gruesome scenes".' The picture was screened in New York for the Normandie Theatre and Radio City Music Hall 'and had a flat turn-down in each case.' It was accepted only by the Trans-Lux, Lexington (albeit 'with enthusiasm') for a 10-week engagement.

The judgement of 'poor technical quality' by the major distributors was less a comment on McLaren's competence than on the pixillation technique itself, and perhaps on the progressive degradation of the quality of the image near the end of the film, when its colour drains into harsh polarization.[66] The NFB's New York representative, Janet Scellen, reported that:

[T]he 'Marquee' people . . . are very much impressed with the film and with the genuine appreciation with which it is being received by their audiences, but they do feel that the people are bewildered and that a short explanation of the technique involved would be helpful. . . . As you remember, Ezra Goodman of Time Magazine made a similar suggestion after he had seen the film.[67]

Scellen endorsed the request that 'a short introductory explanation . . . be placed in front of NEIGHBOURS'.

This viewer uneasiness, I suggest, stems not just from the film's violence but from McLaren, as he put it, 'tampering with the tempo of human action'. The flickering illusion of 'reality' projected at 24 frames per second is undercut by these 'hyper-natural exaggerations and distortions of normal behaviour'. He achieved this, he wrote, 'by manipulating the acceleration and deceleration of any given human movement'. He played with the limitations of human visual perception:

Once it is assumed that the actor being photographed by a movie camera can stop between any or every 24th of a second, a new range of human behaviour becomes possible. The laws of appearance and disappearance can be circumvented as can the laws of momentum, inertia, centrifugal force and gravity; but what is perhaps even more important, the tempo of acting can be infinitely modulated from the slowest speed to the fastest. Apart from the apparently spectacular feats . . . it is possible to use the technique in a concealed way behind what appears to be normal acting. Or . . . in a less concealed way . . . a caricature type of movement . . . tampering with the tempo of human action.[68]

Pixillation in *Neighbours* does not, as elsewhere, signify the exhilarating forward rush of modernity; rather, it signifies the breakdown of civil society. At the outset the two neighbours light their pipes in 'real time' while reading their papers, and one man casually hands matches to the other in an unforced gesture. Only when the flower sprouts behind them on the property line does the tempo change. The trees exhibit the characteristic shakiness of time-lapse photography, and the neighbours 'skid' across the grass without leg movements, 'fly' around their yards like dancing Cossacks seized at the peak of a jump. A disjointed parody of balletic choreography ensues until the camera relaxes into real time once again as the neighbours attempt to negotiate ownership of the flower. As chivalric fencing with pickets degenerates into brawling, the pixillation effect returns to exaggerate their wild struggle, culminating in the vicious clubbing of wives and children with the pickets. With the expiry of the by now ghoulish neighbours, the inanimate elements—pickets and flowers—themselves recompose the scene for the funeral.

Imitative Violence

In June 1955, NFB producer Tom Daly received a letter from Celia M. Anderson, of the New York University Film Library. 'I spoke to Miss Janet Scellen some weeks ago', she wrote, regarding the showing of *Neighbours* to a group of 'disturbed and delinquent children with an average attention span of two or three minutes'. Typically these children reacted to 'ordinary classroom films . . . with restlessness, fighting or a general apathy':

> Since their lives are full of violence . . . at home . . . in the streets and at school, I suggested we try NEIGHBOURS. . . . The results were rather astounding. These ordinarily restless children were completely attentive, and identified deeply with the fighting in the film. The film had to be shown twice and discussion was lively.

The reactions were spontaneous and not the result of a controlled psychological experiment. The teachers explained 'that men who fought like this became savage' but they also directed the children's 'attention to the fact that mountain goats do not "pick fights" but fight to protect their families' and that this 'kind of battle . . . is socially justified.' The children were still talking about the film two months later and 'incorporated it into their spelling, reading, original stories, drawing and painting.' The children decided this was what they called a 'grudge' fight and suggested restaging the neighbours' fight in a 'good' or 'clean' way. McLaren's film both 'flattered' the boys and also made them 'self-conscious'. With the 'desks pushed back into a square . . . both boys fought with fixed smiles . . . they didn't want to look like the men in the picture.'[69]

McLaren's 'music' anticipates the impact-driven, machinic sounds of contemporary video games. It was photographed directly on the film's optical track using his box of indexed sound cards. Aurally, *Neighbours* thus alienated audiovisuality from the reality effects that Michel Chion calls 'materializing sound indices'.[70]

This 'anechoic', or echoless, environment contributes to the neighbours' aura of dislocation, suggesting their infinite transposability from lawn to lawn, suburb to suburb; the scene is 'placeless' except in reference to the disputed property line, a spatial abstraction. In the absence of ambient aural information, the listener is confronted with a transgressive audio apparatus intent on revealing violence in another register: 'It was a silent, hostile, disturbed and mischievous boy', wrote Celia Anderson, 'who became suddenly and intensely articulate, saying: "The music talked. I heard it." '

The patterns of imitative behaviour prompted by the film among these children suggests that *Neighbours* can be read not only as (weak) allegory of war but as a deconstruction of the mimetic desire produced by cinematic images (that so readily lend themselves to war propaganda). To the extent that imitative desire was the conceptual engine of John Grierson's utilitarian philosophy of cinema, McLaren here targeted his old master by disturbing the fetish of film spectatorship.

As an oppositional practice McLaren's 'parable' reveals an invisible continuity between the NFB and the RCMP as ordering or patterning forces in Canadian society. Grierson's wartime documentaries sought to manage the cultural differences between nationality groups by organizing them as observers; the Security Service harried the strays and black sheep in order to scare the 'normal' population into docility. Where Grierson proceeded through the persuasiveness of cinema, the police created disturbance, suspicion, and fear to elicit self-organizing patterns of compliance.

Norm Enforcement

There is no doubt that the Film Board itself was jolted into such patterns of compliance by the security scare. As McLaren and his team worked on *Neighbours* they witnessed Arthur Irwin busily restoring the Board's legitimacy, both in the eyes of the Department of External Affairs (to whose machinations he owed his appointment) and in those of the RCMP (whose continued scrutiny made him nervous). For the former, the 'International Film Program' was designed to meet the secret Psychological Warfare Committee's Cold War objectives.[71] To assuage the latter, dismissals in the order of 40–50 people were obligatory, beginning with three forced resignations for public and parliamentary consumption, the rest to be hacked away at regular intervals.

As I have shown, that there were just three people removed is plainly wrong, a myth perpetuated by Irwin, Pickersgill, Spencer, and even James Beveridge, who perhaps never knew the extent to which he himself had been under suspicion. The public sacrifice of three scapegoats, and the silent removal of the rest, was the price of a clean bill of health, and Arthur Irwin's promised ambassadorship lay on the other side of this unpleasant task.[72]

In April 1950 the NFB terminated the employment of Allan Ackman, Nathan Clavier, and David A. Smith.[73] As far as can be ascertained the three never spoke publicly of the security scare and their scapegoating by the authorities, but it dogged their subsequent careers. Nat Clavier had been active in Montreal's left-wing theatre scene in the 1930s.[74] He joined the NFB in 1944 as a distribution assistant and later directed films and worked as a field representative. After his dismissal he stayed on in Ottawa running a newsreel and photographic supply service. By the 1960s he was working as a real estate agent. Allan Ackman continued as an animator with mixed success, operating a small studio in Toronto through the 1950s. Later, he retreated to a farm near Guelph from which he sold animated advertisements to local businesses.[75] I had no luck discovering what became of Dave Smith. Years later, Michael Spencer, the specially appointed security officer within the NFB, had little to say about the other firings at the Film Board.

KIRWAN COX: So you don't know who was fired?

MICHAEL SPENCER: Shit, I do know, but I guess I'm not going to tell you. Did [Arthur] Irwin say anything about that? He probably wouldn't, would he?

COX: The RCMP wanted to fire forty people?

SPENCER: That's a bit of drama. . . . [Later, as the NFB's security officer] I had a lot to do with the RCMP in this area and they were always correct in this regard. They never said, 'if I were you I'd get rid of so and so,' . . . they would sit there, give you the file.

COX: Arthur Irwin mentioned Inspector O'Neill. . . .

SPENCER: Who spoke to Art? Did you speak to him?

COX: No. But were [the Mounties] acting as agents provocateurs?

SPENCER: Not so far as I know, [chuckles] not so far as I was concerned, anyway.[76]

Those on the winning side of this episode reiterated the shibboleth that there were only three dismissals. James Beveridge, nephew of Norman Robertson, surely was disingenuous when he asked Cox, 'were there really *four*?' Tom Daly transcended to a lofty narcissistic plane when asked about the nitty-gritty of the scare. Jack Pickersgill repeatedly and adamantly stated 'there was no witch hunt, no blacklist' until people believed it. Jack Chisholm of *Associated Screen News* eventually spoke forthrightly, and with smug delight. He told Cox of his confidential meeting in 1949 with Robert Winters, the Minister of Reconstruction and Supply, where he advocated firings beginning with Ross McLean and Jack Ralph.[77] Amazingly, historians Granatstein and Stafford could still write in 1990 that:

> the NFB's executives resisted any wholesale purge, insisted on seeing the evidence collected by the RCMP on thirty-six staff members, and only under duress reluctantly agreed to the compulsory release of three employees. . . . no glorious moment [but] neither was it any great purge.[78]

Even before his Academy Award for *Neighbours* the perennial prizewinner McLaren was considered untouchable, despite his unabashed left-wing background and 'peculiar' lifestyle. Perhaps for this reason his young protégé, Gretta Ekman, was targeted instead. McLaren had first seen examples of her experiments with painted film when he returned from China in 1950. He was 'struck by the kind of imagination behind them, the miniature scale on which she was accustomed to work and her technical skill with fine detail.'[79] He showed her how to make a drawing bench at home and gave her a roll of blank film. She returned a few months later 'with this little animated film . . . a remarkable job, and one which I felt we could well use.' Impressed with her seriousness, he wrote that she was 'the only Canadian artist whom I have tried to encourage in hand-drawn animation.' To McLaren's dismay, the new Film Commissioner suddenly forbade her further work at the Board.

In the spring of 1952 *Neighbours* had grown to be a more demanding project than expected, and as the deadline approached for sending two films to the Festival of Britain, McLaren decided to edit Gretta Ekman's film, still sitting on his shelf, as a 'quickie' to meet the deadline. Setting aside *Neighbours* for a few days, the film *Twirlygig* was produced by McLaren, combining Ekman's animation with music by Maurice Blackburn. It was ready for shipment to Britain when it came to Arthur Irwin's attention that Gretta Ekman's name appeared in the credits. His edict demanding its immediate deletion prompted McLaren's fury to overflow in three memoranda venting rage at the Film Board's abjection before the security authorities.

He pointed out that Ekman had not been on staff or on the premises to make the film. It was 'home-made' prior to her 'resignation'. 'It is true of course that she is left-handed and has reddish hair', he wrote, but although she may have known some Communists 'she herself is not one nor has ever been.' He listed his further objections to Irwin's decision:

- She is not in any way involved in work remotely connected with security.
- Her talent is a rare one, and not available elsewhere.
- The use of her animation eased my problems in meeting a commitment.
- If she is a fascist, anarchist, nihilist, communist or Christian pacifist it is not known [to] those of us who are acquainted with her here, and I should imagine even less to the general public. Her name on a film credit will not mean anything to the public. At least, not until they have seen her work and then it may come to mean a young artist with some promise of talent.
- I would urge that her security status be looked into right away. . . .
- I consider it a matter of grave concern if we have to discriminate against her work or name, without really serious cause.
- I would wish to stand up for the principle that the NFB is interested in the work of an artist for its own merit, irrespective of the philosophic and political opinions of the artist.[80]

McLaren gave short shrift to Irwin's verbal justifications for his decision. The Commissioner argued that by suppressing her name the Film Board might avoid controversy and so continue to buy her films from time to time, hoping that in due course the 'climate of freedom from fear' would improve to the point where 'she may be publicly admitted to be the author of her own work.'

McLaren was not appeased:

The fact of her name appearing on the credits publicly is sufficient in the opinion of the ~~Commissar~~ Commissioner to run a grave risk in the matter of the Film Board's public relations. He has therefore asked that it be removed. In doing so, Maurice Blackburn and I feel quite strongly that we wish to have our names withdrawn from the film too.[81]

He would not concede this point and, in effect having counter-censored Irwin's censorship, sent *Twirlygig* off to England as an anonymous contribution to the festival.

Irwin knew that the significance of Ekman's name to the *public* was irrelevant. What McLaren did not accept was that in the Security Service's universe of significant names the appearance of Gretta Ekman's credit might attract renewed suspicion and cast doubt on Irwin's effectiveness in 'cleaning up' the Film Board. The fact that the young artist was not a security risk was also irrelevant. Unlike law enforcers, the 'norm-enforcing' neighbours at the Overbrook Headquarters watched only for further signs of deviance, never really expecting to find outright illegality.

Evelyn Lambart wrote to McLaren in India a few months later advising him that Arthur Irwin had reneged on a commitment he made regarding Gretta Ekman. 'Yes,' replied McLaren:

Irwin assured me twice that there would be no problem about giving Gretta NFB work, provided she didn't work on NFB premises, nor be given screen credits on films, and naturally provided she was doing an essential job for us, which was

Arthur Irwin and Norman McLaren, at Around is Around *premiere, Ottawa, 1951.*
Damaged negative, NAC, PA 206843, detail.

making use of her special skills or talent. I wonder by what ~~sharp~~ slick diplomatic loophole he has gone back on his word. That he has done so is ~~XXXXX~~
~~XXXXXX XXXXX~~ is disturbing. ~~But I suppose it was to be expected of him.~~ [82]

Ordinary Luck

Even as the Film Board reeled from the RCMP's punch, it continued to order and pattern a national diegesis in the routine production and distribution of its films. Other
than *Neighbours* there was little filmic resistance to Grierson's ideas about audiovisual culture; if anything, the internalization of censorship through the 'red scare'
made the Film Board a *less* effective propaganda agency for a time because its filmmakers became too self-conscious and lost the 'naturalness' he had demanded.

Recognizing the continuity of purpose between cultural and security agencies in
shaping citizenship during the Cold War undercuts the mythologized loss of a progressive nationalism at the Film Board during the security scare. This mythology
misrecognizes Grierson's pragmatic mix of information and disinformation in the
service of government as a pure expression of 'progressive' national culture, and
forgets his conviction that 'Censorship is the central institution by which national
priorities are maintained.'[83] Cultural nationalist historiography thereby forms a
'mirror couple' with the censor's black markers and white corrector fluid. By polarizing culture and security and reinforcing the 'centre-periphery' model of Communist affiliation, it obscures alternative patterns and remains blinkered to
oppositional practices such as McLaren's production of *Neighbours*.

The censor released Mark McClung into historiography forever owing his NFB
neighbours a bottle of the atrocious 'Manoir St. David'. The unrequited gift crops
up like the wobbly marigold that sprouted as the last uncensored 'difference'
between McLaren's homogeneous suburban characters. It signified the prohibited
possibility of intellectual conviviality with his NFB friends, something McClung

desired but instead ridiculed to forestall George McClellan's suspicion. It hints at an aborted cultural future whose full dimension is now difficult to assess.

The NFB's production files record David A. Smith's conscientiousness and rising ability as an employee. There is no hint of dissatisfaction with his work or attitudes prior to his dismissal, nor any suggestion that Smith promoted 'Communism' through his NFB assignments. The closest he ever came to receiving a critical comment was in a script for a 1949 film about Alberta, where he wrote that 'the land has a lot to offer any man who gets an even break.' A superior's blue pencil rephrased this sentence: 'any man who has *ordinary luck*.'

Gretta Ekman's case was also extraordinarily unlucky. Notwithstanding Norman McLaren's shy charm, his fierce perfectionism demanded much from his co-workers, not least his assistant, Evelyn Lambart. It is significant that of all his assistants, including Lambart, only Gretta Ekman received his direct endorsement as a promising animator of hand-drawn abstract films. She did not 'draw large', he said, and this rare praise remains a tantalizing might-have-been in Canadian film history, for after her dismissal in July 1950 Gretta Ekman never drew another animated film.[84]

Perhaps Mark McClung's withholding of any decisive gesture in favour of the Film Board suspects during the security screening contributed to a disturbance he internalized and later sought to quell by criticizing the activities of the Security Service. When I was introduced to him in the early 1980s, in an unrelated context and not long before he died, he struck me as a complex and intelligent man, and one who would have pondered the cultural fallout of Cold War national security. During the same period, James Littleton asked him directly if the 'subversive element' he studied and reported on in the 1940s and 1950s had ever represented a significant threat. 'No,' he admitted, 'inwardly we didn't believe a word of it. It was no threat to the security of the nation.'[85]

3

Remembering To Forget

[T]he essence of a nation is that all individuals have many things in common, and also that they have forgotten many things.

Ernest Renan, *Qu'est-ce qu'une nation?*

Secrecy about secrecy was the British way.

David Vincent, *The Culture of Secrecy*

Denied the intellectual conviviality of his NFB neighbours by the security scare, over the years Mark McClung cultivated a circle of mostly male friends who similarly occupied the liminal zone between national culture and state security during the late 1950s and 1960s. Gathering for weekly lunches at a corner table in Sammy's restaurant in Ottawa's Belle Claire Hotel, rising cultural luminaries such as broadcaster Patrick Watson of the CBC and éminences grises such as Henry Hindley, policy-maker with the Secretary of State Department, were received warmly by representatives of the state security intelligentsia: McClung of the RCMP, Peter Dwyer and Don Wall of the Privy Council Office. Other regulars included, at various times, External Affairs' Arnold Smith, author of the Royal Commission report on the Gouzenko affair, and John Starnes of Defence Liaison II and later the RCMP. From the cultural side, Naim Kattan and David Silcox, Canada Council officers, CBC producer Gordon Cullingham, and Bill Taylor, Director of the Museum of Man, were often present. If women rarely ventured into this fraternity, journalist Starr Solomon was the prominent exception.

As Henry Hindley put it in 1979:

the membership (undocumented, of course) has changed over the years. When I first was allowed in, there was a preponderance of people from the Canada Council, the Privy Council Office, and the Treasury Board, quite a few who had been in the 'cloak and dagger' business of security and intelligence.[1]

Patrick Watson recalls 'a curious frivolity in this intercourse with the security folk'. The security people seemed to enjoy mingling with their counterparts in the cultural sector, perhaps vicariously experiencing their greater freedom of speech and association. They envied the nobility of artistic endeavour by comparison to what both Don Wall and Mark McClung described as 'soul-destroying' compromises exacted by security work.[2] What permanently divided the two spheres were the security group's sworn vows of secrecy, and yet what bound them together was the intimacy attendant to that secrecy. It was a matter of discretion. The Belle Claire stood adjacent to the *Ottawa Journal* offices where the Soviet defector Igor Gouzenko was brushed off as a crank in 1945, but the handful of journalists around the table respected the unspoken publication ban.

This is not to suggest that McClung's circle carelessly shared state secrets. To the contrary, their discussions ranged widely, pre-eminently lighting on cultural or literary topics. Self-consciously patterned after Dorothy Parker's circle at New York's Algonquin Hotel, the literati of this martini-driven, smoky corner indulged in similar displays of wit. Eventually, the group was acknowledged as an informal Ottawa institution when Sam Kauffman installed a round table accommodating 18 or 20 people. In a sense, these lunch parties paralleled the rise of the 'quasi-autonomous non-governmental organizations', or 'quangos', through which the 'arm's-length' formula granted the federal arts and culture agencies limited autonomy from government. The frivolity mentioned by Patrick Watson should not obscure a crucial mapping function underway, elaborating a secure set of discursive practices for the emergent cultural bureaucracy.

Organizations have loci of authority that may or may not coincide with their organizational structures, salary classifications, and decision-making hierarchies. In some cases the executive function is guided directly or indirectly even by relatively junior employees who come to personify the 'conscience' of the organization. Not exactly 'shop floor control', with that term's implication of oppositionality and class consciousness, these localized nodes of influence operate positively, attracting heedful attention from senior figures on account of special knowledge or experience, personal charisma, or recognized genius in a particular field of activity.

Around McClung's table a quasi-official repository of both secret and erudite knowledge combined to influence the profile of the national cultural project. Its key figure was McClung's fellow Oxonian, Peter Dwyer, and its key attribute was a tacit understanding of the relationship between official secrecy and public culture. Sammy's regulars helped to interweave a new cultural sensitivity into the suspicious and xenophobic security establishment, fashioning the supple 'zone of protection' necessary to waging Cold War.

The security aspect of World War II cultural policy intensified during the peak interval of Cold War insecurity, the very years when the Massey Royal Commission on the Arts, Letters and Sciences (1949–51) charted Canada's cultural future. The Massey Report forecast a 'governmentalization' of artistic activity, stitching a national and centrist cultural regimen into the fabric of Canadian citizenship. As a vehicle for disciplinary and surveillance functions, national cultural policy entered here into a Faustian agreement with the national security state. In return for financing the development of a substantial cultural sector these new agencies were expected to foster certain lines of development and foreclose on others. In the tradition of Matthew Arnold's *Culture and Anarchy*, legitimate culture was to neutralize the anarchic potential of popular front culture, the 'ethnic arts', and, to the extent possible, American mass media.

The Anatomy of Secrecy

In his famous 1882 address *'Qu'est-ce q'une nation?'* Ernest Renan explained how citizens must 'already have forgotten' (*doivent avoir oublié*) certain historical events that could jeopardize France's cohesiveness as an imagined historical community.[3] 'Forgetting', Renan reminded his Parisian audience, even to the point of 'historical error, is a crucial factor in the creation of a nation.' By implication, France's humiliation during the Prussian occupation would become yet another historical event citizens must remember to forget in the national interest. National culture never rests on laurels (or disasters), but restlessly reaffirms itself through a 'daily plebiscite', and it is this day-to-day, second-to-second presencing of a nation that presents a paradox.

On the one hand, the model citizen is cued by Renan to be somewhat historically insensitive (to forget the Prussian occupation) and yet a national duty persists to be alert to infiltration, Prussian or otherwise. In this version of civic nationalism, a nuanced tolerance for official secrecy is essential to the ongoing reproduction of the nation as a historically stable entity. It also becomes the site for a collective repressed memory of illiberal actions taken in the national interest.

Early intimations of such cultural conditioning to secrecy can be discerned in the systematic erasure of Aboriginal people from Canada's cultural nationalist regime of wilderness representation.[4] Then there is the complete absence of radio antennas from Canadian landscape art of the first half of this century—the very decades of an unprecedented efflorescence of antennas in wilderness and pastoral lands of Canada. Remarkably, and so far as I know without exception, the radio equipment was filtered from the burgeoning genre of nationalist landscape painting, even as signals intelligence and broadcasting became central organs of Canada's culture-security complex.

Landscape and official secrecy go together, and thus Michael Dorland calls Canada 'a thoroughly hidden country', where 'a territorial configuration of mouths' established 'silence as the cultural norm'. One of Canada's most 'secret corners', David Stafford points out, is Ottawa, where discretion 'can be as thick as the ice in the Rideau Canal.' He attributes this to the residual influence of Whitehall and British bureaucracy, where, as Peter Hennessy writes, 'secrecy is built into the calcium of a British policy-maker's bones . . . it is as much a part of the English landscape as the Cotswolds.'[5]

The relation of official secrecy to national culture raises a question: to what extent was the citizen's 'right to know' preconditioned by a *cultural* imperative to secrecy and confidentiality? From this perspective the current Access to Information Act can be understood as a highly successful *cultural* policy designed to keep Canada's secret landscape underrepresented in its national history. Throughout the

Cold War an internally directed campaign of censorship, intelligence, and propaganda performed quiet and effective work, too, installing a jamming device in Canadian culture that separated the spheres of culture and security, polarizing them in a durable opposition. A chain of binary opposites coded them as light/dark, civilized/uncivilized, pure/contaminated, truthful/deceptive, and open/secretive. Mark McClung described the security function as 'everything that is not civilized' and the arts as nourishing the 'soul' against the corrupting influence of state security services. As Peter Dwyer emphasized, the nation's greatest artistic expressions were to be 'the shining things which really count'.

Understandably, it seemed unconscionable to view arts and culture as implicated in any way with the black limbo of state security and official secrecy that these officials were all too familiar with. Both Mark McClung and Don Wall counted the artistically inclined Dwyer as an exceptional case whose long service in security intelligence never eroded his humanist commitment.

The polarization of culture and security indicates a second order of state secrecy whose presence can be diagnosed only inferentially, like black holes in space. On the external front, for example, Canadians had little knowledge of the ensemble of artistic talent, powerful transmitters, and jamming devices directed towards the Soviet bloc, waging a full-scale 'Battle of the Antennas'.[6] Cultural nationalist accounts hesitate to record similar activities on the internal front: the Canadian Broadcasting Corporation as the instrument of broadcast censorship, the National Film Board as an instrument of propaganda and psychological warfare, the National Library as a clearing house for open-source Soviet intelligence material, the National Archives as guardian of sensitive national security documents, the Multiculturalism program as a nest for immigration investigators, and the National Arts Centre and the string of Centennial auditoria as fortifications against not just American mass culture but the alternatives portended by the Cultural Front of the 1930s and 1940s. The Canada Council for the Arts, above all the others, occupied the loftiest and most unsullied place in the national culture. The unacknowledged links between state security and national culture were tantamount to obscenities in the cultural nationalist regime of historical observation.

A basic distinction between official secrecy and cultural secrecy clarifies this point. Official secrecy is the routine guarding of privy information which, if revealed, might adversely affect the national interest. Official secrecy was enforced by the Official Secrets Act, the Defence of Canada Regulations, the National Archives Act, and in later years by the Access to Information Act and the Government Security Policy. These measures prevented civil servants from making unauthorized disclosures and kept various types of records and information from public review. Less obviously, journalists, academics, and politicians were trained to revelatory rituals that managed publication of state secrets, neutering their potential to excite change. The muted and short-lived repercussions of such releases mark points where official secrecy enjoined this second order of *cultural* secrecy.

Cultural secrecy is not directly enforced by laws or administrative orders but rather circulates through public culture generally, pumped by state information and culture agencies. During World War II and throughout the Cold War, cultural secrecy tacitly combined with official secrecy to regulate the horizon of truth-speaking in Canadian society. Cultural secrecy was the citizen's need not to know in the 'need-to-know' climate fostered by the security state. In Benedict Anderson's phrase it was the citizen's *remembering to forget* information unassimilable to the national culture and its official narrative, a willed amnesia that selected out certain knowledge.[7] Reg Whitaker goes so far as to call such secrecy 'the defining characteristic of the Canadian Cold War on the home front'.[8]

The Right to Know

R. Gordon Robertson is a former civil servant who was influential in security issues for more than three decades. From dismantling Japanese-Canadian internment camps at the end of World War II to the October Crisis of 1970 when he was Chairman of the Security Panel, Robertson learned the rationale for official secrecy from within; indeed, later he helped frame the present Access to Information legislation. Speaking to the Royal Society at a meeting in St John's in 1972, he presented the problem of official secrecy as one of balancing the state's 'need for secrecy' with the public's 'right to know'. In Robertson's opinion, news media too readily published material supplied by whistle-blowers. Frowning on 'the rather festive mood' surrounding a string of leaked cabinet confidences, he 'questioned the action of whoever may have been responsible for an unauthorized disclosure that, if intentional, was contrary to the oath taken by all officials and others who deal with classified information.' He set out four justifications for such oaths, and for official secrecy generally: national security, personal privacy, international relations, and effective government.[9]

Two imperatives to secrecy were axiomatic: all matters concerning national security, he said, are 'pretty generally agreed' to be exempt from public disclosure; second, information whose release might prejudice the interests of the state in its bilateral or multilateral relationships with other states is subject to restriction not just in Canada but in every state. In addition, he said, 'there exist a number of classes of information that most countries accept should be secret . . . where an individual's right to privacy must prevail.' Piggybacking on the usual rationale for privacy considerations—the citizen's right to privacy—he argued that the cabinet's own deliberations present a privacy issue. Cabinet privacy, he argued, is built into the very name *Privy* Council and is essential to yet another justification for secrecy: 'effective government'.

In a parliamentary system, he argued, it is vital that cabinet proceedings be held in camera because its decisions must not be attributable to any single minister but always to the cabinet as a whole: 'Ministers have a right to talk and argue, to be wise or to be foolish, with the knowledge that privacy is accorded to them, too.' In 1980, journalist Tom Earle asked Robertson about his role in developing the Access to Information and Privacy Acts. Robertson said, 'If it were known that their [i.e., ministers'] positions were different from the decision that finally came out, the opposition in the House of Commons would drive a coach and six through government. It would be destructive.'[10]

The official who feels he or she is blowing the whistle over some particular issue in fact frustrates the effective operation of democratic government over the long term:

> In short, the collective executive that is the heart of our Parliamentary system must have secrecy: it cannot work without it. . . . Cabinet documents, whatever their content and whatever their nature, cannot be regarded as 'public' simply because a decision has been reached. They must . . . all be considered confidential until the expiry of whatever period—it is now set at thirty years—will ensure that their publication can have no significant effect.[11]

The checks on any abuses that might be perpetrated under the cover of official secrecy were twofold. The first was that the *outcomes* of confidential cabinet discussions became known in due course when legislation or administrative regulations were tabled and tested by passing through the houses of Parliament under the scrutiny of the media and other interested parties. A further responsibility lies with historians and other researchers not sworn as privy councillors who, upon the release of documents after the statutory period, must develop deeper assessments of governments' confidential activities based on the records themselves. In this way, successive governments are restrained both in the short and long terms from concealing improper, illegal, undemocratic, and illiberal practices behind the screen of cabinet confidentiality.

Shortcomings in Robertson's argument point up deficiencies in Canada's access to information regime. Robertson's first and second justifications—the fact that secrecy concerning security matters is axiomatic—simply accepts that secrecy is in the essence of 'international relations'. The international system itself enmeshes each member state in a binary ambivalence of international co-operation *versus* international competition that makes secrecy unavoidable. Ideally, a state's various alliances and information-sharing agreements hold rivalry and co-operation at equilibrium, forestalling actual conflict. The trouble is that this approach to collective security leads to an escalation of secrecy and thus to distrust with respect to each state's deepest intentions. The secrecy surrounding such intentions is identical with the strength of the state's claim to sovereignty (and this is why, in the era of electronic communications, secret codes and ciphers quietly restored a priestly caste in cloistered halls adjacent to governments).

Robertson relied on the disclosure-in-time principle to justify official secrecy, implying that national security secrets were subspecie to knowable Orders-in-Council. While actual legislation is preferable because it entails parliamentary review, accountability for the raw matter concealed in Orders-in-Council is nonetheless traceable, at least in general terms, to Orders receiving public scrutiny in the manner he described. Yet, the *secret* Order-in-Council is kept secret on a permanent basis precisely to avoid such scrutiny, and one suspects it is a necessary instrument in sustaining his blanket exemption of 'national security' matters. Everyone 'pretty generally' agreed with that, he thought. Yet, by his own logic, should not these secret orders have been *most* open to *ex post facto* scrutiny, as they were the least checked and most open to abuse?

Robertson may have skirted this issue to avoid discussing the threat the secret Order-in-Council presents to civil liberties. Bypassing every check and balance, the secret Order leaves the citizen reliant solely on individual characteristics of decision-makers whose public accountability effectively is suspended. Here, in his characterization of such officials as decent, civilized people, hard-pressed by a bewildering flow of complex developments, he implicitly asked his listeners to take a leap of faith. Where one might wish for a system designed to isolate and expunge bad bureaucratic apples and their illiberal practices, our attention is drawn instead to the goodness of the shiniest specimens. Given the litany of internments, expropriations, clandestine penetrations and manipulations of legitimate dissident groups and ethnic communities, destruction of public documents, and possibly even state murder, one might be forgiven for distrusting this suspension of rights for the sake of the 'efficiencies' necessary to the state's competitive/co-operative jockeying with other states.

In fact, the checks on official secrecy that Robertson mentions are flimsy and solely concerned with cabinet documents. The complete removal of other types of information from public release remains problematic even to this day. The tiny fraction of RCMP security intelligence files transferred to the National Archives, for example, is not released as a coherently archived record group. Rather, these files are pecked open in piecemeal fashion through researchers' individual Access to Information requests.[12] The records are severed not by the Archives staff, but off site, and extensively, by CSIS itself. And who comprises the National Archives Review Unit, which decides the fate of these materials? Oddly enough, it contains neither representation from the National Archives nor from the community of historians. Rather, its members are unidentified former employees of the agencies concerned, the type of document weeders that E.P. Thompson witheringly dubbed 'anti-historians'. This appellation may be too harsh; but given the obstructive methods of release, an assessment of the disposal of documents by CSIS is possible only through the occasional anomalies that crop up in the process of research.[13]

I have mentioned here only the records of the former RCMP Security Service held by the National Archives on behalf of CSIS, but at least several other government departments or their agencies are even more reclusive. The records of the Communications Security Establishment, for example, heir to the CBNRC, are a closed book, as are intelligence agencies within the RCMP and the Defence Department. As John Bryden reports, the individual researcher has the sense of operating against unseen adversaries. He returned to read DND files that he had consulted previously only to find that 'sensitive' documents had disappeared.[14]

On the cultural side, the researcher is not much better off. Agencies such as the Canada Council, the Canadian Broadcasting Corporation, and the National Arts Centre are exempt from the Access to Information legislation and maintain complete control over their own archival records. Researchers find that access to these records is often as restrictive as it is with security and intelligence material.

Can the historical researcher properly evaluate the cultural impact of official secrecy? The *mise en abîme* in public information I have described makes certainty scarce, but the true answer lies less in the flat denial of access to certain documents than in the way the Access to Information function trains researchers to a tightly controlled revelatory ritual. The 'right to know' withers in the calculated damage applied to the documentation, the piecemeal access to it, and its reception into a populace acculturated to secrecy. Furthermore, researchers will be tempted to fill in the blanks with speculation that may magnify the significance of withheld records and hence weaken their accounts.

If Gordon Robertson's presentation avoided any consideration of how secrecy worked culturally, perhaps it is because the state's need for secrecy was *incommensurate* with the citizen's 'right to know'. Fundamental to nationality itself, secrecy is presumed to be an imperative that must precede any such right. The dispersion of official secrets into a widely shared public secrecy thus was a mutually reinforcing process in Cold War Canada. Official secrecy withheld what could never be forgotten if known, whereas cultural secrecy neatly sutured the periodic releases of information inadmissible to its regime of observation.

An Obligation to Remember

Civic memory is now the subject of much historical lobbying. For example, J.L. Granatstein exhorts mainstream Canadians to remember their 'hard' civic obligations to defend the nation. In vilifying the so-called 'zombies'—the conscientious objectors of World War II—he asserts that the state knows best what its citizens should remember and forget.[15] He castigates journalist Zuhair Kashmeri for blurring the hard obligation to national military service with talk of 'multicultural neutrality'. Kashmeri documented how internal security operations during the Gulf War treated Arab Canadians not as citizens but as threats to national security. Kashmeri urges Canadians to remember these recent instances of repressive secret policing against ethnocultural minorities 'before government historians paint the era with the brush of tranquillity.'[16]

Arjun Appadurai's ruminations on 'postnational belonging' lead him to suggest more 'plural, serial, contextual and mobile forms of citizenship' that now seem remote in the aftermath of the terrorist attacks of 11 September 2001. This is precisely the type of thinking that Granatstein would 'throw forcibly into the dustbin'. Appadurai's loose-lipped 'postnational' citizen is likely to remember too much history, and rather too critically. He or she maintains a personal sovereignty and independence of mind akin to the zombies' disinclination to volunteer. Appadurai does not accept that citizenship has to be, like military conscription, a 'forced choice'. For him, postnational belonging means coming to terms with 'the difference between being a land of immigrants and being one node in a postnational network of diasporas'.[17] Postnational processes, he says, undermine the nation-state's ideal of a homogeneous, stable citizenry enjoying simultaneous national presence in a consensual national narrative. On the other hand, Appadurai does not venture into speculation about how the national security state might demilitarize the secrecy, mistrust, and amnesia of national culture, especially in a period of crisis. He asserts, ambiguously, that embracing postnationality 'may mean distinguishing our attachment to America from our willingness to die for the United States.'[18]

No doubt a 'need-to-know' and 'loose-lips-sink-ships' regimen was essential to the elite-driven political and cultural administration that Gordon Robertson called 'effective government'. But one cannot help noticing a certain bypassing of democratic principle in this hitching of the adjective 'effective' to governance. Indeed, Canadian government information policy ever was more 'effective' than it was democratic. My premise is that the right to know will count, as a civil right and as a human right, only when it is met by a concomitant civic obligation to remember.

The role of the National Archives in shaping Canada's civic memory is important in this regard. Significantly, this institution today is not constituted as an arm's-length agency but rather the National Archivist reports directly to the Minister for Canadian Heritage. Its direct public accountability is thus outweighed by its need to comply with government priorities and this orientation is amply reflected in its own historical files.[19] Of course, it is arguable that government departments and agencies would entrust their sensitive records to the Archives if it were a quasi-independent body. Yet, to the extent that historians and journalists have a responsibility to monitor and analyze government's accountability over the long term, this leaves them just the relatively restrictive Access to Information legislation or else sheer accident as the sole means of opening and evaluating secret records.

The Public Information Commissioner thus far has not seriously challenged the blanket exemptions placed on security-related records, but in any case that office cannot hope to substitute for a National Archivist with broad authority and independence to ensure both the retention and the eventual release of all or virtually all public documents. Despite J.L. Granatstein's fulmination, remembering not to forget is a 'harder' obligation than his enforced version of patriotism. Indeed, the question raised by his recent book—*Who Killed Canadian History?*—takes on a different complexion when considered alongside forgotten figures like Paul Robeson, discussed below.[20] After all, if citizens are aware of their history primarily as a branch of government information, they might well be forgiven for forgetting too much.

4

State Security and Cultural Administration: The Case of Peter Dwyer

Espionage is the secret theatre of our society.

John Le Carré

Peter Dwyer. Who can explain him, who can tell the reason why?

Henry Hindley

If John Le Carré is right to call espionage a secret theatre, Igor Gouzenko's defection from the Soviet embassy in Ottawa on the night of 5 September 1945 struck various leading players with stage fright. Indeed, the cipher clerk's defection had so many short- and long-term ramifications for the nascent Canadian security state that its status as a historical event of causal import is almost beyond question. The event caused Peter Dwyer, the British Secret Intelligence Service's liaison officer for North America, to speed from Washington to Ottawa for Gouzenko's debriefing, little knowing that it would place him at the forefront of accelerating developments in both Canada's state security and its cultural administration. The sensational case licensed a tough-minded upgrading of Canada's internal security measures. Culturally, Gouzenko's revelations helped abort the 'progressive' movement in Canada, striking a decisive blow in favour of the national cultural project to be mapped out in the Massey Report several years later.

Yet any portentous 'event' that becomes as axiomatic in historiography as the Gouzenko case nonetheless remains susceptible to an inverse causal reading. Rather than follow up Gouzenko's volition as a historical actor, one can search the density of social forces for the cleft or abscess that drew him forth, irresistibly, without reference to any exercise of individual will on his part. The matter of intentionality, or free choice, in Igor Gouzenko's 'unscheduled' arrival into RCMP care, as will be discussed below, raises the question of how the 'scheduled time' of the Canadian nation, its collective 'cognitive map', was rescheduled by Gouzenko's precipitous action. Peter Dwyer is a commendable guide in this matter because the line management of both the security and cultural dislocations that followed, inasmuch as they devolved on a single individual, fell to him.

Dwyer was not unique in having a dual career in security intelligence and in federal cultural institutions. G. Hamilton Southam, head of the Intelligence division of the Department of External Affairs (DL-2), went on to found the National Arts Centre. Mavor Moore's talents served Military Intelligence and the Psychological Warfare Committee as well as the CBC and the Canada Council.[1] Yet the archive reveals Dwyer's career to have been astonishingly central to post-war Canadian culture and national security. The Canadian career of 'Janus' (his code name in British Intelligence) occupies the crossroads of two ready-made narratives whose mutual repulsion in cultural nationalist historiography surely signals their clandestine attraction.

On the cultural front, the decades-long foment for a federal cultural policy, punctuated by the Kingston Conference of Artists in 1941, finally resulted in the Massey Royal Commission of 1949–51 and then in the eagerly awaited implementation in 1957 of its central recommendation, the creation of the Canada Council.[2] Milestones in the history of Canada's internal security arrangements, on the other hand, include the RCMP finding their anti-Communist *raison d'être* in the Winnipeg General Strike, Canada's investment in signals intelligence during World War II, and the Cold War elaboration of a censorship-intelligence-propaganda apparatus following Gouzenko's defection.[3]

Hypothesizing concordances between these narratives is to enter a historiographical no-go zone associated with that Wesley Wark calls the 'national insecurity state' and what Gregory Kealey describes as 'a popular mentality that stresses insecurity within'. Indeed, Michael Denning goes so far as to call the parallel American process a 'cultural civil war' fought out within the apparatuses of culture and the state.[4] Occupying these interstices, Peter Dwyer's biography forms a hybrid narrative that, by his own design and a measure of good luck, failed to coalesce in public discourse during his lifetime. Dwyer kept significant aspects of his career from public view; but he was lucky, too, that Canada's culture of secrecy safely absorbed various official secrets with which he was associated.

Harry Dexter White

In November 1953, one such secret threatened to upset Dwyer's Canadian career. It concerned Harry Dexter White, the economist and senior American Treasury official who sat opposite British negotiator John Maynard Keynes at the Bretton Woods conference and profoundly influenced the post-war international financial system. Since 1939, when Whittaker Chambers mentioned his name to the FBI, White, along with Alger Hiss, had been under a degree of suspicion of being a source of information for the Soviets.

In November 1945 Elizabeth Bentley provided the FBI with White's name on a list of officials who may have supplied the Soviet Union with confidential government material. White's position gave him access to sensitive data and his possible unreliability posed an immediate question for President Harry Truman when he learned of it in February 1946. Within days White was to be confirmed as American Director of the International Monetary Fund.

Truman resisted pressure to block Harry Dexter White's appointment, suspecting partisan motives behind the information, but White was kept under FBI surveillance for more than a year. When his name surfaced publicly in the spectacular allegations made against Alger Hiss by Elizabeth Bentley and Whittaker Chambers in 1948, White delivered a passionate self-defence before the House Committee on Un-American Activities. His death from heart failure just three days afterwards heightened FBI suspicions that he had betrayed state secrets, but the matter of his innocence or guilt was never satisfactorily resolved.[5]

The Canadian angle on the White enigma emerged on Capitol Hill in November 1953 following mid-term election setbacks for Eisenhower's ruling Republicans. In order to divert attention from both the elections and from the high-flying Senator Joseph McCarthy, Attorney General Herbert Brownell produced new information on 6 November regarding the White case. Speaking to the Chicago Executives Club he accused former President Harry Truman of having promoted Harry Dexter White to a senior IMF post six years earlier despite intelligence reports indicating that White may have been a Soviet informant. Truman dismissed Brownell's charge as partisan demagoguery, but the spat gained altitude when McCarthy flatly stated that the former President was 'a liar'.[6]

Truman ignored a subpoena from the notorious McCarran Committee and instead explained to a nationwide radio audience from his home in Kansas City that Harry Dexter White was permitted to take up his new post in order to facilitate FBI investigations into Soviet espionage rings. That explanation struck most Americans as plausible, but in calling Attorney General Brownell 'mealy-mouthed' and 'phony' Truman hardly placated his Republican adversaries. Following the broadcast one journalist described the atmosphere in Washington as 'charged with political thunderheads'.[7]

FBI Director J. Edgar Hoover obeyed a subpoena to appear before William E. Jenner's Senate Subcommittee on Internal Security and he took the opportunity to challenge Truman's explanation.[8] In unprecedented and gripping televised testimony, he stated that the former President had ignored his Bureau's specific warning about Harry Dexter White, conveyed in a memorandum of 1 February 1946 to Truman's national security adviser, General Harry Hawkins Vaughan.[9] In the concluding paragraphs of this memo Hoover introduced the Canadian dimension, stating that it was a 'highly placed' *Canadian* government source who had:

> reported that the British and Canadian delegates on the International Monetary Fund may possibly nominate or support White for the post of President of the International Bank, or as Executive Director of the International Monetary Fund. It is further commented by my Canadian source that if White is placed in either of these positions he would have the power to influence to a great degree deliberations on all international financial arrangements.[10]

The tabling of this document by Attorney General Brownell jolted the Canadian government. As journalist James Minifie reported from Washington, Canada's

Ambassador Arnold Heeney was 'greatly vexed' by the disclosure; in Ottawa, Prime Minister St Laurent called it a 'disagreeable surprise'.[11] In normal circumstances, they said, such national security matters were handled confidentially between the two governments. But with packs of congressional and senatorial un-American activities inquisitors vying for media attention and partisan gain, circumstances were anything but normal.[12]

Indeed, Brownell's release of this memo was not considered in Ottawa to be accidental, but the by-product of a second issue involving the defector Gouzenko, by then living incognito under RCMP protection. The *Chicago Tribune* had charged (with some truth) that the Canadian government had been less than forthcoming with Gouzenko's information, further asserting that the Soviet defector was in possession of new facts that he would impart only to Jenner's Senate subcommittee.[13] Lester Pearson's reluctance to produce Gouzenko for public questioning infuriated Jenner and his colleagues, and the release of Hoover's memo was just one of several coercive and disruptive measures unleashed to crack the Canadians' resolve. The names of Harry Dexter White and Igor Gouzenko dominated Canadian headlines for nearly three weeks, disturbing the supposedly cordial bilateral relations symbolized by the arrival in Ottawa of President Eisenhower and his wife on 13 November for a state visit.

On 17 November, Lester Pearson learned he would be denounced in New York the next day by right-wing commentator Victor Lasky. The attack was calculated to increase pressure on Pearson to capitulate in the Gouzenko matter.[14] Speaking to a luncheon meeting of the Women's National Republican Convention, Lasky dredged up old rumours to accuse Pearson himself of supplying privy information to the Soviets:[15]

Lester Pearson has long been baiting the U.S. at the United Nations. . . . That's his privilege. We've been baited and insulted by masters. But what is inexcusable is Mr. Pearson's determined effort from preventing accredited American investigators from following up Canadian angles to Soviet espionage. . . . Bob Morris had planned to ask Gouzenko about the Harry Dexter White case . . . but Mr. Pearson, through an underling, can issue a statement that Gouzenko knows nothing more. . . . Mr. Pearson has effectively squelched any investigation into alleged Soviet ties of not only his closest aide, but of himself. . . . [Herbert] Norman has been promoted to the post of Canada's High Commissioner to New Zealand. . . . According to Miss Bentley's testimony, while Mr. Pearson was Minister Counselor in the Canadian Ministry in Washington before the war he transmitted vital information to a Red spy ring she headed. . . . Perhaps Mr. Pearson did not know he was being used. But as soon as word of this testimony got around [the] shocking allegation was stymied.[16]

Pearson dubbed Lasky's charges 'false to the point of absurdity', and the Canadian government responded negatively to the State Department's formal note on behalf of Jenner requesting access to Gouzenko. Within External Affairs, Lasky's description of former high-flier Herbert Norman's assignment to New Zealand as a 'promotion' was noted with grim amusement, but publicly it was pointed out that the FBI had been involved throughout Gouzenko's debriefing in 1945–6 and had questioned him as recently as 1950. By Gouzenko's own admission, they said, he had nothing new to give.[17]

Canadian newspapers were uniformly skeptical of Brownell, the Jenner subcommittee, Lasky and the *Chicago Tribune* (McCarthyism's notorious house organ), and the various attempts to intimidate Pearson and the Canadian government. Editorial writers remained unconvinced of the value of further testimony from Gouzenko. Yet, in order to discount the charge that a Canadian official supplied information to the FBI, at least some clarification by the Canadian government now was essential. As the *Ottawa Journal* put it, if the allegation were true, 'that would leave the inescapable conclusion that Mr. Hoover's "highly placed Canadian" had warned the FBI, but not his own government', about White's impending promotion.[18]

That was the embarrassing and perplexing question for which nobody, including the RCMP, had a ready answer. After checking their records the Mounties were no closer to identifying the mystery official than intelligence officials at External Affairs. Commissioner L.H. Nicholson communicated to Pearson on 18 November that 'an immediate search . . . has failed to reveal any trace that any member of this Force offered any comment on the matter.'[19] Prime Minister St Laurent admitted to the House of Commons that 'so far we have not found anything.'[20]

As front-page headlines shouted of a red scare and muscle-flexing superpowers, the inner pages of the Ottawa newspapers recorded the capillary action of births, deaths, marriages, as well as listings for various entertainments on offer in the capital. Page 10 of the 14 November *Ottawa Journal* contained a brief announcement for Peter Dwyer's one-act play *Hoodman-Blind*, 'a brilliantly-conceived phantasy' that had shared first prize in the Ottawa Little Theatre's national playwriting competition.[21]

Dwyer's little theatre success presents a point of intersection between public and private, front page and local news, between the arts and state security. By the time he arrived at the Ottawa Little Theatre for the premiere of the award-winning plays, the revival of the Gouzenko and White cases had placed him in a situation more fantastic than anything he conceived of in *Hoodman-Blind*. Of all the Canadian security officials, he alone could identify Hoover's Canadian informant, and yet this he was loath to do, for the secret belonged to Britain, not to Canada. His dilemma pitted one nation's Official Secrets Act against the other, underlining his extraordinary status in the Canadian government. Dwyer had sworn the Canadian oath of secrecy on 26 April 1950, but he had not yet formally acquired citizenship and thus had not severed his previous sworn commitments to a foreign government. In effect, he was suspended between nationalities, or else he was the servant of two masters.[22] What of his witty fencing with secrets in *Hoodman-Blind*? That night his actors would wink at the well-heeled Little Theatre audience about '*lettres de cachet*' and 'political annihilation', phrases laden with hidden irony.

Janus

Sixteen years later, in January 1970, the Toronto *Globe and Mail* published a feature-length profile of Peter Dwyer upon his appointment as Director of the Canada Council. Writer John Burns dispensed with Dwyer's prior connections to British Intelligence in his opening sentence:

> Nothing will embarrass Peter Dwyer more than a profile which dwells on his wartime career in the British Secret Intelligence Service. He believes it is no more relevant to his appointment as director of the Canada Council 'than if I had been the commander of an anti-aircraft battery.'[23]

Burns's use of 'wartime' as the locator of Dwyer's intelligence-related activities is reiterated in various biographical sketches, suggesting that it was a standard phrase in the minimal personal information Dwyer supplied when called upon to do so. This diffidence dissuaded Burns from pursuing the connection very far. But then, as *Saturday Night* editor Robert Fulford wrote in 1982, the arts administrator was notoriously reticent about the earlier period of his career. By Fulford's estimate he was 'the least known but perhaps the most permanently important' of the cadre of British imports who created so many of Canada's institutions during the post-war period. Yet, 'Dwyer never wrote his memoirs—he believed to do so would be unprofessional—and his career remains shrouded in secrecy.'[24] Effectively sidelined by illness in 1971, Dwyer deposited his personal papers not with the National Archives but on a burning pyre in his suburban Ottawa backyard. He died on New Year's Day 1973 at the age of 58.[25]

The *Globe*'s John Burns profited from the Soviet double agent Kim Philby's outing of Dwyer as a former British intelligence officer in his 1968 memoir, *My Silent War*.[26] Without Philby's calculated indiscretion Dwyer might have kept details of his earlier career within his intimate circle of friends and associates. Philby recalled Dwyer apparently with fondness, although the sentiment was no longer reciprocated.[27] As Burns enlarged on Dwyer's life, attentive readers may have noticed that the war years formed only a lesser fraction of a secret service career under both British and Canadian governments. In fact, between graduation from Oxford in 1936 and his resignation for health reasons in 1971, Dwyer spent 18 years each in the security intelligence field and in the arts, with notable overlaps. Ultimately, Burns was not convinced that Dwyer's earlier activities were 'irrelevant', and judged instead that 'the qualities which made him an outstanding intelligence agent should stand him in good stead at the Council.'[28]

Oxford Whispers

Peter Dwyer was born in his family's south London home on 17 June 1914, and he was raised to appreciate and value the arts, especially the performing arts. In a biographical note written when he joined the Canada Council, Dwyer recorded that his grandfather was an opera singer and a conductor, his grandmother a member of the chorus of the Royal Opera House, and 'other members of the family were professional actors.' On the other hand, his father was of Irish extraction and worked in the India Office, thus exposing his son to the traditions of imperial administration.[29] Following school years as a day boy at nearby Dulwich College, a school 'steeped in theatrical tradition', the 19-year-old Dwyer left for Oxford in 1933 to take a degree in modern languages.[30]

In the 1930s, Oxford's Keble College was an all-male Anglican college, accommodating 'gentlemen intending to live economically', and presided over by its 'ecclesiastical worthies'.[31] There Dwyer acquired fluency in French, Spanish, Italian, and German, and self-assurance enough to live by his wits in that famously wit-infested conclave.[32] Although he was a bright student, studies yielded to extracurricular commitments to the undergraduate paper, *The Cherwell*, the Oxford University Dramatic Society (OUDS), and the University Opera Club.[33] As a member of the Dramatic Society, he acted in and provided musical accompaniment for various productions. His one-act play *The Mask on the Wall* was deemed the 'most outstanding' in the OUDS 'Smoker', an annual one-act play festival.[34]

Dwyer's particular family background and education made him easily conversant with cultural matters. He had the tastemaker's sure command of aesthetic knowledge and cultural practices, and in English Canada, at least, his accent itself flagged things as valuable in the realm of legitimate taste. At Oxford, Dwyer also became aware of an unwritten code of silence that David Vincent calls 'gentlemanly secrecy'.[35] In 1923 Graham Spry, the Canadian broadcasting pioneer, had enthused to fellow Canadian Arnold Heeney: 'There is not a world like the Oxford world. It is the clearing house of intelligence, the whole knowledge of man is concentrated, invisible, but ever present to the view.'[36] By naming this visible/invisible 'intelligence', Spry pointed not just to a certain ordering of knowledge but to a tacit discretion that lay behind the Oxonian wit.

All accounts agree on Peter Dwyer's civility and charm. In presenting the *Diplôme d'honneur* of the Canadian Conference of the Arts (CCA) to Dwyer in 1971, CCA Director Alan Jarvis voiced his 'affectionate admiration', pointing out that Dwyer had 'acquired that characteristic which marks the true Oxford man—a refusal to take oneself too seriously!'[37] While at Oxford, 'Dwyer began to polish a wit that has indeed become internationally famous, as well as a critical faculty which prefers a keenly honed rapier to the bludgeon', and then Jarvis invoked the hush of secrecy surrounding Dwyer's 'wartime' service:

> Peter would not wish me to dwell at any length on his career in British intelligence. . . . Suffice it to say that the mind which earned such high praise in war continues to serve with equal brilliance in more peaceful areas. . . . I see he is already blushing and displaying that so well-known wry smile.[38]

On the other hand, charm did not detract from Dwyer's underlying firmness. 'Tough, in a quiet way', recalled one of his superiors; 'warm, courteous, strict', according to one of his subordinates.[39] Something pre-emptive about Dwyer's charming firmness was characteristic, too, of the positive construction of secrecy into civic culture. This style of prohibition, tacitly enforced through accents, looks, and gestures, correlates official secrecy with the arbiters of cultural choice. As Graham Spry and Arnold Heeney no doubt knew, English Canada was enmeshed for much of the twentieth century in a generalized socio-political discourse in which 'Intelligence' and 'intelligentsia', gathered together under signs like 'Oxford', governed cultural development in English Canada.

If Dwyer's extracurricular writings at Oxford may have tempered his academic standing they won him other, perhaps more useful, distinctions. Mixed exam results were offset by his appointment as *The Cherwell*'s sub-editor in December 1934; his succession to the editorship followed six months later. Over the next three years he contributed more than a hundred items, including poetry, reviews, essays, experimental theatrical dialogues, short stories, and a weekly diary.

His first *Cherwell* essay argued precociously that almost all of Shakespeare's plays lend themselves to cinematic treatment, announcing that '*Hamlet* must be produced by Eisenstein, *Henry IV* by Korda, *The Merry Wives of Windsor* by René Clair.'[40] Film audiences are drawn effortlessly through Shakespeare's rapidly shifting scenes, he wrote, minus the upstage 'thunder of stagehands removing a courtyard'. His own dramatic dialogues showed real promise. In deft renderings he recorded the voices and banter of fellow students, exhibiting a talent for close listening and a level-headed approach to the rival ideologies on offer in the mid-1930s.[41] If he betrayed a degree of personal political uncertainty and flirted with Oxford's chic nihilism, it was superseded by his pursuit of the class fraction that determined taste in legitimate culture. As announced in 'Shakespeare and the Cinema', he anticipated a career disseminating high culture through the new mass media.

Dwyer's weekly comic diary, 'Samuel Pepys—Undergraduate', embellished his social activities in seventeenth-century phrasings, unwittingly supplying that most valuable type of information: lists of names, associations, and records of travels. The device of 'Pepys' is telling, too, because its comedy derives from the diarist's disarming indiscretion. At his lightest, Dwyer's Pepys was the inconstant courtier both of the 'fair Eliz.', a frosty Scottish beauty, and the fiery Italian, 'Luccia'. In darker moments, Dwyer recorded his disaffection with the world—'Ours is essentially a tragic generation'—and he expressed apprehension at its likely sacrifice in an impending world conflict.[42]

As he learned languages and developed as a writer and actor, his *Cherwell* contributions also trace a submergence into the 'wizardly' domain of national security. The sociable Pepys began to include names whose connections with British Intelligence eventually surfaced in the open literature.[43] The circle around a don named Gilbert Highet and his wife, novelist Helen McInnes, opened to include the young Dwyer. A few years later he and Highet would work together in British Security Co-ordination.[44]

Through the Oxford University Dramatic Society, Dwyer began to mix with BBC drama producer Val Gielgud and actors John Gielgud, Vivien Leigh, Peggy Ashcroft, David King-Wood, and Gyles Isham. Gyles Isham was a decade older than Dwyer and heir to a baronetcy whose country seat was Lamport, situated not far from Warwick. In the 1930s, Isham was also a successful stage and film actor.

In 1935, the year 'Pepys' first mentions him, Isham appeared in David O. Selznick's *Anna Karenina*, with Greta Garbo. That year he also made *Regal Cavalcade*, based on a short story by Val Gielgud and Eric Maschwitz. Maschwitz's writing and directing skills were later employed in the 'black' propaganda unit of British Security Co-ordination, 'Station M', secreted within CBC's Toronto plant during the war.[45] In 1937–8, Gyles Isham went on to appear in Edmond T. Greville's anti-German propaganda films *Under Secret Orders* (1937) and *I Married a Spy* (1938), and when war broke out he served British Intelligence in the Middle East. It appears he hinted at his Intelligence connections to Dwyer in 1935 at Oxford, and Dwyer reported the contact cryptically in *The Cherwell*.[46]

'Words and People' appeared during a week when Dwyer dined with Gilbert Highet and Helen McInnes. For some reason Dwyer's habitually secure and easy-going manner turned to a caustic account of fellow students' misuse of the word 'wizard' (as in: 'He's a *wizard* Rugger Player' or last night's film was *'wizard* cinema'). Dwyer's uncharacteristic stridency suggests that there was something more on his mind. Sure enough, the final paragraph veers off into a strange aside:

> Do you know my friend *Eusebius*? You would never think to look at him that his life was one constant round of diabolic machinations. You would think he was a normal individual: his grey trousers for instance never have a crease in them, and his jacket is of a very ordinary brown tweed. You would never see him dressed without a club tie—he belongs to so many clubs and is fond of beer. He has a pleasant face, kindly and good-natured, with a mop of thick black hair above it. He is himself well-made and good at games, and likes on sight every-one who does not sway at the hips in walking—and they like him. And yet everything with which he is associated has magical significance; poor fellow, he is hemmed in by wizardry. He has pictures of his school on the walls of his room, and respect in his heart for God. Who would have thought he had dealings in horrible magic, that everything he touched was 'Wizard, wizard, wizard'?

Dwyer supplied no other clue as to who this mysterious friend might be, or which 'school' was pictured on the wall of his room. Internet genealogy came to my rescue by suggesting that Dwyer's ecclesiastical reference to Eusebius is probably a feint, for in all likelihood this refers to *Euseby* Isham of Pytchley, founder of the Lamport estate, whose descendant through his fourth son, John, was Gyles Isham.[47]

Dwyer's detached observation that Eusebius was 'hemmed in' and somehow restricted by his secret powers suggests that Dwyer himself was brushed by but not yet seized with the 'wizardry' that gripped some people around him. 'Words and People' marks a general shift in the tone and substance of Dwyer's *Cherwell* contributions. The threat of a European war figures more frequently, and his short fiction concerns mysterious characters gifted with supernatural powers, meeting secretly in Italy or France for opaque purposes. His tone is more cutting, tracing a new edge of confidence and superiority beneath his habitually self-effacing humour.

That a sea change was pulling Dwyer away from the artistic world is best captured in 'The Bridge in the Parks', a whimsical *Cherwell* essay:

There is perhaps no more pleasant pastime than that of listening to the conversations of other people. There are, of course, those lucky few who can place their ear at the keyhole without any moral qualms; but these superhuman creatures are few and far between. . . . There are places where one has excellent opportunities for this fascinating method of listening in; cocktail parties, for instance— but this is most half-hearted eavesdropping, for your real eavesdropper gives his complete and undivided attention to the matter. . . . And your honestly disinterested listener could do no better than to take up his station on the top of the bridge in the parks. Here he can overhear the most delightful snatches of talk. . . . Here he can meditate on humanity.[48]

A week later he returned to the theme of eavesdropping from the bridge: 'gathering the character and interests of a man from a few chance words'.[49] If not supernatural, Dwyer's heightened faculties of awareness must have been a source of satisfaction to talent-spotters; but by then, his Canadian friend Don Wall says, Dwyer was being 'cultivated' in MI6's 'country house system'.[50]

Pepys, undergraduate, busily recorded hijinks with the likes of Gyles Isham. Crammed in the front seat of Vivian Leigh's car, Dwyer and Val Gielgud recited the 'Lay of Horatius':

and we just get to 'like an eagles nest hangs on the purple crest of purple Appenine,' when Milady Vivian goes to sleep and the car goes up on a bank. . . . Look, says Milord Gielgud, we be going awry. . . . La, what a todo.[51]

A starry outing, but Pepys interjects tersely: '*Saturday:* with Milord Rob Long in a car to Warwick, And drives back through the night at a fearful pace, so that my stummick turns to water.'

Secret Intelligence Service

Dwyer's career did not gel immediately. After graduating with a third in 1936, he stayed on in Oxford for a summer as actor and publicist with the Repertory Theatre. In May, he went to London to record the part of the Welsh Captain for a BBC broadcast of *Richard II*; later that month Fascist leader Oswald Mosley visited Oxford and his uniformed bodyguards forcibly ejected hecklers from the meeting. That autumn Dwyer joined 20th-Century Fox's European Story Department as an assistant editor.[52] He told the *Globe and Mail*'s John Burns in 1970 that this involved 'touring the Continent scouting new plays and novels and rewriting them in short story form for consumption in Hollywood'. Dwyer 'did not say so,' mused Burns, 'but the job would have proved a perfect cover for an intelligence agent, which is what he became in a formal way in 1939.'[53]

He was instructed to 'go to Broadway', MI6's London base, and he trained in its temporary quarters at Bletchley Park.[54] He served as an intelligence officer behind the lines in France, where evacuation from the coast in 1940 followed hard upon a frenzied drive from Paris, pursued by German military police.[55] Stationed in Latin

America, he witnessed the Imperial Censorship at Bermuda, where his duties included monitoring the Duke and Duchess of Windsor from an adjacent yacht. In June 1942, while serving as second secretary of the Panamanian consulate (in reality, MI6 station chief), he married Nora Darlington, a colleague from the consulate, at the First Municipal Court of Panama City.[56]

By the end of 1942 Dwyer was in Washington where he befriended Mark McClung in the 'men's bar of the Mayflower Hotel'. McClung had a risk-free 'luxury job' editing a confidential intelligence bulletin for the Canadian Navy; Dwyer was attached to British Security Co-ordination. According to McClung, Dwyer became 'second' under its chief, William Stephenson, the so-called 'quiet Canadian'. Under the BSC rubric, Dwyer headed the Security Intelligence Service's counter-espionage division (Section V) in North America.[57] Dwyer is credited with smoothing relations between British Intelligence and the FBI, as well as with the FBI rival, the fledging OSS (Office of Strategic Services, precursor to the CIA). From 1942 onward he was the frequent guest of his RCMP counterparts in Ottawa.[58]

After the war Dwyer stayed on in Washington as MI6's liaison to American and Canadian security agencies. It was during this transitional period that the 31-year-old officer flew to Ottawa on 9 September 1945 with colleague Jean-Paul Evans for the debriefing of Igor Gouzenko, and he remained in the Canadian capital for extended periods through the arrests, detention, and interrogation of the espionage suspects.[59] Dwyer probed Gouzenko with questions through RCMP interviewers, most particularly, according to McClung, to 'get [Alan] Nunn May', a British physicist working on atomic research in Canada and leaking secrets to the Soviets.[60]

According to Chapman Pincher, Dwyer's telegram conveying the substance of Gouzenko's revelations was received at MI6 headquarters in London by Kim Philby, who promptly relayed it to Moscow.[61] By any measure, it was a devastating act of treachery from someone Dwyer counted as a friend. Unaware of Philby's duplicity, Dwyer continued his work, impressing his Canadian hosts to the extent that his recruitment into Canadian service three years later by Norman Robertson was considered a coup. When he traded Washington for Ottawa, Dwyer gave up what a historian of MI6 calls 'the most important field post in the Service'.[62]

As Clerk of the Privy Council, Robertson chaired the Security Panel, an interdepartmental committee formed after the Gouzenko debacle to co-ordinate the government's internal security. Robertson deemed Eric Gaskell, the Privy Council officer assigned to security matters, too inexperienced and he had angled for Dwyer, a proven counter-intelligence specialist. Dwyer, on the other hand, was mindful of his young family, and by then knew that the British SIS was unsound, even if the unravelling of the Cambridge spies Burgess, MacLean, Philby, and Blunt had not quite begun.[63] Most importantly, Dwyer was expert in a field Canada sorely needed to upgrade: the security of atomic research.

Dwyer's guardedly informative Canadian Civil Service application, dated 29 November 1949, cited three Canadians 'well acquainted' with his work: George Glazebrook, G.G. Crean, and Edward M. Drake.[64] The latter was a Ukrainian Canadian from Saskatchewan who headed the Communications Branch of the National

Research Council (CBNRC). He was Dwyer's superior upon arrival in Ottawa. Significantly, Drake's name appears only with a residential address, whereas Glazebrook's workplace was identified as the Department of External Affairs. That Dwyer associated Crean with the National Defence College hints at Dwyer's little-known teaching function in Canada.[65] The form required further that he list 'three British Subjects' who had known him for 'at least three years'. In addition to Norman Robertson, Dwyer named Thomas Drew-Brook of Toronto, formerly with British Security Co-ordination, and Sir Robert Mackenzie Barr, Security Officer for North and Central America in the British embassy in Washington.

Despite such impeccable bona fides Dwyer's application was *pro forma*. Fred T. Rosser, the NRC's Director of Personnel and Administration, was personally responsible for recruiting secret communications personnel, and he wrote on 30 November 1949 that Dwyer's 'appointment has been approved by the President [Chalmers Jack Mackenzie] in conversation with Mr. Glazebrook. It is expected that Mr. Dwyer will be ready to take up his duties about March 1st.'[66]

Before leaving, Dwyer introduced Kim Philby to Washington. His successor arrived from London in September 1949 and over the next several months the brilliant Soviet mole could only watch on as Dwyer 'nailed' Klaus Fuchs, a German-born British atomic physicist who had leaked Manhattan Project secrets to the Soviets during the war. Using deciphered Soviet communications as a cross-reference, Dwyer turned up Fuchs's name on a list of train reservations. In 1972, Dwyer explained to cartoonist Ben Wicks (avoiding any mention of the intercepts) that Fuchs once made an error by changing his reservation from a bunk to an apartment, leaving a trace that years later revealed him to have been in the wrong place at the right time.[67] The exposure of Fuchs as a long-time Soviet agent tarnished the reputations of the British Intelligence services, but it boosted Dwyer's mettle as he travelled to Ottawa with his family in March 1950.[68]

The Bridge in the Parks

Dwyer formally joined the Canadian public service on 21 April 1950. He reported to the Privy Council Office in the late afternoon of 26 April to swear the oath of office and the oath of secrecy and to pose for his security pass photo.[69] Nobody understood better than he did the gravity of these oaths and the consequences of breaching them. They account for his destruction of personal papers many years later:

> I do solemnly and sincerely swear that I will faithfully and honestly fulfill the duties which devolve upon me and that I will not without due authority on that behalf disclose or make known any matter or thing which comes to my knowledge by reason of my employment. So help me God.[70]

A further declaration recorded his understanding 'that these provisions apply not only during the period of employment but also after employment . . . has ceased.' He further undertook, 'on leaving the Department, to surrender any sketch, plan, model, article, note or document acquired by me in the course of my official duties'.

Peter Dwyer, security pass photo, 26 April 1950. NAC, PA 192730.

Nominally a 'research officer', Dwyer in fact served in a senior capacity at the government's top-secret signals intelligence (SIGINT) establishment. The CBNRC was born when Gouzenko's timely disclosures saved Herbert Norman's wartime Examination Unit from an order to stand down.[71] Instead, the unit was placed on permanent peacetime footing under the cover of the NRC. Fred Rosser recorded on Dwyer's personnel file that '[t]he members of the Selection Sub-Committee are agreed that Mr. Dwyer is admirably qualified to head one of the main sections of the Branch.' Dwyer's exact function was not specified, but Rosser's euphemism for CBNRC work—'non-scientific research in the field of communications'—hints at the true job description.[72] Initially, Edward Drake's unit was nestled behind the De la Salle Academy, the auditorium on Sussex Drive used by the fledgling Canadian Repertory Theatre. One electronic eavesdropper recalls mingling from time to time during breaks with actors such as Christopher Plummer and Amelia Hall, who apparently had no inkling of their neighbours' secret

Novitiate at Hurdman Bridge, ca *1922.* Archives, Soeurs de la charité d'Ottawa.

work.[73] But by the time Dwyer arrived in March 1950 the Communications Branch had taken up larger premises on the southeast perimeter of the city near Hurdman Bridge, which spanned the Rideau River and led to open countryside to the east of Ottawa.

Photographs of CBNRC's 'Nunnery', as it was called, are not available in official archives. One must visit the Soeurs de la charité to view their former novitiate, for decades an idyllic country sanctuary before the Department of National Defence commandeered it in 1941 to serve as the Rideau Military Hospital. Reluctantly, the sisters ceded the building and relocated their novices to the Mother House in Ottawa's Lower Town.[74] By war's end the novitiate had outlasted any usefulness as a religious institution, too worn down by hospital service. Yet the building's situation in a sequestered field overlooking the embassy district of Sandy Hill made it an ideal site for Colonel Drake's Communications Branch. In August 1948, after Drake had called to complain 'about his cramped office space', C.J. Mackenzie wrote in his diary: 'I think we may be able to get the Rideau Military Hospital for him.'[75] If it is true that nursing sisters still occupied the novitiate's lower levels when radio equipment was installed behind the upper windows, then the military hospital already harboured an intercept site for some period of time prior to late 1948 or early 1949 when the Branch's personnel moved in.[76]

Dwyer was welcomed to the Branch by Mary Oliver, recently returned to her administrative post after a year as CBNRC's liaison with the British government's Code and Cipher School.[77] C.J. Mackenzie's diary allows that during her absence an initiative was taken to create a new section in the Branch, apparently devoted to counter-intelligence and to be equipped with the latest technology. He made reference neither to this section nor to Peter Dwyer after visiting the 'Nunnery' for the first time on 13 April 1950, but it is unlikely Mackenzie overlooked the opportunity to meet a new employee with star status in the secret world.

When Dwyer arrived Drake was embroiled in a struggle with the Joint Intelligence Committee, and he lobbied Mackenzie at lunch that day not to concede to National Defence the NRC's authority over the Branch. Drake kept Mackenzie on side by dropping by his office from time to time with tantalizing tidbits of news, and he was supported in this particular interdepartmental scuffle by External Affairs' Bill Crean. Knowing that Crean was 'not anxious' that the CBNRC be drawn into the direct purview of the Defence Department, Mackenzie could write with some satisfaction: 'We are neutral.'

The NRC deserves more vibrant accounts of this period than those provided by former Chief Censor Wilfred Eggleston; the reasons he was selected by Mackenzie to write them are obvious.[78] The NRC's creativity in scientific research and its quasi-independence from government made it an obvious administrative model for any new arts and humanities council. Invited to participate in the discussions of the Massey Commission in 1949, C.J. Mackenzie professed disinterest, but he hosted the commissioners to a sherry party around the fire in the neo-colonial ochre-coloured Council Room. In fact, Mackenzie was not as unaware of cultural affairs as he seemed. He had known and liked Grierson, occupant of an adjacent office during the war. And when Arthur Irwin dropped by after his appointment as Film Commissioner in 1950, the NRC chief judged him 'very sound and an attractive person who should get on well'.[79]

Dwyer worked for almost two years under the rubric of the NRC, although he rarely had reason to visit its main headquarters. The focus was on the Chalk River atomic facility, Canada's high-stakes gamble in nuclear technology. Mackenzie visited the Chalk River nuclear research station frequently and met regularly with Crean, Glazebrook, and Drake to discuss nuclear security and counter-espionage. 'A certain friendly rivalry has developed', wrote Dwyer in his play *Hoodman-Blind*:

> They are trying to ruin our universe; we are trying to ruin theirs. Of course, we could probably tamper with its atomic structure, we might even try that in a couple of hundred years or so. However, at the moment we are concentrating on the destruction of that small part of its spiritual structure which has so far become apparent to the mind of man. The attack is more subtle, more satisfying. Certainly more civilized.[80]

'Get Thee to a Nunn'ry'

On the fourth floor of the CBNRC's 'Nunnery', radio sets were still mounted in walnut cabinets. The spire of Parliament was clearly visible, rising above the embassy district across the river.[81] Just beyond the limits of the novitiate's grounds, Hurdman Bridge connected Ottawa East to the open country on the east bank of the Rideau. During the early 1950s the Hurdman Bridge facility was the nerve centre of Canada's Cold War, allied with the larger American and British SIGINT establishments. The Branch's administrative sections occupied the Nunnery's lower levels, preparing briefs to be transported twice daily by armed courier across the bridge and downtown to the Privy Council Office in the East Block of the Parliament.

Dwyer's *Hoodman-Blind* was written during his two-year stay at the Nunnery and, given that official records remain tightly closed, it has special allegorical significance.[82] He set the action 'on the outskirts of Paris on a summer's eve, 1788', with a dramatis personae consisting of just two characters: Adelaide, Comtesse D'Alembert, and Lupus, an antique dealer. Its epigraph—'what devil was't that thus hath cozen'd you at hoodman-blind?'—is from *Hamlet*, Dwyer's favourite Shakespeare play. In Act III, scene iv, the Danish Prince begs his mother to see how the 'devil', his uncle, has cheated her at 'hoodman-blind' (blind man's buff). Her good faith has blinded her to the murderous truth of his uncle's succession, and Hamlet challenges her to break the grip of secrecy, assaults her willed forgetfulness, and rails against the truth-resistant atmosphere that has descended over Elsinore.

'Hoodman-blind' was also an apt metaphor for signals intelligence, as Dwyer knew from his wartime training at Bletchley Park and now from his work at the CBNRC's 'Nunnery'. This was true especially during the late 1940s and early 1950s when accurate radio direction finding remained a serious technical limitation. The lines following in Shakespeare's 'hoodman-blind' stanza reinforce Dwyer's oblique analogy to electronic surveillance:

Eyes without feeling, feeling without sight,
Ears without hands or eyes, smelling sans all,
Or but a sickly part of one true sense
Could not so mope.[83]

The allusion is double. The practice of signals intelligence itself suffered from imperfect sensory faculties, he hints, but moreover, the very existence of these electronically sensory organs of the state depended, paradoxically, on the dulling of human senses. Where the Official Secrets Act reminded security workers to have 'ears without feeling', another reflex jogged the public to blank out antennas, secret installations, and radio-related research.

According to Naim Kattan, who served as Dwyer's literature officer at the Canada Council, *Hamlet* was the focal point in Dwyer's lifelong passion for Shakespeare. He recalls a car breakdown in the late 1960s en route to a conference in Muskoka when, to his delight, as rain ran down the windows, Dwyer recited the play from memory, inflecting his voice to play each role in a virtuoso solo performance.[84] To what extent did this fascination with *Hamlet*—par excellence the Shakespearean discourse on intelligence and national security—reflect Dwyer's affinity for a man detained from fulfilling his artistic promise by dark matters of state? Kattan laughed, deflecting my question: 'The Canada Council was very small then . . . he was not at all that way.'[85]

Like Shakespeare, Dwyer wrote *Hoodman-Blind* in the context of a state capital riddled with intrigue. Dwyer's memory brimmed with its secrets, just as Hamlet, too, is burdened by the knowledge of what amounts to an official secret, namely that his uncle poisoned his father in order to succeed to the throne. Hamlet's secret is contained within a social context of cultural secrecy that is by no means receptive to such a revelation. The rot of Denmark lies not just within the walls of

Elsinore but in the minds and language of Danes themselves, rightly insecure about their country's future. Even stout-hearted sentry Marcellus, an early witness to the apparition of Hamlet's father, warns ruefully of 'ears fortified against our story'.

Like Hamlet, Peter Dwyer was the carrier of great secrets against which all ears were fortified. Even if he broke sworn oaths and violated the unwritten code of gentlemanly secrecy, publicizing his knowledge of Canada's secret immigration cases, the eavesdropping upon citizens and allies as well as enemies, the extent of its security and intelligence capabilities and the names of its personalities, or the true story of Gouzenko's defection, his words would be absorbed by civic secrecy. In reality, his relationship with secrecy was too advanced for him to contemplate breaching it; at least, not directly. Like Hamlet, he dealt with his secret burden through wordplay.

As readers may have noticed already, the 'hoodman-blind' passage from *Hamlet* alliterates racily on the 'most secret' location of the Communications Branch at 'Hurdman Bridge'. This was not an inconsequential matter; the Canadian government successfully concealed the existence and location of the CBNRC from its own citizens for three decades.[86]

When the ghostly patriarch swears Hamlet and his frightened companions to secrecy, he impresses upon Hamlet that he must *remember* the secret. Famously, Hamlet's vacillating 'purpose is but the slave to memory'. And yet there is something implausible about Hamlet lacking 'will' to exact revenge on his uncle. Is it not rather that his father's anguished spirit knows Hamlet cannot successfully reveal this most potent of all state secrets in Denmark's present culture of secrecy? With 'the people muddied: unwholesome in their thoughts and whispers' and honest men counted 'but one in ten thousand', how can Hamlet act before the rationale for his action is expressible in the discourse of his fellow Danes? Only through the players, and the play within the play, can Hamlet provisionally articulate his 'official secret' and so bring to light the guilty conscience of the king without invoking outright censorship.

I questioned Don Wall, Peter Dwyer's close friend and colleague, and also an actor of small parts at the Ottawa Little Theatre in 1952–3, about *Hoodman-Blind*. He whistled and shook his head, saying, 'we couldn't figure out what Peter was up to with that one.'[87] In Janus's two-faced play, the players, like those in *Hamlet*, uttered certain guarded truths regarding which Dwyer himself was sworn to secrecy.

Hoodman-Blind

Ottawa's lack of a proper theatre troubled Mayor Charlotte Whitton. To little avail she lobbied her reluctant federal counterparts to invest in a substantial national theatre complex containing 4,800 seats in two auditoriums on an eight-acre site at Landsdowne Park.[88] Another decade of discussion intervened before the impending Centennial celebrations in 1967 and the personal impetus of G. Hamilton Southam brought about the construction of the National Arts Centre. It was Whitton's initiative that prompted Peter Dwyer to draft what likely is the first sketch for what became Canada's premiere performing arts centre. Dwyer's knowledge of theatre was unique in the Privy Council Office, as was his active role in the Ottawa arts community where he promoted children's concerts, wrote program notes for the Ottawa Philharmonic, and sat on the Board of Directors of the Little Theatre.

His paper on the proposed national theatre was taken by the Minister of Citizenship and Immigration, Jack Pickersgill, to his meeting with Whitton to discuss her proposal.[89] 'Ideally,' wrote Dwyer:

> a new auditorium in Ottawa should provide once and for all and in one attractive place the present make-do facilities which are scattered about the city. That is to say it should provide accommodation for meetings up to convention size, for plays, opera and ballet, and for concerts.

A generous lobby was essential because 'one of the real pleasures of theatre and concert going is the meeting of friends.' An auditorium in Malmö, Sweden, inspired his sketch of a 1,600-seat hall suitable for opera, ballet, and concerts, with a movable partition that reduced it to an intimate 800-seat theatre. If less magnificent than Whitton's scheme, his was more substantial than anything Robert Bryce, the secretary to cabinet, had in mind. At most, Bryce thought a modest hall attached to the planned new National Gallery would suffice. Dwyer warned Bryce that '[a]nything new which might be built must never repeat the mistakes made in the small stages of the Glebe and Tech [high school] auditoriums. The stage must be bigger than the average theatre goer ever suspects.'[90]

On the evening of 18 November 1953, Dwyer was in the cramped backstage of the Ottawa Little Theatre on King Edward Avenue, formerly the Eastern Methodist Church. Nervous excitement spread through the dressing rooms as word arrived that the Governor-General and his entourage had taken their seats. Dwyer and director, Julia Murphy, offered last-minute encouragement to their formidable Countess, Florence Fancott, and to Lupus, Donald Shepherd, by day a Carleton University professor.[91]

Founded in 1913, the Ottawa Drama League was incorporated in 1952 as the Ottawa Little Theatre, a voluntary organization that was (and remains) a true theatre club, in the sense that such amateur clubs once existed across Canada before the Massey Report recommended the development of professional regional theatres.[92] The national playwriting contest began in 1939, attracting high-profile adjudicators and promising writers of the calibre of Robertson Davies. As a result, it would be a mistake to imagine the audience waiting to see *Hoodman-Blind* and the other winning plays as a gathering of strangers. Rather, they formed a tightly knit social network whose canon of good taste was embodied in their grand patron, Vincent Massey, the first Canadian-born Governor-General, who attended that evening to present the playwriting awards.

When the main curtain glides open, the opening moments of the play perform a customary Dwyer manoeuvre. The Countess Adelaide, in her boudoir, is in front of a large mirror on the wall, which is concealed by an ornate screen. Sensing intrusion, she runs her hand along the proscenium line, searching for the fourth wall, gasping at its compete disappearance. 'Really,' she says, acknowledging the public's gaze, 'this is quite intolerable.' She scolds the audience for 'intruding on my privacy without so much as a by-your-leave.' But her agitation is due to something else, and she elects 'to imagine that all of you are just one person and invite you in so that I can talk to you in absolute confidence. I know I can rely on your discretion.' Thus she draws the audience into her confidence, and with this charming invitation into a magic circle the spectator feels the embrace of secrecy. Once they are 'inside', the Countess seems to forget about her audience, and indeed *they* forget they are inside. Wizardry requires above all the drawing of such magic circles, and this was Peter Dwyer's charming pattern, both in his security and cultural work.

With discretion assured, the Countess discloses to her invisible visitor an illicit liaison earlier in the afternoon with Pierre, the Marquis de Longueville:

Well, yes, perhaps it was a little unwise. But you can have no idea what has happened. We were standing in front of the mirror there . . . (pausing) Perhaps you'd better go and look at the mirror behind the screen . . . Sh! For heaven's sake don't scream like that or you'll bring the servants in! No, you idiot, of course it isn't painted on. It's a reflection which has simply remained permanently on the glass . . . just stuck there! Naturally, I look as if I were enjoying myself. I was, at the time—and so was Pierre, I assume.

She doubts it possible that help can arrive before her husband returns in just half an hour, but she has sent for Lupus, vendor of the offending mirror. 'Frightened?' she muses. 'No, I don't think I am frightened of Lupus.' Even as she speaks a 'rather brilliant flicker of summer lightning' ushers in the antique dealer, 'a man of middle age, white-faced and rather puffy'.

The Countess does not 'relish anticipation which oversteps the limit of what is possible', but heavy-lidded Lupus, his mouth full and red, protests that he just happened to be passing by her house. He examines the screen placed before the mirror, chiding her for not having consulted him before she bought it:

At the moment it rather obscures the Venetian mirror you had from me. Now there is a rarity . . . Murano craftsmen, of course. However, like all quattrocento mirrors the quality of the glass leaves something to be desired, madame . . . (casually) or not?

Lupus anticipates her wish to return the mirror to him immediately, even letting him keep the money she paid, but: '[t]his remarkable generosity is offered provided I remove the mirror now?' he pauses, 'before your husband returns?'

Dwyer explains that the Countess's 'whole attitude to Lupus changes.' She invites him to sit and offers him brandy: 'You and I must have a long, pleasant talk.' She observes that he seems 'remarkably well-informed about an intimate and unusual occurrence which took place in this room not more than one hour ago.' Lupus tells her expansively, 'I make it my business to be well-informed, my dear countess', adding that 'the essential of this particular indiscretion is that while the substance of it has passed, the shadow—shall we say?—remains.' He enjoys the closing trap, imagining that 'in these days of *lettres de cachet*—of scandal and moral rectitude, political annihilation . . . you would miss these rather charming surroundings, the luxury, the comfort.'

The glass is a surveillance device that Lupus boasts 'is entirely new, something I invented myself as a matter of fact.'[93] Indeed, Lupus will remove the offending image only on the condition that Adelaide signs a document consigning her immortal soul to him. 'You may recall that Faust paid it. A mere nothing, of course.' Adelaide is unimpressed: 'Why yes. I believe that tedious Marlowe wrote about it . . . I never could tolerate the Elizabethans. So many scenes, so many people and all that shouting. Very untidy, really.'

With this reference to the playwright/spy Marlowe, Dwyer hints that there is more to the Countess than Lupus imagines. Lupus faints when she holds up a crucifix, but can she look at it herself? When Lupus lights the candles behind her back with wizardly prestidigitation, she scoffs, telling him to save his trickery for the servants. Preparing to sign the agreement, she shows complete disinterest in its contents: 'I never read papers before I sign them, they always commit one to something tiresome which of course one has no intention of carrying out.'

Lupus's 'brief instruction in moral principles' ensures that she knows which ones she is breaking by signing the contract: 'At the moment we are working with the ten commandments as our standard. Of course there have been other standards.' The essential 'is that they should be believed and disregarded in action.'

Adelaide receives his tutelage demurely, like a schoolgirl:

ADELAIDE: The last lessons I had were from a nun.
LUPUS: Bah! The time I've wasted with nuns. . . .
ADELAIDE: I suppose this is rather like an extension course. The nuns used to teach us about embroidery and men.
LUPUS: All about men?
ADELAIDE: No, all about embroidery.

Exasperated, he exhorts her to understand that 'the spiritual values which are established in this universe (he gestures to the windows) were devised by a group of which I am not a member. . . . I will call this particular group the Good.' His group, 'The Evil', resides in 'another part of the space-time continuum . . . an entirely separate universe [created] on very different physical and moral principles, because the entire structure was planned down to the smallest detail.'

'All I ask', he pleads, 'is that you believe what you are doing is wrong—and yet do it, believing it to be wrong.'

Only moments before the arrival of her husband, Adelaide's mood changes. She hears nightingales and looks into the garden, where cypress trees sway like 'black flames burning darkness'. She turns to Lupus, 'No, no, I shall not sign your little paper.'

LUPUS: But surely you understand? Believe me, madame, it would be better.
ADELAIDE: But I do not believe you, Lupus. I do not *believe*, Lupus. And so I cannot sign your little paper to any purpose. I only *know*, Lupus. I know all

Florence Fancott and Donald Shepherd in Hoodman-Blind, *1952.* Photo by Van. Fancott
Collection.

the things that please me. The nightingales in my garden, the tall cypress and the stars. But I believe in nothing.

Her soliloquy continues for several minutes, naming delights of the five senses, reiterating six times, '*I believe in nothing.*' She knows 'the instant pleasure of bright morning . . . the blessing of firelight uttered over a lover . . . the oboe of the wind in a courtyard, and the sound of a lute which is faint in an inner room'; she revels in the 'murmur of voices before a high old evening, and the pulse of music temperately timed', and 'the half delight of a lover's hand along the thigh, lingeringly withdrawn'. Yet, she believes in nothing:

> I know the dark divisions of the rose, the antique scent of marjoram, sage and thyme; the subtle distillation of perfume meticulous in vials, and the bright blazon of all summer flowers. I believe in nothing. I sail in the quinquereme of my senses, and I believe in nothing. (Triumphantly) Non credo, Lupus, *non credo.*

The antique dealer reels backwards, astonished. Adelaide is 'wicked beyond thought . . . you have consigned belief to a limbo where you belong yourself. . . . We must look at you and pass.' The image in the mirror vanishes, for 'nothing evil can withstand the onslaught of a mind that does not believe in evil', and Lupus reflects on his failure. 'My reputation will suffer. My prospects for the future will be damaged. The word will go around the lesser fiends: Lupus has lost his cunning. . . . I shall be ruined.' He eyes her closely. 'The only thing that could have defeated my purposes . . . One might almost think that you yourself were . . . oh, but that's impossible.'

The Count's carriage is heard pulling up, but Lupus lingers, grumbling at the nightingale's song—'One of my opponents' more successful efforts'—and he exits, moaning, 'how the Archangel will laugh.' Then, using the same wizard-like gesture that she could not have seen him use earlier, she douses the candles, and the main curtain closes, leaving her in silhouette before the window, uttering 'a strange harsh laugh'.

Vincent Massey presented the awards to the winning authors that night. Yet Dwyer's appearance on the stage beside Massey did not mark a beginning but rather the end of a writing process begun in his student days. *Hoodman-Blind* proceeded to the Eastern Ontario Drama Festival, and in 1959 the Ottawa Little Theatre gave it a new production, again with Fancott, updated to an art deco setting. But that was the end of it. Dwyer submitted no further scripts and, as far as can be seen, he ceased writing plays altogether. In the fall of 1954, two of his poems were published in *Saturday Night*, and as 'Janus' he continued to write about television in the *Ottawa Citizen*. His most lasting literary legacy would be his richly detailed contributions to the Canada Council's Annual Reports.[94]

So then, what message is encrypted in this artifact handed by Peter Dwyer from behind his veil of secrecy? Examined in terms of straight 'traffic analysis', obviously it reiterated the cultural norms prevailing during the period before the arts in Canada were fully professionalized.[95] As a play of manners 'steeped in the European tradition' it won the praise of adjudicator John Hoare for not having 'anything to do with Canadian life', for eschewing realism and being 'beautifully stylized'. Hoare judged that Dwyer had 'raised the whole standard of the competition to the plane of imagination, schooled to form and style.'[96] But there is more encoded here. It is a case of getting past that controlling accent that has power, in and of itself, to discourage the intent to discern what something is in reality. Dwyer's allusions to secrecy, surveillance, blackmail, political ideologies, spies, and supernatural beings amount to a call to discretion and tacit understanding: 'Hush-hush.'

There is also something jarring about Adelaide's passionate renunciation of 'belief' in favour of the 'quinquereme' of her senses—a five-masted metaphor evoking the CBNRC's five-point Adcock antenna arrays. Perhaps in that autumn of hysterical patriotism this speech signalled the playwright's own fatigue with obligatory 'belief'. It is uncertain if Dwyer addresses his audience from inside or outside the Cold War belief system, and the intrusion of his own autobiographical voice presented a practical difficulty for Florence Fancott in delivering the lengthy and slightly clumsy 'non credo' soliloquy.

This point is made even more clearly in a passage cut from the script during rehearsals. What Dwyer intended to be Lupus's final speech presented actor Donald Shepherd with a similarly difficult shift in tone. At no other time does the antique dealer betray an introspective voice that speaks in Middle English cadences. Standing on the threshold of the apartment as the Count's carriage arrives, Lupus was to have spoken, aside:

Now like a hawk my heart, not poised at pitch, sits hooded at wrist; and the agile falcons of the blood are tassle-gentle to my will. (Gesturing towards the mirror) There, my true fletcher, there was my quarrel over the thumb-rest—into the windless precincts of summer, fallen to the gold of my years. Here at the turn of the stairs the laughter is faint from the anterooms, where bishops and lamp-lighters, pieds-en-l'air, are playing at Hoodman-Blind.

Dwyer excised this passage even though it contained the sole reference to the play's title. This 'third' voice from the threshold intruded a little too obviously into the fiction. The mirror, a wizardly surveillance technology used for entrapment and blackmail, the 'lamplighters' (a trade term for secret service technicians), the previous reference to the hapless Gouzenko suspect Matt 'Nightingale', references to Marlowe and the embroidery of 'nuns' were double entendres calculated to appeal to intelligence insiders. Don Wall recalls that he and Dwyer, upon entering the CBNRC's 'Nunnery', sometimes would pause on the threshold at the turn of the stairs and listen to a strange acoustical reverberation in the central stairwell.[97] Within the anterooms 'bishops' and 'lamplighters' indeed played at an electronic version of hoodman-blind.

In Lupus's final excised words, the allegory culminates in the author's brooding on his own condition. When Dwyer wrote these lines in 1952, during his time at the 'Nunnery', his career had reached a threshold. After a two-year waiting period he was poised to take responsibility for the general co-ordination of internal security for the Canadian government. On the night of *Hoodman-Blind*'s premiere in November 1953 he was well into this new role. Even as the play subtly normalized the Cold War's culture of secrecy, it also sent back to its author a fresh reminder of his own ambiguous status, uncomfortably hemmed in by his own wizardry.

Culture and Security

Dwyer had taken up his PCO position in March 1952 during a period fraught with Cold War paranoia. It was remarkable that someone not yet a Canadian citizen could occupy such a sensitive post, and indeed, Norman Robertson obtained special permission from Prime Minister St Laurent to waive the citizenship requirement in Dwyer's case.[98] Dwyer alluded to his promotion from Hurdman Bridge to the East Block of Parliament in *Hoodman-Blind* when Lupus boasts: 'I handle all the cases of minor sensuality—a sort of third secretary of our mission here':

> Of course it does call for a certain delicacy of touch, and I flatter myself that I've done rather well since I was first posted. . . . I have great hopes of being moved up to the blasphemy desk as soon as it falls vacant.

The line likely drew a laugh, but of all people Norman Robertson was best positioned to appreciate it. Having stationed Dwyer downtown at the 'blasphemy desk', he now had a capable secretary for the Security Panel, a civilian of sufficient heft to handle their military and police counterparts, someone well able to head various security subcommittees and to serve as instructor in counter-espionage techniques. In these duties Dwyer redefined and expanded the position of his predecessor, Eric Gaskell (also an author, incidentally, and a former secretary of the Canadian Authors' Association), who Robertson assigned to censorship planning on a full-time basis.[99]

In fact, Dwyer brought his own distinctive approach to a whole range of cultural and security matters. In both spheres his modus operandi comprised four notable features that amount to what might be called 'intimate sensing', a cultural corollary to the remote-sensing technologies employed in signals intelligence. First, there was open-mindedness. Dwyer's natural curiosity made him a collector of diverse information. Second was his capacity to focus. Not a dilettante, he eliminated non-essential aspects of any problem. Third was indoctrination, confiding information selectively to secure loyalty and discretion. Finally, he installed multiple and highly specific feedback mechanisms in order to obtain high-grade information from narrowly defined targets.

He employed this approach with his departmental security officers in a course given at the Rockcliffe RCMP barracks in 1952. These were no mere security guards but senior officials, often with military service backgrounds, appointed confidentially to serve as security liaisons to the RCMP and the Security Panel. To pique their curiosity, Dwyer suggested they read Noël Coward's story 'The Wooden Madonna' to understand how ordinariness itself ought to be regarded with suspicion. He taught them to notice:

the secretary who for no apparent reason stays after office hours, the filing clerk who occupies himself for an unreasonable length of time at one particular cabinet, the office messenger who takes too long to carry papers from one room to another, the charwoman who consistently stays behind in a room when others have moved on.[100]

He advised them that 'the presence in a file of documents which have been folded for no apparent reason should always be a cause for suspicion.' (Alas for him, Philby's folding of his crucial Gouzenko telex in 1945 caused no such concern at MI6 headquarters.) He confided in the assembled officers, laying out the organizational plan of Soviet intelligence and its range of targets, but he stressed that '[w]hat has been set out here is not the blueprint of an organization, but the salient features of a pattern.' With these salient features in mind the officers should be sensitive even to minor anomalies in their departments, but on no account was any action to be taken by a security officer until both Dwyer and the RCMP's Special Branch had been notified.

In the matter of security of Arctic defence installations, he persuaded the Joint Intelligence Committee to rescind a blanket security cordon placed over the entire District of Franklin in favour of concentrating security measures around sensitive installations. He explained that this not only provided better security for the air defence and wireless intercept sites but also a greater chance of detecting the presence of enemy agents. For example, passengers on the five Arctic supply ships were required to submit personal history forms to the Department of Transport on the pretext of preventing diseases from spreading among the Inuit. In reality the information was forwarded to Dwyer.[101]

In October 1952, the *Globe and Mail* disclosed that for five dollars any foreign intelligence agency could obtain the *Canada Air Pilot* and discover the location of every Canadian airfield, including the secret ones in the North. 'Strange thing, security', wrote reporter George Bain.[102] Dwyer soon received a report from the Department of Mines and Technical Surveys that a suspicious-looking man with a Russian accent had attempted to purchase the said publication. The man was Mr Ogorodnikov, the Ottawa representative of Tass, the official Soviet news agency. Half a century later the incident seems comical, but it prompted serious discussions about restricting public access to open-source information. Air Intelligence Chief Edwards thought it 'one of those problems peculiar to our democratic way of life'. George Glazebrook advocated a principle of step-to-step reciprocation with the Soviets. RCMP counter-intelligence officer Terry Guernsey allowed that other Russian attempts to purchase the *Air Pilot* had been monitored and he suggested the whole question of open sources be put up to the Security Panel. Reading these responses, Dwyer proposed that a group of influential journalists be given an off-the-record briefing to demonstrate how Bain's story was detrimental to national security. At the same time he recommended better measures to enhance feedback when Soviet agents attempted to acquire public documents.[103]

Scholars have speculated that Dwyer took a hand in organizing or perhaps even led a top-secret intelligence group in the 1950s whose existence still remains

secret. He is also touted as a possible conduit for spiriting selected Nazi war criminals with special anti-Communist credentials into Canada along so-called 'rat-
lines' set up after the war.[104] These speculations continue to circulate but no
available records prove or disprove such claims. Dwyer's full workload as recorded
in open documents from his years in the Privy Council Office suggests that such
speculations may be exaggerated. What has been overlooked in the open files,
I suggest, is Dwyer's pivotal role in bridging Canadian cultural policy to national
security during the Cold War.

For example, Dwyer's security and culture briefs coincided perfectly in the
induced birth of Soviet Studies and Russian-language programs in the Canadian
universities. This became a high priority in the 1950s, and Dwyer chaired a
subcommittee of the Security Panel whose task was to co-ordinate the rapid
development of Soviet expertise for Canada's intelligence-related agencies,
including External Affairs and the Defence Research Board. Dwyer brought in
National Archivist W. Kaye Lamb, and the fruit of this association can be found in
the National Library's extensive collection of open-source Soviet material. The
universities were major partners, particularly the University of British Columbia.
The entire project was 'put up' to the Canada Council immediately after it was
created in May 1957. Robert Bryce wrote to John Deutsch, his successor as Secretary of the Treasury Board, that Canada Council Director 'Albert Trueman
should be prepared to consider proposals in this field as possibly one of the most
important and imaginative projects in the field of the humanities.'[105] Always a
skilled navigator, Dwyer restrained the PCO officer assigned to co-ordinate the
new program from unilaterally implementing the subcommittee's suggestion for a
summer school of Russian-language studies. 'Better to have this come from the
universities', Dwyer advised.[106]

On the cultural side, Dwyer's pattern of 'intimate sensing' influenced various
developments following upon the Massey Commission Report. During the weeks
and months of security reorganization Dwyer's influence in cultural matters
widened, and in 1953 he entered an almost schizophrenic period of rapid development on both fronts.

The incoming Clerk of the Privy Council, Robert Bryce, knew of his security
expert's artistic background from having reviewed and approved Dwyer's pay
reclassification before leaving the Treasury Board. Later he recalled that 'we were
fortunate to obtain Dwyer', whose security intelligence experience made him especially sensitive to what Bryce called 'degrees of confidence' in civil servants.
Soviet agencies targeted Canadian officials, particularly homosexuals, to 'get them
into compromising positions, take pictures and then blackmail them'.[107]

The public announcement that Bryce had replaced Pickersgill in the PCO coincided with *Hoodman-Blind*'s premiere on 18 November 1953.[108] Almost immediately upon his arrival in the East Block, Bryce received Dwyer's brief on the
Massey Report's recommendations for fostering the arts and culture in Canada.
During the subsequent months he came to respect Dwyer's passionate vision for an
engaged federal arts program that might achieve tangible outcomes. There was no
shortage of interested parties willing to draft legislation for the prestigious Canada

Council, but Bryce deemed Dwyer the ideal officer for the job, adding this task to his security responsibilities.[109]

By the autumn of 1953, the proposed arts council had been mooted for almost two years. Discussion had focused on the proposed council's governance and executive structure, and its line of reporting to Parliament. The temperature rose slightly when Escott Reid of External Affairs squared off with the PCO's Gordon Robertson to defend the arm's-length principle. Robertson felt that the new council would be accepted more easily if it were placed under the direct control of the Minister of Citizenship and Immigration and characterized as a practical arm of the citizenship apparatus. Anything less directly accountable might seem to be imposing 'Culture' upon Canadians. Reid countered that the council must be visibly free from government interference.[110]

Dwyer set his mind to fashioning an outline for legislation to create an arm's-length Canadian council along British lines, but his initial proposals went further, injecting a fresh and non-bureaucratic perspective into the deliberations. His first eight-page brief on the subject circulated from Gordon Robertson to Jack Pickersgill (by then Minister of Citizenship and Immigration) and on to Prime Minister St Laurent. It had a twofold thrust: (1) the new council should take a strong and imaginative line on arts education, and (2) it should foster professional rather than amateur development in the arts. In both cases, argued Dwyer, it was a matter of cultivating *taste*.

The formal recognition of children in the mandate and functions of the Canada Council was crucial to a society lacking a strong cultural tradition. He pointed out that what may 'determine the ultimate success or failure of the Council's work' is the creation of future audiences:

> The forms of expression used by the various arts are, as it were, languages; and these, like any languages, are more effectively absorbed in childhood when the natural receptiveness and innate good taste of children has not been debauched by long exposure to bad entertainment.[111]

Culture, he argued, should not be thought of in pedagogical terms, but rather as something *sensual*. Mere pedagogy emphasizes 'learning rather than pleasure', he wrote, and 'one observes how the glory of Shakespeare is laid waste for examination purposes.' Appreciation of the arts ought to be based on pleasure, in which case children 'should absorb the media effortlessly.' Over time, Canadians might acquire 'culture', which he defined as 'an ability to enjoy (with the vagaries of personal taste) what previous generations of dedicated people have agreed provides our most profound pleasures, and . . . to apply that ability to the works of one's own generation'.[112]

He warned that Canada's tradition of amateurism in the arts presented a barrier to 'culture' in this strong sense of art appreciation. Channelling government funding through the new council to the 'voluntary groups' that traditionally had supported the theatre, ballet, and music presented the 'very real danger' that they might 'impose their own taste on the artists', thus undoing the central purpose of the new council:

In some cases this does not matter: but in many cases it does, because a willing-ness to ring doorbells or organize ladies' teas in a good cause provides no assur-ance that the people who do so should be arbiters of taste. It can be particularly damaging in the theatre where, in addition to limited taste . . . an unduly strict moral outlook can come between the actor, the writer and their livelihoods.[113]

Prior to the Industrial Revolution, he reasoned, the aristocratic patron 'was usu-ally a man of taste whose direct relations with the artist were sympathetic.' As patrons, the present voluntary groups cannot be said 'to have replaced the stimulus of his culture'. Indeed, 'would it not be our hope', he asked, 'that in the course of some years a good many of the less valuable voluntary groups would, like the Marxian state, wither away?' To the greatest extent possible the new arts council should deal *directly* with artists and their professional organizations to achieve the highest possible standards. Working solely through existing voluntary organiza-tions 'might well serve merely to perpetuate one of the conditions which it is being set up to correct.'

Dwyer's play on the 'Marxian state', in conjunction with his doubts concerning the existing voluntary arts organizations, is a cue to understanding what made the Canada Council project so important within the PCO, and why someone of Dwyer's background was detailed to co-ordinate its development. It was not enough simply to create the new council; it had to be given firm and dynamic direction if it was to have the desired effect on Canadian society.

For its part, the Labour Progressive Party trumpeted a very different aspiration for the new Canada Council. Its 1955 report *The Rising Tide of Democratic Cana-dianism and the Fight to Put Canada First* assailed St Laurent's government for not acting quickly to create the Canada Council.[114] 'Cosmopolitanism', the report stated, 'is the anti-Canadian philosophy of St Laurent and his ruling class' who dominated the cultural industries. This cosmopolitanism 'imbued Canadians with a sense of submissive inferiority' and represented a 'betrayal of the culture of Canada . . . and its national interests'. The LPP disputed the 'supine views' of liberal intellectuals like Frank Underhill, Marcus Long, and Bruce Hutchison, arguing that 'Canadians have accomplished great things . . . a long list leading across Canadian history to Bethune.' Despite the fact that 'the ruling class of Canada has always been spineless on questions of culture . . . [and has] compromised with British and U.S. imperialism', this report noted persistent examples of a true people's culture:

Reuben Ship's famous satire against McCarthyism, *The Investigator*, mirrors the undying bonds of friendship that unites the peoples of Canada and the U.S. in their common struggle against reaction, fascism and war. When 40,000 people gather at the Blaine Peace Arch to hear Paul Robeson sing it is a proof of that solidarity.[115]

The LPP Cultural Commission demanded the immediate passing of the Canada Council legislation, so that 'when it is established the people can make use of it to press their cultural demands upon the government.' Through the new Canada

Council 'Canadian participation in UNESCO . . . can contribute to the increasing cultural exchanges between Canada and the Soviet Union.' A thousand copies of the report were printed 'for circulation among cultural workers'.

Needless to say, the LPP's views were not shared by the 'cultural workers' within the Privy Council Office busily drafting the Canada Council legislation. For Peter Dwyer, in particular, it was high culture's enhanced sensibilities in combination with a liberal 'moral conscience' that dissolved competing claims to cultural legitimacy by all of these 'less valuable' groups. A commitment to professionalism was essential in the face of a threat from a popular formation that, as the LPP claimed, at times had been vibrant and appealing. Dwyer knew that Vincent Massey's desiccated and aesthetically conservative notion of high culture would never be stimulating or engaging enough to grip Canadians' imagination in the way that the progressive Cultural Front once had done. This is one reason he so energetically emphasized pleasure and enjoyment, produced through a commitment to professionalism, and linked these to the idea of a national conscience.

This blending of professionalized culture with a national conscience perplexed Robert Bryce when he read the opening sentence in Dwyer's draft for St Laurent's speech introducing the Canada Council legislation. In retrospect it seems understandable that Dwyer, busy revoking or denying citizenship to persons capriciously tagged as security risks by the RCMP, purging socialists and perhaps the earliest of the homosexuals who would subsequently be eliminated from the civil service, and generally weighed down with suspicion, distrust, and secrecy, should have introduced the enabling legislation as he did. Paraphrasing Anatole France, he called the Council's creation 'a moment in the conscience of Canada'.[116]

In preparing the Canada Council legislation Dwyer also prepared his escape hatch from security work. In writing the Council's bylaws he shaped the role and functions of the Director and Associate Director, whom it was assumed would be an anglophone/francophone pair, towards straight executive functions and supervision of the university funding programs. There was no doubt about who was the ideal person to fill the yawning gap in arts supervision that emerged during the first year of the Council's operation. Moreover, Robert Bryce was not overly impressed with Albert Trueman's 'shilly-shally' attitude to the Council's parliamentary accountability. The Council needed a trusty hand guiding its potentially controversial arts funding programs.

At the same time, Herbert Norman's suicide in April 1957 had touched Dwyer's credibility as the government's internal security co-ordinator. While not directly Dwyer's responsibility, American suspicions regarding Norman had a way of attaching themselves to the 'liberals' around Pearson and in the Privy Council Office.

In any case, privately Dwyer was fatigued by his security role, and his disenchantment deepened when one day he opened the door of his suburban Ottawa home to find MI6's Maurice Oldfield and his team of mole hunters 'on the doorstep'. Oldfield, reputedly a model for John Le Carré's character, George Smiley, was an old accomplice of Dwyer's, but the two-day interrogation (presumably part of Oldfield's investigations, code-named 'Fluency', tracing Soviet penetrations of British Intelligence) left him exhausted and irritated with security intelligence and its bottomless well of suspicion.[117] In sum, there is no shortage of reasons for his departure from the Privy Council Office in 1958 to become the Canada Council's supervisor of the arts program.

Laudatory memoranda in his personnel file confirm that Dwyer's departure from the PCO and the cessation of his formal status as a civil servant were regarded as a qualified loss by senior bureaucrats Robert Bryce and Arnold Heeney—qualified, that is, in that they reserved the right to call on him from time to time with 'special matters'. Once engaged in Canada Council affairs, Dwyer applied his full organizational and analytical faculties to patterning government subsidies to the arts. Positioned to implement his plan for a professionalized cultural sector in an enduring way, his influence reached ahead into the Canadian cultural scene for the next decade and beyond.

Soundings

Eighteen months after moving to the Canada Council, an inquiry from Governor-General Vincent Massey reached Dwyer's desk, wondering about the bona fides of the Canadian Council of Authors and Artists: 'They have asked me to accept a life membership . . . I am very reluctant to accept such invitations unless I am certain of the standing of the body concerned.'[118] Dwyer replied that the Council 'is a radio and television union . . . and holds its charter from the Canadian Labour Congress.' Albert Trueman forwarded this information to Massey, writing that he could 'not say anything about the standing of the Council', but he added meaningfully: 'perhaps that is a matter which is evident from the nature of the body itself.'

Part of Dwyer's application of 'intimate sensing' in the arts sector was to elaborate a multi-faceted interface between artists and government. He pioneered the use of 'soundings', bringing together selected representatives of a particular artistic discipline for a weekend of off-the-record exchanges with Council officers. At one such meeting in 1969 with English-language publishers at an apartment rented by the Canada Council in Montreal, Dwyer told the dozen or so initiates that:

> we have had a fair number of soundings of this kind. They have been with actors, painters, *peintres et sculpteurs*, ballet company managers, singers . . . and we have found them extremely valuable.

He joked about Dr Spooner, of New College, Oxford, quipping that even 'tenors' had occasionally changed 'the tenour of our ways'. But there was just one caveat: 'About what is said here—we think it should not be in any way secret, *but private.*' If any participants wanted to publicize any information arising from the sounding, Dwyer requested that they 'please say so, and we will be more circumspect.'[119]

Styling himself as 'a jack of all trades and master of none', he deferred the detailed discussions to literature officer Naim Kattan, stressing how in general the Council was concerned with the artist 'as an individual' and had devised 'pretty elaborate systems' to take 'good professional advice and follow it as far as we can'.

Peter Dwyer (left) with Alan Jarvis, April 1959. Photo by Lunney. NAC-PA 206458.

Services to the arts, he said, form 'the hidden part of the iceberg', and he mentioned that information services were now centralized within each discipline through the Canadian Theatre Centre, the Canadian Music Centre, the National Theatre School, and French and English book publishers' councils. For several years he had lobbied for the creation of a similar information centre for the visual arts.

If each sounding with artists formed a new 'magic circle', off-the-record briefings of his Canada Council officers formed an even tighter one. In an undated and unsigned page of notes in the Canada Council's 'Soundings' file from 1969, the outline of 'PMD's paper . . . "right & known"' survives. He drew on his counter-intelligence experience to explain the importance of the distinction between what is 'right' and what is 'known'. That is, counter-intelligence information concerning suspect individuals or organizations often becomes 'known' but cannot meet the legal test as evidence in a court. What is not knowable to a court about a certain individual may nonetheless be known to be 'right' by officers of the state, who also know that 'any government would permit measures to stop his activities.' He mentioned the American CIO leader Walter Reuther, an anti-Communist, asking, 'is Reuther a <u>reasonable</u> man?' The note-taking officer scribbled down Reuther's formula: 'if it looks like duck, walks like a duck, has webbed feet & quacks—then I say it is a duck! (a communist).'[120]

To 'know' definitively if such unofficial criteria of selection helped officers guide grant monies away from politically problematic individuals or organizations is not possible. It seems 'right' to raise the suspicion given the RCMP investigators' obvious chagrin at not being able to spot in the Council's activities any pattern of subversive activity.[121] Of all the cultural organizations during Dwyer's period of arts supervision, the RCMP's heavy hand fell lightest on the Canada Council. If Dwyer's security connections, regularly refreshed around the table at Sammy's, or his thorough knowledge of the RCMP's anti-subversive activities and personalities unduly protected the Council, documentary evidence for it is sketchy.

The usual blanks may or may not harbour the answer. In 1965, the Director of Security and Intelligence, William H. Kelly, wrote to the RCMP's 'A' Division:

> Reference is made to your report of November 25th, 1964, in which you suggest that there may be some ____ [one line exempted] ____ Canada Council. We do not share your doubts in this connection for the following reason.
>
> 2. As we understand it the Canada Council is a relatively small and compact organization. The ____ [four-line exemption] ____ .
> 3. In view of the above will you please ____ [one line exemption] ____ . [122]

Confession

From the outset, Canadian government officials had never doubted Peter Dwyer's reliability or his loyalty. Yet, while he was in Ottawa in 1946 representing British Intelligence on the Gouzenko case, he had not informed the Canadians about British and American security concerns over the appointment of Harry Dexter White to the IMF. Seven years later, in November 1953, J. Edgar Hoover's startling reference to a 'Canadian official' as the source of negative information about White's reliability placed Dwyer in the uncomfortable position of knowing the answer to a riddle that confounded his Ottawa colleagues.

Between leaving the Ottawa Little Theatre with his playwright's award on 18 November 1953 and arriving at the Privy Council offices in the East Block the next day, the pressure increased on Peter Dwyer to disclose his involvement in the Harry Dexter White imbroglio. The morning newspapers provided no comfort. The gadfly George Bain explained to *Globe and Mail* readers that the Jenner subcommittee's pressure tactics against Lester Pearson and their demand to re-interview Gouzenko were products of their lack of direct access to FBI files. Deprived of that database by statute, their publicity machine required fresh inputs and Canada presented a likely target for their bullying tactics. Secretary of State for External Affairs Pearson daily bore the brunt of American press attacks that Dwyer's information could help deflect.

In the *Ottawa Journal*, a front-page story covering the Gouzenko case and the Harry Dexter White mystery reported the Prime Minister's doubt that J. Edgar Hoover's reference to a 'highly placed Canadian official' was accurate. Nonetheless, Louis St Laurent assured reporters that a thorough document search was underway. On page two, columnist Judith Robinson cited an anonymous source who had called

THURSDAY, NOVEMBER 19, 1953.

PRIZE WINNING PLAYWRIGHTS MEET **E GOVERNOR GENERAL**—Three of the ur top prize winners in the 1953 Workshop nadian Playwriting competition received eir awards from Governor Géneral Vincent Massey following the opening performce at the Little Theatre last night. Left to right are Aubrey C. Green of Winnip Norman Williams of Toronto, the Goverr General and Peter Dwyer of Ottawa. T other prize winner among the top fo Robert MacLeod of Toronto, was unable attend the opening.

— (Dominion Wide Phot

igh Standards Are Revealed t Prize Plays Competition

Will Show Film At Rockcliffe Home and Schoo

n unusually high triple-}tion could improve this other-dard of playwriting, acting wise well-presented play.

"Coral Wonderland" will shown tonight at the first

Ottawa Journal, *18 November 1953.*

her with a 'strange story'. According to her source, Igor Gouzenko had fingered Harry Dexter White in 1946 when shown a letter from the US Treasury, personally dictated by White, refusing to exempt Gouzenko's magazine royalties from an excise tax. In the letter, White referred to the cipher clerk as 'that Gouzenko', prompting the excitable Russian to take offence and to name White as a Soviet spy. This dubious information appeared alongside equally confusing stories naming variously Mackenzie King and Norman Robertson as Hoover's secret source. None of this could have been welcome breakfast reading for Peter Dwyer.[123]

It is reasonable to think that he did read the papers that morning. On page 15 of the *Journal*, above the headline 'High Standards Are Revealed', Dwyer appears with the other winning playwrights beside Vincent Massey on the Little Theatre stage, and with this report the hapless *Ottawa Journal* failed once again. On 5 and 6 September 1945 its editors had dismissed Igor Gouzenko as a crank and a world-shaking scoop slipped from their grasp. In this case the answer to the question dominating the front page—which highly placed Canadian official tipped off the FBI about Harry Dexter White in 1946?—lay inside the *Journal* itself. The paper even had a photograph of the culprit, since that person was Peter Dwyer.

In January and February 1946 Dwyer indeed *had* been in Ottawa, deeply engaged in the Gouzenko case. Apparently without the knowledge of his RCMP counterparts he had sent a telex through secure British communications links to the FBI's Lish Whitson. It passed through Dwyer's Canadian-born assistant in Washington, Miss Geraldine Dack. She had transmitted Dwyer's warning regarding Harry Dexter White to Whitson, thus prompting Hoover's letter of 1 February 1946 to President Truman. Dwyer's telex stated that his information emanated from 'informed diplomatic sources' and he claimed to have the 'blessing' of the RCMP, as well as the FBI's Ottawa liaison, Glen Bethel, in passing it on. This 'blessing' was not a matter of record with the RCMP, and, with the urgent attention given to Pearson's request for a document search, one wonders whom Dwyer did consult.

Events unfolded quickly in the days following the premiere of *Hoodman-Blind* in November 1953. First, Dwyer learned that his FBI telex concerning White's election to the IMF had completely muddled the actual procedure for IMF appointments. On 19 November, Dwyer received a copy of a memorandum on this subject from Bill Crean to Arnold Smith. Smith had been involved in intelligence and propaganda from the time of his wartime work for the British in Cairo and afterwards at the Canadian embassy in Moscow. He wrote the Kellock-Taschereau Report on the Gouzenko affair in 1946 and later was a regular with Dwyer at McClung's table at Sammy's. In 1953 he was in Lester Pearson's office fielding the various incendiary national security issues for the minister. Crean reported to Smith that according to the Bank of Canada's Louis Rasminsky it was constitutionally impossible for the Canadian or British representatives to have influenced Harry Dexter White's appointment to the IMF in 1946. Furthermore, as a Canadian delegate at the time, Rasminsky assured Crean he received no advice regarding White from anyone.[124]

Also on 19 November a ciphered telegram was received in External Affairs from Arnold Heeney in Washington reporting on an 'exceedingly frank and private' conversation with General Walter Bedell Smith, Undersecretary of State, who formerly served as CIA director and as ambassador in Moscow. Bedell Smith (whose 'cold fishy eye' and 'precision-tool brain' had rattled Kim Philby) allowed to Heeney that normal diplomatic channels would provide little recourse to stem the attacks on Canadian officials by the un-American activities committees. Such charges were 'purely political' and the administration would do well merely to keep President Eisenhower 'above the dust and dirt'. Regarding Hoover's letter concerning Harry Dexter White, he said, 'it must be remembered that J. Edgar Hoover was a power unto himself, that he would never "go out on a limb" by divulging on one hand or withholding on the other information which he thought might be to his own political advantage and that of the FBI.' Although Bedell Smith promised to follow up the matter, Heeney judged that 'no satisfactory result is likely.' And, '[i]n view of the exceedingly frank and private nature of some of the remarks,' he cautioned, 'I would be grateful if only the minimum circulation were given this telegram.'[125]

With such pressures at play, to whom did Dwyer elect to make his confession? He may have warned MI6's liaison officer that he felt obliged to reveal his involvement in the affair. This may well have prompted exchanges in London between the new 'C', Sir John Sinclair (the recent successor to Dwyer's former chief, Sir Stewart Menzies), and Canadian High Commissioner Norman Robertson. There is no available record to confirm this or to suggest where Dwyer may have turned next. It was unlikely to have been his immediate superior, Robert Bryce, new to the PCO and apparently not involved in this case. Possibly Dwyer spoke with Crean or Glazebrook in External Affairs and the matter was discussed by these parties before or after the Security Panel meeting on Friday, 20 November. What is clear is that over the weekend these Canadian officials became aware of Dwyer's role and by Monday they had in hand his 1946 telex to Lish Whitson.

As journalists continued to spin the story in various directions, Pearson's aides began the damage control process. To prevent the issue from opening up another stratum of state secrets the hard-boiled Arnold Smith was assigned to prepare Pearson's statement. With Smith, Crean, Glazebrook, and R.A. Mackay to assist him, it hardly seems credible that Pearson needed more help. Norman Robertson's hurried recall from London perhaps indicates the importance attached to the intertwined problems posed by the Harry Dexter White and Igor Gouzenko cases.[126] Robertson denied to reporters these were reasons for his return, but the documents show his full involvement.[127]

In Washington, George Ignatieff assembled the transcripts of relevant testimony before the various un-American activities committees and also obtained assurances from Robert Morris (secretary of the McCarran Committee) that, despite Victor Lasky's recent provocation, Lester Pearson would not be targeted personally.[128] R.A. MacKay instructed Charles Ritchie that he and Crean be called out of the Security Panel meeting if any new development warranted it. Crean and MacKay thought it dangerous to state there was reciprocity of information with the Americans since it might force the Canadians to permit the publication of information better kept secret. As well, they pointed out:

> there is the previous note in which we deleted the references to Stettinius and in this instance, at least, we did not give the Congressional committee all the evidence about an American citizen which was received from the Gouzenko testimony.[129]

As secretary of the Security Panel and with his unparalleled knowledge of the Gouzenko affair's significance to Western counter-intelligence, Dwyer was acutely aware of the issues raised by revealing his role in the White case. Yet, when he disclosed his centrality in the intrigue and supplied his Canadian colleagues with the actual telex to Hoover, he failed to remember many relevant details. He wondered if the entire matter 'may have been inspired by Sir William Stephenson', leaving unanswered such questions as which British 'informed diplomatic sources' had provided the information in the first place, why he had not shared this information with the Canadians at the time, and if his primary duty lay with the Official Secrets Act of Canada or Britain. It appears that the Canadian officials chose not to pursue these questions, though puzzling loose ends remained.

On 24 November, as Arnold Smith put finishing touches on Pearson's statement, he sent urgently to Crean: 'Please let me know immediately whether Harry Dexter White's name or any reference to him did figure in any of the evidence obtained from Gouzenko, or else obtained in Canada as a result of his evidence here, e.g., did it figure in the famous notebook . . . within the next hour or so.'[130] White's name, according to a telephone reply from Inspector Hall of the RCMP, 'was not in the [Halperin] notebook and did not appear in the evidence.' Apprised of Dwyer's telegram, Smith was left to ponder where the misinformation regarding White's nomination to the IMF had originated from.[131]

Finally having in hand the exact ciphered telex Dwyer had sent in January 1946, the External Affairs team worked in earnest to protect Pearson. In New York, Pearson told a UN correspondents' luncheon on 24 November with obvious relief that the 'Government has found the document' and that he would be returning to Ottawa to make a full statement.[132] From Britain, the Intelligence-friendly Reuters wire doused the North American media with headlines such as 'US Allies Perplexed, Dismayed Over White Case' and 'What Has Got Into Our American Friends?'[133]

Prior to Pearson's public statement on 25 November, the entire matter was presented to 'C', Sir John Sinclair, in a comprehensive top-secret communication that quoted Peter Dwyer's entire 1946 cable verbatim ('in case you are unable to trace the message in your files').[134]

The Canadian dispatch reviewed the entire situation, including Dwyer's inability to remember all the relevant details. 'C' was put on notice that Pearson would present the true information to the House of Commons on the following day, irrespective of possible repercussions to the British secret services. Crean warned Sinclair that a member of the parliamentary press gallery had worked in BSC during the war 'and if he wishes to publish Dwyer's name, he is probably aware of Dwyer's official position at that time.' The dispatch concluded by saying that 'the only security information Canadian authorities ever possessed on White came from American sources.'

It is likely that enough disinformation had already circulated in the press for Pearson's team to have left the matter to decay on its own. Mindful of American witch-hunters, the minister insisted that the air be cleared with a full public statement. Addressing the print and broadcast media downstairs from Dwyer's office in the East Block, an obviously tired Pearson was forced to stop repeatedly because of problems with the broadcast equipment. He rehearsed the Gouzenko case in detail, regretting the American Senate subcommittee's public airing of security information normally exchanged confidentially. He explained that the FBI had always had access to Gouzenko, that they had interviewed him as recently as August 1950, and that Gouzenko possessed no further information, notwithstanding the claims published in the *Chicago Tribune*. He extended an offer to the Jenner subcommittee to interview Gouzenko in Canada, but 'quietly and confidentially' and under strict Canadian auspices.

On the matter of Harry Dexter White and the mysterious informant, he stated that the American claim that a highly placed Canadian official had transmitted information regarding White was incorrect. 'The fact is that the only information which the Canadian authorities had . . . came from the FBI.' It was not from Gouzenko, he insisted, nor from any other Canadian source. The tip to Hoover, rather, was:

> a personal reminder . . . that is all it was . . . from a security official not of the Canadian government, but who was stationed in Ottawa to maintain liaison with the Canadian security authorities on behalf of the security services of a friendly third power.

Beyond this Pearson did not go, and his tone was conciliatory: 'It is clear that in the stress and tension of the moment—and it was a difficult time—the author of the telegram must have misunderstood the details of information regarding the prospective appointments to the IMF.' Pearson found it 'easy to understand and sympathize with this mistake'. He concluded with a lengthy paean to the bonds of friendship and co-operation between two countries that shared the world's longest undefended border, vigilant partners in the struggle against World Communism.

These latter remarks in Pearson's lengthy statement passed without press commentary. Indeed, the Harry Dexter White case disappeared entirely and no further mention was made of the 'highly placed' Canadian informant. The unidentified reporter who might have publicized Dwyer's name remained silent.[135] George Bain and the other parliamentary journalists following the story shifted their attention to the American response to Pearson's Gouzenko offer. Brooke Claxton, Minister of National Defence and soon to be first Chairman of the Canada Council, seized newspaper headlines the next morning by warning of the imminence of a 'Red H-Bomb'.[136] Claxton's announcement reminded Canadians of the near-war relations with the Soviets and reinforced Pearson's more subtle call to discretion.

Pearson had emphasized that security information was normally exchanged *confidentially* between the Western allies' security agencies, implying that further breaches of confidence by American politicians might result in less than frank exchanges. His careful exoneration of the liaison officer also was a cue to reporters that further questioning about his identity was unwelcome. The official secret was left undisturbed even though it obviously led on to further and more difficult questions about Canadian relations with foreign intelligence agencies, and about the Gouzenko affair itself. To what extent were such foreign intelligence agencies, especially Dwyer's British SIS employers, using Canada as a field for covert operations against the Soviets? What other secrets had been withheld from the Canadians in their own capital? Why had Norman Robertson returned to Ottawa from London in such haste on 23 November? The filtration of cultural secrecy ensured that the friendly liaison officer's role in the White case was erased. Like the ubiquitous hill-top antennas, it was marked as information to remember to forget, and the train of inquiry ground to a halt.

Although Pearson's admission that Hoover's source was a foreign liaison officer is publicly available—albeit buried in his tediously long statement—intelligence historian James Barros makes no mention of it in his 1977 article on this subject. Reviewing these events, he states merely that the information in Hoover's 1946 memo to Vaughan 'evidently originated in Ottawa', although this was 'impossible to prove'.[137] In an unsupported footnote, he writes: 'In 1946, one well-placed official in the Canadian government believed White was the more serious problem [than Alger Hiss] since he was closer to the policy-making apparatus.' Is this mere speculation, or was Barros provided with what he thought was inside information? Either way, for those still interested in the matter he restored Hoover's disinformation about a 'Canadian source' with the aura of historical fact.

The Secret Theatre

The secret theatre of national security indeed has a 'backstage' larger than any theatre-goer ever imagines. Cultural secrecy is the absorptive black masking that boxes in its sightlines, obscuring the backstage technical plant where bishops and lamplighters, actors and stagehands mingle. It is the limbo against which shining things are made really to count. It entrains the citizen as a perspectival observer to view human action as if the stage represents a complete world and not merely a confection arranged for a willing and naive audience. It is a theatre whose illusion is durably enthralling and eminently transposable into every new medium.

On the other hand, it falsely glamorizes national security to describe it as a 'secret theatre'. Granted this metaphor, spies and informants become consummate actors, and the sometimes harrowing consequences of their actions seem make-believe. It also implies a reversal of the optics of Jeremy Bentham's panopticon. Instead of watching the prison population from a central tower, the watchers flatter themselves that their actions are indirectly witnessed, or at least imagined, by that population. Indirectly, the 'secret' domain of state security broadcasts its truths through the artifice of theatre, film, and television, neutralizing any possibility for their critical examination in an unaesthetized public memory.

Dwyer's impresario role in national culture and state security mirrors the secret theatre metaphor. As Naim Kattan says, 'He was an artist. He loved the artist, in a candid way.' Dwyer is remembered by his contemporaries with admiration for his dedication to cultivating high achievement in the arts and for his sensitivity to each new artistic development. Alan Jarvis regarded Dwyer as an arts administrator who achieved 'true objectivity', citing Dwyer's own words: 'mature enough to give thoughtful opinion, young enough to embrace what is new'.[138] And yet, despite such praise, the motif of Dwyer's success nonetheless is woven into some larger and more obscure pattern that comprehends his parallel commitment to state security.

By the time of Dwyer's appointment as Director of the Canada Council in 1970 the emphasis had shifted to cultural relations with Quebec. He wrote confidentially to Michael Pitfield, Clerk of the Privy Council, to the effect that attempts by the Secretary of State Department to increase its direct control of arts funding outside the arm's-length relationship with the Canada Council were ill-advised. There is no evidence that his friends from Sammy's, Mark McClung or Henry Hindley, supplied him with inside information obtained through their offices in the Secretary of State, but Dwyer certainly stayed well informed.[139]

'The arts are one of the binding forces of the country', he reminded Pitfield:

> Our relations with Quebec are extremely difficult and, as you know, Jean Knowall Tremblay [Jean Noël Tremblay was Quebec's Culture Minister] is impossible. Nevertheless we have managed to keep a very large percentage of Quebec artists along with us and we even manage informal meetings on the private ground of Montreal with officers of the *Ministère des Affaires Culturelles*. I should take it ill if anyone else goes galumphing across these tenuous links as long as we can hold them together.[140]

Notwithstanding the arm's-length principle, Dwyer wondered if Pitfield might, in speaking with ministers, mention Council officers' skill in traversing the 'fertile field for public misadventure the arts present' and remind them of the Council's record of protecting the government from embarrassments that can easily occur when grants are misplaced.

During the October Crisis in 1970 Jacques Ferron, medical doctor, writer, and political agitator, brought his fabular novel *Le salut de l'Irlande* to completion in a frantic week-long writing marathon. Like Dwyer, Ferron was an allegorist. He set his novel in the Front de Libération du Québec's home turf on Montreal's south shore, aligning local anti-English sentiment with the liberation movement in Northern Ireland. C.D.A. Haffigan is an Irish-*Canadien* 'effelquois' with four sons, of whom Tim, Buck, and Mike appall their father by joining either the RCMP's anti-subversive squad or the Canadian Army. The fourth, Connie, is swayed to FLQ activism. (These names unmistakably refer to Tim Buck, Louis Kon, and Mike Buhay, leading Canadian Communists of the forties and fifties.)

Ferron was a socialist organizer and perennial political candidate (eventually leaving the Rassemblement pour indépendence nationale—RIN—to form the parodic Rhinoceros Party). In the 1950s he was a director of the Canadian Peace Congress, and no doubt the subject of a sizable RCMP file. In every respect Ferron was the type of engagé political author whose outlook was diametrically opposed to that of Peter Dwyer. Thus Ferron's dedication of *Le salut de l'Irlande*—'À monsieur Peter Dwyer'—is as surprising as it was well-aimed. With one stroke Ferron triangulated Dwyer's part-Irish heritage, his previous associations with British and Canadian security services, and his pivotal position in Canadian writing and publishing and placed them against the background of the current crisis.

Ferron correctly intuited Dwyer's hostility to 'effelquois' aspirations. After students occupied *La Maison Canadienne* in Paris during the October Crisis, the Canada Council Director approached Freeman Tovell and the External Affairs' Security and Intelligence Liaison Division to 'ask whether any progress had been made in identifying Canadian students [in Paris] who had indicated sympathy with FLQ objectives during the recent kidnapping cases.' That British diplomat James Cross remained in FLQ hands obviously was a matter of great concern for British as well as Canadian security services. Dwyer explained that it would be a 'matter of considerable delicacy for the Canada Council' if any of the students in question were found to be its grant recipients. He did not personally feel they could be penalized by the Council unless specifically charged with an FLQ-related crime. The inference, albeit presented 'in rather vague terms', was that the Council's files contained fairly extensive information on such persons. In view of the fact that the Canada Council 'was known to be averse to receiving classified information', Dwyer's inquiry was passed to Marc Lalonde in the Prime Minister's Office. Lalonde had already requested this information, and through him Dwyer could have the 'fragmentary intelligence' already received from various Canadian observers in Paris.[141]

Final Curtain

Peter Dwyer's tenure as Canada Council Director was cut short by illness in 1971. While convalescing he spoke from his home with political cartoonist Ben Wicks, who was preparing a broadcast item for the freewheeling and unserious *Max Ferguson Show*. Wicks dabbled in journalism and his unlikely telephone conversation with Dwyer was the high point of a rambling account of the Kim Philby case. Dwyer's slow and cautious responses betrayed his declining health (during pauses birds can be heard chirping in his backyard), but his mind was as acute as ever. One striking aspect of the conversation is its play of accents: one hears Wicks, a British war evacuee who retained a distinctive cockney lilt, in dialogue with Dwyer's smooth Oxonian voice, still charming, habitually discreet, and prone to slightly florid turns of phrase. In the lead-up to the interview Wicks narrates the Philby story, gleefully emphasizing how the exalted idiocy of the British upper classes led not only to high-profile intelligence debacles but to hopeless filing systems maintained by pedigreed secretaries with no patience for detail.

No doubt Dwyer sensed that Wicks's re-creation of the Philby case was to be a verbal caricature equivalent to his political cartoons. Dwyer could not expect to have the same 'English English' affinity with Wicks that he felt with Henry Hindley, for example. The interview proceeded awkwardly, with Dwyer signalling both a willingness to talk and yet cueing Wicks, in that complex paralinguistic call to discretion, not to ask the penetrating questions. Wicks's cheerful admiration for Philby's audacity drew from Dwyer an expression of bitterness at having had his own work compromised:

WICKS: Do you ever correspond [with Philby]?
DWYER: No, we don't correspond. . . . I think what he did was, well, *treason* of a form, wasn't it? And it's not something I wish to have anything to do with.

Intrigued and confused, Wicks lurched through the remainder of the interview without discovering Dwyer's exact role in Philby's exposure or the precise ramifications of Philby's treachery to the Gouzenko and Fuchs cases. 'So it was

Peter Dwyer, 1970. Photo by D. Campbell. NAC-PA 206960.

completely wasted', Wicks concluded, speaking of MI6 activity during Dwyer's
tenure. 'Well, I wouldn't put it as high as that,' Dwyer replied, 'but I would say he
did a great deal of damage indeed.' With that the window for further questions
closed, and when Dwyer died on New Year's Day 1973, he carried most of his
secrets with him. It was also Kim Philby's sixty-first birthday, typically celebrated
with 'a small circle of senior KGB officers in his Moscow apartment'.[142]

Mark McClung's table at Sammy's has an ambiguous place in Canada's cultural history. Three of its leading figures, McClung, Dwyer, and Wall, brought artistic affinities to the security intelligence component. After Dwyer left the Nunnery for the Privy Council Office, Wall hankered after something 'a little more real' than SIGINT. In September 1953 he went to work in McClung's section in the RCMP where his assignments included screening the CBC International Service and the National Film Board. He and McClung monitored the CBC radio and television broadcasts for signs of Communist infiltration. Before long Wall went on to work as Dwyer's assistant in the Privy Council Office, and took over as secretary of the Security Panel when Dwyer joined the Canada Council. Mark McClung resigned from the RCMP after an altercation with incoming Director of Security and Intelligence Cliff Harvison, the tough interrogator of the Gouzenko suspects in 1946.

Estimates of the effects of secrecy on civil servants vary. Robert Bryce shrugged it off, telling Donald Brittain 'you learn to live with it in due course.'[143] On the other hand, Don Wall and Mark McClung agreed it was corrosive to morale, leading in some cases to substance abuse and shortened lives.[144] If Dwyer survived the Harry Dexter White crisis of 1953 to reinvent himself at the Canada Council, one senses that he never completely eradicated a feeling of loss lingering from that Faustian contract first presented him by Gyles Isham or someone like him at Oxford. The whole process of culture and security was blended in him, and inextricably wound him into the cult of official secrecy.

In his final memorandum to his colleagues at the Canada Council, slowly pecked out on a typewriter and signed shakily with his left hand, there is a catch in his voice, and a tremulous tone that suggests dismay at having been carried so far off track by that larger pattern:

> I have to let everybody in the office know that I shall not be returning to work with the Canada Council. There is one essential reason: the doctor [says] it would be at least April before I could come back to work. This is obviously unacceptable to all, and I have informed the Prime Minister.
>
> I shall miss what you do in the arts very much. These are the shining things which really count. So always remember that when some blast-off goes through your hands, ill-written and on paper torn from a notebook, it may be from someone who will give his name to our time. Which I certainly shan't.
>
> Good luck to you all.[145]

Which I certainly shan't. Peter Dwyer's ambivalent legacy in state security and cultural administration remains, as Robert Fulford noticed, shrouded with secrecy. One mystery associated with him—the 'Canadian source' in the Harry Dexter White mystery—is now solved, but other secrets, particularly concerning the Gouzenko affair, have proven to be extremely durable.

5

Pulp History:
Repossessing the Gouzenko Myth

The [painter's] ability to reproduce a given object with photographic accuracy is not the only criterion of good art. . . . Though when one says 'like,' one usually means visually like, there are other ways of identifying objects. What about like by atmosphere, like in sound, like by touch, like by smell; to say nothing of more abstract tests, which are best made by saying, 'what does the picture convey?'

Elizabeth Harrison, *Self-Expression Through Art*, 1951

[Churchill] stressed very strongly what realists [the Soviets] were. He called them 'realist lizards,' all belonging to the crocodile family. He said they would be as pleasant with you as they could be.

W.L. Mackenzie King, Diary, October 1945.

The Painter as Sensor

Elizabeth Harrison's 1944 painting of lunch hour in a wartime Ottawa cafeteria patterns and prefigures impending events with considerable prescience.[1] At the tail end of the queue, shuffling towards the distant buffet, the balding Norman Robertson, heavy-lidded and prematurely stooped, appears lost in his own thoughts, oblivious to the crowded scene. At the head of the circuit of lunching officials, George Glazebrook bears his tray across the centre of the cafeteria. The University of Toronto historian was seconded to work under T.A. 'Tommy' Stone in the fledgling intelligence branch of the Department of External Affairs in January 1942.[2] Glazebrook's weak-chested frame, sunken shoulders, and high forehead project a cerebral air that is nonetheless slightly insipid. Trailing him at the far left is Jack Pickersgill of the Prime Minister's Office, leaning backwards as if caught off balance. Although not exactly reeling, Pickersgill, like Glazebrook and Robertson,

'Cafeteria, Chateau Laurier, 1944' by Elizabeth Harrison. NAC, accession no. 1994–224–5.

lacks the poise of other 'shrewd and correctly dressed' figures in the crowded scene. For instance, the unsmiling M.R.K. Burge, the British High Commission's information officer, stands directly ahead of Pickersgill and raises a reproving eyebrow at the viewer.[3]

At a table at the far right are two other British officials, Mr Laugharne and Joe Garner (later Lord Garner). Garner, languidly forking his cake, leans close to discuss some private matter in tones low enough to escape the notice of Norman Robertson. Standing directly behind them, Robertson seems shut off even from the backhanded whisper of Jack Barwick, civil servant and concert agent, directed to the uniformed Wren on his left. Painter Grant Macdonald, clear-eyed and tall, patiently waits behind Robertson, but Trudy Janowski of the National Film Board—the dark-haired woman standing four places ahead of him in the queue— casts a concerned look over her shoulder in the direction of George Glazebrook. The three British representatives project an alertness and confidence notably lacking in the three isolated and introspective Canadian officials. Significantly, these civilian overseers of the Canadian security establishment were to play key roles in the Gouzenko affair.

Elizabeth Harrison creates a separation between the upper area of the painting containing the figures just described and the five figures who dominate the foreground, one of whom represents herself. Just off-centre, she is the young woman with tightly pinned hair whose head partially obscures the loping Glazebrook. Her attitude is that of a listener, tuned in not just to the swank soldiers dominating the conversation at her table but also to the general ambience of the room. Aurally (for this is above all an *aural* painting), it is Harrison herself who connects her four friends to the officialdom around them. Except for her cocked ear the young subalterns betray no inkling of the invisible forces and burdens stressing their secretive and divided elders.

Two years earlier, while lunching here in the cafeteria, Norman Robertson and Judge T.C. Davis discussed the idea of centralizing the cable, radio, and postal censorship units under the Department of National War Services.[4] Perhaps they touched, too, on the matter of Davis's troublesome protégé, Tracy Philipps. Believing the room noise sufficiently absorbed their voices, the two mooted Robertson's censorship plan in some detail before noticing that a man next to them obviously was listening in. Once observed, the eavesdropper picked up his tray and left, but before long Robertson learned that the man worked under chief telegraph censor L.S. Yuill. Apprised by their incautious conversation, Yuill sought to pre-empt any restructuring of his department. Within a few months he was relieved of his post in favour of the trustier Wilfred Eggleston.

A year passed before Robertson's attention was drawn to the fact that before his departure Yuill had instructed his department to monitor the telephone communications between the Soviet embassy and their Halifax consulate.[5] This practice was noticed only when George Glazebrook deduced that an unattributed intercept received from the RCMP was an exchange between Soviet embassy staff.[6] In retrospect, one marvels that the rather suspicious conversation it contained did not immediately step up concern in External Affairs regarding surreptitious Soviet intelligence-gathering in Canada. Yet Robertson's concern was not for counterintelligence. Rather, he sought to forestall any potential embarrassment to External Affairs should the RCMP's interception of foreign legations' communications come to light.

Glazebrook had expressed concern just a month previously that the RCMP operated its own telephone censorship, pointing out that its 'total extent is not known.'[7] He felt that External Affairs would best be protected if all interception of landline calls fell under the Director of Censorship, Colonel O.M. Biggar. Robertson agreed, but when Glazebrook broached the matter with Commissioner S.T. Wood, the implacable police chief divulged neither the extent nor the specific targets of RCMP in-house censorship facilities, and he discouraged any idea of centralization under Biggar.[8] That was October. Now in November, with the Soviet Ottawa-Halifax phone intercept in hand, Robertson wrote firmly to Wood that 'it would hardly seem necessary at the moment to monitor calls between these two offices.' Evidently the Commissioner complied, ordering an immediate cessation of telephonic monitoring of 'various foreign consular officers in Halifax'.[9]

These records demonstrate that the RCMP maintained an anti-Soviet counterintelligence effort even after the Soviets became allies of Canada. They qualify the government's public attitude of hurt surprise following Gouzenko's disclosures. On the other hand, some 20 months prior to Gouzenko's defection, Norman Robertson restricted one means of sensing vibrations of Soviet intelligence activity in Canada. Indeed, Gouzenko would marvel at the ease with which Colonel Nikolai Zabotin's military intelligence (GRU) contacts in the Halifax legation obtained sensitive information.[10] To what extent is Elizabeth Harrison's Norman Robertson—a man with his eyes and ears closed—more accurately rendered than biographer J.L. Granatstein's omnipresent 'man of influence'?[11] Harrison observed an official inundated with the stimuli and information generated by war mobilization, one who had absorbed the gruelling war emergency to such an extent that he no longer could process all of its implications.

Mapping the lunchtime cafeteria with a palette of greens, browns, and yellows, Harrison acknowledged the crowd itself as camouflage for concealed forces.[12] The action flows around three hubs. The buffet queue forms the largest circuit, looping around from Robertson to Glazebrook. This counter-clockwise movement is replicated in the flow of conversation at Harrison's table and in Joe Garner's and Mr Laugharne's tight circle at the right. These circles of influence are so forceful that they seem to exert a kind of bio-power, further hunching Norman Robertson's shoulders and comically contorting Pickersgill's midriff. If the surface of a lunchtime crowd seems innocent enough, the camouflage tones reveal a fluid swamp replete with quicksand and lurking predators.

In 1944 Elizabeth Harrison worked as a press reader alongside Kathleen 'Kay' Willsher, deputy registrar in the British High Commission. Although Willsher was probably unaware of it, the confidential information she occasionally passed to LPP MP Fred Rose and Treasury officer Eric Adams made her one of Colonel Zabotin's prize informants.[13] Harrison knew nothing of Willsher's clandestine activities, but her wartime assignment to the British High Commission explains why these officials figure so prominently in her painting. It accounts for her noticing a certain superior attitude in their deportment and demeanour. She was as surprised as anyone when, perhaps 16 months after composing this image, Kay Willsher suddenly vanished into RCMP custody. When Harrison learned of the government's ruthless treatment of her colleague and the other suspects, she helped found the Ottawa Civil Liberties Union to protest their secret detention and interrogation without right of counsel. Harrison became Willsher's prison visitor, helping maintain her spirits through three years in Kingston Penitentiary.[14]

In his autobiography, Igor Gouzenko records that he, too, visited the Chateau Laurier cafeteria during this period to drink a glass of beer in the company of Anatoli Kirsanov. An engineer-economist with the Soviet embassy, Kirsanov had been the Gouzenkos' neighbour during their first year in the apartments at 511 Somerset Street.[15] Sensitive as she was, Elizabeth Harrison could never have plucked from the crowd the Russian cipher clerk who would soon short-circuit the flows of energy she imaged so accurately. This tableau leaves the troubling suggestion that even a year before Gouzenko's defection a young artist sensed in these Canadian officials their vulnerability to 'friendly' as well as hostile manipulation. Her painting serves as a corrective to nationalist historiography that routinely de-emphasizes the residual anglophilia and colonial dependency that formed the other half of officials such as Robertson, Glazebrook, and Pickersgill. These accounts provide endless coverage of Zabotin and his ring of informants, but what of their equally predatory British counterparts?

Papier Mâché History

Historians of the Cold War agree that Igor Gouzenko's defection in September 1945 and the subsequent spy scare that gripped North America were of paramount importance in the development of Canada as a 'national security state'. As James Littleton puts it, Gouzenko's exposure of GRU intelligence activities 'helped to precipitate Canada's plunge into the Cold War' and 'set off a reaction that would have reverberations for years to come.'[16] Within the Canadian government the case underlined the need for enhanced sensory capacities in both electronic and human intelligence. On one hand, the wartime Examination Unit, the signals intelligence and cryptography section slated to be disbanded, suddenly gained permanent new life as the Communications Branch of the National Research Council; on the other hand, an interdepartmental Security Panel was created along British lines as a nerve centre to co-ordinate and tighten the government's internal security. As seen in the previous chapters, the Gouzenko fallout prompted purges in agencies such as the National Film Board and it altered the career paths of various cultured security professionals such as Peter Dwyer and Mark McClung.

Apart from the silent upgrading of security and intelligence in government priorities, the Gouzenko case marked a decisive shift in public sentiment hitherto favourably disposed towards the Soviet ally. In place of Canada-Soviet friendship an alarmed public now agreed that Canada's national culture must be purified of Soviet influence. How coincidental was it that the sensational publicity accorded the Gouzenko case coincided almost exactly with Winston Churchill's resounding 'Iron Curtain' address in Fulton, Missouri? The two events provided durable images of ideological polarization and physical partition, images that persisted until the fall of the Berlin Wall in 1989. As has been recounted in the now huge literature on the Cold War, repressive tendencies followed swiftly upon the breakdown of the anti-Fascist alliance at the end of 1945, culminating in the purges of McCarthyism, loyalty tests, a proliferation of secret police surveillance, and the operation of 'star chambers' north and south of the forty-ninth parallel.

That the Gouzenko affair was catastrophic to public trust in the Canadian Left is axiomatic. For example, the RCMP files concerning the American singer Paul Robeson's visits to Canada, discussed in the next chapter, record a polarization in public culture that damned virtually any dissenting opinion as Communist-inspired and somehow in the service of Soviet national interests. Concurrently, Canada's postwar federal cultural policies, prefigured in the influential Massey Report, sought to commandeer 'culture' as the civilian arena for a similar process of national purification and the 'whitest' form of psychological warfare. In contrast to negative and preventive measures taken in areas such as immigration policies, police penetration of dissident groups, and extensive civil service security vetting, these positive and pre-emptive measures saw the establishment or enhancement of federal *cultural* institutions to shape and guide national cultural development.

This is not to say that Gouzenko's action alone was a sufficient or even necessary condition for the demise of the progressive movement during this period, but his defection crops up uncannily at this break in social discourse where an entire set of beliefs, attitudes, and cultural practices were tagged as security risks. The sign 'Gouzenko' came to serve as a memory jogger, prompting legions of Canadians to remember to forget their former progressive affiliations. If other Soviet defectors brought information to Western intelligence services, perhaps even more sensitive information than Gouzenko's, no such case had such an impact on public culture as his. It is the almost perfect efficacy of the Gouzenko affair in the Western propaganda-censorship-intelligence complex that invites further attention.

Five decades of accumulated historiography concerning the case have failed to quiet a gnawing sense that the received narrative is incomplete. Indeed, its uncanniness cannot be contained within the explanatory model assigned to it in such texts. One version of Gouzenko's defection has become a litany reiterated at every opportunity as justification not merely for the government's illiberal internment of the espionage suspects but also for its actions generally in the face of covert Soviet hostility. Cold War 'national history' thus had an interest in maintaining a specific rendering of the Gouzenko case, adding layers to an already thick tissue of disinformation.

The stakes vested in Gouzenko's story are not negligible. One could argue that the slow defeat of the Left since the 1940s has been nudged ahead at every turn by some aspect of his legend. Any suggestion that it is laced with falsity—a charge made from time to time since 1946—typically is heaped with derision.[17] Professors Bothwell and Granatstein write that:

> Some skeptics on the Left still believe the Gouzenko case was an elaborate ruse designed to encourage the advent of the Cold War. There is no evidence that this is so or that the Canadian government eagerly seized on the role that had been given to it.[18]

The event is considered beyond re-evaluation. But is it? If another interpretation were to emerge, particularly one that finds this monument in national history to be a papier mâché construction, might this help to reactivate intellectual and cultural freedom it helped to suppress? Examples of such suppression are numerous enough, but it is not often remembered today that at the time of Gouzenko's defection a 'people's artist' like Paul Robeson routinely filled arenas with 10,000 excited listeners, swept up by his call for human rights and progressive social change.

April 1997

At my usual seat in the reading room of the National Archives, I worked facing several document storage boxes, each containing a volume of files. I had opened and begun to study a volume from Record Group 25, the records of Canada's Department of External Affairs. These particular files were from the top-secret 'small s' series, normally cleared on a case-by-case basis by the National Archives' Access to Information officers. Many files in this series are permanently closed, and open volumes have been thoroughly vetted prior to release. In these particular files, though, I noticed a superior quality of documentation. The material concerned Canadian officials and the US un-American activities committees, the use of passports to control the movements of Communists, and certain activities of Igor Gouzenko under RCMP protection. As I began to work through the material, I paused to order up another series of files garnered from cross-reference indices on the covers.

I traversed these pages not knowing that my second request had triggered alarm bells behind the scenes. Due to a handling oversight I had been provided with still-classified material, and within 15 minutes an agitated Access to Information officer appeared at my table and without warning swept the box away. She advised me that all notes abstracted from these records must be erased from my computer's memory. 'I don't think so', I replied. 'You'd better check about that.' Half an hour later, the section head for military and intelligence records invited me to accompany him to a meeting room where the resident CSIS liaison officer was waiting. He closed the door behind us, and they peppered me with questions about what I learned from the closed volume and requested that I show them my notes.

As I listened to their inquiries, not saying much, I thought about the mass of information that I have been refused permission to view, and an even greater trove sent to destruction with only the Security Service's word that it was not of historical interest. I thought of the then-current scandal of document destruction by officials in the blood system and the government's high-handed hobbling of the Somalia Commission inquiry, itself a product of Ottawa's propensity for secrecy and disinformation. When asked directly to hand over my notes, I refused. It was claimed that the National Archives had the right to exact them forcibly but they chose not to press the issue.

Later, I pieced together what I had learned before the files were seized. The significance of what I had read was not immediately apparent, but certain details led me to question Gouzenko's story. And if his tale as we know it is only partially true, might the missing aspects cast new light on Cold War Canadian culture?

Realist Lizards

To begin, I will rehearse what has become the standard account of the case, provided by Sir William Stephenson, 'Intrepid', the so-called 'quiet Canadian' who headed British Security Co-ordination during World War II. Stephenson subsequently took credit for masterminding various intelligence episodes during the war, including the initial handling of Gouzenko at the time of his defection.[19] The various books propagating Stephenson's reputation as a great spymaster are fine examples of 'pulp history'. Lacking any shred of documentary basis (Stephenson claimed to have ordered the destruction of all BSC records), the books freely crow Intrepid's para-democratic machismo and his penchant for British imperialism. Stephenson's self-image projected in these books is the empowered white European meeting secretly with men of his type in gentlemen's clubs, serving at once the interests of plutocracy and imperial self-preservation. The clubbable Stephenson had his writers. H. Montgomery Hyde, Dick Ellis, and later William Stevenson render a consummate insider, self-consciously attuned to the Churchillian attitude.

Stevenson's *A Man Called Intrepid* is tightly written around its subject's own political warfare objectives. In Stephenson's correspondence these objectives were simply called 'AMCI', the catch-all acronym for A-Man-Called-Intrepid literature, a distinctive blend of security intelligence history, shameless self-aggrandizement, and subtle disinformation. 'When you reach the philosophy of the purpose of an AMCI book', biographer Stevenson was instructed by his subject, 'the lesson is surely made clear by what comes via the news media today from various parts of the world: "that the survival of the English-speaking peoples rests mainly upon their unity of purpose, thought and action in all fields." '[20]

Over the past decade or two Stephenson's role in wartime intelligence has gradually been cut back to size. Disgruntled with the Winnipeg-born millionaire's flagrant breach of the intelligence community's professional code of silence, former intelligence professionals have furtively attacked Stephenson's self-directed hagiography from the wings, casting doubt on his claim to greatness, albeit without providing greater access to any relevant documents still in existence.[21] In spite of their efforts, though, Stephenson's version of the Gouzenko case remains dominant insofar as this episode in Canadian history is popularly remembered, affirmed over a period of decades in at least 20 printed accounts, his own sales running into the millions. Through sheer weight of copy his remains the most widely known description of the defection and the Canadian government's response to it.

H. Montgomery Hyde, a former BSC officer, set out Stephenson's version of events in his 1962 book, *Room 3606*.[22] In this work, later reissued as *The Quiet Canadian*, Hyde celebrated Stephenson's secret wartime career, drawing variously on his own knowledge, Stephenson's recollections, and a secret BSC history. This history was compiled at Stephenson's behest at 'Camp X' near Oshawa in the dying days of the war by, among others, classicist Gilbert Highet and children's author Roald Dahl. As they wrote, original documents were destroyed and the organization itself was wound down.[23] When an independent scholar, John Bryden, examined this history he judged that 'it was deliberately cooked to cast BSC in the best possible light at the expense of both the Americans and the Canadians.'[24] That Hyde's account of the Gouzenko defection was similarly cooked is now a matter of record.

'Late on the night of September 6, 1945,' Hyde began, 'William Stephenson, who happened to be on a routine official visit to Ottawa, called on Mr. Norman Robertson, Under-Secretary of State in the Canadian Department of External Affairs, at his private residence.' Stephenson had learned earlier that day that a Soviet embassy employee had contacted the Justice Department 'through the RCMP' offering to furnish information and he wanted to know if Robertson knew anything about it. Robertson told him that a Soviet cipher clerk named Gouzenko indeed had presented himself to the Justice Department but that the Prime Minister had instructed officials 'to do nothing for the time being for fear of the diplomatic repercussions'. According to Hyde, Stephenson immediately understood the unique opportunity the defection presented and he advised Mackenzie King to have the cipher clerk brought into the RCMP's protective custody the following morning.

Hyde explains that Gouzenko, after receiving final notice of recall to Moscow, made the momentous decision to defect to Canada rather than return home to an uncertain future. He did so not only to enjoy Canada's higher standard of living, but also to 'do something big for this country' by giving 'complete documentary proof of the Soviet spy system in Canada'. With this ambition in mind:

> he went through all the secret files, turning down the edges of those telegrams and other documents which seemed of particular interest. Then, on the evening of September 5th—the day before he was due to hand over—he surreptitiously abstracted all the documents which he had marked, tucked them under his shirt and quietly left the Embassy for the last time.[25]

That Gouzenko took his story directly to the *Ottawa Journal* 'says much about his belief in the democratic processes of the country', wrote Hyde, but as luck had it the newspaper's night editor brushed off the agitated Russian and told him to go to the RCMP. 'The next day he returned to the newspaper to no avail and then trudged from office to office with his wife and child, seemingly getting nowhere.' That night he watched through a neighbour's keyhole as Vitali Pavlov, the NKDV station chief, and three others from the Soviet embassy forced their way into his apartment. Confronted there by two Ottawa police constables, Pavlov and the others retreated from the scene:

> At 4 a.m. there was another knock at the door, this time a low careful one. 'But whoever it was left before I could identify him,' Gouzenko wrote afterwards. In fact it was [Sir William] Stephenson and [External Affairs's Thomas] Stone, who had come to reconnoitre the position.

The next morning Gouzenko was debriefed at RCMP headquarters while his wife and child remained in his neighbour's apartment under police protection. It was only then, on 7 September, that the RCMP Special Branch learned the details of a network of GRU informants operating in Canada, most crucially that it included a British scientist, Dr Alan Nunn May, who possessed knowledge of Anglo-American atom bomb research. Stephenson, Hyde recounts, sent 'two of his most experienced staff to help with the inquiries' at a 'remote country location' where Stephenson placed his 'secure telekrypton facilities at the disposal of the Canadians for the purpose of communicating with London and New York'.

The 'Corby Case', code-named after the whisky that sustained 'the tired group of men' directing the investigation from Norman Robertson's office, was to remain secret for five months 'due to the discovery of further evidence of similar espionage in the United States'. In February 1946, the Washington columnist Drew Pearson 'got hold of the story through some leakage, the source of which was never discovered.' The arrests and publicity followed and Gouzenko painted 'the most remarkable picture of international espionage to be presented in this century'. Hyde concluded his account of Stephenson's supposed role in the case: 'It is not generally known that but for the intervention at a critical moment of [Stephenson], who never sought the limelight, Igor Gouzenko might not have been alive to tell the story.'[26]

Aspects of the foregoing account have at least an air of reality, and these essentials along with a few more facts are reiterated in accounts by the key people involved: the

RCMP's Charles Rivett-Carnac and Cliff Harvison, as well as Malcolm MacDonald, the British High Commissioner to Canada at the time. This version appears, too, in renderings by numerous historians. Presumably, Gouzenko did follow the itinerary Hyde described and was twice rebuffed by the newspaper staff as well as by the various Canadian officials with whom he came in contact. No doubt he and his family were in danger for a period of time, and once in RCMP hands the interrogation team did include British Intelligence officers Peter Dwyer and Jean-Paul Evans. The debriefing occurred primarily at Camp X, the wartime BSC sabotage training centre near Oshawa, where the 'telekrypton' encryption device and the powerful Hydra transmitter provided secure communications. Yet, as John Bryden has shown, important aspects of the Stephenson/Hyde account are deliberately misleading.

The key point is that Stephenson was not in Ottawa at the time of the defection. He arrived from New York two days later to play a minor role. Bryden's signal contribution has been to prove beyond reasonable doubt that Sir Stewart Menzies himself, the head of the British Secret Intelligence Service, or MI6, who was customarily known as 'C', was in or near Ottawa at the time of Gouzenko's defection, and that Menzies is the British Intelligence chief referred to by Mackenzie King in his diary. In an inspired piece of detective work Bryden located Menzies's signature in the registry of the Seigniory Club at Montebello, Quebec, entered on 6 September 1945.[27] This startling indicator, so at odds with Stephenson's widely propagated version of the events, leads on to the possibility of a deeper deception that Bryden leaves dangling: namely that the defection was not purely Gouzenko's 'choice' but rather a product of a British intelligence operation conducted on Canadian soil without the knowledge or consent of the Canadian government. If this hypothesis has merit, the entire edifice of propaganda, censorship, and intelligence built upon Gouzenko's 'choice of freedom' must be attributed not simply to the natural unfolding of the latent Cold War rivalry but to an intentional policy pursued by elements within the British intelligence establishment at the end of the war.

Stephenson told his biographer that he became involved 'quite indirectly, in that particular case, it was a fortuitous circumstance.' Despite his claim to have been the subject of Mackenzie King's diary reference, he personally had 'never read King's published diaries.' King and Pearson, he recalled:

> were frightened mice in the Gouzenko Affair. Norman Robertson and Tommy Stone of External acted upon my advice rescinding prior orders to RCMP to stay clear. My intervention occurred from one a.m. to dawn on relevant day.[28]

Involvement solely in the early morning hours explained why nobody in the waking world laid eyes on him at the time, and it made Intrepid's story difficult to refute. But then, as Sir William explained in another telegram, a basic premise used in an AMCI-type book was this: 'the possibility is in the highest degree unlikely [of adverse government] publicity, as any argumentative discussion that field would require divulging most secret and strongly classified information in any effort to rebut.'[29]

Perhaps Bryden's and others' deflation of Intrepid's claims to greatness overlook his more general significance. To be sure, Stephenson was meddlesome and manipulative, an empire-builder whose disrespect for human rights and international law is laid bare in the Hyde and Stevenson hagiographies. Indeed, the Stephenson legend cultivated in popular non-fiction sits uncomfortably with his reputation for public service.[30] In the end, he is an embarrassing figure, whose activities reflect badly on national history as it is overtaken by more heterogeneous historical perspectives. On the other hand, it is worth attending to certain details that differentiate him from his contemporary who caused such embarrassment, Tracy Philipps.[31]

Where Philipps was shaped by experience with racial pacification in the imperial governance of Africa and the Middle East, Stephenson's formation was marked by a particularly Canadian orientation to communications technologies. He must be seen as Canada's pioneer *polluter of distances*, in the sense that Paul Virilio identifies speed and the collapsing of distances by electronic communications as an ecological concern.[32] Not just a saboteur and propagandist by disposition, Stephenson dedicated himself to the acceleration of informatics. An airman in World War I, he made a fortune during the interwar years exploiting the invention of radio photo transmission, thereby revolutionizing the global dissemination of visual information. Behind his interest in cryptography and wireless technologies was a pronounced interest in television, and eventually, in surveillant telepresence. It was not as an intelligence specialist that Stephenson entered high circles of influence but rather as a telecommunications pioneer.

So, even if revisionists are right to reduce his contribution to the Gouzenko case to merely the provision of secure communications via the telekrypton machine and his Hydra transmitter, it is arguable that these are not mere technical details. As a high priest of Cold War (dis)information, Stephenson helped desensitize civic culture to the implications of electromagnetic omnipresence.[33] Thus the prominent Hydra antenna at the top-secret Camp X sabotage training centre near Oshawa in Ontario was explained away as a transmitter site of the CBC.[34]

Notwithstanding Intrepid's high-grade use (and at times clever evasion) of communications technologies, in the 1940s public uneasiness regarding the migration of the human sensorium into the radio sphere found uncensored expression only in the utterances of the mentally disturbed. For example, take the man who presented himself to the *Ottawa Journal* during the period just prior to Gouzenko's defection warning of secret radio signals. Editor Ken Parks justified his failure to recognize Gouzenko's importance by recalling that 'we had all kinds of nuts come into the office. We had one guy who used to come in and claim that they were watching him from an empty building across the street and putting electric waves on him.'[35]

Was that man's paranoia so different from that of senior officials of the Department of External Affairs? In the years preceding the defection there was growing concern about a whole range of issues associated with invisible 'electric waves'. The Canadian government's success in intercepting and deciphering foreign wireless traffic, for example, was proportional to its own officials' escalating paranoia regarding the security of their own communications. Lester Pearson wrote nervously from Washington to Norman Robertson in March 1943:

We frequently suspect that the U.S. Censorship listens to and interferes with even calls between the Legation and Ottawa. . . . Quite apart from censorship, we suspect that some agency . . . listens in to our calls for intelligence purposes.[36]

After conferring with Tommy Stone, Robertson admitted he was resigned to the situation and 'inclined to the view that it would be better not to bring this matter up with the United States authorities.' Even if somehow induced to acknowledge the existence of such surveillance, J. Edgar Hoover was unlikely to accept any Canadian exemption when 'we have reasonable evidence that the FBI goes to the point of monitoring calls from one United States Government agency to another in Washington.'[37]

. . . A Little Naive in England

Tommy Stone's absence from Elizabeth Harrison's painting is conspicuous. 'I hardly need to tell you that if I can I shall thumb a ride on the first available aeroplane', he wrote in March 1944 to C.D. Jackson in London, although it was not until August that he slipped Norman Robertson's grip to become Canada's senior political warfare liaison in the British capital.[38] Finding himself somewhat lost on the talent-crowded stage of Allied propaganda, Stone occupied himself lobbying his British and American counterparts to include Canadian content in their broadcasts and sought to persuade Ottawa to make more aggressive use of prisoners of war in propaganda activities.[39]

Soon after his arrival in London he met with the NFB director, John Grierson, inviting along the High Commission's enforcer, Campbell Moodie.[40] Stone dispensed with the 'my dear John' familiarity of previous salutations and staked his turf as the lead Canadian propaganda co-ordinator in London. Grierson's private conversations with Sydney Bernstein, chief of the Films Division for the Political Warfare Directorate and former film director of the Ministry of Information, rankled Stone, who wrote to Robertson:

My impression is that between the two of them, they have worked out some kind of plan for the complete re-education of Europe through the medium of film and they decided the political thesis on which this education was to be based. You will notice that there is a tendency in the correspondence, of which I enclose copies, to discuss matters in which, to put it mildly, we should at least be informed.

Stone complained that Grierson 'was as slippery as the proverbial eel . . . and it was difficult for me to get anything definite out of him as to the subject of these conversations.'[41]

Stone's immediate superior was Vincent Massey, another anglophile susceptible to British honours and recognition. 'My chief in London in this work, the High Commissioner, has asked me to convey an expression of his appreciation', Stone wrote to Robert Bruce Lockhart upon his departure in November, 'Mr. Massey is, as you know, very interested in political warfare matters and in the development of a close liaison between London and Ottawa in this field.'[42] Dreaming of British honours, Massey's and Stone's 'close liaison' did not ensure sensitive critical feedback to Norman Robertson. Rather, their pawn-like availability to British political warfare objectives left them only dimly aware of British intentions. A young captain with intelligence and psychological warfare training who shouldered the actual liaison work for Stone was Mavor Moore, years later chairman of the Canada Council. He still marvels how Britain's propaganda co-ordinator, Ivonne Kirkpatrick, completely withheld from Stone that 'MI5 engineered the whole [Rudolf Hess] caper.'[43]

The Department of External Affairs' wartime Psychological Warfare records are shaded with such anglophilia. From London, Stone wrote to Glazebrook, his deputy in Ottawa:

> It was really very amusing about the [NFB] film called A MAN AND HIS JOB. After the film was over Walter Adams quietly remarked that, in view of the fact that they had had unemployment insurance in Germany since the time of Bismarck . . . he doubted that German prisoners would be very impressed by the fact that Canada had instituted legislation to this end in 1940 and he felt rather inclined to the view that they might even make mock a little of the implication that Canada was a pioneer in this field. [I]n parentheses, I would add that I do not think this picture should be shown outside of Canada. It is even a little naive in England.[44]

Canadian forays into the world arena of political warfare are a fascinating subject, but they bear on the Gouzenko question precisely as an index of the diversion of Canadian intelligence officials from their own government's sovereign interests in this field. The Department of External Affairs' senior officer assigned to propaganda and intelligence, T.A. 'Tommy' Stone, sought to expand Canada's political warfare and propaganda role in Europe at the expense of *domestic* censorship and intelligence functions. Anglophilia, and a desire to be at what he perceived to be the centre of activity, appears to have blinded Stone and Glazebrook to 'realist lizards' lurking in their own camp. Thus, despite his presence in Ottawa on the night of the defection, Stone had been absent during crucial counter-intelligence failures, adding to the lack of preparedness recorded in painter Elizabeth Harrison's perceptive brushwork.[45]

Explanans

Clearly the Canadians were vulnerable, but what are the points that favour the hypothesis that Gouzenko's defection was the product of a British intelligence operation? Since papier mâché history is crafted from mulched documents—often the fate of security intelligence records—unequivocal empirical support for the hypothesis is not immediately available. If definitive records of prior British involvement in the Gouzenko defection exist they are out of reach, locked in classified British archives. The hypothesis forms by piecing together other traces and fragments that are present, and by examining the pattern of absence formed by closed and missing documents.

Why might a British intelligence agency have wished to provoke an espionage crisis in Canada in 1945? An answer to this question forms if one hypothesizes that the eminence grise behind the defection was not William Stephenson, nor even Stewart Menzies per se, but rather Menzies's immediate superior, Winston Churchill, the wartime British Prime Minister whose appetite for covert operations was matched with long experience with security intelligence matters. As David Stafford demonstrates, Churchill's enthusiasm for dirty tricks and sabotage betrayed a certain immaturity and a 'Boy's Own Fiction' approach to the use of intelligence in high politics and war.[46] According to Stafford, operations directly inspired by Churchill tended to misfire, and if the present hypothesis is correct the Gouzenko defection failed in part because it did not produce instant publicity. On any longer view, though, the operation surely must be credited as a brilliant success.

In July 1945 Churchill's first term as Prime Minister ended in a surprise electoral defeat in part because the war-weary British public demurred from his unflagging military attitude—famously, he compared the British Labour Party to a Gestapo.[47] Out on the election stump Churchill, already resigned to post-war East-West tension, found the Ribbentrop-Molotov Pact forgiven or forgotten. Britons warmly credited the Red Army with absorbing the Axis blow and rallying valiantly to rout Hitler's forces. The most important personages graced the platforms at Soviet friendship rallies.

On the other hand, it had been obvious to Churchill for months that from Britain's perspective the West's post-war relations with the Soviet bloc ought to become defensive as soon as possible to curb growing Soviet influence. It appears he relished the thought of renewing the anti-Bolshevik *cordon sanitaire* policed by Menzies's organization during the interwar years. It was a policy that potentially— if the Americans could be induced to endorse it—lent new life to the Empire. But Churchill's paranoia and renewed militarism did not appeal to exhausted Britons turning to rebuild their nearly bankrupt nation.

SIS chief Sir Stewart Menzies forged a close working relationship with Churchill during the crucial years of the war.[48] It was he who supplied the Prime Minister with daily ULTRA briefings on intercepts decoded at Bletchley Park. Churchill's at times amateurish interpretation of raw decrypts provoked irritation in the intelligence services and enmity towards Menzies for placing his personal influence with the Prime Minister above sound intelligence practice. By the summer of 1945, with Tito proving less than malleable in the Balkans and Stalin's cynical betrayal of the Polish Resistance, Churchill and Menzies both swung around to the familiar pre-war anti-Soviet stance. Internally, they began eliminating left-leaning elements in their own services as early as the spring of 1944.[49] After Labour's resurgence in the summer of 1945 there was every reason to jolt public opinion and demonize the 'Soviet friendship' movement.[50]

A biography of Stewart Menzies states erroneously that 'C' left London just twice during the war. The man who 'never went anywhere beyond St. James's unless in the Imperial interest' flew to Algiers in 1942, and climbed to a rooftop to hear an assassin's pistol fire three shots into the stomach of Admiral Darlan below in a nearby building.[51] The Allies had reluctantly embraced the Vichyist Darlan to keep the French fleet out of Axis hands, but this embarrassing association undermined the Allies' credibility with European resistance movements. The unfortunate young assassin, led by his SIS handlers to believe his act would make him a national hero, instead met summary execution. That Stewart Menzies took a personal interest in rectifying the Darlan situation has only one thing to do with Gouzenko: 'C's' presence in Ottawa, too, on the day of what became the most sensational defection of the century. It brings to mind Peter Dwyer's Countess who did 'not relish anticipation which oversteps the limit of what is possible.'

As it transpired, Winston Churchill was far from Downing Street making oil sketches on the shore of Lake Como when Gouzenko absconded with his trove of secret documents in Ottawa. The former Prime Minister could have had no official knowledge of the defection, and yet one gains the impression he was not as isolated as it seems. The Field Marshal's villa where he stayed no doubt had good communications facilities, and a letter from Churchill to his wife mentioning Lord Beaverbrook perhaps intimates advance knowledge of impending events concerning the Soviet Union.

Churchill's friend and rival Max Aitken, Lord Beaverbrook, had struck up surprisingly cordial relations with the Soviets during his characteristically dictatorial stint as Minister for Aircraft Production. A Toronto newspaper put it tactfully, writing that the Canadian-born plutocrat could be in no way considered sympathetic to Communism, but 'Stalin soon discovered in him a kindred spirit who shared his realistic outlook.'[52] Beaverbrook passed the dismal election evening with Churchill, and he was widely blamed for the Conservatives' election defeat. Afterwards, the disconsolate Churchills received his gift of hens for their country residence, Chartwell.

It is Beaverbrook's short but intense interlude of 'Soviet friendship' that makes the phrasing of Winston Churchill's letter to Clementine from Lake Como on 5 September 1945 noteworthy. On the night of Gouzenko's defection Churchill wrote:

> How are the Beaverbrook chickens? *Have they laid any eggs yet? Is there any particular flavour about the eggs that you do not like?* I fear you must be very near the end of the lemon-scented magnolias.[53]

Of course, this is highly speculative, and indeed the reference to Beaverbrook's chickens may strictly concern poultry. But the passage 'Have they laid any eggs yet? Is there any particular flavour . . . you do not like?' sits rather oddly. Recall that in his landscape paintings Churchill did not worry unduly if he gave the horizon a distinct tilt. He was perfectly capable, too, from time to time, of suddenly tilting an opponent's horizon, and perhaps this was the case with Gouzenko's malodorous eggs. Lord Moran, Churchill's doctor, dutifully noted in his diary his patient's declared disinterest in seeing any newspapers, but also that the sidelined statesman devoured them voraciously at every meal. Churchill's mind was fixed on Stalin, wrote Moran, and on Russian conditions. Yet, on the day of Gouzenko's defection, he was suddenly smug, elated even, and that night, for once, he slept soundly.

At the Chateau Montebello the following day, Stewart Menzies's apprehension must have risen at the farce unfolding in downtown Ottawa. His mounting concern that Gouzenko might be recovered by the Soviets perhaps led to intense frustration at the Canadian officials' inaction and particularly the obstructive behaviour of Ottawa police constables McCullough and Walsh. This duo first stopped their 'prowl car' in front of Gouzenko's apartment at 511 Somerset at about nine in the evening, responding to a radio call to attend the 'Kirsanoo' residence in apartment 5.[54] Sergeant Bayfield of the RCMP Special Branch was there watching them from the park across the street, along with a second officer—someone he knew but never publicly identified. (Later Bayfield admitted recognizing by sight some of the British agents involved.)[55] The Gouzenkos themselves had been moving around by means of their back porch and its staircase to the ground until they became aware of being observed from the rear by another agent in a blue suit, a man whose identity also has remained undisclosed. Bayfield recalled that Gouzenko was 'a very frightened boy' by the time the Ottawa police came on the scene.

When Constables McCullough and Walsh entered 511 Somerset they accosted Vitali Pavlov and his associates ransacking the Gouzenkos' apartment (#4). Looking back on the events later, McCullough was struck by two points. First, that his inspector had showed no interest in the intruding embassy officials but rather disappeared straight into the adjacent apartment 5: 'he didn't talk to the Russians at all.' Second, two persons who arrived later claiming to represent the Department of External Affairs demanded that Gouzenko, his wife, and their infant child be released to them so that they could take them to 'the big lodge on the other side of Gatineau'. The two men were so insistent, McCullough told John Sawatsky, that he began to wonder what was behind it:

They were trying to get Gouzenko placed somewhere. The head guy from the Department of External Affairs at that time was there. They wanted to move the Gouzenkos away to Quebec—to the big lodge on the other side of Gatineau.

. . . .

External Affairs wanted to take them away that night. Tom and I wouldn't let them move them at the time. They were trying their damnedest to take Gouzenko over into Quebec to a big lodge there. But they didn't get them because we wouldn't let them take Gouzenko out of the apartment. We didn't know what we were going to do with him. The guy said he was from the Department of External Affairs, but who was he? He didn't show any credentials.[56]

Knowing now that 'C' himself was stationed there, it is hardly surprising that every effort was made to extract the Gouzenkos to Montebello. The whole episode brings to mind Kim Philby's derisive 'fish and game' metaphor in his memoir, *My Silent War*. Although he makes no specific reference to Gouzenko, nor to Menzies's absence from London at the time, he does describe SIS activity during this period as merely 'casting flies' over Soviet and Eastern European diplomatic personnel:

> During my period of service, there was no single case of a consciously con-
> ceived operation against Soviet intelligence bearing fruit. We progressed only
> by means of windfalls that literally threw the stuff on our laps . . . defectors . . .
> who 'chose freedom,' like Kravchenko who, following Krivitsky's example,
> ended up a disillusioned suicide. But was it freedom they sought, or the flesh-
> pots? It is remarkable that not one of them volunteered to stay in position, and
> risk his neck for 'freedom.' One and all, they cut and ran for safety. (134)

Gouzenko's reason to cut and run presumably was his imminent recall to
Moscow, or perhaps it was timely for other reasons—if, for example, certain
British elements sought to set anti-Soviet feelings ablaze. If that was the hope, the
Ottawa Journal quashed it by failing to seize the story, thus leaving an opening for
Prime Minister Mackenzie King to put his clamp on it. There the matter rested,
wrapped in secrecy, stifled by what one *Journal* reporter later called the 'ambiance
of controlled news'.[57]

It is possible that King continued to delay publicizing the matter after his October visit to Britain precisely because he suspected that Churchill had deliberately
visited this diplomatic nightmare on him. The Canadian Prime Minister found it
odd that when he unofficially disclosed the above-top-secret case to Churchill in
October 1945, 'it did not seem to take him by surprise.'[58] Indeed, Churchill seemed
better briefed than Attlee, Britain's new Labour Prime Minister, and mentioned his
plan to make a speech 'of some significance to British-American relations' in Fulton, Missouri. Churchill flattered King, telling him that other Canadian leaders
were 'as children' compared with him, and he added a pointed message: publicize
the Soviet espionage case as soon as possible.[59] To the contrary, King happily
accepted this praise but turned delay to his advantage by using Gouzenko's disclosures to secure the very top-level meetings from which Churchill had excluded him
during the war.[60]

The Canadian Prime Minister found himself the most senior statesman in the tri-
angle with Attlee and Truman, and it appears he put his experience to good use. In
London, 'C' pressed Foreign Secretary Ernest Bevin and Attlee to arrest the suspects without delay, or 'the scent will get very cold.' Bevin was swayed, lobbying
Attlee to agree with his security officers that King's delay went against the
'straightforward course in these cases, namely that the network should be broken
by ordinary legal means and that we should not be afraid of diplomatic repercussions.'[61] Perhaps Attlee suspected that these cases rarely followed any straightforward course but for whatever reason he sided with King, telling Bevin 'it would be
inadvisable to break it prematurely.'[62]

What astonished 'C' and the other security officials involved was King's proposal to present to the Soviet government an opportunity to 'turn over a new leaf'.
The Canadians, British, and Americans would agree to hush up the Gouzenko case
if Russian leaders would 'agree to abandon all these [espionage] activities'. Bevin
reported the general feeling that 'the Canadians have got a bit excited over an issue
of a kind very unfamiliar to them' and that King's ideas were 'unrealistic', to say
the least: 'It is not difficult to imagine what sort of reply the Russians would give to

an invitation to abandon their espionage system, or indeed what reply we ourselves would give in a like case.'

If, like Mackenzie King, rank-and-file Canadians were shocked when they eventually learned of the espionage cases six months following the defection, it cannot be said that the Western intelligence community had been unduly surprised. That NKVD and GRU networks were then operating abroad was well understood within the British intelligence services, who indeed ran their own such networks and routinely intercepted Soviet wireless communications.[63] In the days leading up to Gouzenko's defection the Soviets noticed that the 'greens'—Western counter-intelligence agents—were trying to 'turn' some of their sources, and at about the same time the Americans were close to achieving 'complete encirclement' of the Soviet consulate in New York.[64]

Yet if Churchill and Menzies perhaps possessed means to expose Soviet agents operating in Britain or in the United States, they shied away from anything so directly provocative. *Indirect* means to secure long-term British influence in American policy were preferable. Canada's 'in-between' status as a junior partner in the Anglo-American alliance, along with its full integration in that alliance's media and propaganda circuits, would have recommended Ottawa as an appropriate setting for such an operation. Furthermore, Canada's counter-intelligence capability was disproportionately small in relation to the role its agencies then played in atomic research. To adapt historian Wesley Wark's phrase, Canada's wartime loss of innocence in security intelligence was ripe for a grand dénouement.[65] Inducing a Soviet defection in Canada under the noses of the RCMP presented little difficulty and relatively little risk. At worst, the Canadians would be taught a useful lesson in counter-espionage; at best, it might promote a slide in Western public approval of the Soviet Union at a moment when Britain was being humbled by the US in post-war reconstruction negotiations.

This Was My Choice

If Gouzenko was induced to defect by British operatives, one would have thought that by now the secret would have emerged in secondary accounts. Not necessarily. Few would ever have known for certain, and disclosure of this fact would be especially resisted if Gouzenko, as has been suggested, brought with him more extensive code and cipher information than has been admitted. Such materials have further-reaching implications than simply his naming a number of informants. Indeed, as Bryden speculates, if he brought a code book it may have provided the Venona cryptographers with essential keys that accelerated their decryption of years of intercepted Soviet communications. Each government and security agency, including the GRU, had reasons not to press the matter in public.[66]

In terms of propaganda, disclosure of the full extent of the operation would have undermined the multi-faceted Gouzenko campaign to harden Western attitudes externally against the Soviet Union and internally towards the Left in general.[67] The widely distributed Kellock-Taschereau Royal Commission Report attracted immediate international publicity, but over the longer term the Gouzenkos' serialized articles and books (in addition to Igor's novel, both he and Svetlana each published an autobiography), a Hollywood film, various television appearances, and steady media coverage over the years added up to an unparalleled anti-Soviet propaganda coup.[68] As a result it was virtually impossible for anyone to be heard when they asked what seemed an obvious question: was Gouzenko's motto 'This Was My Choice'—the title of his autobiography—an example of Orwellian doublespeak?

Interviews conducted with Gouzenko's contemporaries in the 1980s by journalist John Sawatsky reveal that both *This Was My Choice* (1948) and Gouzenko's epic novel, *The Fall of a Titan* (1954), were team efforts.[69] Various figures, such as journalist A.W. 'Andy' O'Brien and Mervyn Black, the RCMP's chief Russian translator, wrote parts of these two seminal works of anti-Soviet propaganda. The bulk of *This Was My Choice* describes Igor's upbringing and career prior to his assignment to Ottawa. In each episode Stalin's brutal regime is laid bare, revealing Communism to be a cynical ideological cloak for tyranny. The miserable condition of the Soviet people, half-starved and persecuted by Stalin's secret police, is matched only by their incomprehension of the true freedom available in the West and their own government's implacable campaign to destroy it. Experiencing democratic life while stationed in Ottawa, it strikes Gouzenko that duty to his infant child obliges him to defect and further the fight for freedom.

Certain facts are added to colour Gouzenko's claim that he acted alone, impulsively, and at the last possible minute. For example, he is warned by Colonel Zabotin that British agents have arrived in Ottawa to assist the RCMP's counter-intelligence efforts, and that 'as a cipher clerk, the counter-espionage is liable to become interested in you and make life uncomfortable as well as dangerous.'[70] Other passages seem intent on explaining certain irregularities in his work habits prior to defecting. It is claimed he was meticulously careful in the suspicious embassy environment, assiduous in his work, and often remained at his post after regular hours: 'The tension was severe', he wrote. 'We began locking up loose papers in the safe or in desk drawers even before leaving for a quick visit to the washroom. Several times I returned to the office after being nearly halfway home, just in case I had left some paper on or around my desk'(236).

Where the autobiography is vague about what may have triggered Gouzenko's recall to Moscow, Malcolm MacDonald's memoir recalls that Gouzenko once accidentally left a secret document exposed on his desk, and, although excused by GRU chief Zabotin, the charwoman (an NKVD watcher) spotted the omission and reported it to the 'neighbours'.[71] The autobiography allows that Gouzenko overheard his colleagues discussing Dr Alan Nunn May's meeting in Montreal with his Soviet contact. Nunn May, he learned, was terrified because already he suspected he was being watched by the RCMP. Gouzenko's recall may have been simply a routine staff rotation, but the propaganda writers' intensification of detail around his handling of documents, the specifics of his work schedule, and the activities of British counter-intelligence betray the papier mâché quality of disinformation. The question forms of itself: had Gouzenko pilfered documents for the British prior to 5 September?

Letting pass the internal contradictions, exaggerations, and paranoia that reduce *This Was My Choice* to the level of pulp history, it is important to note its effort to let no doubt accrue as to Gouzenko's motivation, to explain oddities in his behaviour during the period before his defection, and to justify irregularities in his subsequent actions, not least his taking the story directly to the newspapers rather than to the police. He claimed to have feared the RCMP as much as he did the NKVD. Yet if truly he believed that Canada ran its own version of the Soviet police state, why defect? His information included no indication that he should fear Soviet penetration of the RCMP, although this possibility was given great play later by Intrepid's chronicler, William Stevenson. Gouzenko went to the *Ottawa Journal* first, according to the present hypothesis, because his British handlers sought to detonate an anti-Soviet media explosion. If so, they were dupes of their own propaganda extolling the virtues of a free and unfettered Western press.

The Propaganda Voice

In retrospect, the marks of multiple authorship in *This Was My Choice* are obvious. Perhaps they resist effacement because propaganda's 'public voice' eradicates the writer's personal specificity. The autobiographic subject in propaganda notably lacks either the 'fictional' or 'historical' truth that is achieved when a narrative has a fine consistency with the surrounding context.[72] On the one hand, the possibility for 'fictional' truth in *This Was My Choice* evaporates in direct proportion to the difficulty of casting Gouzenko as a hero when equally he was a traitor and an informant.[73] To satisfy fictional truth in this case, the structure of myth requires that Gouzenko make some sacrifice, and probably a fatal one, to resolve the plot. But Gouzenko, by his own admission, became 'a small but happy pebble on the democratic beach', adequately pensioned, 'with the entire security system of a free country ranged solidly behind him' (294, v).

On the other hand, even if the multi-authored 'autobiography' misrepresents certain events, it never was intended to be read as fiction but rather as history. This points up the problem for characterization in propaganda: how to satisfy readers with the complex resonance of 'historical truth' while still meeting propaganda objectives. Historians are ethically obliged to regard their historical characters as *actual subjects*. In the case of Gouzenko's 'autobiography', the unethical aspects of his self-characterization were not directly or solely detrimental to himself as a historical subject, but rather to *readers* drawn to misconstrue his true motivations. This suggests that disinformation is distinguishable from propaganda by the nature of change intended. Disinformation is directed against an object, person, or organization in order to undermine, restrict, or provoke some action affecting that object. In short, it meddles with the *sovereignty of its object*. Propaganda, on the other hand, is specifically directed against *readers*. It seeks to reconstitute their subjectivity through their acts of reading.

The character 'Igor Gouzenko' was the product of both disinformation and propaganda. The disinformation regarding his intentionality (i.e., exaggerating his volunteerism) was essential to the efficiency of the propaganda (i.e., persuading readers to view Gouzenko as a guide for their own conduct). Gouzenko and/or his ghost writers fashioned a character who apparently without outside interference chose a dangerous course because he had come to believe in the liberal capitalist way of life in Canada.

This disinformation meddled with Gouzenko's sovereignty by prescribing his 'free choice'. It also served the broader propaganda objective to cast 'progressivism' as the folly of misrecognized Soviet self-interest. Helping to package the loose coalition of social movements that constituted North American progressivism as *unpatriotic* was the central propaganda achievement of the Gouzenko revelations, even though it flew in the face of Gouzenko's rather ambiguous status in this regard. In fact, the character 'Gouzenko' in *This Was My Choice* sits uneasily with the man described by friends and acquaintances. Leslie McKechnie came to know the defector well and later remarked, 'I always wondered how he had the courage to defect. Because he didn't look the type.'[74]

In his cabin on the *Queen Elizabeth*, steaming across the North Atlantic to America on the last day of October 1948, Mackenzie King 'read for some little time from Gouzenko's book "I Chose Freedom"':

> It is a book everyone should read. Very revealing ... of Russian communist methods. The more I think of it, the more it seems to me that it has come about through Canada having opened her legations and subsequently Gouzenko's actions and disclosures of what he saw in true Democracy in Canada, that our country would have been the spearhead to free the Nations of communist activity.[75]

King's syntax leaves the meaning of this entry a little obscure. One gathers that, after three years, he felt that he had recuperated the Gouzenko case for Canada's national interest. The sting of surprise had settled into a tone of self-congratulation. Through a lucky chance King had seized the propaganda spearhead from the British and claimed for himself and for Canada the distinction of freeing 'the Nations' from Communist activity.

Further down the chain of responsibility, though, Lester Pearson and G.G. 'Bill' Crean had treated the production of Gouzenko's autobiography with great caution. In late 1946, Pearson thought Crean 'would have to be pretty discreet' in disclosing any information to would-be ghost writers of Gouzenko's story and counselled against providing them with direct access to the principals in the case or to the primary documentation.[76]

The genre of ghost-written defector narratives reached its dubious apotheosis a decade later with the Petrov case in Australia. This parallels the Gouzenko affair, not least because it is widely thought to have fractured the Australian Left for a generation or more. Vladimir and Evdokia Petrov's *Empire of Fear* (1956) likely owed its commercial failure to its cloying portrayal of an unflappable Australian intelligence service smoothly masterminding the defection. Robbed of any vestige of heroism, Vladimir Petrov is characterized as an amateurish and ineffective agent lucky to have such enterprising Australian friends (it is his wife Evdokia who achieves a moment of real drama by defecting only at the last possible moment, at the Darwin air terminal, where she is strong-armed away from the burly Soviet couriers escorting her home). This celebration of Australian Cold War security casts light on the Gouzenko case of a decade earlier inasmuch as the Petrovs' defection narrative so obviously wants readers to appreciate that the Aussies engineered *their* Soviet defection just as effectively as if the British had done it for them.[77]

The Fall of a Titan

Gouzenko's novel *The Fall of a Titan* takes the same crude anti-Soviet propaganda line, but here it is underscored by an oblique self-reflexivity lacking in the autobiography published six years earlier. *The Fall of a Titan* won a Governor-General's Award for Gouzenko in 1954 and by any measure it was a highly successful first novel.[78] Of particular interest here is its almost obsessive concern with the processing of disinformation in national history. Gouzenko's protagonist, Feodor Novikov, is a young historian whose spectacular rise to academic prominence is orchestrated by the NKVD as a means to silence the national poet, Mikhail Gorin.[79] Novikov is not only their informant and operative, but he has no professional objections to 'remaking history' for propaganda purposes. During a Party official's speech, Gouzenko writes:

> They all realized that they were present at the remaking of history. The expression on their faces became strange, not so much surprised as embarrassed, or perhaps wary . . . [for] after the remaking of history follows a purge. . . . Feverishly [Feodor] began to search his past for the least hint, for the smallest reason why he might be in the path of this remaking of history. But his whole career was concerned with ancient history; he had nothing to fear. He looked at Gorin with interest. 'Will he swallow this lie like all the others?'[80]

The novel hints, on one hand, that history is subject to manipulation (suggesting implicitly that Gouzenko as author knew more than he disclosed about his own place in history); on the other hand, it recasts the Soviet project as a self-interested nation, conforming to the principle of nationality while disguising itself in a cloak of world Communism. Gouzenko's readers learn not only that the Bolsheviks' Marxism secreted an intense nationalism, but that it had done so from 1917 on. His conclusion? Any sympathy for Marxism in the West willy-nilly supports not international socialism but the belligerent Russian nation-state.[81]

Feodor Novikov's ruthless intrigues outclass the politics in most university departments, fictional or real. With NKVD help he navigates his 'brilliant' thesis *On the Sources and Origins of Ancient Slav Culture* past the ossified Academic Council to win lofty favour in the Politburo itself. Anticipating a shift in the Party's orientation, Novikov 'proves' that the Russian Empire was born of an ancient Slav culture 'conceived in the south of Russia' far from Western influences. 'While all the historians around him were still beating the old drum, Novikov suddenly introduced a new and startling rhythm', exposing the orthodox accounts as mere inventions and 'fairy tales' (77).

Stalin takes a personal interest in Novikov's career: 'Give him plenty of help. In everything.' His deputies are told:

I know that many historians disparage him among themselves, because he is breaking the faith with established truth. But that, I think, is tommyrot. Truth! Truth! What good is it to people who have convictions? From people such as Novikov all young specialists should take an example. (219)

Stalin's endorsement dissolves the university director's former condescension and aloofness towards the neophyte lecturer. Now the man fawns over Novikov, names him a full professor, and of course soon must concede him his directorship. The price of such swift ascent emerges in Stalin's ominous wish, conveyed through the NKVD, that Novikov befriend the eminent writer and poet, Gorin. Cynically, he courts and later rejects the poet's daughter and in the novel's climax he suppresses self-disgust and obeys the instruction to murder Gorin. Thus falls the 'Titan' of Russian letters who personified the conscience of the nation, brutally silenced by Stalin's favoured historian.[82]

Gouzenko's readers are estranged from Novikov, whom they witness suspending his humane or liberal inclinations. But by positioning the reader within Novikov's divided consciousness the text opens up an unintended reading of the historian's relations with the secret police, showing how each supports the other in propagating certain misrepresentations of the past. Irresistibly, for students of Canadian historiography, the novel brings to mind Professor George Glazebrook, the University of Toronto historian whose ascendancy in Canada's intelligence-censorship-propaganda complex coincided with the novel's publication in 1954.[83]

There is no available evidence that Glazebrook took a personal hand in the production of *The Fall of a Titan*, but doubtless it was a matter of interest to him as Head of External Affairs' Defence Liaison (2), Director of Communications Security, Chairman of the Psychological Warfare Committee, and member of the Committee on Censorship Planning. J.L. Granatstein records a memorable exchange with Glazebrook concerning the latter's role during the wartime years:

The method of operation was that Stone and Glazebrook saw Robertson to seek his permission to do some particular job. Robertson offered his comments, almost always helpful, and assented or refused. Nothing was written down. Intelligence, said Glazebrook, 'is handled like no other subject. It's purely personal and almost entirely oral.'[84]

As the testament of one professional historian to another this is a remarkable statement. The historical value of the 'purely personal and almost entirely oral' is weak at best.[85] Glazebrook's bare-faced lie to Sawatsky regarding the presence of William Stephenson at the Royal Ottawa Golf Club on 6 September 1945 changes its terms altogether: 'I have a photographic memory of Robertson and Stephenson sitting on a sofa', he said, 'and Stephenson having [Gouzenko's] story told to him for the first time. Later on he went and hid behind the bushes, watching the building where Gouzenko was hiding.'[86] With this statement Glazebrook disclosed a megalomania, perhaps peculiar to historians, that quests not for an omniscient 'total history' but rather subverts and if necessary reinvents historical signs to *influence* historical events as well as to chronicle and interpret them. Like Gouzenko's Feodor Novikov, George Glazebrook audaciously blended his authority as a historian with his prejudice as a historical actor.

One of Gouzenko's minor characters, Alexei, is a 'literary man' who only imperfectly controls his dissident impulses. Over dinner Alexei jabs at Feodor Novikov, 'I have always thought that historians described revolutions but did not make them.' Novikov agrees coldly that the 'task of historians is to write about facts of the past, and not to imagine them.' But then, Novikov adds, often historians tend merely 'to repeat each other':

> 'As you know, frequent repetition is still not evidence of truth. Particularly when the disclosure of new historical facts—'
>
> 'Have you uncovered such facts?' Alexei asked him outright. Red spots suddenly appeared on his cheeks. . . .
>
> 'Yes some facts have been uncovered. But most of them were known long ago. Only they were concealed or presented in a distorted form. No, I haven't made any revolution. I have simply re-examined the facts.'[87]

Feodor Novikov rises in the Academy of Soviet Russia because at once he controls the representation of the past while having direct access to unseen forces that shape the future. His condescension toward Alexei and 'literary people' in general is part of a deadly disciplinary rivalry coursing through *The Fall of a Titan*. Writers and poets are fatally disconnected from the empirical realm, condemned to an endless and endlessly dangerous 'sputtering of saliva and quotations of Shakespeare and Pushkin' (99). The competition within the academy for influence in affairs of state pits the emotive force of literature against the empirical and conceptual authority of social science. The frostily analytical Novikov encounters the passionate and moralistic Gorin over the chessboard to play out an epic struggle between history and literature, witnessed by the architect Shchusev.

This 'simple game of chess' becomes 'a satanic game with fate itself', and Novikov's opening move claims the game for his discipline: 'History and chess', he remarks, 'are very much alike.' Gorin counters, pointing out that in history 'all the moves have been made' whereas the essence of chess 'lies in creative work, in the knowledge that one can alter its course. The game of history, unfortunately, one can only contemplate.' Novikov responds by defending history as a science 'always moving forward, developing and each day drawing nearer to its goal—the highest objectivity'. History *does* require creativity, he maintains, and is not merely retrospective contemplation. Gorin is unmoved. He holds up a castle and asks, 'What about historical facts? . . . What more can you do than contemplate them?' (189) 'Only in fantastic novels can scientists alter the past.' Tiring of these manoeuvres, Novikov takes the upper hand on the board and in the conversation with a move to doctrine: 'Marxism defends Partyism from the historian, to understand it as the highest form of objectivity, to repudiate the acceptance of apparent facts' (191). Gorin is thus right to view historical facts as chess pieces to be 'combined and moved around without end'. Facing checkmate, the poet is suddenly plaintive: 'we writers, artists, what should we do?' Novikov relents just slightly, allowing that 'the intuition of the artist is sometimes worth the logic of the man of science.' But this does not appeal to the architect Shchusev, who interjects that artistic intuition combined with precise historical procedure 'wouldn't be history, but porridge.'

The novel's engagement with the venerable problems of historical objectivity and history's relation to literature has greater sophistication than is required either for its plot or for its propaganda message. Gouzenko introduces an intertextual dissonance that inevitably frets at the veracity of his own legend. This is exacerbated by making a literary hoax crucial to the novel's plot development.

The discovery of a lost 1907 manuscript miraculously proves Stalin's anticipation by two years of Lenin's thesis in *Materialism and Emperiocriticism*. The unveiling of Stalin's early treatise occurs in an atmosphere of strained belief at a gathering in a magnificent new archive, an edifice that Feodor Novikov suddenly understands was built purposely for 'the discovery of Stalin's work' (139). Even the cynical Novikov marvels how 'History is being changed before my eyes.' He cannot suppress theorizing about how the Soviet intelligence-censorship-propaganda complex has created a society where survival depends on dodging a scapegoating mechanism run amok. Moreover, it strikes him that whatever might appear in the dubious realm of government information, *architecture* itself cannot lie (117).

Not everyone involved was prepared to go so far as George Glazebrook in propagating disinformation concerning the Gouzenko case. Malcolm MacDonald, former High Commissioner, does not affirm William Stephenson's presence in Ottawa but simply refers to 'a senior figure in the British secret service'.[88] Charles Rivett-Carnac of the RCMP Special Branch is even more circumspect. His leaden and self-absorbed memoir, *Pursuit in the Wilderness*, contains just one quotation from another work, a lengthy passage setting out the circumstances of Gouzenko's defection in the words of none other than H. Montgomery Hyde, Stephenson's appointed scribe.[89] Joe Garner reported merely that Gouzenko 'escaped' the Soviet embassy and that MacDonald's deep involvement in the case 'provided an apposite example of the close understanding between Canada and Britain in an unfamiliar situation.'[90] Other insiders, such as Peter Dwyer, chose to leave no written memoir of the case at all. In his 1952 course for government security officers he allowed that Colonel Zabotin was overconfident in believing he could safely run agents directly without employing an 'illegal resident' to act as intermediary.[91] Dwyer's only public comment occurred in a 1960s television interview, and it is curious in light of Gouzenko's apparent fascination with the use of toilet tanks in public washrooms as dead letter drops and Dwyer's penchant for coded allegory. Yes, Dwyer grinned, Gouzenko had information that led to the arrest of Alan Nunn May, but 'the rest was crap.'[92]

Primary Records

If the secondary accounts leave some doubt as to the reliability of Gouzenko's story, available primary records weaken it further. These records will be treated as three classes: inconsistencies, hidden agendas, and absences.

Inconsistencies

Among the files I was given by accident in April 1997 at the National Archives of Canada was a file called 'Request of U.S. Sub-Committee on Internal Security to interview Igor Gouzenko'.[93] Lester Pearson, as was seen in the previous chapter, was forced to capitulate to the Americans' request to interview the defector, but it was a Pyrrhic victory for Jenner's publicity-hungry subcommittee. With little choice but to accept the Canadians' terms, they met Gouzenko in conditions of utter secrecy and under a media blackout. The American investigators agreed to limitations on the nature of their questions and to the mediation of Gouzenko's responses through the auspices of a Canadian chairman. The venue provided by the Canadians for the meeting was the Seigniory Club at Montebello, Quebec, the 'big lodge on the other side of Gatineau'. More specifically, they met in the Manoir Papineau, the old Seigniory itself nestled in the tall pines on a point a few hundred metres downstream from the famous Chateau.

The Chateau Montebello is an architectural curio, a massive log structure with a central vaulting tower with bedroom wings projecting from it like spokes from the hub of a wheel. It was built in 1930 almost exactly on the original penitentiary plan, an elaboration of Bentham's panopticon design that permitted surveillance from the centre tower down each corridor of cells. Of course, this floor plan was the Chateau's only resemblance to a penal environment. With its famous golf course and wilderness hunting range, in every other respect it was a luxurious and highly exclusive resort—exclusive to the point that the membership page in its handsome promotional booklet stated outright that 'racial and social restrictions apply'.[94]

During the war anti-Semitism marred the Seigniory Club visits of American high officials, and the policy persisted even in 1962.[95] Throughout the Cold War an annual meeting on Canadian Information Abroad was sponsored at the Seigniory Club by the Information Division of External Affairs. These luxurious encounters of 30 or 40 top communications officers, held in secret, refined the government information officials' personal contacts in the realm of news media and corporate communications. At the 1962 meeting *Star Weekly* editor John Clare voiced a concern that cropped up from time to time over the years, deeming it 'ironically inappropriate for a conference called to discuss Canada's image abroad to meet in a club that does not welcome Canadians of all religions and racial backgrounds.' Nothing was said about this in veteran diplomat Marcel Cadieux's keynote address, but Clare added, facetiously: 'perhaps it is a good idea that the proceedings are secret, in case word of this somehow got overseas and became part of our image.'[96]

Insofar as these elites were concerned, historian Chad Gaffield's apt description of eastern Ontario as the 'buckle of the bilingual belt' is geographically misplaced.[97] The intersection of French and English political cultures occurred not in the low-lying farmland south of the Ottawa River but rather on its north shore, in the forested hills cradling the Seigniory Club. The exclusivity of that club, and also its American origins and affiliations, fused a socio-political accommodation in which French-English differences receded in favour of complacent class interests and corporate dynastic genealogies. The companionable qualities of secrecy and exclusivity made Montebello a wilderness annex of metropolitan club land, and a haven for the intelligence brethren.[98]

It would be possible to pass over these unpleasant aspects of the Chateau Montebello, whose days of extreme exclusivity ended when the operation was taken over by Canadian Pacific in 1970, had it not served as base camp for the Gouzenko adventure. The decision to interview Gouzenko at the Seigniory Club in December 1953 resonates with the presence there of Stewart Menzies, the SIS chief, at the time of the 1945 defection.[99] In 1953 it presented obvious advantages of comfort, seclusion, security, and close proximity to Ottawa (it was an easy two-hour drive), but still well outside the 25-mile radius around Ottawa beyond which Soviet embassy staff required permission to travel. It had the merit, too, of special secure phone lines running directly to the East Block in Ottawa, whose privacy was ensured by Bell Canada.[100]

By the time Igor Gouzenko arrived at Montebello in an RCMP motorcade he was highly agitated and fearful that an attempt would be made on his life. His insistence first on bringing a young student with him from Toronto as a witness and then on switching cars just before entering the Montebello grounds struck his RCMP handlers as bizarre precautions. One wonders if he truly feared assassination by his former *Soviet* employers.[101] As it turned out, he arrived without incident. After keeping the assembly waiting for some minutes he finally took his place at one end of a table presided over by Canadian Judge James C. McRuer, flanked by Bill Crean. The Americans had accepted Pearson's condition that only Senators Jenner and McCarran and their counsel Robert Morris attend; the RCMP was represented by Mark McClung, the Justice Department by David Mundell, and External Affairs by Arnold Smith.[102]

Later McClung scoffed that the entire process was an embarrassment and that Gouzenko, as predicted, had absolutely nothing new to add.[103] Indeed, the transcript of the proceedings records a very different Gouzenko from the assertive man portrayed in the Kellock-Taschereau Report. Shy, faltering, and mumbling, he seemed intent only on pointing out that richer incentives would surely entice more Soviet embassy staff members to defect. This was hardly riveting testimony from a man who had shaken the world seven years earlier. That is, except for one small inconsistency. At one point Gouzenko blurted out that he had told 'them'— a group whose identity passed unspecified—that 'they must go in and get the other cipher clerk.' That is, as the GRU's clerk, Gouzenko had no access to NKVD traffic. Soviet espionage in Canada would have suffered an even more severe setback, he said, if Vitali Pavlov's cipher clerk, Farafontov, had been induced to reveal the NKVD's networks.[104]

Two questions are likely to strike the reader of this testimony. When could Gouzenko reasonably have made this suggestion except *before* his defection? And to whom might 'them' refer except British Intelligence? Once Gouzenko fled the cipher room with secret documents it was nonsensical to suggest either to the RCMP or to anyone else that a second cipher clerk might be induced to defect from the same embassy. Setting aside the unconvincing argument that Farafontov lacked diplomatic immunity and could have been arrested, Gouzenko's statement at

Montebello is intelligible only if it referred to a discussion prior to the defection, and it recalls obvious seams in Gouzenko's testimony before the Royal Commission in May 1946.

In one instance, speaking through RCMP interpreter Mervyn Black, Gouzenko responded to the commissioners' invitation to ask any questions or introduce any other matters not already raised in the proceedings:

> GOUZENKO: I can't think of anything now . . . but just something occurred in my mind which I told Mr. Black I wished to tell you, and to tell people. I still worry, and I just expressed surprise to Mr. Black that there were not taken steps to expose the NKVD system and other systems.
> Q. What steps would you have in mind?
> MR COMMISSIONER TASCHEREAU: Mr. Williams, I think if the witness tells us exactly what he knows about the NKVD, as to steps, we will see to that.
> THE WITNESS: Of course I do not think it is up to the Commission. First I asked Mr. Black to arrange some more or less private conversations—
> MR COMMISSIONER TASCHEREAU: I would not like to hear the witness on that, I think, Mr. Williams. [105]

Taschereau cut short Gouzenko before he ventured into a more secret layer of discourse than is reflected in these transcripts, themselves 'top secret' and kept under wraps for 35 years. The second commissioner, Kellock, subsequently steered the matter of NKVD cipher clerks off in a harmless direction.

Is it plausible that Gouzenko suggested his idea of turning an NKVD cipher clerk to someone prior to 5 September 1945? It seems possible that he did.[106] That it might have been an agent of the Canadian government hardly seems likely. From all the available evidence one must agree with J.L. Granatstein that the surprise of Canadian officials on all levels was genuine, as was their initial reluctance even to accept Gouzenko into custody. Given the architecture of the situation it is difficult to imagine that the relevant party was of any other stripe than British.

Would Deputy Registrar Kathleen Willsher not have learned of this counter-intelligence fly-casting over Soviet cipher personnel? Joe Garner appeared before the Commission to describe security arrangements in the British High Commission and the extent of Willsher's access to classified documents. He allowed that although she read materials held in the 'lower vault', the 'upper vault' was out of bounds to all except the most senior officials and its contents were circulated in locked blue boxes. Willsher herself explained that *above-top-secret* communications bypassed the registry altogether. Garner easily diverted the commissioners' curiosity about the purpose of the upper vault, the locked blue boxes, and above-top-secret communications; his testimony concluded without these subjects arising again.

The British Mission celebrated the opening of the Canadian Parliament with a garden party on the afternoon of 7 September 1945. The previous night Pavlov and the others had broken into Gouzenko's apartment only to be discovered and detained by the Ottawa police. The next day, High Commissioner Malcolm MacDonald greeted Soviet Ambassador Zaroubin: 'You look as if you'd been out fishing all night. The fish can't have been biting.' MacDonald records that Pavlov, who was accompanying the ambassador, 'looked startled'.[107] This supercilious remark was later explained away merely as MacDonald's uncanny power of observation. By his own account, he did not know about the defection until Norman Robertson's phone message reached him 'a few minutes later'. Or is this yet another instance of anticipation that oversteps the limit of what is possible?

Hidden Agendas

Next are the deeper implications of Peter Dwyer's backstage activities in Ottawa in January 1946 concerning Harry Dexter White, senior US Treasury official and suspected Soviet informant. Information presented in the previous chapter definitively identifies Dwyer as the mysterious 'Canadian source' who tipped off J. Edgar Hoover regarding Harry Dexter White's appointment to the International Monetary Fund in 1946. The FBI chief, it will be recalled, jolted the Canadian government in 1953 by revealing, in an ingeniously deceptive manner, that *Canada* had been the source for doubts regarding White's loyalty. Dwyer, of course, was neither Canadian nor in Canada's employ in 1946, but his role in the matter suggests several points that concern the Gouzenko affair.

The Careful Silence of Peter Dwyer

Foremost, Dwyer's role in regard to the Harry Dexter White issue shows that he was eminently capable of pursuing a separate British agenda not disclosed to top Canadian decision-makers. In 1953, RCMP Commissioner 'Nick' Nicholson maintained closer relations to the External Affairs intelligence set-up than did his predecessor, S.T. Wood, and undoubtedly he was truthful in a memorandum to Lester Pearson professing the RCMP's inability to trace the source of information purportedly given to Hoover. The text of a top-secret telegram sent by Peter Dwyer (accidentally released to me, as described earlier in this chapter) does suggest that he may have confided information regarding Harry Dexter White to some intimate RCMP counterpart who kept the matter to himself.

Within the Department of External Affairs the Harry Dexter White intrigue clearly came as a surprise to Arnold Smith, George Glazebrook, and Bill Crean. The crucial point is that in January 1946, when Dwyer had the information about White's appointment, he was in almost daily contact with these Canadian officials. Why did he conceal it from them? When he very reluctantly admitted to it, and presumably turned over his original telegram, why was his memory so faulty?

One possible answer to this riddle is that Dwyer feared disclosing any information that might indicate pre-defection contacts with Gouzenko. If the British initially withheld any information passed to them by the cipher clerk prior to 5 September 1945, this material could not subsequently be introduced into the Canadian inquiries. Dwyer's incomplete recollection of the exact circumstances of his Harry Dexter White telegram, and his careful suggestion that perhaps it was inspired by Sir William Stephenson (a default figure to whom such mysteries seem to be magnetically drawn), at the minimum leaves some doubt about the reasons for his reticence.[108]

By 1953, in addition to Dwyer, at least Pearson, St Laurent, Robertson, Pickers-gill, and Glazebrook likely knew or strongly suspected an ulterior British hand behind Gouzenko's defection. Others around them might have deduced this, too. Bill Crean's telex to 'C' regarding Harry Dexter White leaves no doubt they would protect such secrets. If this handful of Ottawa officials had become keepers of Britain's Gouzenko secret it explains their consternation when possible connections between Harry Dexter White and Igor Gouzenko were mooted openly in the press in November 1953. Their concern was such that Norman Robertson returned from London to help with the crisis. Robertson brought only one thing not already available to Pearson's competent team of officials: an encyclopedic grasp of the true facts of the Gouzenko case as opposed to the layers of disinformation it had accumulated. Robertson was best equipped to sort out the myriad implications for Canada's foreign relations if unruly committees south of the border somehow prodded Gouzenko to reveal these concealed facts.

The slight tone of irritation in the Canadian's telegram to 'C' is consistent with the sting Robertson must have felt from the very moment he began to equate Menzies's presence at the Seigniory Club on 6 September 1945 with having been the dupe of British SIS in his own capital. If Robertson nearly suffered a nervous breakdown over the Gouzenko defection it must have come as a further blow in 1953 to learn that Peter Dwyer, his hand-picked internal security specialist, had kept him in the dark about Harry Dexter White in 1946. On the other hand, Pearson's gentle treatment of Dwyer suggests that a view was taken that he had merely followed orders.

Other Oddities

Another file in External Affairs' top secret 'small "s"' series contains a brief correspondence that evokes the neurotic ' "state" within the state', wherein madness can lift constraints on truth-speaking. In the 'Klaus Julius Emil Fuchs' file are three handwritten letters dated in May 1950 from an unemployed aviation mechanic, James Stephens, of 931 Cathedral Street in Montreal, who claimed to have secret knowledge of the Gouzenko case.[109]

Stephens read in a newspaper report that a British MP had demanded to know why British Security Services failed to notice Klaus Fuchs's name when it first surfaced in the Gouzenko evidence, and wondered if perhaps the Canadian government had suppressed this information. Stephens wrote to Lester Pearson advising him that the British knew more than they were saying, because he had supplied them with a crucial piece of intelligence prior to September 1945:

Allow me to inform you that Scotland Yard got their information from Somerset House. From a friend of mine who was a clerk there. I told him that the top men who the government was employing for Atomic Energy Research would still have their hatred for the British and would he consult his chief at Somerset House to ask Scotland Yard to have them watch[ed]. As he would make one false move and they would have to watch him for a long time as he would go to the Russian Embassy. And then to go in and get him. My friend['s] name was William Hoitt.

Now the denial of the Labour Attorney General in the British House of Commons that no information had been obtain[ed] from Canada (Written in Hansard) And then his retraction of that statement for the benefit of the Intelligence Service afterwards [is] stealing another cake. As I am the man who told to consult his chief at Somerset House. I am the writer of the letter that went through the post (Censor) to Bristol and on to Scotland Yard. When the present Prime Minister, the Rt. Hon. Mr. St. Laurent was Minister of Internal and External Affairs in the Rt. Hon. Mackenzie King's Government. The substance of the letter was written thus.

Dear Lilian and Clara
Etc. Etc. Etc.
    Stop

Commence.
Now the Russians are getting hold of the Atomic Energy Secrets. And theirs a Canadian Member of Parliament envolved in it, and others. And if they want any more information they will have to go in and get the Russian Chyper [sic] Clerk. As theirs not a Socialist or Communist has cannot be bought by a good job or Gold. You can let Scotland Yard have this letter if you like. Hoping everything is alright in Bristol.

Now I went to the R.C.M.P and ask the Serg. in charge of the subservid [sic] squad to get me an interview with Chief Commissioner. But he refused. As he stated if I had read the papers I would have read that they caught [Gouzenko] going round to Newspaper Editors offering the information. But the present Prime Minister know's where the real information came from. And the Serg. ask me to bring him some nice cake like that.
Well if Canada can look after a Russian, Canada can certainly help me.[110]

George Glazebrook did not file a copy of his initial reply to this strange missive. Whatever he wrote did not satisfy Stephens, who provided further 'cake' in a second letter stating his knowledge that secret wireless personnel were trained at 'the old Restanton Home on Queen Mary Road'. Stephens believed that his wartime achievements warranted Pearson's obtaining him employment, as his benefit was shortly to run out. Replying over Arnold Heeney's signature, Glazebrook suggested that Stephens 'get in touch with the local office of the Department of Labour'.[111]
    Glazebrook's brush-off of Stephens as a crank is not surprising. If a kernel of truth lay behind Stephens's allegations, clearly he was not a man whose tale would be widely credited. On the other hand, Glazebrook handled the matter personally during a very busy period. Moreover, he took the precaution of placing Stephens's letters in a top-secret file rather than in a file for crank correspondence. This 'top-secret' designation removed the letters to the highest known category of confidentiality. He assigned them to his working file on the Klaus Fuchs case.
    In fact, James Stephens's correspondence arrived at an irritating moment for Glazebrook, just as he was piecing together the Canadian government's acquisition

of knowledge concerning Klaus Fuchs. It had become public knowledge that Fuchs's name had appeared in Israel Halperin's notebook, seized during the Gouzenko espionage inquiries in 1946.[112] This information cast further doubts on the reliability of MI5 and MI6, whose remaining credibility with the Americans would shortly evaporate when Soviet moles Guy Burgess and Donald Maclean bolted to Moscow in 1951.

Had the Canadian government failed to pass on Fuchs's name in 1946? If it had been passed on, why had the British failed to notice the connection and as a result left Fuchs in place until late 1949? Pearson fielded such questions while Glazebrook rifled the files searching for facts. Oddly enough, MI5 staff in London were unable to find any references to Halperin's notebook in their own files. The British Foreign Office formally requested clarification from Canadian External Affairs regarding what, if any, information from the notebook was provided to their own intelligence services during the espionage inquiries.

As best as Glazebrook could discern, both MI6's Peter Dwyer and the FBI's Lish Whitson were apprised of and given free access to the notebook throughout the inquiries. As the Canadians were not party to the actual reports sent back to London or Washington, he could not determine if Fuchs's name had been noticed. It was pointed out that evidence seized from the suspects filled an entire room. If, in retrospect, the notebook entry of Fuchs's name seemed an obvious oversight, at the time it was just one particular in a huge assemblage of data. Only later, after decrypts permitted Dwyer and his associates to deduce Fuchs's guilt, did it stand out from the background. This rather inadequate explanation was the best Glazebrook could offer.

There is a circular connection here between Dwyer's use of decrypts in the Fuchs case in 1949 and Gouzenko's presumed assistance in breaking Soviet ciphers. Stephens's correspondence touched on both matters, although his central claim was to have supplied British authorities with the tip regarding the cipher clerk. Did Glazebrook have knowledge that Gouzenko's cipher information contributed to the eventual capture of Fuchs? If so, any disclosure linking Gouzenko to Fuchs's capture risked exposing the extent of Soviet vulnerability to Western cryptography. At that moment, the slight possibility of Stephens succeeding in reopening these questions was taken seriously by Glazebrook in the immediate context of the Fuchs case.

Shielding the Gouzenkos

The occupants of 511 Somerset were told to keep quiet about the events of 5–6 September, and for several months afterwards their building was kept under police surveillance.[113] Some of the residents later spoke of these events but never those principally involved, Frances and Edwin Elliott, whose apartment was used by the Gouzenkos during the defection. The only direct record of their involvement lies in the Mackenzie King Papers and it raises further questions about the received version of events.

Frances Elliott was a nervous woman suffering chronic health problems. Supposedly, she ventured to shelter the defectors in her apartment across the landing at number 6. She evidently witnessed at least some of the exchanges between the various police and intelligence representatives present that night. Her testimony before the Royal Commission and at trials of the espionage suspects caused her significant stress. On 25 March 1946, after news of the case had broken publicly, her husband Edwin wrote to Mackenzie King:

> As you no doubt are aware Mrs. Elliott afforded protection to Mr. and Mrs. Gouzenko and child, on the night of September 6th, 1945 when they were desperate and in need of a friend. The incident occurred when I was out of town on Government business. All the excitement and worry happened at period when Mrs. Elliott should have been resting as much as possible. I know that this affair with its responsibilities has aggravated her condition so much that the ailment has to be, on the advice of her Medical Adviser, corrected, and that an operation is necessary. Mrs. Elliott acted as any good Canadian soldier would—the result of which she is subject to ill health, and carries a load of worries. I can definitely state Mrs. Elliott's physical condition has deteriorated rapidly in the last seven months. . . . Her condition has been hastened by the strain and worry of the Gouzenko case.
>
> If your Government could, in some way, absorb the expense of Mrs. Elliott's medical treatments and the added cost of a trip, everything would be allright. This would be a great relief to us. If this is not possible I offer the following suggestions—that I be granted a War Duty Supplement of at least $60.00 per month, retroactive to April 1st, 1945. . . . There may be other possibilities, such as a new permanent position at $700.00 per annum more than I am now receiving. I am well known to your colleague, Honourable J.J. McCann . . . at my home town, Kingston, Ontario.[114]

It took more than two months for King's secretary to reply coolly that 'Mr. King has asked me to express his sympathy [but] he is afraid there is no way in which it would be possible for the government to make available any assistance.'
Elliott immediately responded with greater force:

> It was very appropriate that you tended your sympathy but sympathy will not pay for medical treatments. . . . I would suggest that you reconsider the case. There is always a solution for every problem. . . . You place me in an awkward position as *there is an oath to be considered* and I cannot discuss the contents of my letter of the 25th with senior officials in my division. *I wrote you fully aware that you knew all the details of the case and did not divulge any secrets.* I do not know of any way in which I can request a War Duty Supplement *without breaking certain confidences.* You place the onus of trying to obtain adjustments solely on myself. I feel doing as Mrs. Elliott did there should be some assistance coming from your office. Perhaps it would have been better to allow the Foreign Agents to get hold of the Star Witness or allow him to carry out the plan he had in mind rather than risk the health of Mrs. Elliott, but in the interest of Canadians and Canada she stepped into the breach and as a result has suffered impaired health.

I am fully aware that the least written about this subject the better and I would like to suggest that you contact Mr. L.J. Trottier, Chairman of the Unemployment Insurance Commission, outlining the reasons why in the interest of the writer consideration should be given to a War Duty Supplement, retroactive to April 1st, 1946. I will take no action until I hear from the Chairman of the Commission.[115]

The passages I have emphasized are puzzling, given that this letter was written after the case was made public. They make sense only if Mr and Mrs Elliott had been exposed to a deeper layer of secrets surrounding the case. The cautious reply reiterated 'that you follow my suggestion contained in my letter to you of the 6th of May' to contact the pensions bureau directly. Yet the matter was not left there. Behind the scenes Igor Gouzenko (whose staunch refusal to remunerate his RCMP ghost writer, Mervyn Black, purportedly prompted the latter's fatal heart attack) freely gave the Elliotts $550 from his book royalties.[116] Furthermore, in Mackenzie King's file is a personal letter of January 1949 from Edwin Elliott to J.W. McConnell, publisher of the *Montreal Star*:

It is with grateful appreciation and heartfelt thanks that I, on behalf of my wife, Frances Doris Elliott, acknowledge the information that on January 28th you deposited at the Civic Hospital, Ottawa, your cheque for $1000.00 to take care of present and future medical and hospital expenses in connection with her illness. . . . In affording protection to the Gouzenko family [Mrs. Elliott] did what any good Canadian mother and housewife would have done. . . . It was not this action which accelerated her malady, but the great emotional strain of appearing before the Royal Commission and spy trials in Montreal. . . . Your kind consideration is now doubly appreciated as it gives us much needed moral support, coming as it does from an interested Canadian citizen.[117]

These moneys flowing through unofficial channels suggest that steps were taken to quiet the Elliotts down. No doubt Mrs Elliott's ailment was genuine. One can only imagine the stress placed upon her if in fact she was bound by some prior and secret oath to testify incompletely either before the Royal Commission or in court during the subsequent spy trials.

Absences and Withholding

The status of government information concerning the Gouzenko affair might best be described as one of selective withholding. Files recording attitudes and decisions of key Canadian officials in the RCMP, the Privy Council Office, the Prime Minister's Office, and the Departments of Justice and External Affairs even after 50 years simply are not available. On the other hand, there is a surfeit of relatively innocuous material, some of it published by Professors Bothwell and Granatstein in *The Gouzenko Transcripts*. Certain files have been opened that provide insight into the Gouzenko propaganda phenomenon, such as 20th Century Fox's securing film rights to film the Gouzenko story as *The Iron Curtain*.[118] A slender file exists concerning Igor Gouzenko's autobiography, but it ceases before the crucial period during which the text was written and published.[119] Another file contains a four-page essay, evidently by Gouzenko, called 'My Literary Tastes'.[120] But where are the files containing the traffic between the Canadian principals involved in the case: Norman Robertson, G.G. Crean, George Glazebrook, Tommy Stone, and Charles Rivett-Carnac, not to mention Dwyer and Whitson?[121] The pattern of documentary release suggests that elements of the story have been withheld.[122]

In the Mackenzie King Papers held at the National Archives in Ottawa there are various records relating to the case, some of which were released in 1981. Volume 417, though, has perplexed researchers for many years, containing as it does a cardboard notice that the following items have been removed and are closed permanently:

Espionage. Corby Case Report 1948
Espionage. Memoranda. 1945–6
Russian Intelligence in Ottawa. British Security Report. 1945
Soviet Espionage in Canada. 1945[123]

Through a gaping exemption in the Access to Information legislation it is possible for the Archives to retain government records such as these in *private* manuscript collections such as the King Papers, thereby removing them altogether from the purview of the Access Act (researchers are not entitled to file access requests for material held in personal manuscript collections). Furthermore, this particular restriction is maintained not by a private donor or literary executor but by the Canadian Security Intelligence Service itself. Clearly, this is altogether contrary even to the relatively restrictive spirit of the Act, and the relevant academic councils and associations should seek remedial legislation on this point. Otherwise, public documents may be sequestered forever with impunity.

Blocked from viewing the documents themselves I requested and received (severed) copies of correspondence held by the National Archives that concerns the restriction on this particular volume of the King Papers.[124] I discovered that from the accession date in 1977 onward scholars have been rebuffed continually when seeking access to these four files. In each case, indications were given that the material would be released after 30 years had expired, and then after a further five-year extension, and then after a further extension, and so forth. In my case, an off-the-record offer to release some of the material has yielded nothing to date.

Perhaps the most interesting aspect of my formal inquiry into the background of the restriction is that the refusal to release the material derives not from Canadian government departments, whose officials apparently would gladly rid themselves of a persistent headache, but from an unnamed foreign government (clearly, the United Kingdom). Despite the current British Labour government's commitment to 'open government', these documents seem no closer to leaving the vault than they were when the Archives received them 25 years ago.

Picking the Lock

This brings the train of inquiry to the famous missing Mackenzie King diaries and their canny executor, J.W. 'Jack' Pickersgill. While George Glazebrook and Norman Robertson have loomed large in this account, Pickersgill, the third Canadian official in Elizabeth Harrison's painting, has remained in the background. His significance to the case rests in his proximity to Mackenzie King, a Prime Minister who until the Gouzenko case preferred to remain uninformed of the details of intelligence and security. Pickersgill occasionally fielded such matters for the Prime Minister and it was he who supervised the editing of King's diary for publication as the *Mackenzie King Record* after King's death in 1950.

It has long been known to scholars that Pickersgill's edition of Mackenzie King's diary glosses various events and withholds a certain amount of material in order to downplay King's eccentricities. Now that the unexpurgated diary is available, it is possible to wade through King's punctilious and candid chronicle of his activities over the period of almost six decades, from 1893 to 1950. Of the entire span *only* the folders containing 10 November to 31 December 1945 are missing. This blanks out that most crucial period of King's role in the Gouzenko investigation, when he travelled to the United States to confer with Clement Attlee and Harry Truman. Perhaps the disappearance of these diary folders is accidental, but it is uncannily consistent with the pattern of documentary absence I am describing.

How tenable are the conflicting explanations that circulate: (1) that the folders were removed and destroyed to save reputations because the elderly Prime Minister at the relevant dates was intensely paranoid, seeing a Soviet spy in every associate; (2) that he was trying to make a secret deal with the Soviets to bury the case; or (3) that over the years they disappeared through some mundane handling oversight? The latter explanation may well be true, but it leaves the nagging question of why, of all the folders in King's massive diary, *the most security sensitive* folders should have been lost. The other two explanations also strain belief, even if one accepts that King may have passed through a phase of extreme vacillation in the fall of 1945. Pickersgill carefully pruned the published *Mackenzie King Record* precisely to withhold such embarrassing details and not one other folder or page went missing. It is reasonable to suspect that the lost material was compromising on a larger scale to have warranted its permanent removal or destruction.

Notwithstanding such doubts, it would be incorrect to assume that there has been an ongoing systematic cover-up of these and other secret Gouzenko records. My assessment is that a selective removal of records was subtly effected long ago and in such a way that subsequent generations of police and civilian bureaucrats have been unable to account for their disappearance. In 1981, after J.L. Granatstein called publicly for the release of relevant PCO and DEA records, Cabinet Secretary Michael Pitfield launched an internal inquiry to determine the actual status of records concerning the Gouzenko affair. RCMP and civilian researchers combed their respective archives and turned up little in the way of the documentation Granatstein rightly asserts must have been routinely generated in such an important and protracted case.[125]

In August 1969, when a Mountie investigator in search of the missing diary folders attended the Public Archives to examine Mackenzie King's papers and diaries, he 'found therein a few useful pieces of information', including the insight that Norman Robertson 'seems to exhibit an approach to the problem entirely consistent with the best interests of the country and security in general.' This allowed for 'a clearer assessment of his attitudes towards security matters than we have been able to gain from some of his subsequent administrative decisions, i.e. his personal clearance for George Vickers HAYTHORNE.'[126]

This indication of the RCMP's lingering distrust of Robertson speaks volumes about the almost cult-like isolation of the RCMP's Security Service. Apropos the Gouzenko mystery, though, the RCMP's investigator clearly set forth the state of the Mounties' knowledge of the matter as it stood in 1969:

[The diary] shows that someone representing the British in New York came to the Seigniory Club on the 6–9–45 and on to Ottawa that night to confer with Norman ROBERTSON. This person is not identified but obviously is not STEVENSON [sic], head of B.S.C. but could possibly be Peter DWYER who was subsequently here regarding the investigation.[127]

By 1969, then, the RCMP Security Service itself did not have ready knowledge that Stewart Menzies had been in Ottawa on 6 September 1945. But Sir William Stephenson's claim to have been on the scene was somehow known to be spurious.

It might be thought that this question would have been pursued in the usual diligent manner of police inquiries; that it was not reflects a more sinister aspect of the RCMP's interest in the missing King diaries. In fact, the Mounties hoped to recover the diaries in order to target civil servants who may have been mentioned by King as suspects before their names were hushed up. Astonishingly, the RCMP's provisional explanation for the disappearance of the diaries centred on the usual suspects: supposed 'reds' at the National Film Board. Specifically, they focused attention on the common-law wife of an NFB staff member who had 'lost his job in mid-1946' before 'descending into debt and drinking'. She had worked as a secretary in the Prime Minister's Office from September 1945 to January 1946 and it was thought she may have purloined King's diary entries in order to protect other Communist civil servants. One wonders if there is a better example of the Security Service's anti-Communist reflex blinding them to the subtleties of a particular problem.

Jack Pickersgill told researcher Kirwan Cox a few years later that he had considered police suspicions regarding the NFB after the war as exaggerated, but in 1969 both he and National Archivist Kaye Lamb were most anxious to co-operate with investigators in unearthing any former leftists still active in the civil service:

Mr. PICKERSGILL then agreed to serve as not only a source of information concerning the time and the personalities in his sphere of direct knowledge, but was invited to contribute advice as to research areas of greatest benefit. The atmosphere was most cordial with no signs of animosity whatsoever throughout. He felt that he was of the school which may hold some skepticism as to what secrets Canada may hold, but that the principle we were working under was a valid one.

. . . .[C]oncerning the type of attitude exhibited by the Wartime Information Board and the National Film Board during the war, Mr. PICKERSGILL stated that he had been a little dubious about the NFB and both he and Dr. Lamb felt that the CBC policy which is so blatantly anti-American cannot be a mere accident.[128]

Was this the same Jack Pickersgill who told Cox that he had been 'very concerned' about the NFB security scare and 'didn't want a precedent for extending police methods'?[129] How reliable are Pickersgill's oft-repeated claims that he knew nothing of Gouzenko until two days before the roundup of the espionage suspects in 1946, or that he knew nothing regarding the fate of the missing diaries?

Adding to the intrigue regarding the diaries, and to the diversion of police attention from the probable true explanation for their disappearance, it was learned that Public Archives employee Jean Daviault had secretly bootlegged microfilm copies of portions of the diaries (though apparently not the missing ones) and had attempted to sell these to a journalist. The intrepid journalist immediately contacted not his editor but, who else, Norman Robertson, with the result that Kaye Lamb forced Daviault's resignation. Ten years later Daviault again floated material from King's diary on the black market, and once again police were notified. That Daviault had misled them on the earlier occasion and retained a secret cache of microfilm did not please the Mounties. Shortly after this, and before any sale was completed or any charge was laid, Daviault committed suicide.

In sum, the RCMP investigation of the missing diaries never once raised the question of who, other than imagined subversives, might have benefited from this crucial information gap. And Jack Pickersgill had no intention of enlightening them.

During his interview with the NFB's Kirwan Cox, Pickersgill wanted to explain how security matters really work in order to justify the repressive measures taken and the ongoing secrecy in the Gouzenko case. 'It is not a pleasant task,' he explained, 'the security people want to take no risks . . . maximum precautions; but there is a political responsibility against this to ensure the maintenance of freedom.' It is remarkable, he said, that the majority of the public always *approves* of repressive measures at the time and 'only speaks up later', long after the crisis has passed. This was as true for Japanese-Canadian resettlement, he said, as it was for the use of the War Measures Act during the October Crisis. The Gouzenko case, he concluded, 'undoubtedly was a very cold douche for ordinary people [and] a real crisis for fellow travellers.'

As he paused for breath, Cox caught him with a brilliantly precise question: why was William Stephenson present in Ottawa on the night of Gouzenko's defection? Pickersgill answered, cautiously, 'I think he came here specially, because of this business, but I'm not sure.'

> COX: I don't follow. He would have had to know about it in advance, wouldn't he?
> PICKERSGILL: I must be wrong . . . it seems to me he just happened to be here for some other reason, when you recall it for me.

COX: Stephenson is given some credit for talking Norman Robertson into taking the man in, when they were waffling—

Pickersgill is audibly uncomfortable, and he interjects, 'Well, I don't want this recorded' and asks that the tape be stopped. It resumes with Cox's question, 'Would you say the King diaries are a complete record?'

'Well of course they are not', Pickersgill is imperturbable, 'because there is this missing volume for November and December 1945. The whole account of King's visit to Washington is missing, and nobody's been able to find it anywhere . . . a very serious gap.'

To understand the pattern of absent documents perhaps it is useful to examine King's actions, or rather his inaction. At first, the Prime Minister wanted no part of Gouzenko—innate caution warned him away from all the implications that the cipher clerk's defection presented to the Canadian government. Indeed, it is a measure of King's character that he hoped the problem would be obviated if Gouzenko became desperate enough to commit suicide. Yet the extended delay between Gouzenko's debriefing in September and the RCMP's roundup of the suspects the following February, a delay that went against all British advice, hints that another quality in Mackenzie King took precedence: that maddeningly recessive intransigence that made him a crafty leader, one who took the necessary actions but not necessarily the actions expected. He may once again have turned the tables on an opponent.

Recall that the Gouzenko story was forced into the open only when Washington columnist Drew Pearson was leaked details of the case just prior to Churchill's 'Iron Curtain' address in Missouri; left to King's discretion the matter would have dragged on in secrecy.[130] King may have confided excessively paranoid views to his diary while also trying to dispose of the case quietly; it is also possible he understood perfectly that only a fluke had frustrated the British plan for Gouzenko to receive instant publicity. If this was the case, prolonging his own importance and centrality in the matter at the expense of some frustration for Churchill became his policy, a policy perhaps recorded with satisfaction in the missing pages of his diary?

The Task of the Translator

One final irregularity, a crucial one, concerns Michael Petrowsky, the RCMP's Ukrainian specialist whose activities in relation to Tracy Philipps were discussed in Chapter 1. The Philipps papers reveal Petrowsky performing not just translation but actual undercover fieldwork for the RCMP. Indeed, Petrowsky styled himself 'Special Constable RCMP' when first listed in the *Ottawa City Directory* in 1941. (Subsequently he was listed simply as 'translator'.) During the period relevant to the Gouzenko case, 1944 to 1946, Petrowsky apparently had gone undercover, and he supplied a false address in the city directory. This would in itself be unremarkable except that in depositing his papers with the National Archives after his death in 1982, his widow, Yvanna Petrowska, mentioned two important facts. First, some of Petrowksy's papers were removed by officials (presumably from the RCMP, although this was not specified) prior to her depositing them. Second, she reminisced about the years when she had taken an active role in her husband's undercover work, including, she claimed, *sheltering the Gouzenkos during their defection in an apartment in the same building.* In fact, she claimed for herself and her husband a role in the case that has never been noticed or recognized.

Is this anecdote true? It is supported to some extent by the fact that Petrowsky appears among the RCMP guards in the background of a Gouzenko home movie filmed during the months after the defection.[131] It is not refuted by other available sources. Unlike the other translators, for example, chief translator Moïse Arnoni (Yiddish), E.W. Elfvengren (Finnish), George Steffen (German), Georges Cliche (French), and Mervyn Black (Russian), Michael Petrowsky was notoriously evasive about where he lived during the Gouzenko period. A close study of the pattern of residency in the six apartments at 511 Somerset and also in the surrounding buildings reveals no definitive clue, but beneath the Gouzenkos there existed a seventh apartment neither listed in the city directories nor on the buzzer panel in the vestibule. Nor was it mentioned or included in sketches of the building layout tabled at the Royal Commission hearings. Only in 1946, some months after the defection and five years after the building was erected, was this apartment included in the city directory listings. Might this have been occupied by the Petrowskys? Or did he and his wife still occupy their previous residence just several doors up the street at 535 Somerset West?[132]

Gouzenko himself may have nearly stumbled into revealing his connection with the Petrowskys during his testimony before the Royal Commission. He described the sequence of events following his flight from the embassy, the various points of call he, Svetlana, and their infant made in their desperate attempt to gain Canadian asylum. On 6 September, after a day of fruitless trudging from office to office, their baby was tired and they left him with a neighbour while they went out again to the naturalization office. Later that night he went to his immediate neighbour, Harold Main, 'and he readily agreed to keep the child.' This part of his account confused the commissioners:

Q: Was that the same neighbour with whom you had left the child earlier in the evening or afternoon?
A: No.
Q: Was there another neighbour?
A: The first neighbour was in a house.
Q: The first neighbour was in a house.
A: Yes, it was a woman.[133]

In no treatment of the case has this neighbour ever been identified. Was it Mrs Petrowska? If so, was she actually living in 511 Somerset or, as Gouzenko said, in a nearby house, perhaps at 535 Somerset? This unexplored angle on the Gouzenko affair is all the more urgent and tantalizing because Mrs Petrowska is alive and well and remembers these events with clarity. My initial telephone interview with her produced one of the strangest moments I encountered during my research for this book. I spoke first to her son-in-law and had no sooner introduced myself than a harsh, beeping alarm sound intervened and the line went dead. When I restored the connection, he said, dubiously, 'apparently someone doesn't want us to talk', but Mrs Petrowska came to the phone. I had a page of questions ready but I got no further than asking how clearly she remembered the wartime period before she interjected, fiercely and in a low voice, 'I helped people, but I'm not allowed to tell.'[134]

Several months elapsed before the circuits cooled sufficiently to arrange a face-to-face meeting. In the meantime, she had moved and taken an unlisted number and it required ingenuity and some good luck to find her again. Although surprised, she received me graciously in the sunroom of her home and immediately told me again that there were matters she is not permitted to discuss. Instead, she outlined vividly her family origins in Hungary and the Ukraine: a saga of artistic achievement and social prominence dashed by savage persecution by Communism in the 1920s, finally leading to evacuation to safety in Canada. Photographs of herself at the outbreak of World War II show a glamorous young singer and fashion model by then engaged to a promising Ukrainian-Canadian writer, Michael Petrowsky. At about this time Professor Preston Manning of Edmonton, a mentor to Petrowsky, put the 33-year-old author in touch with the RCMP, who were looking for a new Ukrainian and Russian translator.[135]

Michael Petrowsky and Yvanna Maroz were not without contacts in Ottawa. First, there was the Ukrainian community, which provided an instant network of friends and acquaintances. On the other hand, Petrowsky's participation on the executive committee of the Canadian Authors' Association introduced him to a wide circle; indeed, the couple's 'CanLit' credentials were solemnized by their 1940 marriage in the home of veteran writer Sir Charles G.D. Roberts. Petrowsky had survived lean years during the 1930s before accepting his 'bread-and-butter' RCMP post, as his friend Watson Kirkconnell called it. In the early 1940s the aquiline-faced writer and his striking wife circulated easily in Ottawa's literary and security intelligence communities.[136]

In 1941, when Petrowsky was assigned to cover a major Ukrainian convention in New York, Inspector Jack Mead called just before he left with a change in plan. Because Petrowsky was known to be with the RCMP's Special Branch by some Ukrainians who thus were unlikely to speak candidly in his presence, the Mounties would pay for Yvanna to travel with him. His wife's anonymity gave her a distinct advantage over her husband, and John Leopold told her, 'don't talk; just listen.' This began a pattern of activity wherein Mrs Petrowska became an effective intelligence-gatherer on behalf of the RCMP. This was particularly useful during the wartime interval when the Soviets extracted full advantage from the Soviet-Canadian friendship movement. In one instance, Mrs Petrowska recalls preventing Laurence Decore, future Alberta Liberal leader, from becoming enmeshed in the Soviet net. It prepared her, too, for a pivotal role in the Gouzenko affair.

Mrs Petrowska clearly knows a great deal about the case; indeed, her first-hand knowledge of the actual events may now be unique. She is prohibited from speaking about the details of what transpired but she assured me that it is true that she and Michael Petrowsky were actual *neighbours* of the Gouzenkos at 511 Somerset

Street at the time of the defection. 'You lived next door to them?' I asked. She smiled and nodded affirmatively: 'Across the hall. Our apartment was here, and their apartment'—she pointed to an adjacent space—'Then I moved to another house. Then Gouzenko—well, Leopold took over his case.' She spoke of seeing two men in front of the building, 'day and night, something fishy'. But her husband would not tell her who they were, suggesting that 'they just needed fresh air.'

None of this made any sense to me. If the Petrowskys' apartment had windows *facing* Somerset Street it could only have been #6, yet that was impossible because Edwin and Frances Elliott lived there. But she would say no more. She talked about her role as a curator at the Ukrainian Institute in New York City and how this brought her into contact with diplomatic personnel from Soviet-bloc countries. It was in this guise that she gathered intelligence for the FBI and the CIA. As I rose to leave, Mrs Petrowska brought out one of her embroidered images, an accomplished work crafted fastidiously in the Ukrainian tradition. She spoke of the notice her works have received from museums—recognition of her artistic work. As an after-thought, standing on the doorstep, I asked her, point-blank: 'Mrs Elliott. Frances Elliott. What did she have to do with it?' Mrs Petrowska's face froze. 'I cannot tell you', she almost whispered, 'I cannot speak about that.' I mentioned that Mr Elliott had written several puzzling letters to Mackenzie King regarding the Gouzenko case. She gripped my arm tightly, and said with greater force, 'No, I told John Leopold, I promised him I would never talk about that.'

Explanandum?

I have not drawn the definitive blueprint of an explanation for the Gouzenko defec-tion but rather I have tried to elicit the salient features of a pattern. I have sifted the fine grain of the event in order that thoughtful readers may judge for themselves how likely it is that Gouzenko 'escaped' or else was extracted from the Soviet embassy in 1945. A legitimate objection to the hypothesis I have presented is the lack of decisive empirical corroboration. I have merely lifted the corners of the papier maché layered over the secret or missing documents. The beauty of the Access to Information Act, from the point of view of keeping official secrets, is its pincer movement that tightly circumscribes researchers' access to documents on the one hand, while creating the appearance of freedom of information on the other, thus setting them up to be dismissed for not producing solid empirical evidence to support their arguments. But the same objection applies equally to the official ver-sion of the story. Exactly the same classified documents must be released to clarify if Gouzenko acted alone or with outside connivance. In the absence of direct evi-dence, the circumstantial evidence better supports the hypothesis that Gouzenko did not 'spring forth unarmed'. Nonetheless, the disinformation circulated by William Stephenson and George Glazebrook and repeated in countless 'pulp histo-ries' now has the air of historical truth.

It is now clear that this *was* disinformation. Stewart Menzies, not William Stephenson, was the British Intelligence chief present in Ottawa; Peter Dwyer was *not* working in full co-operation with his Canadian hosts at the time; Gouzenko,

Yvanna Petrowska, as sketched by Margaret Frame, ca *1940s.* Petrowska Collection.

Mackenzie King, and others hinted repeatedly that there was more to the story than was ever told; the role of the Elliotts clearly was different from what historians have told us; and finally, the Petrowskys' participation in the defection as Gouzenko's *neighbours* entirely changes the terms of the case.

The disinformation casts into doubt not only the content of received accounts but also their form. In terms of content, British involvement in Gouzenko's defection ought to form a working premise pending the release of further information. Formally, the historiography that established Gouzenko's 'choice of freedom' in civic memory must be analyzed as part of a conceptual device that helped foreclose on legitimate dissent during the Cold War and sought to contain it within Canadian cultural nationalism.

Repossessing this inaugural event in Canadian Cold War discourse might unblock the excavation of alternative histories its propaganda helped to suppress and the futures it helped to avert. Taken as a set of outcomes, social discourse is, to borrow from Gouzenko, an architecture that cannot lie. The re-examination begins not with apologetics for the failures of Soviet Marxism but rather with critiquing the architecture of the Canadian cultural nationalist formation. This thought-limiting project conjoined culture with security in order to establish the Canadian state as an intellectually sanitized zone. Slowly, the arch villains of the Gouzenko saga, the so-called spies of Zabotin's network, are being recuperated into a post-Cold War historiography as the idealistic young progressives that they were, barring a few highly cynical exceptions.[137] These were people who intended no harm, and did no actual harm to other Canadians, but who were in most cases deeply scarred by the scapegoating impulses of an insecure society, exacerbated by reactionary elements in the British Establishment. Their folly was to accept any direction to act in secrecy.

Painter Elizabeth Harrison sensed the pattern. 'The intuition of the artist', as Feodor Novikov admits in *The Fall of a Titan*, 'is sometimes worth the logic of the man of science.' When she painted the Chateau Laurier cafeteria in 1944 her husband Eric Harrison was in Italy serving as a war historian attached to the Canadian forces. Twenty years later he tried to put her sensory acuity into words:

> It has always been my good fortune in life to be a friend of artists. I married one. It is a unique indebtedness. For as my masters at school taught me to read, my artist friends have taught me to see. They have not given me the analytic and commanding visions of a painter, confident in perception and technique. But at least they have cured me from being purblind to some of the facts before me . . . the complex revelation of a face, the colour of a mood.[138]

Elizabeth Harrison's image prefigures the 'loss of innocence' Canada experienced as a result of Gouzenko's defection. The jolt it supplied to Canada's infant censorship-intelligence-propaganda complex rescheduled the development of national culture and state security. It secured a substantial post-war commitment to signals intelligence and continued censorship, it prompted the rapid intensification of counter-intelligence measures and internal security vetting, and it implicated the Canadian government in the full orchestral range of internally directed propaganda produced by British and American allies. In sum, it jogged Canadian officials to remember their place in the international sphere of security intelligence and propaganda, and it helped integrate Canadian culture into a highly strung Cold War security regime. After Gouzenko, Canada would mark off an entire set of cultural practices as a restricted zone that its citizens would henceforth remember to forget.

6

'I Came To Sing':
Paul Robeson on the Border

Man has no internal sovereign territory, he is all and always on the boundary.

Mikhail Bakhtin

On a typically damp autumn day in November 1995 I drive with my father over to Peace Arch Park, nine hectares of manicured flower beds, trees, and lawns that separate Blaine, Washington, from White Rock, British Columbia. We park near the Canadian customs station and walk down the long gentle slope to the Peace Arch itself, a whitewashed concrete monolith planted in the middle of the intermediate zone between the two border stations. In theory, the park is under continuous surveillance, but I notice that it feels like a voided space, a lull in the overlap of two formidably policed jurisdictions.

My shoes have absorbed the grass's wetness but as I walk I think, absently, that apart from the ubiquitous nineties minivans trickling past, it could easily be the 1950s. The condos of White Rock that stare out blankly into the bay are masked from view by the tall trees of the Semiahmoo Indian Reservation hemmed in along the shore. Beyond the railway tracks, on the seaward side of the park, the beach casts a scent of brine and wet cedar and small insistent waves churn up pebbles and broken clamshells.

The citizens of White Rock, on my informal poll, are mostly retired white-collar workers from other parts of Canada. Strolling the boardwalk and the pier, they seem anxious to preserve the homogeneity of their lives and, for the most part, they appear to have interest neither in local history nor in the prehistory of the Straits Salish who once summered in this bay. It is virtually unknown among the occupants of the condominiums and gated communities that in the 1950s the singer and actor Paul Robeson gave a series of outdoor concerts at the Peace Arch, sponsored by the BC District Office of the International Union of Mine, Mill, and Smelter Workers (IUMMSW). Like so many of its battlefields, the cultural civil war left no obvious trace here.

Recalling the presence of thousands of British Columbian workers and their families to hear Robeson sing and speak on the afternoon of 18 May 1952 is thus to recuperate many small gestures of courage. And yet my rapport with this audience is an uncertain one. Although born in the almost superhuman grandeur of this Pacific coast, I grew up at the far end of the international boundary in the gentler landscape of Atlantic Canada.

I was recruited into the burgeoning cultural sector shaped by Peter Dwyer and his associates around the table at Sammy's. In the mid-1970s Canadian cultural nationalism was tantamount to a religion in newly professionalized regional theatres, flush with Canada Council munificence. Even Atlantic folk cultures were caught up in a process of governmentalization, leaving precious little space for the old progressive cultural front to engage with a new generation. Under this lowered thought ceiling, the post-war federal cultural policy built its secure infrastructure, and I had no idea that the Robeson records in our family collection once counted as political dynamite. As a result, my steps towards the Peace Arch do not follow a well-worn path of local knowledge but one long overgrown in the National Archives, retracing the steps of secret policemen, union officials, journalists, and audiences.

The 1952 Paul Robeson Peace Arch concert already occupies a tiny historical niche.[1] Gary Marcuse and Reg Whitaker place it in a wider pattern of censorship: Sir Ernest MacMillan's summary dismissal of the 'symphony six' from the Toronto Symphony Orchestra and the cancellation of the Royal Winnipeg Ballet's performances in Sudbury for Mine-Mill union workers. One could mention innumerable (but often almost traceless) cancellations, dismissals, demotions, and transfers of broadcasters, filmmakers, musicians, and other cultural workers who dared to display progressive tendencies in the post-Gouzenko period. As was discussed above with reference to the NFB, the Cold War meta-narrative tests the strength of a person's Party affiliations against the state's illiberal practices, finally arriving at measured judgements of what was proper or improper conduct.

Yet there are aspects of the Peace Arch concert that exceed this configuration. Even half a century later, Robeson's border intervention is a memory that, in Walter Benjamin's phrase, 'flashes up at a moment of danger.' Amazingly, Robeson's 'dangerousness' is not considered by his traditional enemies to have abated even with his immobilization by poor health in the early 1960s, his death in 1976, or even the passing of the Cold War. Their sustained attacks suggest that his legacy remains a wound not so much to 'Americanism' as to the system of nationality itself, calling forth severe criticism of his 'wrong-headed' and 'irrational' political aspirations and his 'flawed' interdisciplinarity.[2] These critics emphasize the stereotypical figure of a Communist stooge, a political naif, and a man of limited talent who nonetheless presented a veritable risk to national security. These writers react forcefully when any retrospective softening of Robeson's uncompromising positions recuperates him as an American cultural nationalist hero.[3] The two mutually antagonistic stereotypes breathe life into the durable opposition of 'American/un-American' while remembering to forget deeper challenges that Robeson posed. Five decades on, the unreconstructed Robeson remains intolerable to conservatives and liberals alike.

Looking south from the Canadian customs point to the US terminal, 18 May 1952; the audience gathers at the Peace Arch to hear Paul Robeson. Photo by W. Chass. Mine-Mill, University of British Columbia Special Collections.

A Cultural Deficit

November has come again to the Peace Arch, but in fact the long winter of Cold War passed without the arrival of spring. For decades the Cold War saturated the paradigmatic relation between Canada's 'nationalism' and its 'nationality', forbidding any separation of the two in political discourse. Canada's sovereign uniqueness (*nationalism*) and its integration in the system of nation-states (*nationality*) were stapled together and filed away. In 1995, with the security barometer restored to fair weather, it seems that any relaxation of that urgency, any exhumation of that particular file, portends 'a return of the repressed' and a legitimation crisis. No one wants to speak of the *cultural* deficit accumulated by the Canadian state during the post-war decades.

I pass through the centre of the Peace Arch examining the comparatively flimsy iron gates fixed to the inner walls in a permanently open configuration. It strikes me that the shrill expressions of nationalism in Canada and the United States during the Cold War obscure the longer-tracking rise of 'nationality' as the discourse governing cultural difference and mobile populations. One realizes how oft-discussed 'alliance politics'—from the Concert of Europe, through the League of Nations to the United Nations—also served to reinforce a less obvious and even mundane systematization of national administration. The blurring of nationalism and nationality allowed Cold War alliance politics to pulverize the constituency that once ventured here to listen to Paul Robeson, reducing them to a condition of more or less silent individuation within the security state.

Of course, many people continued to act according to the general attitude of progressivism, but these acts were sharply circumscribed by the imperative to cultural nationalism. What the Cold War placed in a state of detention, by branding as Russian-inspired and unpatriotic, were potential alternative authority structures. In the absence of such structures, communities or constituencies could form only after passing through what amounts to a 'forced choice' of a 'shrewd and correctly dressed' rationality of Canada, one hub in the international system of nation-states.

Narrative I: Coliseum

At eight-thirty in the morning of 17 May 1947, Paul Robeson arrived at Malton airport near Toronto on a Trans-Canada airliner from New York. He stepped into a posse of reporters seeking his reaction to the Toronto Police Commission's speech ban on his concert the next night in the CNE Coliseum. 'This is practically unbelievable', he told them. 'I expect to sing tonight, but if I wanted to speak and I was not allowed to do so I would think it was a fascist act.'[4]

Just a few weeks earlier in Peoria, Illinois, Robeson had found 'the whole town under a wave of terror'. The city council cancelled his concert and 50 policemen blocked access to the hall. In a small frame house on the town's south side the singer held a press conference: 'I have been around the world and the only time I have seen hysteria reach these heights was in Spain under Franco and Germany under Hitler.' Peoria's Mayor Treibel called the 49-year-old, six-foot three-inch, Columbia-trained lawyer and former football star 'a pretty smart boy'. The mayor claimed that 'all the council and I were trying to do was prevent riots. . . . It was only common sense . . . certainly not fascistic.' Then he rescinded permission for the Citizen's Committee to host a reception for the singer in a room at the City Hall.[5]

Leaving Peoria, Robeson proceeded to the Progressive Party Convention in Chicago, sharing the stage with presidential candidate Henry Wallace, before defiantly returning to perform in a venue not controlled by the mayor and his council. 'I am not easily frightened', he announced, but in truth such expressions of courage increasingly brought persecution upon his local sponsors and supporters.[6] Now in Canada, on the tarmac at the Malton airport, he told the reporters that he had 'been saying all over the U.S. that Toronto people would find this harassment unbelievable.'

Unbelievable or not, Annie Buller, publisher of the *Canadian Tribune* and promoter of the Coliseum concert, was browbeaten at a Police Commission hearing into agreeing that Robeson would not speak during his performance. Controller John Innes instigated the ban, stating:

> He's anti-British, and as far as I'm concerned he won't appear here. . . . Some of the veterans associations might go in there and break a few heads of these Communists. . . . Anyone who has his son educated in Russia has no place in our democratic set-up.[7]

CNE manager Elwood Hughes assured the press that 'Robeson couldn't get any more than about 15 subversive words out of his mouth before he would be stopped.'[8] At Malton airport Robeson offered no further protest, but before being driven into Toronto to prepare for the concert he diagnosed what he viewed as a principal source of the hysteria: 'I think the trouble in Peoria was a direct result of the Russian spy scare you had here in Canada. You are looking for a spy under every bed. If the Canadian and American people aren't careful there will be no democratic privileges of any kind left.'[9]

That evening at the Coliseum, as 6,000 people waited with nervous expectancy, they observed a phalanx of security officers taking up positions around the arena. At last the lights came up and cheers and applause erupted as the singer mounted the platform. Robeson's easy confidence and infectious smile dissolved the edge of fear that had formed. When finally the ovation subsided, he winked and stepped up to the microphone.

Seven years earlier, in October 1940, Sub-Inspector George B. McClellan suggested that Robeson be barred from entry to Canada under the War Measures Act. McClellan wrote that 'in view of Robeson's definitely anti-British feeling, it is considered the Immigration Department may wish to give some consideration to his entry to the country.'[10] The singer's RCMP file commenced even earlier, in June 1937, when he sang for the Republican troops in Spain. At a rally in London's Royal Albert Hall he announced he had withdrawn his son, Paul Jr, from a Massachusetts school in 1935 'after he was subjected to a policy of racial prejudice'.[11] The boy, Robeson stated, would receive his education in the Soviet Union.

Vancouver immigration officials declined to act on McClellan's suggestion in 1940, but the same advice would be renewed with mounting insistence in the coming years as Robeson's Canadian following grew. At a Vancouver rally of the Anti-Fascist Mobilization Committee for the Soviet Union in 1941, an RCMP informant estimated that 2,500 persons packed the 2,300-seat hall for Robeson, the 'real attraction'. The singer spoke of 'his own background and made a plea for closer relations with the Soviet Union [and] called for a second front.' He called attention to the plight of imprisoned Communist leader Earl Browder, and then sang 'the old Wobbly song "I saw the ghost of Old Joe Hill". . . . It was noticeable that only a few of the old-timers understood and led the applause, and old Bill Bennett was kept busy answering questions about it in the section where he was seated.' Robeson's appearance 'received considerable publicity in the local press.'[12]

The following spring Robeson's tour of eastern Canada prompted similar enthusiasm. In Quebec City on 20 May 1942 he sang for the Quebec Committee for Allied Victory, drawing an audience of 12,000. Dr Raymond Boyer of the National Research Council acted as master of ceremonies.[13] Constable J.E.M. Barrette's report stated that Robeson provided his services for free, and that 'his renditions . . . consisted of songs mostly depicting the sufferings of slaves and the oppressed.' After renditions by the Quatuor Alouette and the Negro Guild Choralities, Robeson returned to speak of his father, born a slave in the American South, and of his own travels around the world. He applauded President Roosevelt for releasing Earl Browder and dedicated a song to the USSR. Ovations met his references to the 'magnificent stand taken by the Red Army soldiers', whereas Robeson's dedication of a song to 'the bombed persons of London brought very little applause' except from a thousand members of the Armed Forces in attendance. Inspector H.A.R. Gagnon credited the observed lack of support for 'our British cause' to the fact that '80% of the audience were of foreign origin.'

The press, telegraph, and telephone censors intercepted invitations sent to Robeson by left-wing Canadian organizations, providing the RCMP with early indications of his movements in Canada. In the summer of 1942 he visited Toronto for an 11,000-strong rally of the Dominion Communist Labour Total War Committee at Maple Leaf Gardens. A week beforehand, the *Canadian Tribune* complained of organized interference with the distribution of tickets for the rally and encouraged attendance by all possible means, promising that the evening would contain 'a dramatic surprise'. For its part, the Intelligence Branch of Toronto 'O' Division assured Ottawa headquarters that 'this Rally will be fully covered', and indeed Constables Coulson, Jones, Raby, Shields, Spriggs, and Weston attended in plain clothes.[14]

Of this group Norman O. Jones was destined to rise high in the Security Service, and his report of the rally alluded to a certain 'Robeson effect': his air of dignity, physical impressiveness, and charisma mingled with an ineffable vocal authority. Jones wrote that 'the "dramatic surprise" was a twenty-five minute speech by Paul Robeson entitled "The Armies of Freedom" ':

> Mr. ROBESON is a fluent speaker and stressed the fact that he has for years been interested in the struggle against Fascism while singing in many countries. He praised the common man in England, the Loyalist army in Spain and the Chinese. He spoke of Russia in glowing terms telling of the vast improvement of the lot of the common man in that country. This speech was well received by the audience and can only be described as clever and subtle Communist propaganda. Mr. ROBESON then sang several more selections and the Rally ended at 11 P.M. with the playing of 'O Canada' and the marching out of the Armed Forces.[15]

If the RCMP remained deeply suspicious of these Soviet friendship rallies, it is apparent from their size and warmth that this was not a view shared by sizable sections of the public. Robeson's visits provided a focus for the progressive cultural movement at the peak of its popular appeal in Canada, bringing together a diverse public united by common, if vaguely defined, pacifist, anti-Fascist, and egalitarian convictions. When he returned to Toronto in the winter of 1943, the *Star* reported Robeson's address to a welcoming party of 'hundreds of Toronto negroes' with an impromptu speech:

> 'Sometimes Negroes grow discouraged and decide to remain alone in their fight for equality, but this is a mistake,' Mr. Robeson said. 'The Negro problem is part of the problem of unfortunate people in every country.' Only in Russia did he find no discrimination. . . . His years in Britain interested him in the problems of the people of Africa, India and the West Indies, but he was unable to understand how the aristocratic or leisure class of colored persons from these countries

sometimes allowed themselves to be divided from the lowest-placed people. . . .
'My father was a slave,' said Mr. Robeson. 'So how can I do otherwise than
work for those who are in the lowest positions today?'[16]

The CBC carried an interview with the singer on the topic of cultural arts and
education in Russia in which he cited the 'Russian Eskimos' as an example of how
Aboriginal people flourish when they have adequate social and educational
resources. This portion of the discussion took up less than a minute and a half of
the interview but it prompted Commissioner Wood's request for a transcript. Reid
Foresee, talks producer for CBC's Ontario region, briefly summarized the discussion but declined to produce 'an exact typewritten transcription of the recorded
interview'. He pointed out that Robeson was briefed on censorship requirements
prior to the interview and that a careful check of the recording prior to broadcast
had found nothing objectionable.[17]

The RCMP did not press the matter, but their concern over the presence in
Canada of Robeson's voice on sound recordings, in films, and on the radio grew as
the years passed. Gregory Vlastos, an academic serving as an Air Force 'morale
builder', drew negative police attention for mentioning Robeson favourably in his
addresses. Pro-Robeson remarks by singer John Goss in an informal lecture on
'The Negro in the World of Music' were added both to Goss's and Robeson's
files.[18] At a gathering in a Vancouver studio, Goss reportedly played cuts from various recordings and 'eulogized' Robeson. In Montreal, police studied a *La Victoire*
story, 'Courage is Always Right', that mentioned the Paul Robeson Club, 'a group-
ing of young negroes of Montreal who have progressive ideas'. Press censors supplied the RCMP with more than a hundred pro-Robeson articles from *Liaudies
Balsas, Ludove Zvesti, Novosti, Srpski Glasnik, Ukrainske Slovo, Wöchenblatt,
Vapaus, Veestnik*, and other minority-language periodicals.[19]

At the end of 1944 Robeson crossed back into Canada for a day during the
Detroit run of *Othello*.[20] He sang for and addressed striking auto workers in Windsor and joined their pickets. An RCMP informant was present in Robeson's luncheon
party to report the singer's off-the-record conversations. According to this informant, the singer told his Canadian friends of a recent encounter with an Oklahoma
university president who said that Jews were perpetrating a Communist conspiracy.
Robeson had repudiated the charge, telling the president that while not Jewish he
called himself a Communist.[21] The RCMP, following the usual routine, apprised FBI
liaison officer Glen Bethel of this damning admission, and Commissioner Wood's
office sent copies of the reports to the FBI in Washington, adding that 'Robeson
mentioned the United States Federal Bureau of Investigation, stating that he was
not afraid of them, and would continue to fight fascism.'[22]

By the time Robeson returned to Toronto in November 1945 for three concerts
at the Eaton auditorium, Igor Gouzenko had divested himself of Soviet secrets just
an hour away at BSC's Camp X. Already, Peter Dwyer and the others had pieced
together the evidence of Soviet penetration and the RCMP's anti-Communist attitude had hardened. If they had kept close tabs on Robeson before, after Gouzenko
they followed his every move, opening new files on every person he came into

contact with during his stay. Excisions from the released surveillance reports make it impossible to state with certainty that Robeson's telephone at the Royal York was tapped, but informants circulated around him at social functions, including a festive party at the apartments of Beatrice Marks and Lucy Giscombe at 469 Palmerston Boulevard.[23]

The party fell quiet as Robeson gave an impromptu performance, singing 'Joe Hill' and speaking about the anti-Soviet mood of American troops he met in Bavaria, including men of a Negro Regiment. 'He alleged . . . definite reactionary anti-Soviet forces at work . . . placing Nazi leaders in positions of influence by the U.S. Army. He feared that America might . . . MIGHT . . . become a centre of fascism.' At RCMP headquarters the following passage was highlighted: 'He emphasized real danger of fascist growth in America. He said he felt so keenly about this situation he plans to abandon his present concert tour . . . and devote his whole time to fighting American fascism.'

Among Labour Progressive Party luminaries noticed by the informant at the party was Mrs Sam Carr. By then the Special Branch knew from Gouzenko's documents that her husband had supplied information to Colonel Zabotin, and Carr himself was keeping a low profile. Their names and the substance of Robeson's remarks were provided to the FBI. These reports indicate that Robeson sensed the political climate changing, but he had no idea of the tectonic shift underway in Canadian culture and national security. The defection of Gouzenko made the happy occasion on Palmerston Boulevard the last carefree afternoon he would spend among his friends and fans in Toronto.[24]

At Christmas, as the RCMP guards presented gifts to the Gouzenko family, Toronto's 'O' Division noted the singer's return to Windsor 'to help provide Christmas dinners for needy members of Ford Local 200 UAW-CIO'. The police identified union members appearing with Robeson in surveillance photographs taken at the picket line and inside the Capitol theatre. While Canada's foreign-language presses delighted in Robeson's high-profile support for the Ford strikers, the RCMP made special note of Nathan Cohen's praise for the singer in the Jewish weekly. Within weeks the spy scandal erupted in the press, and the tide of popular opinion turned against Robeson and his progressive Canadian friends.[25]

Furor in Quebec

On 4 November 1946 controversy swirled around the singer's date at the Palais Montcalm in Quebec City. The source of the trouble lay in Robeson's remark while leading a seven-person anti-lynching delegation to the White House. Despite a terrifying wave of recent lynchings, this joint initiative by Robeson and Dr W.E.B. Du Bois found President Harry Truman unsympathetic; indeed, he was unwilling even to hear out the group's prepared statement. When Mrs Harper Sibley inquired how the government's commitment to punishing Nazis at Nuremberg was consistent with the conspicuous lack of prosecutions of lynchers at home, Truman replied irritably that the United States and Great Britain are 'the last refuge of freedom in the world'. To the contrary, interjected Robeson, the British Empire was 'one of the world's greatest enslavers of human beings', a remark that elicited press commentaries doubting the rationality of anyone making such a statement.

Two reporters from the Quebec *Chronicle Telegraph* bypassed Robeson's designated spokesman, Lawrence Brown, and bribed their way to the singer's suite in the Château Frontenac. The singer desired privacy but the pair of reporters coaxed him to answer questions. Their scoop the next morning reaffirmed Robeson's criticism of the British Empire, and he added new explosive statements.

Singing and acting, they reported, were Robeson's means of aiding a fight against 'a fascism that is much wider than the bonds of race or religion'. Consider the social conditions in the colonized world, the singer told them, pointing to South Africa, Nigeria, Kenya, the Malay States, and the West Indies. Even in Canada, he charged, 'the basic source of all oppression is the concentration of the great resources in the hands of a few privileged people.' America supported the remains of Fascism all over the world because the 'big industrialists, financiers, and captains of industry are very frightened of a so-called Socialist world. Their greatest weapon in confusing the common people is . . . the Red bogey.' The West should let the Soviet Union build its own way of life, he said, and the extent of personal freedom there compared favourably with many parts of the British Empire. How could South Africa be, in the words of Jan Smuts, 'a model for the world' when like 'Hitler he does not consider the black Africans to be people . . . certainly they have no rights . . . except the right to work as slaves.' Greece, Spain, Indonesia, and Palestine had conditions of enslavement, too, and in Canada he decried 'hysterical attempts' to break the back of labour.

The *Chronicle Telegraph*'s editors bristled with rebuke:

> Where we think this artist makes a grave mistake from the point of view of ordinary courtesy is that while touring the British Empire countries . . . he does not hesitate to attack the British Empire in terms he can hardly expect to be other than offensive to many people in these audiences.[26]

The editors were outraged at his likening Welsh miners to the 'poor whites' in the American South, and rejected any British connection to the inferior position of non-whites in South Africa. He seems to have in mind 'a moral rather than physical slavery', they allowed, but 'he will have difficulty in proving that the British Empire is a sinner before anyone else . . . by comparison with the Soviet Russian republics for instance, it will have nothing to fear.' How could Britain's Labour-Socialist government have enslavement as its policy? They accused Robeson of 'very poor judgment and singularly bad taste', suggesting that in the future he keep 'his artistic career and political activities separate'.[27] *L'Action Catholique*'s Louis-Philippe Roy sided with his English 'confrères':

> If ever the ARTIST returns to Quebec to raise money and further 'his fight' he'll find Quebecers will not have forgotten the POLITICIAN. False notes marred the harmony of his presentation. Quebecers are people who remember. You will be held to what you say, Mr. Robeson.[28]

Behind the scenes such views were conveyed to the RCMP at the highest levels. Reporting at length on the difficulties Robeson's visit portended, Constable J.H.F. Chénier explained that James Halpin, the concert promoter, was the victim of a smear campaign of a disgruntled competitor. Seizing on Robeson's anti-British comments, the 'frustrated impresario' circulated a rumour that Halpin and Laval University 'were bringing a Communist to sing in Quebec.'[29]

This was just the beginning:

> The rumour spread like wildfire so much so that it was circulating in the Cardinal's Palace and very soon, Mr. Charland, the Assistant-Deputy-Director of the Québec Provincial Police phoned this office . . . and requested that we had an interview with Monsignor Pelletier, the [Bishop] of Québec who was to be the guest of honour with the Premier of the Province at the concert.
>
> His Eminence accorded an audience to the writer. Monsignor stated that he did not want us to state if Paul ROBESON was a communist or not as he knew of his socialist ideas. What he requested was a certain assurance that ROBESON would not make any statement in Québec, as he (Mgr.) enjoyed very much Paul ROBESON's singing and added that he was in a delicate position, inferring that the Heads of Faculties of the University had declined their invitation to the concert on the ground that ROBESON was a communist. His Eminence was answered that we could not give him any such assurance but that the impresario had ascertained a promise from ROBESON that he would not make any declaration during the concert.

Monsignor Pelletier's final words on the matter are excised from the released copy of the report, but Chénier went on to detail the physical surveillance placed on Robeson from the moment of his arrival by train from Montreal. The fact that the secret of the singer's presence in Quebec was poorly kept, he noted, resulted in the intrusion of the two reporters into Robeson's suite.

Constable Chénier's description of the evening as 'a brilliant success' perhaps betrayed his personal feelings:

> Mgr. Pelletier did not attend but Premier Duplessis was presiding. The artist did not make any statement except before an 'encore' in the third part of the concert. He stated: 'And now, a piece dedicated to a great all[y] in wartime and certainly a great all[y] in peacetime, the Republic of Soviet Russia' and then he went on to sing a Russian marching song by Moussorgsky. . . . This comment of ROBESON electrified the assembly, the concert hall was jammed to the rafters and many had come, it is believed, with the idea to witness a little 'scandal' and everybody felt that it was probably the beginning of it; two priests and a young man went out, an English-speaking person behind the writer exclaimed to his party of three: 'The dirty pig.' But the commotion was of short duration and soon ROBESON had the audience nervousness subdued and obtained overwhelming applauses by his great rendition of this Russian march. He did not make any other allusion for the rest of his concert and it was ascertained that no other statement[s] were made till he left on the morning train the next day.[30]

The encounter across the footlights in the Palais Montcalm between the great left-wing activist and the arch anti-Communist Maurice Duplessis, instigator of Quebec's notorious Padlock Laws, could hardly be more dramatic. The two retired separately to their respective suites in the Château Frontenac. Robeson never returned to Quebec City.

In Toronto the Special Branch assessed Robeson's visits in light of 'renewed fraternal activity' observed among the numerous Mackenzie-Papineau veterans now returned to the city from the various theatres of war. Their places of employment were noted and, judging from the exemptions and the tell-tale phrase 'information believed true', phone conversations were monitored. With Robeson's help the Mac-Pap 'is coming to life again', warned Constable Winmill:

> an organization of this nature forms a good nucleus for a trained organization in an underground movement in case of a war with Russia and doubtless these same veterans will infiltrate into branches of the Canadian Legion.[31]

Citing Chénier's 'report containing the furore created in Quebec City', Winmill wondered if 'an immigration stop could be placed against Robeson when he attempts to enter Canada from the USA or elsewhere.'

Robeson's appearances in Quebec, Montreal, Toronto, Winnipeg, and Vancouver produced negative reactions in the mainstream press. The *Ottawa Journal* doubted his claim that Fascists existed in Canada, and even if they did 'we can deal with them ourselves.' Women Liberals meeting in Toronto turned aside from their agenda to discuss the 'harm' Paul Robeson was doing to Canada, agreeing he was more dangerous than LPP leader Tim Buck because of his charm and popularity as a singer: 'If we Liberals don't bestir ourselves we might find ourselves in a Camp Belsen.'[32] The *Globe and Mail* claimed that college campuses were 'Stalked by a Red Spectre', noting that HUAC had named Paul Robeson in particular as 'exploiting to the advantage of a foreign power the idealism, the inexperience, and the craving to join, which is so characteristic of our college youth'.[33]

On the other hand, 4,000 students at the University of British Columbia gave Robeson a tremendous welcome and listened as he encouraged them to 'attend the Communist Forum to get a better insight into the struggle against fascism.' The RCMP's 'D' Division reported that in Winnipeg Robeson told students that 'he intends to devote more time in future to the support of so-called "progressive" organizations, labor dramatic groups, etc.'[34]

These statements, placed against the background of the Gouzenko case, attest to the hardening of mainstream opinion against the singer as he prepared for his Toronto Coliseum date in May 1947. Yet, by amplifying the element of agitprop in Robeson's speeches, both the media and the RCMP reports downplayed a visceral appeal conveyed through his concerts and informal appearances. This unstated quality posed the true threat: for Paul Robeson disarmed people's cynicism, and he stirred their hopes for a better society. The consensus to silence him in Canada did not form around fears that he led a Communist fifth column. Rather, the worry was that he might activate a broad spectrum of resistance to Canada's emerging national security culture. With Robeson on the scene it was more difficult for people to *remember to forget* their nation's colonial residue of race discrimination, its compromised sovereignty, and its structural inequality.

Forbidden Speech

Toronto Star reporter Wessely Hicks noticed that the Coliseum crowd was 'restless and nomadic' as they waited for Robeson to appear. Milling around the improvised stage even the 6,000 people in attendance seemed lost in the vast 'hall of steel girders, thousands of wooden chairs and a lot of space' punctuated by 'white-coated attendants selling soft drinks'.[35] Arthur Walker admitted in the *Tribune* that the Coliseum 'dwarfed the great Jewish Folk Choir' whose massed voice failed to overcome the acoustics. Reginald Godden's four piano pieces fared better, as did virtuoso teenage violinist Joseph Pach. He rounded out the first half with Saraste's 'Fantasy of Carmen' and 'Der Zephir' by Hubay. Disoriented by the Coliseum's resounding echo, Pach noticed neither the policemen nor the restless mood of the crowd.[36] His fiery violin technique won the audience's attention in spite of the poor acoustics, preparing the way for 'the favorite of the evening'.

Familiar with the Coliseum from singing there for Canadian troops during the war, Robeson strode onto the stage to what the RCMP report called 'a prolonged standing applause'.[37] With the Police Commission's ban in the air the crowd 'sat expectantly waiting for him to make the forbidden speech.' They saw Robeson's lips move, but the microphone was off. As he stepped back, shrugging to the sound technicians, members of the audience reacted, unsure of what was wrong:

> 'Go ahead and speak!' a voice exhorted. 'It's a free country!' another shouted. 'Whisper' advised a third. When the microphone was live, Robeson stepped close to it, the crowd stilled.[38]

'I'd like to tell you how happy I am to be here tonight', he told them. 'I'll start with a song called "Over the Mountains, Over the Waves—Love Will Find a Way".' This cued the audience to understand that Robeson was far from silenced by the ban. As Hicks put it, '[h]e sang it and made every phrase vibrate with suspense and hidden meaning.' When Robeson introduced a selection from Mozart's 'The Magic Flute' he said 'Mozart based this song on freemasonry—an idea that was subversive in its time.' 'That brought the crowd to its feet', wrote Hicks:

> He sang 'Oh God, Why Hast Thy Foresaken Thy People?' and made a great lament of it that was genius. He followed it by the Negro folk song 'Scandalize My Name' and at each repetition of the title the crowd roared its approval.

The report of an RCMP undercover agent echoed the *Star*'s story, albeit without Hicks's enthusiasm. Despite Annie Buller's agreement that he would not make a speech, 'it was apparent from Robeson's selection of songs, and emphasis on certain words, he was able to convey to the audience their political meaning.'

Hicks wrote that Robeson 'needled the police commission through its representatives, the score of uniformed men who guarded the exits of the Coliseum.' Time
after time the singer, in announcing a number, 'stepped up to the microphone and,
pausing dramatically, eyed the crowd which sat waiting tensely for him to make the
forbidden speech':

> Then Robeson would eye the nearest policeman, draw a deep breath and say:
> 'And now, from the concert stage—' and announce his number. The intent was
> obvious and the audience . . . applauded his every inflection.

The RCMP undercover agents, busily identifying and recording names of persons
in attendance, had no intention of intervening, though they took special note of
Robeson's short speech at the close of the concert. 'Toronto has always been one of
my favorite cities, and it still remains so', he said:

> I know I'll come back many times to sing—and to speak here (loud applause).
> I sang all over Canada for Canadian troops during the war and I remember those
> days with affection. I stand for true democracy and I will fight to the end for the
> right kind of world—and for the people—with all the strength that is in me.[39]

The Coliseum concert echoed in the press for a number of weeks, sparking the
most intense civil rights debate since the government's extraordinary detention and
interrogation of the Gouzenko suspects the year before, and it added momentum to
John Diefenbaker's campaign for a Bill of Rights. On the whole, a slender majority
held that the Police Commission, goaded by Controller Innes and Mayor Saunders,
wrongly imposed the restriction on Robeson's right to speak at the Coliseum. Even
the mainstream papers objected to the Commission's threat of interference, though
taking care not to endorse Robeson's political views.[40]

The *Toronto Telegram*, *Peterborough Examiner*, and *Ottawa Journal* defended
the speech ban and published letters to the editor supporting even more stringent
anti-Communist measures. The Toronto municipal politicians who created the crisis played it both ways, continuing to vilify Robeson while denying that they
placed any actual ban on him. They claimed that the whole affair was cooked up by
Communists as a publicity stunt. Annie Buller, they maintained, willingly agreed
that Robeson would not speak and then lied to the public in stating that it was a
Police Commission ruling. Mayor Saunders said that he and Controller Innes were
both 'trapped' in an elaborately constructed 'Mare's Nest'. Innes's fuss had helped
block an appearance by American writer Theodore Dreiser in 1942. Now he stated
with considerable insouciance:

> I am here to serve the people of Toronto. I don't think anybody should put me in
> the position of saying whether or not he should be allowed to Toronto. Why ask
> me? I have nothing to do with it. Why should I object?[41]

Disinformation choked the issue as the question of Robeson's civil rights gave
way to whether or not he was a Communist provocateur. The off-duty policemen, it

was reported, did not represent the city but were paid for by Annie Buller as part of the Coliseum's rental contract. They received no instructions from their chief, Inspector Harrison, to stop Robeson if he spoke, or to take notes. Furthermore, it was charged that Buller had protest leaflets printed *prior* to the Police Commission hearing. The mayor maintained there was 'not a tittle of evidence . . . that the Police Commission should apologize for anything.'[42]

Within two weeks the issue had lost all clarity amid the recriminations, evasions, and exaggerations. Of all the newspapers only the *Prince Albert Herald*'s editors kept sight of the fact that 'while technically correct, Mayor Saunders did not adequately reveal the coercion exercised against the concert promoters.' Quoting from a *Saturday Night* article, they pointed out that the Commission's coercion was implicitly financial in nature. Alone in a closed hearing, facing the (all-male) Police Commission, clearly Buller had been intimidated.[43]

Andrew Brewin of the Civil Liberties League had accompanied her to the hearing but he was kept outside in the corridor. He told the *Star*:

> We were not invited into the meeting . . . and do not know what took place there. The Mayor, however, saw us shortly after the meeting and assured us the board had taken no action. There is no doubt that he is technically correct. The question arises, however, whether the board did in fact exact a promise from the sponsors of the concert that Mr. Robeson should not speak. If they did, the argument that they took no action is surely specious. To require or exact such an undertaking as a condition of proceeding with the concert would surely be just as much an interference with freedom of speech as a direct prohibition.[44]

When Annie Buller emerged from the Commission hearing, visibly shaken, she had defended Robeson to the reporters present 'with considerable fire in her voice'. Following the concert she explained, rather tortuously:

> All my life I have fought for free speech. . . . I gave the assurance we would not make any subversive speeches. We have never made subversive speeches. I interpreted the commission's decision that they okayed the festival but did not okay a speech. I don't want the interpretation placed on me that I separate free speech from music. They go together.[45]

Was Robeson free to speak his mind? Technically, yes, but a political speech might have exposed Buller to censure, possibly through the post-concert financial settlement with Coliseum manager Elwood Hughes. The visible police presence was required, as the mayor said, ostensibly for the security and safety of the audience and not for censorship purposes. Yet in every statement leading up to the concert he and other city officials warned of police intervention if Robeson spoke. In fact, the box office noticed a drop in ticket sales as prospective concert-goers were frightened off by Innes's prediction that anti-Communist veterans would start a riot.

The conflicting reports of note-taking policemen are easily explained. True, Robeson puzzled Inspector Harrison's off-duty municipal officers by implying that they were somehow poised to stop the proceedings, and it is also true that they took no notes. On the other hand, as the RCMP reports demonstrate, federal secret police in the persons of Constable J.J. Cranney and other agents did attend, well-armed with pencils and notepads. But press articles such as Mary Lowrey Ross's inane 'Left, Right, Left' in *Saturday Night* kept attention well away from the RCMP. Her fictitious interlocutor 'Mrs. Nettleby' demanded to know 'why police *with note-books* should attend the concert of a great artist like Mr. Robeson.' Ross mused, 'maybe they wanted his autograph.'[46]

In Ottawa, the RCMP's John Leopold reviewed these reports and clippings and wrote to the Director of Criminal Intelligence that 'the only solution I can see is to keep a man of this calibre out of the country, to refuse him admittance on the grounds that he is creating disaffection among his majesty's subjects.' L.H. Nicholson agreed that 'some steps should be taken to keep troublemakers such as this out.' But he doubted 'very much if we could expect any centralized action through External Affairs and Immigration.' Nicholson told Leopold:

I have a feeling there would be a hesitation in laying down a policy and we would get nowhere if we pressed for it at this stage. I have in mind particularly what I have been told recently by Immigration as to the Government's desire not to impede the flow of visitors across the international border.[47]

Eighteen months later Leopold tried again, and this time Nicholson wrote, 'I agree.' A detailed brief was prepared for the cabinet committee reporting Robeson's controversial statements, his memberships in five organizations considered to be 'totalitarian, communist, or subversive' and attaching copies of adverse American HUAC reports. Of the Toronto Coliseum concert, Leopold maintained that 'the whole controversy was engineered' by Communists, despite the fact that his own file material clearly pointed to the Police Commission's intimidation of Annie Buller as the true source of the fiasco.

In External Affairs, G.G. Crean wrote to Escott Reid, Acting Undersecretary, stating that 'it seems that Robeson is taking part in Canadian politics in a manner unbecoming to any foreigner in this country. . . . This is not the first time.' Crean recalled that Louis St Laurent, as Justice Minister during the war, ordered Dreiser ejected from Canada the day after the American writer spoke of 'the degenerate British aristocracy'. Reid thought this 'irrelevant since we were compelled to do in war a lot of things we would not contemplate doing in peace.' But Crean backed the RCMP's bid to block Robeson's entry:

We . . . should do something to prevent Mr. Robeson continuing to make political speeches in Canada. We might approach the United States Embassy or the State Department, but there is little that they can do to prevent Robeson from entering Canada as he does not need a United States passport. I would be reluctant to see Robeson, the singer, refused entry to Canada but it is going to be difficult to separate him from Robeson the political propagandist . . . the only effective way is . . . to refuse them permission to enter this country, by putting them on the list issued by the special Cabinet Committee.[48]

Crean had the blessing of Eric Gill in the Privy Council Office and Leopold of the RCMP, who attached his brief to the submission. Nonetheless, Escott Reid replied:

I am opposed to taking action to refuse Robeson permission to enter Canada or giving him permission only to sing. However, I would like to take it up with the Minister. Please therefore do a memorandum giving me text of cabinet decision on the exclusion of certain types of Communists, the interpretation given in practice to this decision, the memo of the previous Cabinet decision on Robeson, & pros and cons of neutralising him.[49]

Leopold discussed his Robeson brief with Robert Forsyth in the Justice Department. Forsyth was that department's security officer, and also acted as Igor Gouzenko's press agent. He arranged with Deputy Minister Varcoe that Leopold personally hand him the Robeson brief on 1 December 1948. Yet, even this direct overture failed. Eric Gill wrote from the PCO to S.T. Wood that 'the Minister of Justice raised the question with the Cabinet at their meeting yesterday. Their decision was that Robeson should not be refused permission to enter.'[50] Leopold had lost another round, but now he was certain that top decision-makers were fully apprised of the intelligence agencies' jaundiced estimates of the singer.

Robeson arrived in Toronto as scheduled and joined Dr James Endicott on the platform at a Peace Conference in session at the Bathurst Street Church. The *Globe and Mail* derided the conference and castigated Robeson personally for his 'dreadful nonsense', dismissing his speech as the 'sophistries of a blatherskite'. Slavery was abolished in British North America in 1793, the editorial huffed; 'Canada has no need of lectures from him in racial tolerance.'[51] After his concert at Massey Hall, Robeson spoke to the B'nai B'rith Lodge of Toronto, saying, 'If speaking for my people and other oppressed peoples makes me a radical, I choose to be a radical.' The *Telegram* reported that Robeson:

would 'shut up' in Canada only when he saw strikers at Windsor given enough food to eat, or when Anti-Semitism disappeared and Asiatics were permitted to live in full equality. 'It's not so good here for Negroes either—I can say it where they can't,' he declared.[52]

Cognitive Maps

The preceding narrative carries Paul Robeson back and forth across the international boundary, periodically generating traces in Canadian newspapers and government records before disappearing again below the forty-ninth parallel. The 'space-building' that occurs through this narration consequently emphasizes the international boundary as well as certain common elements on either side of it.

During these darkening years his travels stitched together a waning social solidarity among North American progressives, American and Canadian, and yet his presence also marked such people as security risks for both sets of authorities. My syntax has placed these events in familiar spatio-temporal frames, and this requires caution, for these very frames helped to neutralize Robeson's popular impact and destroy his constituency.

As cognitive linguist Gilles Fauconnier points out, words such as 'meanwhile', 'already', 'simultaneously', and 'then' situate everyday language in shared cognitive maps. From the maze of mental spaces, phrases such as 'in 1947', 'at the border', or 'sent to his American counterpart' foreground the cognitive domains associated with the nationalities of Canada and the United States.[53] The internal structuration of these two domains, while not identical, corresponds sufficiently such that a term like 'progressive' can activate a cross-space mapping, reaching into both domains to denote similar groups.

Yet in the social discourse of the 1940s and 1950s the word 'progressive' circulated as what mental space theorists call an *underspecified sign*. That is, it presupposed an order of things never actually achieved in Canada or the United States. Enunciating potential or hypothetical cognitive mappings, it tended to 'float up' to less determinate spaces unless blocked by operators such as 'but', 'however', or 'despite'. Progressives typically used what Fauconnier calls the 'analogical counterfactual' to open a hypothetical mental space for imagining and discussing social change. For example, Paul Robeson consistently attacked American race discrimination by invoking the Soviet Union as a place where minorities enjoyed the dignity of equivalent citizenship. Since the analogical counterfactual requires the analog (in this case 'Soviet egalitarianism') merely to be *propositionally* true, Robeson created pressure within the space of the hypothesis for its empirical referent (i.e., Euro-America) to achieve parity with the posited analog. The upward presuppositional float had this effect until blocked by signs demanding specification of the analog.

Robeson wrote in his memoir, *Here I Stand* (1958), of his London years in the 1930s:

> The British intelligence came to me one day to caution me about the political meaning of my activities. For the question loomed of itself: if African culture was what I insisted it was, what happens to the claim that it would take 1,000 years for Africans to be capable of self-rule?[54]

In this case Robeson used the analogical counterfactual to establish a *hypothetical* Africa at odds with the stereotype of colonized Africa. The key phrase 'what happens [if] . . .?' launched Robeson's hypothesized Africa as putatively self-governable. The counterfactual applied pressure on readers to agree that it should not take '1,000 years' to achieve. Yet, when the authorities came around precisely to caution him with an implication of reserved force this was not to prove his counterfactual 'wrong', but rather to block or jam the upward float of his analogy. I will argue that this is exactly what happened to the sign 'progressive' when it was capped by the powerful Cold War discourse of 'nationality' through such phrases as 'must decide between' or 'foremost allegiance'.

So far, this chapter has avoided creating any cognitive dissonance between what typically is written and read together from this 'base space' of the nation's imagined community and its territory. Yet, following Fauconnier, there is no reason why significations buried under the 'base space' of Canada's nationality cannot be unearthed. Indeed, the political implications of Fauconnier's analysis of presuppositional floats are striking. He notices that although such presuppositions may be prevented from 'floating all the way up', they are not *cancelled*:

> A presuppositional float will float up into higher spaces until it is halted. It will then remain in force for the mental spaces into which it has floated. In other words, inheritance is not an all or nothing process.

Historical pragmatics, then, far from ensuring seriality and closure, *reserve* the capacity to reactivate presuppositional floats halted at some previous point. Although dormant they are nonetheless still alive, seeds waiting to sprout again in natural language.

On this view, any base space, no matter how pervasive and weighty, is not immune to the reawakening in its own language of differential practices of signification. It is worth pausing to see how cultural nationalism was used to block presuppositional floats such as 'progressivism' and to suppress their occurrence in natural language. By reductively assigning the entire cluster of signs in that group (progressive, Communist, etc.) to *Soviet* national interest, this device subordinated all public utterances to a forced choice of nationality, neutralizing alternative possibilities.[55]

This is evident throughout the proceedings of the 1946 Kellock-Taschereau Royal Commission. The suspects' exchanges with the authorities show how their cognitive maps became decontextualized, disallowed, and purified through strict reaffirmations of the base space of nationality. In Kay Willsher's examination by Commission Counsel Gerard Fauteux, one finds preventive 'structure-building' at work, efficiently propagating nationality as the base space for their dialogue:

FAUTEUX: You have been a member of the Party for a long time, have you not?

WILLSHER: Yes, but I mean I do not have any close contacts.

FAUTEUX: You must have some idea as to the inspiration of the theory of that Party, where it comes from?

WILLSHER: Well, there are similar parties in all countries.

FAUTEUX: From where would you say that those parties receive their instructions?

WILLSHER: I do not know that they receive instructions, I think they exist—

FAUTEUX: Do you know if they are federated?

WILLSHER: I do not know that there is any federation.

FAUTEUX: Or put it another way, what would be the interest of the Soviet Union in those parties?

WILLSHER: Because they are similar to the Party itself in its own country.

FAUTEUX: Because it was similar to what?

WILLSHER: Its own party. I mean, it is natural that they would not be antagonistic. I think each country carries out its own policy as far as possible. Naturally, they would support each other's policies to a certain extent. I mean, I believe, as I have read in *The Tribune,* the executive are Canadians, and they have a policy.

Fauteux uses space partitioning ('where') to limit Willsher's interlocutional possibilities. She finds him foreclosing on her scene of utterance, but her attempts to predicate a 'base space' on 'similar parties in all countries' will be blocked. The Commission is bent on isolating her cognitive map and preventing it from 'floating up' to authorize a new supranational base space. Fauteux demands of her: do the Communist parties in each country comply with the principle of nationality or not? If they do not comply, de facto they must be treasonous. If they *do* comply with the principle of nationality then one nation must predominate, and which one if not Soviet Russia? As Willsher was forced to adopt this syntax she slid into greater difficulty, speaking of 'the Party itself in its own country'. Did she mean that the Party did indeed emanate from one country? Fauteux's assertion of a cognitive map predicated solely on the actually existing pattern of nationalities thus had disastrous consequences for Willsher, whose actions were then explicable only in terms of treason:

FAUTEUX: [B]eing called upon to make a decision as between your master and the country you were working for [Great Britain], on the one hand, and the Communist Party on the other, you told us you decided in favour of the Communist Party.

WILLSHER: Yes.

FAUTEUX: Whom do you think the Communist Party held loyalty to?

WILLSHER: As I say, I think they are in their own country, they are all connected because they all have the same aims in view? . . . I do not think of it in the sense of one country versus another; it was part of all countries.

FAUTEUX: I do not think of it as one country against another. . . . What about the effect if the information that you passed on to Mr. Adams was passed on to Russia; what about that?

WILLSHER: That would be a great misfortune. I did not think that was going to occur. . . . I think the Communist Party has done itself a great deal of harm. I do not think it has—there would be an effect on public opinion which would be very strong over this kind of thing.[56]

When Willsher stated 'I do not think of it in the sense of one country versus another; it was part of all countries', Fauteux trumped her invocation of a supranational base space as the cognitive frame for 'progressivism'. Indeed, his 'I do not think of it as one country against another' saturated it with the implication of Soviet national interest, preventing Willsher from relieving her distress by building upon a supranational ideal. Indeed, with nationality and nationalism totalizing the field, and with any upward movement blocked, Fauteux left the Englishwoman no alternative but to refuse to answer or else accede to the Commission's delimited speech situation and so supply, irresistibly, everything necessary to her subsequent court conviction.

Willsher admitted to attending a study group at the home of Agatha Chapman, a young economist with the Bank of Canada. The RCMP seized Chapman, too, and brought her before the Commission. See how Commissioner Kellock neutralized the word 'progressive' during her examination:

CHAPMAN: No I am not a Communist.

KELLOCK: Are you sympathetic?

CHAPMAN: I am—I do not know how to describe myself. Let us say I am progressive in my sympathies. That is how I would describe myself, and if you want to define progressive—

KELLOCK: I cannot define anything for you . . . we are interested in facts. You say you are not a member . . . would you describe yourself as a sympathizer?

CHAPMAN: Is this question relevant?

KELLOCK: The witness is not putting the questions.

CHAPMAN: I described my sympathies as progressive.

KELLOCK: If you want to dodge the question that's your privilege.[57]

To begin to recuperate the space foreclosed upon by these means is not to rehabilitate the Soviet experiment, nor even the term 'progressive' itself. Rather, it is to reawaken ways of discussing and analyzing social and cultural history that is *not* already prefigured by any particular nationality or by the spatio-temporal connotations of 'progress'. At the moment they were caught up by the Gouzenko disclosures these 'progressives' were developing fresh cognitive maps—albeit half-formed and intuitive—within which the tenets of the 'base space' of nationality and the concept of progress were matters of concern and discussion. It was their misfortune to have had these tentative political imaginings so easily and cynically mapped onto the sovereign interests of a rival state.

After their arrests, the suspects were interrogated at the Rockcliffe RCMP barracks by C.W. 'Cliff' Harvison and M.E. Anthony. Norman Robertson's 'Corby' group knew that Gouzenko's documentary evidence in itself had minimal probative value. A secret Order-in-Council authorized the extraordinary suspension of the suspects' rights to legal counsel, counting on the shock effect of dawn arrest and secret detention to scare them into quick confessions. The illiberal handling of the case has been the source of debate ever since.

Cliff Harvison described the interrogations as 'intensely interesting'. With the Soviets' own personality estimates of the suspects in hand, he had a unique opportunity to probe their political motivations. He was surprised by the high calibre of these 'ideological spies' and came to doubt they were 'true Communists'. To explain their treachery he turned to the Kellock-Taschereau Report's account of 'organized indoctrination' that sought to:

create in the mind of the study group member an . . . acceptance at its face value the propaganda of a foreign state . . . a gradual development of divided loyalties.

[They] begin by feeling that Canadian society is not democratic or equalitarian enough for their taste . . . without reference to whether that other country is more or less democratic or equalitarian than Canada.

Indeed, a sense of internationalism seems in many cases to play a role in one stage of the course. . . . The Canadian sympathizer is first encouraged to develop a sense of loyalty, not directly to a foreign state but to what he conceives to be an international ideal. This subjective internationalism is then usually linked . . . through indoctrination, with . . . the national interest of the foreign state.[58]

According to Mark McClung, Harvison epitomized the anti-intellectualism of the RCMP.[59] Yet, despite his downplaying the psychological brutality and dubious legality of the detentions, and despite his call for Security Service activities to be kept under the wraps of official secrecy, Harvison's account nonetheless acknowledges a differential space of political signification, one that exceeded the Cold War formulation. Of course, Harvison believed this was a space wherein 'the disintegration of normal moral principles, beliefs and character' ultimately exposed the suspects to exploitation by the Soviets. What is remarkable is his admission that 'nationality', and not Communism, was the root issue.

Churchill's Security Metaphors

Winston Churchill's address at Fulton, Missouri, on 5 March 1946 followed swiftly upon the arrests of the Gouzenko suspects. Titled 'Sinews of Peace', it announced a post-war global partition with its compelling image of the 'iron curtain'. Today Churchill's mighty metaphor is as effaced as its material referent, the Berlin Wall. Yet to nervous North American radio listeners in 1946 Churchill's address dampened any remaining post-war euphoria with its tone of renewed militarized sobriety. It rang down the fire curtain in the make-believe theatre of Soviet friendship—converting it to Le Carré's 'secret theatre' of espionage—and the speech pointedly emphasized the 'sinews' of national security in the English-speaking countries.

Deftly, Churchill justified the weighting of Anglo-American culture with renewed secrecy and security-consciousness in order to achieve parity with the Soviets' formidable secret political police agencies. The enemy within must be ferreted out, while externally, vigilant sentries must track Soviet movements in the shadows. Less obviously, Churchill's iron curtain augured a *virtual* system, that is, as a new regime of information. He called for reciprocal national measures to project the Atlantic alliance into future decades, predicated not simply on the opposition of East and West but on an accentuated regime of nationality within which the Anglo-American alliance might hold sway.

The two central metaphors of his speech—'sinews of peace' and 'iron curtain'—worked together as a masterpiece of political indirection.[60] Behind Churchill's theatrical 'curtain' image was his call backstage to muscle up *all* national frontiers, particularly those of 'the fraternal association of the English-speaking peoples'. As he predicted, the post-war period would see 'the continuance of the intimate relationship between our military advisers, leading to a common study of potential dangers', and a covert elimination of Communist fifth columns by a strengthened and integrated intelligence-censorship-propaganda complex. Securing Anglo-American hegemony within the United Nations organization was 'an open cause of policy of very great importance'.

People knew the speech was boundary-raising. Even as Mackenzie King telephoned Churchill in Fulton that evening with effusive praise, demonstrations were afoot in Britain and America protesting its warlike tone. Churchill encountered placard-waving protestors when he arrived back in New York.[61] In San Francisco, Paul Robeson's reaction to the speech was recorded on an FBI wiretap. Speaking with Max Yergan in New York, the singer demurred from Yergan's strident wording for a letter denouncing Churchill, but in subsequent public addresses Robeson warned that the Fulton speech presaged a 'more highly developed kind of benevolent Anglo-American imperialism'.[62] In fact, as he was painfully to learn, Churchill's 'iron curtain' would descend relentlessly on his own concert career.

Party Line

Paul Robeson remains anomalous in the general pattern of Left disenchantment following the USSR's war against Finland, its pact with the Nazis, the purge of Trotskyites, its interventions in Czechoslovakia, Hungary, and so forth. Although he became aware of the serious and ultimately fatal flaws in 'actually existing' Soviet socialism, he renounced neither the Party nor the Soviet Union. Knowing of systemic anti-Semitism in the Soviet Union, for example, he did not speak of it in the West, and even denied that it occurred. This silence and his failures to speak up in favour of the Finns or the Trotskyites have been used to discredit him ever since.

Recently a recording has surfaced in a Moscow archive supporting Paul Robeson Jr's claim that his father antagonized Stalin during a special Moscow concert in 1949 by dedicating the song of the Warsaw ghetto to Soviet Jewry and singing it in Yiddish. Everyone in the hall and not least Stalin understood Robeson's message perfectly. In the stunned silence that followed one brave person began a slow clap that gradually grew into a thunderous applause. Stalin abruptly shelved plans to release a record of the concert. In later years Robeson believed that this type of action had made him a target of Soviet as well as Anglo-American security services.[63]

Certainly he remained a target of RCMP security intelligence, whose copious Robeson files reflect a considerably more complex subject than their own characterization of him as a mere mouthpiece of the Party line. In general, Robeson emphasized repeatedly his primary concern for the civil rights of black Americans. Second, he attacked European colonialism and, like W.E.B. Du Bois, he confronted the liberal democracies with their illiberal tendencies, particularly in their treatment of minorities. Finally, he earned his friendships with labour through personal associations, often irrespective of the Communist Party, and by operating well beyond its limited sphere as a rare point of intersection for a divided oppositional culture.

In the matter of Fred Rose, Robeson ran directly against the Party line. As a Labour Progressive Party member of Parliament, Rose's six-year prison sentence for espionage came as a catastrophic blow. He and the party paid dearly for his covert liaison with Colonel Zabotin. In retrospect, his actions on behalf of Soviet intelligence seem not only treasonous but craven and deluded when measured against his responsibilities as the LPP's first elected representative. Voicing no such qualification, Robeson became his staunch defender.

The sinister villain in Zanuck's *Iron Curtain* does not match up to Rose's actual description. He was not primarily a spy but rather part of the organized Communist Party structure that tried to keep to windward of the progressive movement as a whole through the 1930s. Rose worked zealously on behalf of labour and minority groups, attempting to sway them to the Party, but also to raise the alarm against rising Fascism, and not least what he viewed as Fascist tendencies of the RCMP. His 1938 pamphlet *Spying on Labour* attacked the promotion of 'disunity and prejudice inside the labour and socialist movements' through the use of stool pigeons and provocateurs: 'Spy-promoters always try to give the impression that all their investigators look for is the so-called "subversive" activities of the Communist Party' when the actual field of surveillance and interference knew no such bounds:

> These same 'gentlemen' never limited their activities to this one section of the labour movement. . . . *Every one of them was also engaged in industrial and general espionage against the entire labour and progressive movement.*[64]

If any doubt remains that the RCMP's 'centre-periphery' model of Party affiliation deeply exaggerated the influence of the Party in the labour and progressive movements, Rose himself dispenses with it here. Nobody would have been quicker to describe his party's activities as forming its centre, and he did not do so. On the other hand, Rose's attempts to sensitize progressives to the covert destruction of their movement by governments and industry were neither fanciful nor fearmongering. If anything, he perhaps underestimated its scope.

Rose emerged from prison a broken man and he fled ostracism in Montreal to exile in Poland.[65] Jack Pickersgill, while Minister of Citizenship and Immigration, took the opportunity to revoke his citizenship and cancel his passport, and henceforth denied his requests to visit his family in Canada. With considerable ruthlessness, Tim Buck's Labour Progressive Party also abandoned Rose to his prison term and subsequent stateless limbo. Yet the RCMP Special Branch recorded, almost with disbelief, Paul Robeson's repeated public expressions of support for the disgraced MP and his steadfast refusal to participate in the scapegoating of Rose. In Montreal, he looked out at an audience that included both Tim Buck and RCMP undercover agent J.E.M. Barrette, and said, 'Tell him I was here and that I'll be back—I mean Fred Rose.'[66]

Robeson's presence in someone's home or in a vast assembly gave people courage to turn and resist illiberal tendencies in the Western democracies. The complexity of this turning against the flow of public discourse exceeds his assignment in Cold War historiography to the battery of Soviet propaganda.[67] Even the reports of undercover policemen betray signs that Robeson touched them personally with his performances. One aspect of this singular ability was his disinclination to use irony. Pointing out obvious fabrications and distortions in the press was one thing, but cynicism only very rarely marred his statements and performances. Perhaps this lack of irony explains postmodernist critics' contemporary disinterest in Robeson. If so, that disinterest is inversely proportional to the wide admiration his unironic and uncynical encouragement of progressivism commanded during the dark years of the 1940s and 1950s.

Reviewing a Robeson concert in the University of Toronto's *Varsity* in 1949, student William Glenesk struggled for words to describe a voice that was 'a medium through which a principle was proclaimed . . . the equality of man'. Although Robeson 'confined his message to song', Glenesk wrote, 'one sensed from the supraliminal cues manifested in his performance and stage presence, an aura of vindication, a mind and soul harrowed by the piercing shafts of critical crowds.'[68] As Weisbord writes of the Montreal progressives: 'Raymond, Irene, Fred and Gilles, Robeson belonged to them, he was them. They called him Paul.'[69] Long after Robeson was silenced, Irene Kon kept reactivating memories of his legacy: 'Young people today should rediscover this man, who, long before they were born, was fighting for the rights of black people.'[70]

Alas, Robeson's own stamina and resources were finite, and the suspension of his passport privileges in 1950 restricted opportunities to earn foreign income. Across America, concert promoters, record producers, and broadcasters shied away from his name, cutting him off from audiences and exacerbating his financial problems. Canadian newspapers carried stories such as 'The Red Pose of Martyrdom' and 'Alien Propaganda not Welcome Here'. Yet there were helping hands, too, not least those of his son, who assembled a makeshift recording studio in his uncle's New York home. Robeson's lawyers exhausted every possible avenue to restoring his passport in a war of attrition with the US State Department. Over the next eight years the singer gradually sank below the surface of world fame, unable to tend to his domestic or overseas followings. His health suffered, and his sure vocal command gradually eroded. Robeson's 1952 Peace Arch concert thus has special significance as his last great public performance for Canadian listeners.

Passports

Dr Robert Boyer was released from Montreal's Bordeaux prison in 1950 to a ruined scientific career and the annihilation of the Canadian Association of Scientific Workers he had laboured to create.[71] He decided to travel abroad. Citing four countries he intended to visit, he applied for and received his new Canadian passport. Unfortunately, this decision coincided with nuclear scientist Bruno Pontecorvo's disappearance from Chalk River and re-emergence in Moscow. Similarly, scientist Leopold Infeld decided not to return to Canada from a trip to his native Poland.[72] To make matters worse, the travel company handling Boyer's booking, either as a matter of course or because of his notoriety, passed on the information to the Canadian authorities. Meeting in Ottawa on 25 October 1950, George Glazebrook and George McClellan executed a cabinet decision to block Boyer's exit from Canada, ordering RCMP officers in Montreal to relieve him of his passport.[73]

Three months earlier, two FBI agents had sought out Paul Robeson in New York with the same purpose. On his lawyer's advice he refused to surrender his passport, but this had no practical effect because the State Department had it voided and notified all border points to prevent his departure. Robeson was not the first left-winger to suffer such a bar, but his fame brought renewed international attention to the US government's anti-Communist consular practices.[74]

That the American government and to a lesser extent the Canadian government sought to control movements of their citizens by revoking their passports indicates the growing importance of consular policies and practices. Documents of safe conduct are of ancient provenance, but the notion of a world population identifiable individually through a nationally administered global passport regime is a recent concept, approximately coterminous with the creation of the United Nations.[75] A striking aspect of this regime is the secrecy that attended it. As one scholar of international law puts it:

> Our knowledge of state passports depends directly on the policy of the state to make its practices public. Unfortunately, the attitude in this particular area, with few exceptions, is to remain reticent.[76]

One reason for reticence was the close integration of passport systems with intelligence services. British and Canadian passport officers abroad were agents of MI6 and the RCMP, combining consular duties with other information-gathering activities.[77] In this sensing system the passport was a crucial contact point between the travelling citizen and state authority, marred only by citizens' stubborn misapprehension that bearing a passport was their right, not state prerogative. Of the *apprehension* they experienced at the customs point, Paul Fussell writes:

> For the modern traveler it is a moment of humiliation, a reminder that he is merely the state's creature. . . . It would be depressing to estimate the amount of uniquely modern anxiety experienced by the traveler returning to his own country when the passport officer slowly leafs through his book of pariahs.[78]

Travellers, immigrants, refugees, and defectors course through a great self-organizing consular system whose basic unit is the passport. Canada's position in these developments during post-war decolonization and its population displacements was dubious. The racism that divided the subjects of Britain's Empire into white and non-white categories, despite palliatives about differential rates of progress towards self-government, had all along precluded any pan-Empire citizenship status. Moreover, because the Colonial Office discouraged internal migration within the Empire there could be no invariable issuance of passports to all persons subject to British rule. Canada's Citizenship Act of 1946 unilaterally forced Britain to treat the Dominions as distinct nationalities, as opposed to its protectorates and colonies. Ambiguity about post-colonial nationality and citizenship would persist as a fracture line within the Commonwealth.

Canadian consular practices remained closely tied to British and American policy. British consular policy reflected the tradition of common law. As Sir David Maxwell Fyfe, Secretary of State for Home Affairs, told a meeting of American correspondents in 1953, 'we do not think in terms of mobilising the whole country towards a particular problem called cold war, but rather how to face the individual problems as they arise.' Naturally, the Canadian officials took Fyfe's implicit message that discretion, and sticking to particular cases, helped forestall counter-mobilization from forming up in opposition to illiberal consular practices.

For their part, the Americans preferred to isolate, perhaps even invent, Communists as a group and to treat them with a well-publicized policy of considerable harshness. The Internal Security Act of 1950 named 'a world-wide Communist revolutionary movement' whose purpose was global domination: 'Individuals in the United States, by participating in this movement, in effect repudiate their allegiance to the United States and transfer their allegiance to the foreign country which controls the Communist movement.' The right of Americans to receive 'protection and good offices of American consular officers abroad is correlative with the obligation to provide undivided allegiance.' As a result, any person whose activities 'promote the interests of a foreign country should not be the bearer of an American passport.'[79]

During a trip to China in 1951, Canadian Dr James Endicott accused the US-led force of using bacteriological weapons against the North Koreans. Endicott's charge exercised Canadian officials less with the matter of its truth or falsity than with possible US reprisals aimed at Canadian policies that had permitted Endicott to travel abroad in the first place. But the tight clamp-down contemplated by hawks in External Affairs prompted concern over the potential negative publicity it might cause, and about the dubious legal basis for such action.

The lone voice of Escott Reid argued for a third option that neither suppressed people's movements secretly and selectively nor clobbered entire classes of persons with sweeping controls. In France and Italy there must be 'Endicotts by the thousands', Reid wrote, and 'no attempt is made to prosecute them or to refuse them passport facilities.' He suggested 'that we bear our Endicott with patience as part of the price we have to pay to maintain our democratic traditions.' Canada should lead the free world by example, permitting dissenting voices to criticize even other members of the Atlantic alliance. What better way to build civic confidence in the North Atlantic community? He argued that an administrative order preventing citizens from travelling or expressing opinions had no statutory basis and would only erode civic confidence:

The leader of the free world, the United States, is peculiarly subject to temptations to limit freedom of speech and freedom of movement. It would be unfortunate if Canada were to encourage these tendencies in the United States.[80]

Reid's views met with skepticism, but it transpired that the department's legal experts favoured the British approach, arguing that 'seeming to isolate one group—i.e. communists—for special treatment' was less preferable than the 'more defensible practice of [pursuing] individual special cases'.

Seizing upon Endicott's statements in China, the Jekyll-and-Hyde civil libertarian John G. Diefenbaker made a great show of the government's handling of Canadian Communists. He demanded that the government adopt 'better security measures' to control their exit from the country. Pearson sent Arnold Heeney behind the scenes to apprise Diefenbaker of the fact that since August 1951 Canada tracked its passport holders' movements in Iron Curtain countries. Publicly, Pearson's response was more oblique. Irrespective of Endicott, he said, the broad purpose of consular facilities would remain the provision of assistance to Canadian citizens abroad.[81]

If the truth of Endicott's charges regarding bacteriological weapons remains murky, the incident shows the enhanced importance of the passport regime to the security intelligence function. As with censorship, the greater value of consular practices derived not from the suppression of communications, or in this case, travel, but rather from information gleaned through the consular process. As Reid explained to Pearson, the Passport Office monitored 'the names of 116 active Communists given us by the RCMP, but in fact we do not refuse passports to people on this list.'[82] On the other hand, their passport applications provided valuable personal information not always easy to obtain in other ways.

The Canadians noted with interest the rise and fall of the Australian government's passport campaign against its own left-wingers, requiring every traveller destined for a Communist country to obtain prior approval. 'Legitimate' travelers' clearances inundated the Australian passport office while the tiny minority of suspects easily bypassed the process altogether. Unless legislated as such, passports proved ineffective as exit control documents. As affirmations of identity they facilitated entry elsewhere through visas stamped or placed in the passport by officials of the destination country.[83] As a result of the Australian fiasco, Canadian officials concluded that passports should not be used to control exits except in extreme cases.

In fact, the entire passport question was entering a new international plane, moved not by Opposition questions but rather by a covert drive towards international co-operation between various Western security agencies. The RCMP's control of consular and visa functions and its liaison with other police services placed External Affairs in a client relationship. George Glazebrook cautioned his Consular Division counterparts to treat all information received from the RCMP with the utmost care. Under no circumstances might documents be taken outside the East Block to the Bank Street passport offices, where there were known security 'shortcomings'. In citing such material, officials were instructed that paraphrasing was essential in order to conceal the sources of information.[84]

RCMP visa control officers and liaisons in Canada's foreign legations reached informal reciprocal understandings with their counterparts at the periphery of External Affairs' knowledge and influence.[85] On the other hand, the diplomats themselves sought bilateral information-sharing agreements with certain countries, while giving the cold shoulder to others. Taken as a whole, the Canadian passport regime was ideologically sensitized through a haphazard series of formal and informal agreements and personal contacts, as well as by continued reliance on British intelligence for clearances. The net result of these activities only rarely restricted the travel of Canadians, but it objectified their movements and their identities in a database carrying considerable exchange value in cross-national markets of security intelligence.

In some cases the degree of monitoring depended on the personality of a particular chargé d'affaires. In Moscow, R.A.D. Ford fumed at the failure of Canadian Communists to check in with the embassy upon arrival and before departure: 'it seems to be the general impression of Canadian travelers to Iron Curtain countries that they only have to report in person once . . . when they do care to report at all.' This was true of almost every visitor, reported Ford, 'with the exception of Mr. Pierre Elliott Trudeau who appeared willing to discuss his impressions of Moscow on various occasions during his stay.' Ford forwarded to Ottawa the 'flimsy excuse' provided by Mary Jennison that 'pressure of time has made it impossible to conform with the usual courteous formalities.' When a Canadian trade union delegation visited Moscow, Ford was instructed to verify 'through all the sources available to you . . . the composition of this group'. It was not known which delegates were Party members, but 'the possibility is being considered here of impounding the passports of this group upon their return to Canada.'[86]

In Ottawa, Dana Wilgress embarked on his fourth decade of vigorous anti-Communism by taking a hand in consular policy.[87] His mettle shone once again when Escott Reid queried the Consular Division regarding the passport renewal of radical MP Raymond Arthur Gardner. Pearson was 'holding on to the file' because, as Reid wrote, 'the sponsor of the application is himself a communist.' He wondered 'whether we should accept a sponsor of this kind?'

Usually Wilgress encouraged taking a hard line against Canadian Communists but here he argued against barring known Communists from vouching for other persons' passports: 'We would be hard put to justify our action . . . the latter would almost certainly demand publicly to be shown our authority for taking such action and it would be very difficult to produce wholly satisfactory answers.' Furthermore, wrote Wilgress, the current practice offered distinct advantages:

> The name of every applicant vouched for by a known Communist is referred to the RCMP, who in this way sometimes discover Communists not previously known to them. It would appear to be a mistake to cut off this source of information. These applications are scrutinized more closely than others by the Passport Office. . . . Perhaps if vouchers who are Communists are given enough leeway they may bring their own downfall. We are not likely to have many other opportunities to punish them for their subversive activities.[88]

Externally, Canadian consular policy felt its way towards the most advantageous international co-operation arrangements. In some cases this meant declining the overtures of other nations. During Tommy Stone's ambassadorship to the Netherlands in 1952 he was approached by Baron van Boetzelaer of the Dutch Foreign Office, who allowed that an internal Benelux arrangement monitored the movements of Communists by means of passport and consular facilities. When the Baron wondered if Canada might support expanding the initiative to include all

NATO members, Stone gave him the brush-off: 'We told Baron van Boetzelaer that it might give rise to some objections from the Canadian point of view.' Stone evidently knew without asking where Ottawa's preferred liaisons lay in the field of security intelligence.

These are apparent in a dispatch from Oslo, where the Canadian chargé d'affaires reported a similar approach by the Norwegian police:

I do not think it necessary to provide Inspector Bryhn with lists of Norwegians applying for visas to Canada. We can do as we have done in the past—have such Norwegians screened by British Intelligence. . . . [T]here is less likelihood of a leak by taking this course. Even now, one cannot be completely sure there are not Communist agents in the Norwegian Police Force.[89]

Canada's continued reliance on British intelligence services perhaps explains Irish officials' coolness to a proposed reciprocal notification of the movement of Canadian and Irish Communists. A dispatch from Dublin reported:

We can only take it that the Irish authorities, either because they feel that there is so little Communist activity in Ireland . . . or because of deliberate policy, are unwilling to commit themselves one way or another.

Asked if he wished 'to press the matter', George Glazebrook took the hint and replied, 'not at this stage'.

Given the Canadians' tight interface with the Americans and the British, security advisories of movements of suspect Canadians were a matter of course. Glazebrook set out the procedure in some detail in response to a request from the UK High Commission for information regarding Canadian exit provisions. Already, he had supplied Canada's policy regarding lookout lists and the admission of undesirable persons, but as he set to work on a three-page reply to the second inquiry, he noted, 'this is getting more difficult.'

Under Canadian law, passports in themselves cannot control movements, he wrote, but the cabinet's Standing Committee on External Affairs had determined that in rare instances that threaten national security a passport may be impounded, such as in Raymond Boyer's case. Boyer proved not to be a security risk so his passport was returned, with permission to travel not to 'all countries' but only to the four countries he requested, one of which was the United Kingdom. 'I might add . . . it was thought proper to notify the four countries concerned . . . so they might exercise their right to refuse Dr. Boyer admission.'[90] A 'notice to travelers' in Canadian passports, Glazebrook concluded, required that they appear in person at the relevant Canadian legation or embassy in Soviet-controlled territories to submit their travel plans, and that they present themselves again before their departure.

As for the Americans, External Affairs had to rely on the RCMP to handle Hoover's FBI. For reasons discussed previously, Pearson and his staff did not share the same affinity with the American security agencies they did with their British counterparts. Nonetheless, consular issues were close to the forefront of US-

Canadian relations, with a strong expectation south of the border that Canada would co-operate fully in the anti-Communist crackdown. The US-Canada border presented an obvious point of weakness for the US, which otherwise *did* use passports as a form of exit control.

If Paul Robeson had been a Canadian citizen, the government would have had to return his passport, as they did in the case of Raymond Boyer. As an American citizen, the government had a case for keeping it. Although the Immigration and Nationality Act of 1952 repealed 1941 legislation requiring any US citizen exiting the western hemisphere to hold a valid passport, technically the earlier measure remained in force through a presidential proclamation authorizing a state of emergency. Without a passport no American could travel to foreign destinations other than Canada. As Daniel Turack writes, this resulted in a legally complex situation wherein:

> a citizen of the United states could lawfully leave the United States and enter Canada without a passport, then fly to Argentina and return to Canada before returning without a passport (but not to Africa, Europe or Asia).[91]

Even after *Kent v. Dulles*, a 1952 US Supreme Court decision guaranteeing the right to travel, a passport could still be denied or rescinded if there was doubt concerning the applicant's allegiance to the United States. Despite persistent attempts, Robeson's lawyers could not persuade the State Department to return the singer's passport.

Between the 1947 Coliseum concert and his passport suspension in 1950, Robeson's Canadian concert dates were moments of relative calm in an increasingly bitter struggle south of the border, culminating in 1949 with the singer's performance at Peekskill, New York, where he sang directly into the sights of Klansmen's rifles. The progressives who attended the outdoor concert were beaten and stoned by so-called 'veterans' groups' with tacit encouragement from state police. At a Paris peace conference Robeson electrified the assembly by charging that black Americans would not fight the Soviet Union because their rights were better respected there than in their own country.[92] When the Korean War erupted in the spring of 1950, Robeson again called on his people to demand their civil rights at home before volunteering to fight an imperialist war abroad. It was an intolerable repudiation of the 'hard obligations' of citizenship.

Even as Robeson continued his tour to Scandinavia and then to Poland, Czechoslovakia, and Russia, reports of his statements helped to cement mainstream opinion against him at home in America. On the other hand, North American ears were closed to the systematic obstruction of his recording and concert career by the FBI. The Bureau's relentless persecution of Robeson foreshadows the sinister COINTELPRO operations directed by Mark McClung's friend William Sullivan against Martin Luther King Jr and Malcolm X in the 1960s. Disinformation regarding Robeson and the 'Communist menace' was propagated not just by high-profile informants such as Whittaker Chambers and Elizabeth Bentley but by a host of alarmists and opportunists touring North America with lurid tales of Communist plots. Manning Johnson, for one, dubbed Robeson 'The Black Stalin', playing up race fears by 'revealing' secret Communist plans to seize America and place 219 counties in nine southern states under Robeson's personal control.[93]

Robeson soldiered on, performing in churches, union halls, and at outdoor events, recording and broadcasting wherever a friendly hand permitted it. No one who knew him doubted that the singer, irrespective of the Party line he was accused of parroting, shouldered the burden of 'courage' almost for its own sake during this period of great fear. He became a symbol of resistance to a relentless asphyxiation of the progressive movement in North American culture. When the Progressive Party under Henry Wallace failed in the 1948 elections Robeson did not capitulate. Increasingly isolated, he continued to hold up the socialist world as the analogical counterfactual for black civil rights, social equality for all Americans, and the liberation of colonized peoples.

The singer's arrival at the border without a passport, en route to perform at the Mine-Mill convention in Vancouver, BC, put to the test a complex and not entirely coherent series of measures that had rung down the 'iron curtain' not just at Checkpoint Charlie but even at nondescript American-Canadian customs points like the Blaine Peace Arch. Haphazard as it may have been, a globalized filtration system conditioned the movements of persons according to their perceived allegiances, and Robeson's intention of testing the openness of the world's longest open border had exercised Canadian and American officials alike.

Narrative II: Peace Arch

On 12 January 1952 the RCMP's Special Branch in Vancouver learned from sources within the Mine-Mill Union that Paul Robeson was expected to speak and sing at the Western District Convention on 1 February. In fact, this was not much warning, considering that the union's press release reached Vancouver newspapers just two days later. Reporters demanded to know from the RCMP and the Immigration Department if the Canadian government would permit the singer's entry, eliciting prevarication from Immigration, and a flat 'no comment' from the Mounties. The RCMP's liaison officer in Washington notified the FBI on 17 January that Robeson intended to visit Vancouver in the near future.[94] While the Canadian officials believed the Americans would relieve them of responsibility by blocking Robeson's exit, they took the precaution of seeking approval from the Director of Immigration to prevent his entry, if necessary.

Constable A.E. Thomas's report of 12 January named four other American union officials scheduled to attend the convention, and he contacted his counterparts in the US immigration office in Vancouver to discuss the impending imbroglio. Thomas learned that even without a passport Robeson could easily prove US citizenship and thus it 'would be difficult' to restrict his movements. Meanwhile, Mine-Mill District Chairman Harvey Murphy assured the press that the Canadian Immigration Department 'would not bar the American singer', the truth of which is refuted by Constable Thomas's private conversation with D.N. McDonell, Canada's Superintendent of Immigration for the Pacific District. McDonell assured Thomas that neither he nor his staff had communicated with

Ted Cochrane and Paul Robeson arriving at the Blaine terminal, 31 January 1952.
Rare Books and Special Collections University of British Columbia Library, Mine-Mill
Collection.

Harvey Murphy. Indeed, Thomas advised his RCMP superiors that the Superintendent of Immigration did 'not believe that ROBESON would speak or sing in
Vancouver, intimating that he has made some arrangements within his own Branch,
to prevent ROBESON's entry into Canada.'

In Ottawa, the Deputy Minister of Citizenship and Immigration, Colonel Laval
Fortier, announced on 29 January 'that Robeson has neither been admitted nor
barred' because the department had received no official advisement of his intent to
visit Canada. Either Fortier was unaware of his own officials' plans, or he deliberately misled the public. The latter is more likely, because on the same day John
Leopold wrote from RCMP headquarters in Ottawa to advise Cliff Harvison in Vancouver that '[e]fforts have been made at this headquarters on a very high level to
have these five persons refused admission to Canada and the Director of Immigration has agreed to have Paul ROBESON stopped at the border.' The Minister of Immigration had 'refused to take any action on his own and finally the case was referred
to the Prime Minister' for decision. Louis St Laurent authorized the ban.[95]

Not knowing what might happen, Robeson left Seattle heading north towards the
Canadian border. But even as the car pulled into the customs terminal both Canadian
and American authorities had determined that he would not be crossing. As it turned
out, the Americans did act first. Summoned into the office of Inspector Everett
J. Strapp, Robeson contested the order for an hour, insisting that he be advised of its
legal basis. He was courteous with Strapp even when the latter's studied intransigence flared tempers in the union committee. After conferring with Washington,

Strapp cited a 1918 war measure, and the singer had to accede to what he called 'domestic house arrest'. St Laurent's unexercised decision remained secret.

With reporters gathered around, Robeson broke the news to Bill Stewart, secretary of the Boilermakers union, Ken Smith of Mine-Mill, and the rest of the welcoming committee: 'They used an extraordinary measure, under an old war measures act to prevent me from appearing in Vancouver. I am extremely sorry I won't be able to meet and greet my many friends in Canada.' He added that it was:

> a great moment in world affairs . . . when Negro people in the U.S. are under great pressure in their fight to be treated as full citizens. . . . I have never before been refused access to any country [and] the repercussions of this refusal of the right of an American citizen to enter Canada will be felt throughout the whole world.[96]

In Vancouver, Harvey Murphy led a delegation to the US immigration office to protest the ruling, but Director Boyd merely stated that 'Robeson's departure for Vancouver was not in the best interests of the United States.' Murphy told reporters, 'Everybody is living in a mental vacuum, afraid to hear what's going on.'[97]

The coda to Robeson's denied entry to Canada in 1952 was a technique he resorted to with increasing frequency. Using the same communications grid that carried the advance warnings that frustrated his activities, Robeson cast his voice northward through the telephone lines. From the Marine Cooks and Stewards Hall in Seattle, he kept his date with the miners by speaking over a line connected by George Gee, Electrical Workers Local 213, into the public address system at Vancouver's Denman Auditorium. The RCMP's informant reported that Robeson's 17-minute presentation 'sketched his interest in helping to promote "decent working conditions" and to aid the Negro race.' His voice was 'piped over loudspeakers' and he told the delegates that the exit ban 'was an act of the U.S. administration, not of the American people. . . . I believe in American democracy and I am not discouraged by an incident like this.' The signal faded out at times during his rendition of 'the miners' song'.[98]

Harvey Murphy moved that a protest be sent 'to the Civil Rights Committee of the United Nations, requesting all those in favour to stand'. Constable Thomas reported 'that everyone stood up':

> whereupon he requested that anyone opposed to the resolution should stand up— no one did so. [Murphy] stated that 'it is known that there are some FBI and RCMP agents with us but apparently we are unanimous in support of this resolution.'

Murphy's humiliation of police informants had long since ceased to surprise the Special Branch; indeed, over 23 years his file had grown to such epic proportions that there was not much they did not know about the obstreperous union organizer.[99] Thus Constable Thomas ignored the hilarity with which the delegates passed Murphy's motion. Too hilariously perhaps, since they appear to have underestimated the extent of RCMP penetration of the union. 'E' Division's Special Branch received copies of its executive agenda and a complete list of convention delegates, including a photograph of each. Perhaps most seriously, the Mounties took some hand in foiling a 'possible formation of a new congress made up of . . . unions expelled from the C.C.L.' The relevant passages are deleted from the report, but the informant somehow knew that, behind the scenes, the idea would be 'decisively ruled out and the matter did not appear before the convention.'

Concert Planning

Before adjournment, Murphy proposed to invite Paul Robeson to sing at the Peace Arch. The singer would 'fly to the border anytime we ask him to', Murphy said; 'we will invite all the people and there will be thousands on both sides.'[100] The delegates set 18 May as the concert date and Murphy's staff set about publicizing the event, promoting the image of Robeson standing at the northern extreme of the United States, hailing Canadians across the international divide.

Even though the event was to be free of charge, it would be a challenge to assemble a mass audience so far from Vancouver. While the *Pacific Tribune* exhorted readers to attend, Murphy's assistant, Olive Anderson, chartered 23 buses to ferry people to the border. She solicited support from businesses and fellow unions, and enlisted sound engineers to provide a public address system and to record the performance. Her attention to detail extended to engaging a photographer and a light aircraft from which he might take aerial shots of the concert.

The intangible, continent-wide climate of fear proved to be the most difficult attendance barrier. The Peekskill terror weighed on people's minds, especially after hearing that veterans groups planned to disrupt the concert. Progressives' anguish over the impending execution of Julius and Ethel Rosenberg prompted the RCMP to note with interest 'that Canadian Communists are now being called to support American subversives in their drive to secure reversal of the Rosenberg conviction.'[101] The Special Branch received transcripts of pro-Robeson radio broadcasts, and they seized the singer's recordings from a Sudbury radio station.[102] In Vancouver, the League for Democratic Rights resolved to oppose Justice Minister Garson's Criminal Code amendments clamping down on restive unions. On 11 May, just a week before the Peace Arch concert, Canadian immigration officers detained the octogenarian Dr W.E.B. Du Bois and his wife at Malton airport when they arrived to address a peace conference in Toronto. Immigration officials hustled them back to the US on the next available flight.

Still, the *Pacific Tribune* boldly pegged success of the Peace Arch concert at a turnout of 10,000 people.[103] Indeed, an unspoken understanding held that the concert had to produce a show of strength, even though everyone knew the authorities would take close note of who attended. For their parts, the FBI and the RCMP prepared to record car licence plates and to shoot still photos and surveillance film of the audience for identification purposes. The concert site gathered intensity as a field for image-gathering not just by Robeson fans snapping mementoes, but by national police forces and the miners' union, too.

The Concert Landscape

From an altitude of several thousand feet the Peace Arch locale is clearly marked by diverse cultural practices. The glassy surface of the bay cuts diagonally across the view to leave a triangular patchwork of land comprising three major elements. First, there is the invisible border, the 49th parallel separating Canada from the United States, running across the bottom of the photograph. The portal itself straddles this line just a few metres from the beach where it meets the Pacific Ocean. The boundary is arbitrary with respect to local topography, a geographer's abstraction. The park where people gathered for the concert lies between the two border posts; the maple leaf flower bed is a reminder that this park is a 'geographic' space to be seen from the air, like a map. To the south, at the bottom right, is the edge of Blaine, Washington. Running north from the Canadian terminal the King George Highway exits decisively towards Vancouver, flanked on the seaward side by a Salish Indian reserve and on the other by the Peace Arch golf course. Thus, the international boundary park triangulates the Indian reserve, suburban developments, and the golf course.

Just north of the concert site, the Semiahmoo (Salish) Indian Reserve is marked more by human feet than by car tires. No grid portions off the space and indicates 'planned' development. Trees are felled for fuel; pathways pass from house to house, to the shore, and into the woods. The land surface is a recording medium for differentiated space-time routines, and the pattern of Salish routines suggests centripetal activity at the centre, near the shore, gradually blending into the surrounding landscape.

In 1952 the outermost streets of Blaine were still practically a rural setting. Yet, the cadastry here differs sharply from the Salish land. The automobile is dominant, and the plan of an undifferentiated car-adapted landscape already is well established. Zoning regulations have shaped the pattern of inhabitation around the automobile and the proliferation of suburbs it is opening up. The time-space patterns in this image are conditioned by the invisible international boundary that arraigns local residents in the distant administrative centrifuges of Washington and Ottawa.

The golf course that touches the north boundary of the Peace Arch Park shows that 'town and country' are not polarized but rather fused together in a continuous regime of landscape perception. This 'wilderness' just across the road in the Semiahmoo Reserve has been idealized and tamed to the Arcadian memory of the eighteenth-century English park.[104] Long swaths of forest have been cleared away to create the scallop-shaped fairways, ranged for driving golf balls. As at Oka in Quebec, the golf course acts as a buffer zone between the Indian reserve and surrounding lands.

High above on the north-facing pediment bold characters proclaim: 'BRETHREN DWELLING TOGETHER IN UNITY'. Thus the portal-builders sought to hold in force certain states of existence north and south of the line. The Arch was the first such concrete structure in the world, reports a park brochure, 'reinforced with steel so that in the case of an earthquake, it would vibrate but would not crack.'[105] Rising 30 metres above the ground, the Arch not only commemorates 'the lasting peace between the two countries', but, 'it show[s] the world, in a tangible way that neighbours, whether sovereign states or urban dwellers, can live beside one another in peace and harmony.'

Paul Robeson approaches the stage for the 1952 Peace Arch concert and greets members of the audience. Photo W. Chass. Rare Books and Special Collections, University of British Columbia Library, Mine-Mill Collection.

Despite such claims to 'dwelling', though, the Arch and its open gates perform, in architecture, the ambivalent relation between nationality and nationalism. Just as the statements 'I am a Canadian' or 'I am an American' signify at once systemic unity *and* sovereign difference, so the Arch represents not just its constituent elements but the system that keeps them from the collapsing into, or annexing, one another. 'Your people came on the *Mayflower*, mine arrived on the *Beaver*, we all arrived by ship.' The syllogism is built into the Arch, foreclosing on other possible significations. As a sentinel of nationality, the Arch 'presences' the limits of national territory, poised to eliminate alien phenomena.

When the singer arrived at the Blaine customs terminal he was permitted to pass through into the park. As his entourage converged on the Arch he shook hands and greeted the audience. He mounted the stage where Harvey Murphy and his son William, Al King and his sister Olive Anderson were waiting. The stage was placed 'twelve inches inside U.S. territory', Murphy said, but this was meaningless. As can be seen from the Mine-Mill Union's photographs, the audience moved freely around the monument, irrespective of the actual border demarcation. Despite the boundary-emphasizing function of the monument, the park was in fact a liminal, or overlapping, space wherein the two 'nationalities' cancelled one another out, even as the surveillance function was doubled. FBI and RCMP agents stumbled over each other in gathering intelligence data, obviating the usual liaison functions and introducing a certain confusion that any violence surely would have brought to the fore.

Aerial view of 1952 concert. The Arch towers above the crowd assembling for the concert. The rear platform of a truck pulled up beside the Arch serves as a stage. The roof of a van parked nearby is loaded with horn-style speakers fanned out to provide sound in every direction. The crowd concentrates around these two vehicles, but many people have spread blankets to sit on the gently rising slope. Rare Books and Special Collections, University of British Columbia Library, Mine-Mill Collection.

There was neither violence nor heckling. Al King recalls that he and a party of miners, 'mostly veterans, came the night before and spent the night and all day in the hills around the park, ready with weapons.'[106] Threats of intimidation on the American side reportedly dampened the attendance by residents of Bellingham and Blaine, but the Mine-Mill irregulars met with no hostile elements.

Song Lines

At two-thirty, Harvey Murphy took the microphone and welcomed the throng in his hard-bitten way:

I know that you came to hear a singer, but you also came to demonstrate the brotherhood and fraternity of the peoples of the United States and Canada—we have a common mission in this world to march forward with the other peoples of this world for peace and security for all of us and (applause) for our children.

And we are happy that we were the means of bringing you together, but I know that *Paul Robeson*—that name—what that stands for is what every decent man and woman in the world stands for.[107]

On the Peace Arch concert recording, *I Came to Sing*, Murphy's descending cadence 'we have a common mission in the world' sounds preachy and Party-line. But when he says '*Paul Robeson*—that name', a human warmth returns, and even relief—for this concert was a genuine achievement for the embattled miners' union.

As always, Robeson's performance blended song and speech, civil rights, trade unionism, and the idiosyncratic, diasporic cultural figuration that Paul Gilroy calls the 'Black Atlantic.'[108] In these 'arts of darkness', writes Gilroy, there are 'anti-discursive and extra linguistic ramifications of power at work'. Robeson's and Lawrence Brown's achievement was to transpose the slave spiritual from being a carrier of black consciousness into an intercultural genre of resistance to oppression. Their success in formal concert halls in Europe and America during the 1930s and 1940s had carried the expressive culture of the Black Atlantic into high cultural spaces normally reserved for 'art for art's sake'. Robeson's eschewal of elite stages prompted criticism of his interdisciplinarity and his refusal to separate his art from politics.

The Peace Arch concert, like Robeson's concerts in general, resonates with Gilroy's heuristic of the Black Atlantic. The attribution of a contingent political rationality carried within music and song forms is Gilroy's innovative thesis. Robeson, too, believed that an unofficial understanding about difference and identity was alternatively produced and transmitted by popular musics of the world. Robeson sensed 'a mysterious inner logic' in music that escaped notice in the dominant forms of political rationality. When Robeson was diagnosed with mental illness in the years following the Peace Arch concerts, this 'irrational' belief was thought to be one of its symptoms.

Perhaps biographer Martin Duberman too quickly dismisses the singer's musicological thesis that a common pentatonic structure, as opposed to the seven-tone system of European classical music, underlies and connects much of the world's popular music. This idea, Duberman writes, 'is as true as it is obvious', adding that Robeson's obsession with it became an embarrassment to the singer's friends and family.

In *Here I Stand* Robeson added an appendix entitled 'The Universal Body of Folk Music—A Technical Argument by the Author':

During the recent years of my enforced professional immobilization, I have found enormous satisfaction in exploring the origins and interrelations of various folk musics . . . which further confirm and explain my own and Lawrence Brown's interest in and attraction to the world body of folk music. . . . My people, the Negro people of America, have been reared on . . . pentatonic melodies, in Africa and America. No wonder Lawrence Brown introduced me to the music of

Moussorgsky . . . Dvorak . . . Janacek; to ancient Hebraic chants; to the old melodies of Scotland and Ireland; to the Flamenco and de Falla of Spain . . . Armenia . . . Albania, Bulgaria, Rumania, Hungary, and Poland . . . ancient Africa, Brazil and the Caribbean . . . [and] North American Indian peoples. And I have found my way to the music of China, of Central Asia, Mongolia, of Indonesia, Viet Nam and of India . . . with my 'pentatonic ears.'[109]

Robeson was accustomed to sharing songs in various languages with audiences all over the world, 'living them', he said, for he knew the intense collective emotion they generated. Perhaps the 'obvious' in this case *is* innovative, as a 'performative' wherein the singing of the songs performed their message. Duberman's dismissal notwithstanding, Robeson's ineffable quality as a musical and political performer was unmistakably less in what he *said* than in what his song conveyed in subliminal and visceral ways.

At the Peace Arch, Robeson's bass-baritone drowned the magnetic drivers of the radio engineers' horn speakers with a barrage of low frequencies:

Water Boy, where are you hiding?
If you don't come, I'm gonna tell your daddy.

And after the spirituals, Robeson spoke of his confinement and greeted his 'beloved friends in Canada', acknowledging the audience's courage in assembling at the Peace Arch to hear him. He spoke of the social solidarity of diasporic black culture that long ago extended along the underground railway to Canada. Citing the Christian church as the institutional site for the transmission of black culture, he traced the intellectual provenance of his own father's and brother's church in Brooklyn, tying its history to that of Frederick Douglass, Harriet Tubman, and Sojourner Truth. He wanted to 'leave some feeling of what has influenced me so much' in his wide travels:

I have seen and experienced the oneness of mankind. Not the differences but the likenesses—the common human spirit that we see in the various peoples' songs. I cannot sing these songs today but I will read just a few words from some of them, to leave some feeling.

Sterling Stuckey views Robeson as 'perhaps unique in the modern history of great performing artists' for bringing to 'a fine consistency' the roles of 'performing artist and philosopher of culture'. His influence on 'African peoples on the continent and in the diaspora was substantial materially and spiritually.' Robeson's 'most lasting contribution', he continues, 'may be his most obscure: developing a more *spacious* conception of what being African could mean.' Robeson and Lawrence Brown associated the spirituals they had popularized around the world with American manifestations of the African 'ring shout', an expressive oral and gestural ritual. It is possible, Stuckey writes, that Robeson 'was one of the few scholars of music in the western world—perhaps the only one—to have demonstrated such analogues.'[110] In

Robeson's songs, the memory of the slave experience resonated *within* modernity, inseparably, as one of its constitutive features.

RCMP documents record the 'affection [that] had to be seen to be believed', the 'prolonged standing applause', the 'resonant voice [that] injected fire', the delegations that 'cheered wildly', the 'adulation' of people who 'hung on his every word', the hope placed in him as 'a great world citizen'. The photograph of Robeson performing on a makeshift stage, which was used for the concert album cover, reflects an atemporal grandeur, the performer holding out against the fragility of biographical continuity. That the subject, as an intentional agent, *can* persist through the shifting currents, density, and discontinuities of lived social realities is by no means certain. Here the camera aperture opened to a coincidence of a historical moment with a symbolic configuration that charges the image not with a fleeting instant, but rather with 'duration' and a greater truth.[111]

Cache

Where Robeson sang, near the base of the Arch, just behind his improvised truck-bed stage, rests the monolith's cornerstone. Inside it is a cache containing items no one at the concert knew of, and yet, in a way, they had been obliged to forget. For the Arch holds rare fetish objects of nationality itself, deposited there during construction 31 years earlier in 1921 when Samuel Hill spearheaded the Peace Arch project to mark the first century of peaceful coexistence between Canada and the United States.

The monument secures a breach in the present for the past, attempting to hold in force the set of contexts and conditions that brought it forth. Reposing in the Peace Arch beneath a bronze plaque bearing an image of the Pilgrims' *Mayflower* is a timber from that original vessel of Anglo-American colonialism. It measures 20 inches long and six inches square, and was the gift of the Quaker upon whose property near London the remains of the *Mayflower* lay. When Hill deposited it in the Arch in 1921, he placed it inside a hammered steel chest weighing 172 pounds and fitted with seven locks. The metal chest was born of the Black Atlantic—it was a trophy captured by a British naval vessel from a ship carrying African slaves. The circumstances of its donation are pertinent, too. The chest was the personal gift of Sir Basil Thompson, Scotland Yard's Director of Intelligence, who attended the inaugural ceremony.

The cache also contains a film, 'The Sacred Faith of a Scrap of Paper', produced by Samuel Hill to depict historical events that ratify the claims made above on the exterior of the Arch, namely that the two countries were 'children of a common mother' and 'brethren dwelling together in unity'.[112] Three filmed re-enactments depict General Lafayette in American uniform inspecting French troops and the signings of the Mayflower Compact and the 1814 Treaty of Ghent. The latter defined the initial boundary between the United States of America and British North America. Canada contributed a timber from the *Beaver*, the first steam-powered ship to enter the Pacific Ocean, on 18 June 1836, forerunner of the steamships that would secure British control of the northwest coast.

Samuel Hill sanctified the European occupation of North America with artifacts that reinforce the international boundary as the legacy of shared British heritage:

colonialism, distance communications, naval power, and a filmic audiovisual observer. As fetish objects, they connect the abstraction of nationality and the virtual time-space of film to this arbitrary line upon the earth.[113] Paul Robeson's presence just a few feet away, singing slave spirituals to an audience riddled with camera-wielding secret policemen brings the buried culture-security connection to the surface.

True, Basil Thompson's strongbox was booty from a *captured* slaver. Yes, Hill included the Mayflower Compact in his film partly to recall the Society of Friends' decision to withdraw from the legislature in 1758 rather than support an Indian war. Yet, Thompson's main task in 1920–1, when he donated the chest to Hill's Peace Arch project, was to prevent Communist-inspired subversion at home and in the colonies.[114] The Friends' gesture in favour of Aboriginal peoples in 1758 did not prevent a virtual genocide over the next century. Indeed, the political act of the Quakers is anomalous in America's national development. Finally, Hill's *filmic* offering to the portal's cache, dramatizing the origins of the American nation, invoked a high order of mimetic magic, indeed.

Behind Robeson, and behind the Peace Arch itself, stood another totem of sorts. Tower Beacon #5 served as a guide to shipping in the Georgia Strait and established the marine frontier between Canadian and American waters. The antenna is a reminder that two national radio spheres are joined here in an electromagnetic zone of protection.

Where the CBNRC plucked messages from the Babel of the airwaves and sorted them for processing in the cubicles of its foreign-language experts, Robeson gathered and disseminated songs in such languages as Russian, Chinese, French, Polish, Yiddish, Spanish, and English. At the Peace Arch concert he recited from the Chinese 'Chilai', and in Yiddish, speaking of 'the same brave people who fought back in Warsaw, in that epic of the Warsaw ghetto', and in Russian he recited Shostakovich's call for world peace. Where the intelligence-censorship-propaganda complex wrought a technocratic understanding of cultural diversity in order to manage it, Robeson touched deeper structures of communication, harmonics that respected both the similarities and differences in human cultures. The content of the song form itself resonated with a 'strange inner logic' well beyond the reach of the CBNRC's cryptography.

The Third Space

Martin Duberman's account of the 1952 Peace Arch concert occupies two paragraphs and one footnote in his monumental biography. He recounts the financial difficulties overcome by Robeson's United Freedom Fund associates in arranging the tour and the problem of mobilizing local support in the face of FBI intimidation. The second paragraph concerns the concert itself:

> The most successful single stop on the tour, from both a political and a financial point of view, was at the Peace Arch itself—largely because of the response from the Canadian side of the border. Thanks to the efforts of the Mine, Mill trade unionists, twenty-five to thirty thousand turned up on the Vancouver side

Paul Robeson, Harvey Murphy, beacon tower #5. Photo W. Chass. Rare Books and
Special Collections, University of British Columbia Library, Mine-Mill Collection.

for the concert; no more than five thousand mobilized on the American side (the
American press estimated *total* attendance at five thousand; the Canadian press
put the figure seven times higher). The FBI, predictably, was also there. While
the Border Patrol took license-plate numbers, FBI agents filmed and photographed the event itself. Nonetheless, there were no incidents, and the sponsors
laid plans for making the Peace Arch concert an annual event.[115]

Duberman's account approaches the border from the American side. The Robeson
concert is indexed not just in the biographical sequence of Robeson's life but at a
limit of American cultural nationalist discourse. The Canadians are positioned outside Duberman's narrative voice, exempted from his damning narrative focus on
American repressive state apparatuses.

Compare Reg Whitaker's account, which introduces Robeson as a test of Canadian immigration policy:

Invited to attend the Canadian convention of the Mine-Mill union in 1952,
Robeson was prevented from leaving the US—thus relieving Canada of having

to bar him, which it certainly would have done, given the source of the invitation. Robeson dramatized the situation unforgettably by giving a concert just across the border at the Peace Arch Park in Washington state, attended by 30,000 Canadians on the British Columbia side; this event was repeated annually for the next three years.[116]

Whitaker's sources are primarily Canadian cabinet documents and newspaper accounts. His account mirrors Duberman's but from the other side of the border, and the narrative is focused on the ideological compliance of Canadian officials, indeed, the isomorphism of Canadian and American internal security policy.

What both accounts share is nationality as the 'plane of consistency' on which the event becomes visible. Both Duberman and Whitaker visualize the national boundary as a binarism, reflecting the newspaper reports and the union's publicity. They present the reader with the spatial image of Robeson standing on the American side facing the Canadian audience. Yet the union's photographs reveal that the space was indeterminate, with Americans and Canadians and their respective security agents freely mingling around the Arch. Ironic though both accounts may be, and however critical of their respective governments, they fall short of evoking the liminality of the concert, its complex irruption into the landscape and soundscape of Semiahmoo.

I walked around the Arch, noticing the disposition of the site from a technical perspective. An obvious difficulty was how to place Paul Robeson near the portal itself, exactly at the border, while still keeping sightlines to him clear from the largest possible surrounding space. The trees, foliage, and natural barriers made this location more problematic than if, for example, the stage was placed near the American customs building, allowing the audience to congregate in the full length of the park, and thus taking advantage of the rising ground. Under the circumstances, the US inspection point would hardly have been a suitable backdrop.

How then could 40,000 people be accommodated? In fact, the site chosen limited sightlines to an audience of 5,000 people at most, and the sound engineer's horn speakers would have been hard put to serve more than that number. Standing where the stage was positioned, facing eastward, the scale of the park seems miniature compared to the written accounts (including reports that took into account the possible exaggeration of organizers and scaled the crowd estimate back to 15,000). The union's photographs contain no evidence of even 15,000 people.[117] Through sheer repetition, Harvey Murphy and Tom McEwen in the *Pacific Tribune* fixed their very high estimates on the public record despite caustic press attacks labelling them 'Red Press Agents' directed from Moscow. Yet, of the two organizations reporting the *lowest* figures, the RCMP counted 5,000, but oddly enough the Soviet news service Tass reported just 4,500.[118]

The inflated estimates ought not temper admiration for Mine-Mill and Paul Robeson. To have congregated 5,000 people 35 kilometres from downtown Vancouver under the combined gaze of the FBI and RCMP was a significant achievement by any measure. The post-Gouzenko atmosphere of tension had settled on Semiahmoo, and people were right to worry: the police photographed them, filmed them, and took their licence numbers. Cliff Harvison, by 1952 in Vancouver commanding the RCMP's 'E' Division, intervened during the concert with an undisclosed action that, he wrote, 'will undoubtedly complicate matters within the Union, particularly insofar as _____ are concerned.'[119]

On the other hand, Murphy failed to grasp that the concert's significance had less to do with actual numbers than with opening up a 'third' space between the discourses of culture and national security, brief moments wherein an approximate balance of identity and difference was extricated from the coercive sinews of nationality. Robeson was blocked from exploring and elaborating it any further in Canada, but it is an afternoon that should be remembered, and remembered accurately.[120]

Close-up

Peace Arch concerts were repeated for the next three years, but none matched the success of the first year. In 1956, when he was finally permitted to enter Canada again, Paul Robeson's Massey Hall concert was an emotional occasion. Bruce Mickleburgh wrote of tears welling in the eyes of the overflow crowd 'as the old familiar figure stepped on the stage'. Everyone could see the physical decline he had suffered during his period of internal exile, but Mickleburgh noted that this fragility somehow enhanced his stature and his closeness to the audience. Robeson was clearly moved, too, and he recalled for Mickleburgh in an interview afterwards his very first Massey Hall date, 'one of the first concerts in my life of any importance'. He still kept the clipping of 'a woman critic who wrote a very warm review' that swayed him away from a law career towards song.[121]

His politics had not dimmed. He told Mickleburgh that the Montgomery bus strike 'shows the strongest will to end oppression since the Civil War' and 16 million black Americans protesting firmly but peacefully 'in the Ghandian tradition' would see it done. Canadians, he said, could do something for the people in Montgomery, Alabama: '[t]here are millions of people who have been silent for a few years and who, now that things are beginning to loosen up, will be coming forth again. They are still there, and they will be multiplied.'[122]

Such statements were used by the Mounties to justify intensified pressure on the singer and intrusive surveillance measures, and the RCMP supplied a brief to cabinet that this time succeeded in his being banned outright from entering Canada. One of seven immense manual card indexes used at RCMP Overbrook was titled 'Coloured Persons' Index'. In 1956, the information from Robeson's index cards was transferred from it to the new MacBee punchcard system, both as ROBESON and under his alias, ROBSON. (Not that he ever had used a secret identity—the suspicion came from inaccurate spelling by RCMP officers over the years.) These index cards still exist somewhere in the CSIS complex.[123]

This quiet but ongoing security interference lay behind the cancellation of an invitation to Robeson to sing at Dalhousie University in Halifax in February 1958. Wiretap information had alerted the Mounties to Robeson's planned tour of the Maritime provinces. Deputy Commissioner Rivett-Carnac cautioned investigators

Paul Robeson at last Peace Arch concert, August 1955. Harvey Murphy, Lloyd Brown, and Al King are visible on the platform to the left of Robeson. Photo W. Chass. Rare Books and Special Collections, University of British Columbia Library, Mine-Mill Collection.

not to intervene overtly and to avoid the controversy that would follow 'if the matter became public'.[124] G. Hamilton Southam of External Affairs' DL(2) was advised that the singer's status as an undesirable visitor had not changed, and when N.O. Jones passed on word of Robeson's plans to other offices he requested that the information not be disseminated without prior authorization and that the RCMP must not be named as its source. Then, living in exile in London, Robeson considered moving to Canada, perhaps unaware that its government's antipathy towards him had not abated.[125] Given the way Canadian cultural and security policies intersected, it never did abate to any great extent.

In October 1960, he set off on a three-month tour of Australia and New Zealand. He told an Auckland audience about the Peace Arch concerts near Vancouver when he had been 'shut up' by his own government. American diplomats in Auckland wished they could shut him up once more, particularly when he spoke of Little Rock and the civil rights of black Americans.[126] They organized a disinformation campaign behind the scenes designed to discredit him. Such treatment was the terrifying daily norm for this great artist.

Paul Robeson Jr believes that Western security services went beyond psychological warfare techniques to fatally damage his father's health. In particular, there is the mysterious, massive, and ultimately debilitating electroshock and drug treatment the singer underwent in a private London clinic in 1961–2.[127] The released

Canadian intelligence files shed no new light on this mystery, beyond affirming the alacrity with which the RCMP co-operated with the FBI in pursuing Robeson.[128]

Thanks to maverick producer Ross McLean, CBC-TV's *Close-up* carried Elaine Grand's extended interview with Paul Robeson, taped in London at the end of 1960.[129] Grand and Reuben Ship, writer of the anti-McCarthy radio satire *The Investigator*, had abandoned Toronto and taken up residence in London to escape the clamp-down on left-wingers in Davidson Dunton's CBC. After many months of delay by CBC's in-house censors, Colonel R.P. Landry and W.E.S. Briggs, the politically neutral Robeson item finally aired on 29 August 1961, just a few months after the singer was rushed to the clinic for the treatments from which he would never properly recover.

Martin Duberman sets out the circumstances of his hospitalization, and he weighs the fact that Robeson already was in poor health by the end of 1960 against the suspicions of police malfeasance. In Robeson's conversation with Elaine Grand the singer is animated, but not evidently ill. Certainly, one would not suspect that he would shortly require the most severe electroshock and drug therapies. He is passionate, charming, and speaks of his childhood, of linguistics, and of music. It is difficult to reconcile the vital and loquacious personality in the CBC interview with the broken figure he would shortly become, living reclusively until his death in 1976, primarily under the care of his sister Marian in Philadelphia.[130] By only a few months, his rare interdisciplinary talent outlasted the CBC's ban so that his Canadian friends once more could hear and see him, and recall the great concerts and rallies he once led in their cities.

Beyond the Border

'Man has no internal sovereign territory, he is all and always on the boundary.'[131] Bakhtin's insight, at once simple and ineffable, is perhaps better understood within the security field than in the realm of Canadian cultural nationalism, wherein identity remains a hermetic and self-policing concept. The security forces know better that the nation is constituted far less stably than it appears to be. Short of actual war, it maintains itself restlessly by fear, distrust, rumours, and selective memories, and by sensing, surveillance, subterfuge, sabotage, and secrecy. They know that any national situation is always more desperate than it seems. A character in Raymond Williams's novel, *Second Generation* (1964), captures precisely this unease when he warns, 'if you give it [the nation] up too soon, you will lose it to other classes and other nations.'[132]

Why is it that when Paul Robeson stepped in between the US and Canadian borders at the Peace Arch he triggered every possible alarm merely with a few folk songs sung in different languages? The full resources of the post-colonial 'security state', a feature of 'nationality' that intensified during the mid-twentieth century to the status of a dominant global system, were ranged against him, right down to the fetish objects cached in the Arch's cornerstone. Perhaps the tentative and unfulfilled promise of his songs—the seeds of alternative traces—was perceived as perilous because it was sovereign in some unique and unmanageable way. In the event, Robeson's analogical counterfactual was too perilously hopeful to withstand the crushing revelations concerning 'Soviet democracy'. Yet, this is not the whole story. He came to sing, and his song augured a cultural future so at odds with Canada's security-dominated cultural project that it was necessarily 'forgotten', even if never entirely cancelled.

Conclusion

*Nationalism is not overcome through mere internationalism; it is rather
expanded and elevated thereby into a system.*

Martin Heidegger

Plateaus of Freedom

Cultural theorists are fond of 'surface' metaphors. For Michel Foucault, social discourse produces different 'surfaces of visibility'; Gilles Deleuze and Félix Guattari
write of 'planes of consistency' and of subjectivity as a paradoxical 'folding' on
itself, and Giorgio Agamben toys with the idea of late capitalist culture collapsing
into a 'perfect exteriority'.[1] For liberals, the 'plateau of equality' is a proceduralist
surface upon which civil rights are located and cultural differences are arbitrated.[2]
In essence these are all *visual* metaphors and as such they are susceptible to a common perceptual uncertainty: is a given surface to be seen from one side or the
other? If a surface marks the frontier in a binary relation, do surface metaphors not
always in some way reinforce binary thinking?[3]

Read in a different way, though, surface metaphors also impute a certain
'tension' akin to the 'surface tension' known to fluid dynamics.[4] When a society or
a culture is represented as a 'surface of visibility', one is concerned not only with
what data do and do not appear on that surface but also with the tension that gathers
them together on the same plane and gives them coherence. In this way, 'security'
might be thought of as the *tension* that makes national 'culture' coherent, that is, at
once holding it together and rendering it comprehensible as a social entity.

An internal study commissioned by the Canadian Security Intelligence Service
instructively treats this notion of 'surface tension' with respect to the polygraph, or
lie detector. When Harvard psychologist and lawyer William M. Marston first published the polygraph concept in 1917, the report states, he had 'sought and obtained
a great deal of public attention as the originator of the "Wonder Woman" comic
strip, which publicized more of his fanciful theories, including an infallible lie
detector.'[5] Marston's interdisciplinary sorties were 'prolific and imaginative' but

228

ultimately his 'extravagant public statements brought about an investigation of criminal fraud which ended with his being censured.' Thus, an originator of the most celebrated bio-apparatus of truth was exposed as a fantasist and a deceiver.

This liar's paradox sets the CSIS study on edge and to stabilize these uncertainties the 'tension' principle is introduced. The purpose of interviewing a subject prior to conducting a polygraph test:

> is to explain to the examinee the futility of trying to 'beat' the instrument [and] to create a level of tension sufficient to ensure reaction to the questions. *The ability to create the 'right' degree of tension requires training, skill and experience.*[6]

Applied to state security and cultural administration as a whole, this passage suggests a fundamental pattern: first, there is *persuasion* to prevent the examinee from trying to 'beat' the instrument; then, 'a level of tension' is created as a surface of (mis)trust upon which the subject's reactions register. Metaphorically, this 'surface tension' describes how induced anxiety is generalized to help identify and manage alien phenomena. Conditioned to an optimal degree of intellectual and intercultural tension, Canadian citizens might occupy the 'plateau of freedom' as alert, but also unquestioning, members of a quasi-militarized national culture.[7]

Commencement

At the outset of this book I juxtaposed two convocation addresses by Arnold Davidson Dunton in order to specify a point where cultural nationalism asserted itself as a device closely attuned to Canada's collective security. Dunton felt a responsibility to adapt a public cultural institution like the CBC to the emerging national security culture of the 1940s and 1950s. Indeed, to do otherwise was to 'ignore the sky' or to 'reverse the flow of the St Lawrence'.

In November 1960, Malcolm Ross, Arnold Dunton's former colleague under John Grierson in the Wartime Information Board, assumed a different responsibility in a commencement address to the Kingston Collegiate and Vocational Institute.[8] Ross—a professor of Canadian literature and formerly a staunch promoter of the Soviet friendship movement—was concerned to conserve a degree of intellectual mobility and spiritual playfulness from the frigidity of Cold War paranoia.

Recalling his own commencement in Fredericton, New Brunswick, in 1929, he contrasted the 'end of the money-mad, pleasure-mad, crime-ridden twenties' to the 1930s: 'a mountain on the broken back of the world . . . a new era, long drawn-out, the Depression, [and] the flickering threat of revolution'. He wanted to retrieve from the 'self-deceiving mish-mash of memory' exactly what it felt like 'to grow up in that ruined world'.

He told the students that the hardship of the Depression years induced people to 'make light from dark':

> We had to scratch, mind you, to do it. But this was good for the muscles of the mind. And lo and behold, light broke—or what seemed to be light, what we

thought was light. I know now that [it] finally played us false. But for a while . . . the dream of light took hold of us, shaking loose the centre of the self, imparting sinew and purpose to a vast enterprise, a New Deal . . . a children's crusade in a false dawn, that's what it was. But we marched.

The Kingston students were not 'commencing' in such a world, he said, but their commencement was surely more difficult despite the 'flow of milk and honey' in the 1950s and 1960s. 'There are jobs . . . scholarships . . . we live in the "affluent" society and, to a degree, in the welfare state. Our dream of the thirties has come true, in part, at least.' But he warned them: 'Do not be beguiled by . . . self-pitying middle-aged people who tell you how lucky you are', for beneath the surface of prosperity there is 'a fear more dreadful than I could have imagined in 1929'.

We all feel it now and then in quick spasms. . . . We hide, we hide behind ourselves in our ranch-houses and two-car garages. We rock 'n' roll the fear away . . . we huddle together, herd-like . . . looking like everyone else, talking and acting like everyone else. . . . Thus it is to be prosperous under the bomb.

But Ross was not sure that the nuclear threat fully explained this fear, for there was an even 'more insidious' danger. Even 'if the bomb never falls (and it may never fall)', he said, Cold War inquietude had succeeded in structuring both conformity and anti-conformity, 'and alas, the conformist and his ranch-house, the beatnik and his beard are heads and tails of the same coin.' His experience could offer no simple remedy for the depoliticized version of citizenship that embraced the students in 1960. 'In the false light of the thirties we thought man could be saved from out-side—by new laws, new deals, new political methods and systems. We were wrong, very wrong.' On the other hand, the students could not 'hide forever . . . from political action. As never before we must act, we must be citizens.'

The dilemma, as Ross saw it, could only be resolved by redressing the internalization of fear and the discipline thus imposed. 'Mark the meaning of the thirties,' he warned, 'mark it well. Action from the *outside* will not avail.' Look inward first, he told them:

recover before it is utterly effaced the lost and bright image of the human person cast anciently in the mould of the divine . . . what he is, where he is, and why. There is a call for a new direction in our thought, our feelings and our actions, a direction that is new because it is so very, very old.

Forty-two years on Malcolm Ross's plea seems to resonate with a conception of citizenship that respects and learns from difference, that is finely adapted to its immediate surroundings. It suggests a form of citizenship that is not force-fed by nationalist cultural policies, policed by a culture-security complex, or shadowed by a culture of secrecy.

In the aftermath of the September 2001 terrorist attacks in the US the inter-sections of culture and security have emerged from obscurity to become topics of debate (and occasionally of full-blown polemic when it comes to matters such as intellectual freedom, privacy, national duty, and ethnic profiling). Postmodernism's earliest expressions in Philip Johnson's and Robert Venturi's ironic and playful architecture have been superseded by the terrifying erasure of modernism's crowning achievement: the World Trade Center. Cultural relativism is no longer simply a philosophical canard in academia's 'culture wars' but rather is touted as a serious intellectual weakness exposing Western nations to present danger. In this sense, the ambivalent Tracy Philipps, zealous and jealous protector of an archaic imperial consciousness, scholar of anti-Western secret societies, and fighter for minority rights, has never been more relevant. As an 'electrical engineer' of culture, he always insisted that the successful management of foreign nationality groups would result only from effective imperial censorship, security intelligence, and propaganda.

In *The Man Who Knew*, Phillip Tracey scrambles aloft in a biplane fighter armed with 'tracer bullets' to shoot down an undetectable and deadly Afghani airship before it can unleash its weapon of mass destruction on Europeans. Berserk imperialist and counter-imperialist fantasies of knock-out punches were a stock item of colonial espionage literature that became appallingly and anachronistically real on 11 September 2001. As was the case during the Gouzenko affair in 1946, a majority of Canadians accepted the intrusive security measures put in place after the attacks, the extraordinary detention of suspects, and the suppression of public information. Tracy Philipps's role in early Canadian multiculturalism policy gives pause for thought in light of these events. If a multicultural state is, by necessity, a national security state, then it follows that multicultural policies, and cultural policies in general, should be subject to critical scrutiny for the encroachment of security interests in cultural, artistic, and intellectual freedom. The gap between Canada's cultural nationalist rhetoric of equivalent citizenship and its culturally asymmetrical assignment of security resources surely provides one index of such freedom.

In the 1950s, Norman McLaren made *Love Your Neighbour* to mount such a critique of the emerging national security state. He knew that one of the ways that 'effective government' supersedes democratic government is to shape the citizen's perceptual relationship with the audiovisual apparatus. His film counters John Grierson's view of the 'aesthete' working in the service of the state. Grierson discerned the artist's usefulness as a type of cognitive explorer and trader essential to the progress of modernity and the security of nations. McLaren's film is a complex warning against conformity to the smooth screening of audiovisual 'reality', jogging viewers to notice not just their susceptibility to propaganda messages, but indeed their own construction as (mass) observers. Taking 'screening' in its other meaning, McLaren's film grimly documents the civil war within the NFB staff that occurred during the RCMP's security investigation. Once again, the gap between the government's rhetoric of restraint and moderation and its actual scapegoating and eliminating of Film Board employees did not bode well for artistic and intellectual liberty of expression, particularly within the other federal cultural departments and agencies.

Gouzenko's Choice

Igor Gouzenko indicates in *The Fall of a Titan* that architecture cannot lie, but his case also shows that the structure of a historical situation may not easily be discerned. Canadian ears have been well fortified against hearing certain stories, and one hopes the foregoing chapters will elicit some fresh questioning. If national culture and state security were as interdependent as I have argued, it is worth asking what other histories might be reconstituted out of the Cold War era that bear directly on Canadians' cultural and intellectual lives today.

Ultimately, new material unearthed concerning the Gouzenko case brings the wider 'culture and security' theme into direct engagement with an interpretation embedded in Canadian historiography. Did the 'cultural nationalism' that shaped the post-war development of federal cultural policies and institutions quietly track alongside a wider Anglo-American security agenda aimed at supplanting other less docile social formations? Recall NFB producer Bernard Devlin's dismay at the influx of 'mediocre reliables' at the Film Board during the post-Gouzenko purge of that organization.[9]

A recent book on the CIA's 'cultural Cold War' contends that reliable mediocrity flourished as a result of the CIA's manipulation of the Western intelligentsia, and it would be surprising if Canadian intellectual life was not touched by this hidden hand.[10] Yet, in truth, the consequences of domestic censorship, intelligence, and propaganda activities on Canada's historiography and its cultural development during the Cold War are known only to the small extent that a few commendable independent scholars have succeeded in penetrating the veil of official secrecy. Perhaps the cultural effects of state security were in fact minimal, but the enduring silence of those who acted in this secret theatre, the difficulties in accessing archival documents that might shed light on the cultural Cold War in Canada—including the specifics regarding Igor Gouzenko's 'choice of freedom'—raise concerns about the degree of official secrecy that citizens have been trained over decades to accept.

It is regrettable that Gouzenko's former neighbour Yvanna Petrowska feels constrained from speaking out freely about her part in the Gouzenko affair. The case had a sufficient impact on Canadian culture that it needs to be fully and accurately assessed. Indeed, thousands of women who served as censors have faithfully kept their silence about the extent of domestic censorship activities during the Cold War. One wishes that the historians who have been noticeably circumspect about such matters would publish the full extent of their findings.

Peter Dwyer once wrote in a Canada Council annual report that arm's-length arts councils are 'the servant of two masters, and like Janus we face both ways—up the footpath of the spirit and along the autobahn of efficiency.' The insouciance of his statement should now be clear. After all, Dwyer, 'Janus' himself pulled in both directions throughout his career, knew best at what junctures cultural administration spilled into the surprisingly spacious backstage of state security and 'effective government'. Cultural policies and intellectual freedom present an ongoing concern that did not abate with the passing of the Cold War.[11]

This passing has presented a fresh opportunity for political solidarities to form without the pernicious association to the former Soviet Union and its systems of espionage and propaganda. Rethinking the relationship of nationality, security, and culture is a difficult but essential prerequisite for which historians and archival records may have something useful to offer. In an era of much confusion about the rump Cold War institutions there is a need for historical accounts and area studies that do not take the principle of nationality and its consequent secrecy as given. Canadian studies, for example, can be approached more critically, seeking to recover people's intellectual agency from the blandishments of cultural national-ism, something the Cold War national security state actively discouraged and diverted. In fact, the censorship-intelligence-propaganda complex that proliferated in Canada after World War II played a counterpoint between national culture and state security, with the result that freedom, especially intellectual freedom, plateaued on the principle of nationality. The downfall of Paul Robeson was brought about by his refusal to submit to its 'forced choice', his courage in the face of harassment by state security agencies, and his insistence that 'culture' in its artis-tic sense could be truly popular—that is, accessible and meaningful to people across the social spectrum—while still respecting differences. Robeson and the wider project he represented were stymied by a mixture of security and cultural policy measures, both open and secret, that attests to the fragility and the enduring power of art to effect social change.

Notes

Introduction

1. Raymond Williams, 'The Arts Council: Politics and Priorities', lecture, Arts Council of Great Britain, 3 Nov. 1989, 15.
2. Other writers may come to mind here: Erving Goffman's espionage-inspired 'culture-pattern slips', Pierre Bourdieu's 'habitus', and Homi K. Bhabha's interstitial cultural spaces. Each of these writers supports in his own way Raymond Williams's observation that orthodoxy is *notoriously alert* to what is emergent in a culture.
3. Yi-Fu Tuan, *Landscapes of Fear* (Minneapolis: University of Minnesota Press, 1979), 6.
4. A similar five-mast array was erected at Masset. NAC RG 10, vol. 7789, file 27157–2, Masset—Radio Beam Station, 1943. Initially, the intercept site was located directly above the old village in a playing field cleared by the Haida. In early operations antennas were attached to nearby treetops. During protracted lease negotiations the Haida leaders underlined their demand for electrification of the village as payment for the land by felling a tree across the station's power cable.
5. Herbert Spencer, *Social Statics, or, The conditions essential to human happiness specified, and the first of them developed* (London: Williams and Norgate, 1868), 216.
6. For example, Will Kymlicka, *Finding Our Way: Rethinking Ethnocultural Relations in Canada* (Toronto: Oxford University Press, 1998), remains silent about how the radically asymmetrical liberal state he countenances might mobilize its population for war, or how it might grant asymmetrical rights without a concomitant increase in surveillance and policing of ethnocultural minorities. He counters mainstream fears that multiculturalism erodes national sovereignty by noting that it applies 'pressures both positive (incentives) and negative (barriers)' in order to promote integration. Thus, Canadians are wrong if they associate multiculturalism with the total set of demands of special ethnocultural interests when, in reality, it is a system that reciprocally imposes the state's demand for integration on the individuals comprising such groups. Here Kymlicka seems to perpetuate a bad-faith rationale for multiculturalism as a means of social control. Indeed, his culturally sensitive approach to liberal political theory would be strengthened by opening up the question of special cultural rights to deal directly with state security (even if the result might not so readily valorize grant-winning concepts like 'nation-building'). A liberal theory of citizenship for which 'forced choice' is not axiomatic would have to disassociate 'nation-building' from

cultural rights and thereby repudiate the illiberal and effaced cultural logic of national security that associates cultural difference with risk.

7. NAC, RG 37 vol. 49, file 60–3–RCMP, C. Starnes to A.G. Doughty, 14 Dec. 1926. On 19 Mar. 1928, Starnes offered Doughty a further 'considerable accumulation' of material.

8. Ibid., 8 Nov. 1951.

9. J.L. Granatstein, 'The "Hard Obligations" of Citizenship: The Second World War in Canada', in William Kaplan, ed., *Belonging: The Meaning and Future of Canadian Citizenship* (Montreal and Kingston: McGill-Queen's University Press, 1993), 36–49; A. Davidson Dunton, 'Freedom for Whom?' Convocation Address, University of Saskatchewan, 14 May 1954 (Toronto: CBC, 1954). National Library of Canada.

10. NAC, RG 41, vol. 200, file 11–18–11–41 pt. 2, 'Citizens' Forum', F.W. Park to A.D. Dunton, 21 Feb. 1946. Park objected to Dunton's 'intellectual contraceptive', but Dunton argued that cancelling the 'broadcast on Canadian relations with Russia . . . is right because . . . it would be unreal . . . without bringing in the current spy business.' He added that 'to substitute [the topic of the United Nations in place of Canada's relations with Russia] is likely to be helpful rather than harmful to sensible judgement on the part of the public.' A.D. Dunton to E. Bushnell, 13 Dec. 1946, advising title change. Arthur Siegel, *Radio Canada International: History and Development* (Oakville, Ont.: Mosaic, 1996), 99–101, recounts the Solomon-Griffiths firings. NAC, RG 146, ATIP 96-A-00119, RCMP file, 'CBC—TV Programs', J. Leopold to file, 9 May 1952: 'he realized that if the CBC proceeds . . . it may lay itself open to charges of [assisting] the Communist inspired campaign to celebrate the 100th anniversary of the death of Gogol. . . . Asked what he should do, the undersigned [Leopold] ventured to suggest that if he were in [Dunton]'s shoes he would cancel the contract to avoid any unpleasant repercussions.'

11. A. Davidson Dunton, 'Freedom For Minds', Founder's Day address, University of New Brunswick, 28 Feb. 1957. National Library of Canada.

12. Fredric Jameson, *The Geopolitical Aesthetic: Cinema and Space in the World System* (Bloomington: Indiana University Press and BFI Publishing, 1992), 3.

13. Ibid., 9.

14. Michel de Certeau, *Heterologies: Discourse on the Other* (Minneapolis: University of Minnesota Press, 1986), 186.

Chapter 1

1. NAC, RG 26 (31), vol. 12, file 8–2–2, Irving, 'Report, for the Committee on Morale, of Research of Rumours, September 5th, 1942', 4.

2. NAC, Mark McClung, interview by Donald Brittain, 15 Jan. 1981, ISN 61911.

3. 'The Armenian' was Ladislaus Biberovich, 'the Hindu Kush' was the Reverend Wasyl Kushnir, and 'Dynamite' most likely refers to Duncan Cameron, member of the Committee for Co-operation in Canadian Citizenship and critic of Tracy Philipps.

4. NAC, MG E350, Tracy Philipps Papers (hereafter TPP), vol. 1, file 16, Thomas Cook Ltd. to T. Philipps, 20 Mar. 1941. A representative replied evenly that Philipps had received exactly the accommodations he paid for.

5. 'Distinguished Soldier Is Sure Britain Will Remain Supreme in the Mediterranean', *Edmonton Journal*, 20 Nov. 1940.

6. NAC, TPP, vol. 1, file 24, T. Philipps to T.C. Davis, 7 July 1941.

7. Ibid., file 22, Lawn and Alder, Merchants and Colonial Agents, to Tracy Philipps, 21 Sept. 1942. They apologized about his spectacles: 'Our premises & records were totally destroyed on April 17th & our optician suffered a similar action on May 10th.'

8. Ibid., file 11, Tracy Philipps to T.E. Frost, 18 Nov. 1942. Philipps's serum, 'strictly for my use alone', was obtained through the mail from the Manager of the Army and Navy Club, Pall Mall.

9. Myron Momryk, 'V.J. Kaye (Kysilewsky) (1896–1976): Ukrainian Family Historian', *East European Genealogist* 3, 1 (Sept. 1994): 6–7; also, NAC, MG 32, vol. 445, Personnel File: 'Vladimir Julian Kaye (Kysilewsky)'. When Kysilewsky joined the Nationalities Branch in 1942 he was advised 'for administrative convenience' to change his name to 'Kaye'. During World War I Kysilewsky and Philipps fought on opposing sides, but in 1930s London they formed a fast friendship while Kaye ran the Ukrainian Bureau.

10. Leslie A. Pal, *Interests of State: The Politics of Language, Multiculturalism and Feminism in Canada* (Montreal and Kingston: McGill-Queen's University Press, 1993), 72; RG 35/7, National Records Committee Files, vol. 16, Advisory Committee on Co-operation in Canadian Citizenship, Part II (confidential), 2. Indeed, the Advisory Committee on Co-operation in Canadian Citizenship (CCCC), in its confidential report following Philipps's departure, called this an 'extraordinary situation of an Advisor who was not Canadian, and with a very limited knowledge of Canada, in charge of activities the purpose of which was to teach Canadian citizenship. Being familiar only with the European pattern, he placed his emphasis on the political problems in Europe rather than the cultural contribution of these groups to Canada.'

11. Ludwig Wittgenstein, *Culture and Value*, trans. Peter Winch (Chicago: University of Chicago Press, 1984), 35e, 84e.

12. Ibid., 54e.

13. N.F. Dreisziger, 'The rise of a bureaucracy for multiculturalism: the origins of the Nationalities Branch', in Norman Hillmer, Bohdan Kordan, and Lubomyr Luciuk, eds, *On Guard For Thee: War, Ethnicity, and the Canadian State, 1939–45* (Ottawa: Canadian Committee for the Second World War, 1988), 1–29.

14. Ibid. Davis was seconded from the Saskatchewan bench in July 1940 to establish the Department of National War Services.

15. N.F. Dreisziger, '7 December 1941: A Turning Point in Canadian Wartime Policy Toward Enemy Ethnic Groups?', *Journal of Canadian Studies* 32, 1 (Spring 1997): 21.

16. Ibid.

17. NAC, RG 26 (31), vol. 12, file 8–2–2, Irving, 'Report, for the Committee on Morale, of Research of Rumours, September 5th, 1942', 5. Rumour had it that Lapointe was murdered and that the case had to be hushed up.

18. Dreisziger cites J.L. Granatstein, *Man of Influence: Norman A. Robertson and Canadian Statecraft, 1929–68* (Toronto: Deneau, 1981), 97.

19. Mario Duliano, *The City Without Women: A Chronicle of Internment Life in Canada During the Second World War*, trans. Antonino Mazza (Oakville, Ont.: Mosaic, 1994). Playwright Duliano was interned as a suspected Fascist sympathizer; his Fredericton camp diary records that the internees were of 18 different nationalities. The eight internment camps for Japanese Canadians in British Columbia were established under a separate administrative mechanism.

20. Irving Abella and Harold Troper, *None Is Too Many: Canada and the Jews of Europe, 1933–1948* (New York: Random House, 1983); Valerie Knowles, *Strangers at Our*

Gates: Canadian Immigration and Immigration Policy, 1540–1990 (Toronto: Dundurn Press, 1992); Reg Whitaker, *Double Standard: The Secret History of Canadian Immigration Policy* (Toronto: Lester & Orpen Dennys, 1987).

21. N.F. Dreisziger, 'Tracy Philipps and the Achievement of Ukrainian-Canadian Unity', in Stella Hryniuk and Lubomyr Luciuk, eds, *Canada's Ukrainians: Negotiating an Identity* (Toronto: University of Toronto Press, 1991), 326–41.

22. Vladimir J. Kysilewsky, *Early Ukrainian Settlements in Canada, 1895–1900* (Toronto: University of Toronto Press, 1964). See 'The Problem of the Ethnic Name', xxiii–xxvi: 'A stateless nation which becomes a minority in an alien body politic is invariably exposed to political, social and economic pressure aimed at the obliteration of its identity. . . . Ukrainians within the Russian Empire were subjected to all of these pressures . . . [with the result that] the peasant masses in both politico-geographic areas, Galacia and Bukowina, [who immigrated to Canada] had little national consciousness.' Unification of (anti-Communist) Ukrainian *Canadians* thus may have been encouraged in order to nurture the potential for a Western-friendly Ukrainian government-in-exile.

23. Ibid.

24. NAC, TPP, vol. 2, file 28, T. Philipps to V.J. Kaye, 13 Jan. 1941.

25. In *Son of Abdan: A West African Novel* (London: Hutchinson: 1936) the inscription introduces 'Captain Webster' as 'an officer in the King's African Rifles [who] learned to know and love the African native, of whose psychology he seems to have acquired a haunting understanding.'

26. F.A.M. Webster, *The Man Who Knew* (London: Selwyn and Blount, 1927).

27. NAC, TPP, vol. 1, file 1, 'Personal Dossier', undated autobiographical summary. It states: 'In 1927 the well-known British author F.A.M. Webster made (without consultation) Mr. Philipps, under the thinly veiled disguise of 'Philip TRACY' [*sic*], the principal character of his historical romance, "THE MAN WHO KNEW." '

28. NAC, Robert England Papers (hereafter REP), vol. 3, file 1. Three of Philipps's numerous articles are collected here: 'Pan-Islam in Africa' (1917), 'The Tide of Colour' (n.d.), and 'Nabingi: An Anti-European Secret Society' (1919).

29. See Wesley Wark's introduction to Wark, ed., *Spy Fiction, Spy Films, and Real Intelligence* (London: Frank Cass, 1991). In fact, F.A.M. Webster's post-World War I novel is respectful of German Intelligence exploits, particularly information-gathering carried out under the guise of archaeological surveys.

30. Webster, *The Man Who Knew*, 71. (His scare brackets.)

31. J.M. Coetzee, *Giving Offense: Essays on Censorship* (Chicago: University of Chicago Press, 1996), ch. 9, 'Apartheid Thinking', 163–84.

32. Carole Pateman, *The Sexual Contract* (Stanford, Calif.: Stanford University Press, 1988).

33. Geoffrey Bilson, *The Guest Children: The Story of the British Child Evacuees Sent to Canada During World War II* (Saskatoon: Fifth House Press, 1988), 4. The sponsor for Philipps's Canadian lecture tour was Major Fred Ney, Director of the National Council of Education. An ardent imperialist, Ney promoted the evacuees' cause in Canada.

34. NAC, TPP, vol. 1, file 5, T. Philipps to Lord Halifax, 9 July 1940. During the 1920s the Norwegian Arctic explorer Fridtjoff Nansen (1861–1930) served as the League of Nations High Commissioner for Refugees, and provided relief to many Russians displaced by war.

35. British Foreign Office, document 371/22961, Philipps to Halifax, 6 Jan. 1939. In this report Philipps does indeed mention events in the Ukraine as providing an 'unexpected common ground for collaboration with Germany'.

36. Charles Ritchie, *The Siren Years, 1939–45* (Toronto: Macmillan, 1974), 53–4. Ritchie was with the Canadian High Commission in London. He called it 'a whole social system on the run . . . only the people at the top'.
37. Ibid.
38. Ibid., T. Philipps to Lord Halifax, 25 June 1940.
39. Ibid., T. Philipps to Lord Halifax, 9 July 1940.
40. Carl Berger, *The Sense of Power: Studies in the Ideas of Canadian Imperialism, 1867–1914* (Toronto: University of Toronto Press, 1970), views imperialism in Canada as a 'lost cause' by 1914, but its remnants were still potent when Philipps encountered them in 1940.
41. Lord Milner, ed., *The Nation and the Empire* (London: Constable, 1913), 290. Also see 'The Two Empires', his address to the Royal Colonial Institute, *The Times*, 16 June 1908.
42. NAC, TPP, vol. 1, file 5, T. Philipps to S. Watt, 7 Sept. 1940.
43. T.E. Lawrence, *The Seven Pillars of Wisdom* (London: Jonathan Cape, 1935 [1926]), 384. According to J.N. Lockman, *Meinertzhagen's Diary Ruse: False Entries on T.E. Lawrence* (Grand Rapids, Mich.: Cornerstone 1995), 65, Lawrence's 'insight into Meinertzhagen's essential nature' was accurate, but it elicited from 'Meiner' a lifelong disinformation vendetta against Lawrence and his legend.
44. Col. R. Meinertzhagen, *Kenya Diary, 1902–1906* (London: Oliver and Boyd, 1957), 74. For more of the same, see his *Middle East Diary, 1917–56* (London: Cresset, 1959).
45. TPP, vol. 2, file 23, T. Philipps to Walter Herbert, 19 Nov. 1943. For Philipps the geopolitical definition of Canadian citizenship was a simple colonial formula: 'British subjects residing permanently in Canada'.
46. NAC, TPP, vol. 1, file 19, T. Philipps to S.T. Wood, 20 Sept. 1941; PRO, FO 395/619, TP to Sir Stephen Gaselee, 5 Apr. 1938. Philipps visited South America for several months in mid-1938. This appears to have been another 'personal mission' without official sponsorship by the Foreign Office.
47. W.E.B. Du Bois, *Autobiography of W.E.B. Du Bois* (New York: International Publishers, 1971), 291.
48. Paul Gilroy, *The Black Atlantic: Modernity and Double Consciousness* (London: Verso, 1994).
49. For Webster (see *The Man Who Knew*, 38–9), 1920s London is a patchwork of racially determined prospects and refuges. To escape the giant black man chasing him, for example, Carruthers ducks into a restaurant from which his pursuer is blocked by the invisible colour bar. But recent relaxation of these rules permits a 'Hindu of the student type now so common in England' to enter and watch him from the next table. Du Bois's characters in *Dark Princess* shrug off the bar that prohibits their entry to restaurants.
50. Du Bois, *Autobiography*, 291. This may explain the Colonial Office Library's collection of Du Bois titles.
51. Indeed, in Du Bois's *Dark Princess* (Jackson: University of Mississippi Press, 1995), the protagonist, Matthew Towns, sings a slave spiritual to overcome 'racism within racism' at the Darker Peoples' secret council meeting, where black America is dismissed as having no importance.
52. NAC, TPP, vol. 1, file 24, T. Philipps, unaddressed, 9 Sept. 1941.
53. Ibid.
54. Philip Tracey's cabinet briefing: '[O]n Intelligence service I noticed that natives of South Africa and such advanced communities as Sierra Leone served as transport drivers and in Labour battalions in France. They were, therefore, brought in contact with

the American blacks, who had some personal experience of lynchings and other persecutions. In German East Africa also they came into touch, for the first time perhaps, with East African and Congolese soldiers from the border of the Sudan.

'After the war I was sent to Constantinople, where I came into touch with Eudisch, the Soviet representative. He informed that in the School of Oriental Propaganda at Moscow the Russians were educating and financing twenty-four blacks. . . . [T]he American negro, Elder Smith, who died on his mission to Abyssinia in 1920, had been one of their greatest adepts, although he had taken only a correspondence course. . . . I was told that, through the influence of Smith, four Abyssinians had been sent to America to receive an Ethiopian education.

'I was following up this trail in Asia and India when I was recalled to Central Africa to deal with the Nabingi trouble. . . . I have here a short account of the origin and development of a notorious Anti-European Secret Society of Central Africa. It serves as an excellent example of the type of African Secret societies now tending, with the advent of race consciousness, the development of communications and contact with education to form into widespread organisations of almost Masonic significance and most profoundly disquieting tendencies. To this I have appended the official account of the attacks made by the armed forces of this semi-religious and wholly fanatical organisation upon British, Belgian and German forces, indiscriminately both before, during and after the Great War. . . .

'An elementary form of hypnotism is an important factor in the operations of the Nabingi, or "Expellers" as this society is named. It has, for more than half a century, terrorised, from time to time, large tracts of British, Belgian and German territory in Africa.'(148)
55. NAC, TPP, vol. 1, file 5, A. Phelps Stokes to T. Philipps, 11 June 1940.
56. Ibid., T. Philipps to T. 'Jesse' Jones, 15 June 1940.
57. Ibid., vol. 1, file 19, W.E.B. Du Bois to T. Philipps, 3 Apr. 1941, under the letterhead, '*Phylon:* The Atlanta University Review of Race and Culture'. Du Bois extended a formal invitation to the 'Conference for Cooperation of Science and Work'.
58. Ibid., Du Bois to Philipps, 7 Apr. 1942.
59. W.E.B. Du Bois, 'Chronicle of Race Relations', *Phylon* (Winter 1941): 81–2.
60. Ibid., 82.
61. Du Bois, 'Chronicle of Race Relations', *Phylon* (Spring 1941), 185. The text of Philipps's address follows (185–8) and the quotations cited are drawn from these pages.
62. Ibid. 'Thus, in Africa, the prerequisites for democratic institutions are still lacking. Yet democracy from Europe continues, dangerously and illogically, to be held up to subtropical Africans as an ideal and an ambition worth fighting to attain.'
63. NAC, TPP, vol. 1, file 19, W.E.B. Du Bois to T. Philipps, 10 Apr. 1941.
64. Ibid., file 20, T. Philipps to Sir Gerald Campbell, 1 June 1941.
65. Ibid., vol. 2, file 6, S.T. Wood to T. Philipps, 2 May 1941.
66. Ibid., vol. 1, file 26, Saul F. Rae, 'Minutes of Interdepartmental Meeting on Organization of Proposed Committee on Cultural-Group Cooperation Under Ministry of National War Services, 30 October 1941'. The intelligence interests were represented by Norman Robertson of External Affairs, Insp. D.C. Saul, RCMP, and O. Coderre, Nationalization Branch; censorship by J. Sydney Roe, Examiner of Publications, press censors Wilfred Eggleston and Ladislaus Biberovich, and Edgar T. Read, Custodian of Enemy Property Branch; propaganda/information was represented by Walter Herbert, Public Information, John Grierson, National Film Board, Peter Aylen, Canadian

Broadcasting Corporation, and Saul F. Rae, Department of External Affairs. W.P.J. O'Meara represented the Department of State, responsible for citizenship registration. The others invited to the meeting were experts on 'cultural groups': Prof. George W. Simpson, slated to head the new committee, Robert England, Department of Pensions and Health, and Tracy Philipps, European adviser to the proposed committee.

67. Ibid.

68. Ibid.

69. Ibid., file 24, T. Philipps to unknown correspondent, 7 July 1941.

70. Of these, DeWitt Poole of the Office of Strategic Services was his most regular contact and closest US equivalent. Philipps's friend E. Bisiker, a British diplomat in the US, warned him that the FBI men were 'impossibly tight-lipped' and 'one must be cautious with them.'

71. Nicholas J. Cull, *Selling War: The British Propaganda Campaign Against American 'Neutrality' in World War II* (New York: Oxford University Press, 1995), 117–18.

72. William Stevenson Papers, University of Regina Archives, Sir W. Stephenson to William Stevenson, cable letter, 6 Apr. 1974: 'four floors at R[ockefeller] C[enter] 35, 36 and third. The last was a floor in section of the complex called BEB British Empire Building and housed the Communication Department plant and transmission equipment.'

73. NAC, TPP, vol. 1, file 21, T. Philipps to 'My dear Huxley', 29 May 1941; ibid., M. Huxley to T. Philipps, 2 June 1941; ibid., file 16, T. Philipps to Col. James Mess, 31 May 1941. The pro-Empire Mess responded warmly to Philipps and invited his opinion regarding 'Prince Vladislav Radziwill (New York) and his work organizing 5th column activities behind enemy lines.' Philipps responded that 'You may be sure that in the States, the Gestapo have got Radziwill pretty closely taped and will sooner or later bribe some of his confidantes to let out what is afoot. Then both the Russians and the Prussians will probably shoot any newcomer out of hand.' He wondered, though, about possibly training Ukrainians in Canada for this purpose.

74. Ibid., vol. 2, file 2, T. Philipps to M. MacDonald, 13 Aug. 1942. 'The French Canadian situation is undeniably bad, and undeniably artificial. It is NOT a complicated problem. This does not make it necessarily easier to deal with. . . . If there is an "injustice", it is that their Catholic Church, like the Orthodox in Serbia, is so little cath-olic [*sic*] and so narrowly national and so nearly auto-cephalous that it will not give its Youth an education to enable it to compete on equal terms with "les Anglais". By "les anglais" they mean business-Ontarians, especially Orange-men. The economic inferiority in which they feel themselves, like the Moslems faced by . . . neighbouring Christians, is embittered by their Church's inculcation, like Islam's, of a superiority complex against infidels and heretics. Thus there is bred in them, in everyday life, an envy, hatred and malice. Secondly, the news of the world and of the rest of Canada cannot be got without insinuation or distortion, past the authoritarian Sinn Fein-like village priests, down direct to the peasant farmers and industrial-workers to enable them to exercise their shrewd, soil-rooted and sober judgment. In the narrowest sense of the term, they can be regarded as the best Canadians of all, for they alone have ceased to look back nostalgically . . . beyond and outside Canada to a mother land . . . whose influence will predominate until Canada, as an (English-speaking) nation, can give them a patriotic maternal mysticism as embracing and as exalting as the old.'

75. Ibid., file 9, CCCC, Minutes of the 3rd Meeting, 23 Sept. 1942.

76. Ibid. A typical Philipps report was tabled: 'The Influence Exerted on the Mind, and Eventually on the Actions, of Recent-European Canadians by German-Controlled

Short-Waves from Their Motherlands Appealing to Them in Their Mother-Tongues'. To combat Radio-ROMA Philipps called for 'a positive programme of social restoration of these fellow-citizens of ours'. The discriminatory practices of 'Anglo North Americans [cause] Recent-Europeans in North America to look back, and listen-back . . . by the millions'.

77. NAC, RG 36 (Wartime Information Board), vol. 13, file 8–9–1, J.S. Thomson to J. Grierson, 11 May 1943.

78. NAC, TPP, vol. 2, file 10, C. Lamberti to T. Philipps, 20 Oct. 1942; ibid., vol. 1, file 29, T. Philipps to C. Payne, 5 Aug. 1943: 'Canadianizing broadcasts, decision: *No broadcasting to any special language groups in Canada*. That is, not even in English. (Ref. Memo 21 July 1943).' During the same period the CBC narrowed its labour broadcasts as well. See Marcus Klee, ' "Hands-off Labour Forum": The Making and Unmaking of National Working Class Radio Broadcasting in Canada, 1935–1944', *Labour/Le Travail* 35 (Spring 1995): 107–32.

79. NAC, TPP, vol. 1, file 25, T. Philipps to T.C. Davis, 1 Oct. 1941. Philipps also appears to have underestimated the importance of radio. He complained, 'I frankly regard broadcasting as one of the most troublesome, thankless (and ill-paid) chores which can be inflicted on a busy man.' On the other hand, he felt slighted by *CBC Talks* producers for overlooking him as a commentator.

80. Ibid., vol. 2, file 9, 'Minutes of the 3rd meeting of the Committee on Cooperation in Canadian Citizenship', 23 Sept. 1942.

81. Watson Kirkconnell and A.S.P. Woodhouse, *The Humanities in Canada* (Ottawa: Humanities Research Council of Canada [1944], 1947 edn), 7.

82. Watson Kirkconnell, *Canadians All: A Primer of Canadian National Unity* (Ottawa: Director of Public Information, 1941). Kirkconnell's interest in ethnocultural minorities began during World War I when he served as an internment camp guard in Kapuskasing, Ontario.

83. Ibid., 5–19 passim. See also Watson Kirkconnell, *A Slice of Canada: Memoirs* (Toronto: University of Toronto Press, 1967), 275. 'In January, 1940, I published . . . a series of articles on "War Aims and Canadian Unity," pleading for unity among New-Canadian groups and for a federal statement of war aims that would give coherence to that unity. The Prime Minister, Mr. Mackenzie King, who usually worked by indirection, then asked me through a personal emissary, Leonard Brockington, to write a substantial pamphlet on *The Ukrainian-Canadians and the War*, seeking to expound the issues of the conflict as I saw them and to emphasize the urgency. . . . I did not mince words in my advocacy of community integration in wartime.'

84. Kirkconnell, *Canadians All*, 20.

85. Watson Kirkconnell's *Seven Pillars of Freedom* (Toronto: Oxford University Press, 1944) became a *cause célèbre* on account of its almost hysterical anti-Communism. He viewed Communism as eroding the 'pillars' of religious faith, co-operation, education, justice, discipline, fraternity, and loyalty.

86. NAC, TPP, vol. 1, file 22, W. Kirkconnell to T. Philipps, 24 June 1941.

87. NAC, RG 146, file 93-A-00131 pt. 1, Department of National War Services, 'Extract from THE HOUR, published at 100 East 42nd St., New York', n.d.

88. *The New Republic*, 26 Oct. 1942, 545. This version added an insinuation that Philipps was involved with a secret Ukrainian-Fascist terrorist group, the ODWU (Organization for the Rebirth of the Ukraine).

89. Perhaps it did emanate from Canada, for it seems unlikely that an American writing for a New York publication would refer to 'the American State Department'. Philipps

claimed to possess postal intercepts that proved Biberovich's authorship, but the RCMP did not find the material convincing.

90. NAC, RG 36, vol. 13, file 8–9–1, R.B. Bryce to Clare Moyer, 26 Oct. 1942.

91. Ibid., L.R. LaFlèche to N.A. Robertson, 2 Nov. 1942. On 7 November 1942 T.C. Davis wrote to LaFlèche supporting Philipps: 'I unhesitatingly support Philipps in this controversy, as I am satisfied that he is a loyal citizen, intently desirous of rendering Canada and the United States every possible help in these difficult days.' Ibid. G.W. Simpson wrote to T.C. Davis on 17 November 1942 to explain that 'from the start that Mr. Philipps was working under a huge handicap because of his matrimonial difficulties and the fact that as an Englishman he was interesting himself so directly in the matter of promoting sound Canadianism. I have never had any doubts as to his sincerity and good faith. It is absolutely impossible for me to believe that he had any fascist leanings whatsoever. [W]e were absolutely agreed regarding . . . the principles of free governmental institutions and traditions. . . . It will be very difficult to find anyone with similar experience and talent. Dr. Kaye was of quite different temperament. He was without ambition and I think he joined us entirely out of a sense of duty. No one worked harder or more conscientiously.' The attack continued on 30 November 1943, when Glazebrook wrote to Heeney, Grierson, and Claxton attaching copies of 'another article concerning the Nationalities Branch'.

92. Prior to the war Dunton was editor of the Montreal *Standard*; he was responsible for the Canadian delegation's press relations during the Quebec Conference in 1943.

93. NAC, RG 36, vol. 13, file 8–9–1, A.D. Dunton to D.B. Rogers, 13 Nov. 1942.

94. NAC, TPP, vol. 1, file 33, T. Philipps to G.W. Simpson, 17 Oct. 1943.

95. Ibid., D.W. Buchanan to J. Grierson, 4 June 1943.

96. Ibid. Censor H.W. Baldwin advised Buchanan that while the left-wing press attacked Philipps there was otherwise little or no mention of him: 'The Nationalist Press, however, has been taking up all anti-Russian material, has reprinted verbatim the anti-Communist speech of Watson Kirkconnell.' Buchanan reported that 'Tracy Philipps travels, makes speeches, has personal contacts with editors of Ukrainian papers [and] has been attacked in editorial comment in some of the American Ukrainian papers.'

97. Ibid.

98. Ibid., M. Ross to D.W. Buchanan, 7 June 1943.

99. Ibid., *The Manchester Guardian*, 10 Sept. 1941. Philipps visited Libya in 1939.

100. NAC, RG 36, vol. 13, file 8–9–A, J. Grierson to L.R. LaFlèche, 28 Oct. 1943. The *Hour* article was tabled at the Wartime Information Board with Lester Pearson and others present. File contains Grierson's written notes: 'The interest of the Wartime Information Board is naturally . . . the whole matter of unity, particularly as between the various ethnic groups. . . . We were anxious to operate on a basis of co-operation with National War Services in this matter, but were doubtful of how the facts lay. If you now see fit . . . I feel certain that a formula could be devised which would secure a healthy co-operation. There is only one matter of which I am doubtful . . . [t]he influence of Mr. Philipps.'

101. There is no evidence Philipps had access to the high grade of diplomatic and counter-intelligence material provided by SIGINT or human sources. On the other hand, in one of his files there is a crib sheet he used for encoding his own messages.

102. NAC, TPP, vol. 1, file 21, V.J. Kaye to T. Philipps, 1 June 1941.

103. Ibid., file 31, T. Philipps to O.M. Biggar, 17 June 1942.

104. Ibid., 29 June 1942.

105. Ibid. See also Claude Beauregard, *Guerre et censure au Canada, 1939–1945* (Sillery, Que.: Septentrion, 1998).

106. NAC, RG 24, 'Minutes of the Sixth Meeting of the Security Panel', 6 Sept. 1946.
107. Ibid., vol. 769, file s-1950–21, part 4, N.A. Robertson to C.M. Drury, 14 Feb. 1951.
Canadian officials felt the need for such an organization, and its plan was given higher
priority after Robertson advised Drury, Deputy Minister of Defence, that the United
States government's willingness 'to maintain an open border [in an emergency]
depends on our ability to initiate active censorship on short notice in the event of war'.
Ibid., Minutes of the Sub Committee on Censorship Planning, 23 July 1951. Eric
Gaskell, secretary of the Security Panel, took the co-ordinating role in establishing the
peacetime organization. R.G. Robertson attended the meeting on behalf of the Privy
Council Office.
108. Ibid., G.R. Tottenham to Director of Naval Intelligence, 24 July 1951.
109. Ibid., Appendix to Minutes, 7 Aug. 1951, 'Refresher Training Course in National Censorship'. The DNI circled the word 'women' in the appendix and commented margin-
ally: 'Hang on to our own ex-censors! An eye should be kept on what women turn up
in Gaskell's net, lest they be ex-wren censors.'
110. In his biography of Norman Robertson, *A Man of Influence*, J.L. Granatstein lists Mary
Oliver among his interviewees, and although he must be aware of her significance to
the nation's history as well as to Robertson's career, he has remained silent about her
clandestine work. Also see Chapter 4, note 78. Another Ottawa woman, Lois Moody,
for many years the *Ottawa Citizen*'s jazz critic, spent the early part of her career with
the CBNRC as an analyst.
111. NAC, TPP, vol. 1, file 9, T. Philipps to J. Leopold, 6, 21 May 1943; Leopold to Philipps,
11, 18 May 1943.
112. Ibid., vol. 2, file 38, 'Odd Notes'. Philipps's blunt pencil embossed entire pages with
palimpsests of his overwrought thinking. The spatial organization of his cursive style
has exploded and the reader discerns only broken phrases, such as 'The f-b received us
almost messianically . . . deceived into believing Can-Govt. interested in them . . . One
asks nothing better than a chance to reconcile the divergencies with R.' Written over
these themes are anguished statements concerning his domestic situation. Finally, over
the top of everything and heavily circled is this: 'For all of us, the present is the past
flowing into the future.'
113. Ibid., vol. 1, file 33, T. Philipps to G.W. Simpson, 1 Oct. 1943.
114. NAC, RG 36, vol. 13, file 8–9–1, J. Grierson to G. Glazebrook, 15 May 1943: 'Will you
please keep Arnold [Dunton] posted on your conversation with Norman [Robertson]
regarding the Ukrainian-Canadian affair and the implication so far as the Tracy
Philipps committee is concerned?' NAC, RG 25, file 75(s), 'Government Supervision of
Foreign Language Groups in Canada', N.A. Robertson to W.L. Mackenzie King,
1 June 1943. Robertson advised the Prime Minister that nationalist stirrings of the
Ukrainian Canadian Committee made relations with the Soviets 'more delicate and
difficult'. The government's 'contacts with the foreign language groups generally are
pretty confused and unsatisfactory.' He hoped Grierson would 'straighten out the press
side of the picture, but I am more worried about the [Nationalities Branch]. . . . I do
not think they have the right men for the job [and] the wrong men can do a good deal
of mischief.'
115. NAC, MG 30 D282, W. Eggleston Papers, vol. 17, file 'Biberovich', L. Biberovich to
A.W. Merriam, 15 Dec. 1942, 'Re: Ukrainian Canadian Committee and Mr. Tracy
Philipps'.
116. Ibid.
117. Ibid., W. Kirkconnell to W. Eggleston, 8 Jan. 1943.

118. Ibid., Kirkconnell to Eggleston, 24 Jan. 1943.
119. Ibid., Eggleston to Kirkconnell, 20 Feb. 1943.
120. Ibid., Kirkconnell to Eggleston, 24 Feb. 1943.
121. Ibid., The contents of this file record Eggleston's years of inquiries on behalf of Biberovich. The latter learned from friends as far afield as Los Angeles that RCMP agents had visited them with questions about his political leanings. On 10 May 1951, H. Winkler, MP, wrote to Eggleston that the Minister of Justice, Stuart Garson, 'has drawn the Biberovich file [and] none of the parties suspected by Biberovich of being his worst enemies appear to have anything to do with the file.' The RCMP judged him to be a 'Rightist rather than a Leftist'. In a 'note to file' Eggleston recorded that Paul Gegeychuk of Winnipeg had signed a deathbed affidavit to the effect that, 'at the instigation of Tracy Philipps, he made false charges against Biberovich.' Kirkconnell dismissed Gegeychuck as a 'self-confessed liar'. He was 'frankly astonished' to find 'him now fathering his unsavory tales on Tracy Philipps, whom I have always found the soul of honour.'
122. Ibid., G. Glazebrook to W. Eggleston, 10 July 1951. Eggleston wrote to Glazebrook on 29 May: 'As a liberal I have been much exercised by the injustice [Biberovich] appears to have suffered.'
123. NAC, TPP, vol.2, file 20, T. Philipps to C. Payne, 30 Aug. 1943. 'Lord Milner was kind enough to call me his 'live wire'. . . . If I were not more-than-sometimes right, I should be just as much an imbecile as an experienced Electrical Specialist.' Ibid., 'Culture Clash or Composition? Assimilation or Re-integration?'
124. Ibid., vol. 1, file 25, T. Philipps to T.C. Davis, 22 Oct. 1941.
125. Ibid., vol. 1, file 7. Philipps relentlessly lobbied S.T. Wood until the latter permitted him 10 days of unpaid vacation at Shediac, NB. But on 18 August 1941, Wood categorically refused to pay for valet services, and 10 days later, after learning Philipps was traveling first-class, Wood advised him tartly that 'Officers are not permitted other than standard berths.' Public Record Office, WO 374/53773. Philipps never was a full colonel, as he claimed. What his actual rank and military service were bewildered even the War Office officials who later fielded his various pension claims. He ranked as a captain when he was assigned to Intelligence in the King's African Rifles during World War I but the length of his official military service was less than one year (1916). He once was commended for promotion by Winston Churchill, but without result. There is no file available disclosing his work for the Foreign Office, nor his freelance intelligence assignments in various African districts.
126. NAC, RG 146, RCMP, 'Tracy Philipps'. Two of the 25 existing labour periodicals, wrote Wood, can 'be induced, without running any great risk, to publish material emanating from Government sources.' Neither did Wood subscribe to Philipps's view that international socialism was the outdated illusion of Western leftists who failed to understand that Stalin had fully 'renationalized' the Soviet Union. Wood wrote to Judge Davis, 8 July 1942: 'I cannot subscribe to the contention advanced by Mr. Philipps that Communism is dead in Russia.'
127. Archives of Ontario, Michael Petrowksy Collection. Later the RCMP quietly decorated Petrowsky with an award for outstanding service. His wife, Yvanna Petrowska, befriended and assisted Lubka Kolessa Philipps following her separation, including paying Josef Karsh for a portrait sitting.
128. NAC, TPP, vol. 1, file 12, S.T. Wood to T.C. Davis.
129. Ibid., file 15, Davis to Wood, 6 Nov. 1941.
130. Ibid., vol. 1, files 11, 13, 15. Somehow Philipps obtained Michael Petrowsky's secret report of October 1940 on the Hetman Organization as well as various reports on the

Ukrainian Canadian Committee, the Ukrainian National Federation, and on a Ukrainian convention held in Chicago. Among other things, he learned that Petrowsky was keeping a close eye on Bill Burianyk. Ibid., vol. 1, file 11, T.C. Davis to S.T. Wood, 5 Dec. 1941, agreeing Simpson should be briefed by Saul and that the notes of that conversation might be passed back to Petrowsky.

131. NAC, RG 146, RCMP file 'Tracy Philipps', T. Philipps to F.J. Mead, 10 Aug. 1942.
132. Ibid., Mead to Philipps, 14 Oct. 1942.
133. In the case of one Dr Radwan, an Indian spiritualist travelling through Canada, Philipps advised Mead to contact MI5 in New Delhi.
134. NAC, RG 146, RCMP file 'Tracy Philipps', J. Leopold to F.J. Mead, 7 Oct., 16 Nov. 1942; Y. Petrowska, interview by author. Leopold apparently did not put into writing his own personal involvement in the small group of friends then giving aid to Philipps's estranged wife, Lubka Kolessa. For Leopold's background, see Steve Hewitt, 'Royal Canadian Mounted Spy: The Secret Life of John Leopold/Jack Esselwein', *Intelligence and National Security* 15, 1 (Spring 2000): 144–68.
135. Ibid., 4 Jan. 1943, 'Summary of correspondence re: foreign language broadcasting'.
136. Ibid., F.J. Mead to J. Leopold, 8 July 1943
137. W.E.B. Du Bois, 'Chronicle of Race Relations', *Phylon* (Summer 1943): 377.
138. NAC, RG 36, vol. 13, file 8–9-A, T. Philipps to J. Grierson, 23 Nov. 1943.
139. Ibid., D. Petegorsky to J. Grierson, 1 Dec. 1943.
140. Ibid., T. Philipps to J. Grierson, 16 Dec. 1943.
141. Ibid., Grierson to Philipps, 21 Dec. 1943. Grierson, marginal note to Dunton: 'Should we let Philipps do this, or take other steps ourselves?'
142. NAC, Robert England Papers, vol. 3, file 1, T. Philipps to R. England, 6 Apr. 1944.
143. NAC, TPP, vol. 1, file 4, T. Philipps to V. Kysilewsky, 1 Mar. 1944, referring to Dr W. Kushnir and Ladislaus Biberovich.
144. Ibid., vol. 2, file 7, note dated '1943', 'A country's Civil Service': '[T]here is a moral cowardice in the matter of responsibility and a search for the solution least likely to attract blame on the official himself, *however right the cause may be.*'
145. Ibid., vol. 2, file 25, Col. R. Meinertzhagen to T. Philipps, 26 Feb. 1944.
146. NAC, MG 32, vol. 445, 'Vladimir Julian Kaye (Kisilewsky)', Personnel File, C.P. Holmes to UNRRA, 25-7-44: 'Mr. Payne, the Deputy Minister reports that there is no doubt as to Dr. Kaye's loyalty. . . . His health, however, would not appear to be satisfactory. Dr. H.T. Douglas . . . would consider Dr. Kay [*sic*] a poor risk.' Payne had a second objection, though: he 'could not release Dr. Kaye for some two months at the moment since he is the only man to bridge the gap between an old branch of Nationalities and a new Citizenship Division now being formed.'
147. NAC, Robert England Papers, vol. 3, file 1, N.A. Robertson to H. Wrong, 4 May 1944. On 29 April, Wrong had written to Robertson that 'I doubt Machtig will be helpful.' A week later Robertson replied that he discussed it with Machtig 'to little purpose' since the latter 'cannot conscientiously recommend [Philipps].'
148. Ibid., C. Payne to J. Harris, 4 May 1944
149. Ibid., H. Wrong to C. Payne, 4 May 1944.
150. Ibid., T. Philipps to R. England, 13 May 1944.
151. NAC, RG 146, RCMP file 'Tracy Philipps', T. Philipps to S.T. Wood, 17 Aug. 1944.
152. NAC, Robert England Papers, vol. 3, file 1, press clippings, 20 May 1944.
153. NAC, RG 25, vol. 5772, file 173(s), 'Appointment of Frank Foulds as Director of Citizenship Division of Department of War Services', L. Mayrand to H. Wrong, 20 Oct. 1944.
154. NAC, Robert England Papers, vol. 3, file 1, G. Baxter to R. England, 26 July 1944. In

this letter, Baxter also complained to England that, due to Chester Payne's error, all the new positions in the Citizenship Division were designated as 'males only'.

155. NAC, TPP, vol. 2, file 4, V.J. Kysilewsky to T. Philipps, 14 Dec. 1957. Kysilewsky continued: 'Dad did not like "gossips" and we were reminded to speak about everybody as if the person would be present. . . . How well I remember the discussions about the latest plays of Ibsen or Sigrid Undset. . . . At first I was bored with Maeterlinck, [mother's] favourite philosopher . . . but then we found delight.'
156. Ibid., vol. 1, file 22, T. Philipps to Wasil Swytsun, 22 July 1941.
157. Jacqueline Rose, *States of Fantasy* (Oxford: Clarendon, 1996), 11.
158. Meinertzhagen, *Middle East Diary*, 6 Dec. 1937, 165. Meinertzhagen himself supported Zionism from an anti-Semitic perspective.
159. Archives of Ontario, Petrowsky Papers. In 1941–2 Petrowsky was engaged by Grierson as translator and adviser for the NFB's *Ukrainian Winter Holiday*, one in a series of propaganda films directed at Eastern European immigrant groups.

Chapter 2

1. John Grierson 'The Changing Face of Propaganda', *Free World* (Jan. 1945), and in James Beveridge, ed., *John Grierson, Film Master* (New York: Macmillan, 1978), 218.
2. Ibid., 179.
3. Ibid., 180.
4. Charles R. Acland, 'National Dreams, International Encounters: The Formulation of Canadian Film Culture in the 1930s', *Canadian Journal of Film Studies* 3, 1 (Spring 1994): 7, points to a 'hegemonic moment' in Canadian cultural discourse, well in advance of Grierson's arrival, when Donald Buchanan and others first sought to link education and national culture through film. Buchanan's influence in Canadian cultural policy extended from Canadian cinema in the 1930s and 1940s through the Massey Report era and into the 1960s when he curated the permanent art collection decorating the new National Arts Centre.
5. Ibid., 7–8; Donald Buchanan, 'The Projection of Canada', *University of Toronto Quarterly* 13, 3 (Apr. 1944): 1. Buchanan explained that the 'making of motion pictures is a mixture of mechanism and art, and the mechanism looms large.'
6. Ibid.
7. Donald Buchanan, 'Canadian Movies Promote Citizenship', *Canadian Geographical Journal* (Mar. 1944): 123.
8. Ibid., 125.
9. C.W. Gray, *Movies for the People: The Story of the National Film Board's Unique Distribution System* (Ottawa: National Film Board of Canada, 1977), particularly ch. 7, 45–7: 'Between 1942 and 1946 . . . [i]t was a common experience for NFB projectionists to discover, in their first film round, that one-half or more of the people in their audiences were seeing a motion picture with sound for the first time.'
10. NFB Archives, Montreal, NFB file, 'Peoples of Canada', n.d., Condensed Guide for Film Utilization, Discussion Quiz.
11. Ibid. The actual quiz begins:
    Q. Are there any Canadians of descent purely native to this country? A. The Indians.
    Q. Have they rights of Canadian citizenship? A. They have no vote.
    Q. Where did our first citizens come from? A. France and England.
    Q. Should people from other lands be encouraged to retain their national habits?
    A. As long as they can be useful [and] they are contributing to our culture.

12. Ibid., E. Spice to J. Grierson, 17 Nov. 1939. Spice's letter of acceptance did not exactly coincide with the film's message of multiculturalist tolerance: 'I was reluctant', she wrote. 'To tell you the truth I am horrified at the thought of the fat Jewess in the outer office & the frightful camera outfit who don't know enuf about inside lighting.'

13. Ibid. Grierson struck 'people of Canada' from this sentence and substituted 'white men'.

14. Ibid., J. Grierson to G. Sparling, 18 Nov. 1940.

15. Ibid., J. Grierson to S. Legg, 24 Feb. 1941. Grierson opposed using Lorne Greene as narrator: 'I play with the notion of having [Leonard] Brockington do the commentary . . . his is the best known voice in Canada . . . which is in any case a great deal more civilised than Lorne Green's' [sic].

16. Ibid., S. Legg to G. Sparling, 13 May 1940. When Stuart Legg viewed the rushes sent from Regina he complained to Sparling of excessive 'wobble' resulting from what he deduced was hand-held operation of the bulky Eyemo camera. 'This is fatal', wrote Legg, but Sparling responded coolly that 'the risk of a slight wobble is far out-weighed by getting natural action and expression. . . . Used with discretion and good cutting, the Eyemo shots are not readily identifiable.'

17. Ibid., G. Sparling to S. Legg, 24 May 1940. With this use of the word 'white' one wonders whether Sparling's difficulty finding lively film subjects had something to do with his own attitudes: 'I think that objection can easily be taken care of by the addition of about five words to the script: 'To the English, Irish and Scotch were added many strange new faces.' (Or words to that effect!) . . . We are also taking the liberty of substituting Hutterites for Mennonites since the latter have largely given up their special dress and living methods, while the former still live in their picturesque colonies. We are also on the trail of some Icelanders.'

18. Ibid., G.H. Michell to J. Grierson, Apr. 1941.

19. NAC, RG 25, vol. 32, 11, file 5353-AB-40, 'Canadian Liaison with UK', A. Marshall to J. Golightly, 31 Dec. 1943. The NFB's Ross McLean had written to Golightly on 22 Oct. 1943, asking 'What sort of films are considered [by the Psychological Warfare Executive] fit for use in liberated territories? Should we tell them what beautiful people they are? . . . or that democracy is a beautiful thing and we intend them to enjoy it? . . . or that they had better do what they are told?' His flippancy did not impress External Affairs officials, but Arthur Calder Marshall of the British Ministry of Information thought that *Peoples of Canada* was 'far better than, say, the Frank Capra pictures, which tell the story as it would be seen by God, if God was an American.'

20. Ibid., M. Moore to T.A. Stone, 21 Nov. 1944.

21. José Arroyo, 'John Grierson: Years of Decision', *Cinema Canada* (Dec. 1989): 15–19; Grierson CBC broadcast in James Beveridge, *John Grierson, Film Master* (New York: Macmillan, 1978), 220.

22. John Grierson in *Creative Process: Norman McLaren*, dir. Donald McWilliams (Montreal: NFB, 1991); film documentary.

23. J.M. Coetzee, 'Breytenbach and the Censor', *Raritan* 10, 4 (Spring 1991): 83.

24. NAC, RG 146, Access to information request 93-A-00082, M. McClung to G. McClellan, 27 Mar. 1952.

25. George McClellan in *On Guard For Thee*, Part 2, 'A Blanket of Ice', dir. Donald Brittain (Montreal: NFB, 1981); film documentary.

26. Mark McClung, interview by James Littleton, 15 Jan. 1981, NAC, ISN 61911; NAC, MG 31 E87, vol. 2, file 4: R. Gordon Robertson's double-edged character reference for McClung dated October 1944 praised his 'brilliant mind' and an 'unusual capacity for expressing himself. [I]f he can remain interested in the kind of work involved, I think

he would be extremely good. I make this qualification because I think that otherwise he might be a bit unstable.'

27. Don Wall, 'The Files', in Len Scher, ed., *The Un-Canadians: True Stories of the Black-list Era* (Toronto: Lester, 1992), 127. Wall, a former RCMP analyst, recalls that he reviewed the NFB files and concluded that '[t]here was very little to the scare.' Reg Whitaker and Gary Marcuse write in *Cold War Canada: The Making of a National Insecurity State, 1945–57* (Toronto: University of Toronto Press, 1994), 249, that 'one might almost think there was some deadly game of espionage and counter-espionage going on—until one remembers that the "suspects" were nothing more than documentary film makers.'

28. Rick Salutin, *Globe and Mail*, 25 Jan. 1986, D2. 'I noticed [Peter Pearson] talking to a very nice-looking older woman. She was talking animatedly, and then I noticed she was crying. Later I asked him why the woman was crying. He told me her name was Evelyn Cherry and that she had worked at the Film Board in the early days. He said she was talking about a witch hunt, a purge that had taken place there. . . . I didn't know there had been this explicit attempt to quash the Film Board's interest in social issues.'

29. *The Eye Hears, the Ear Sees*, dir. Gavin Millar (London: BBC Television, 1970); film documentary. NAC, MG C243, Lambart Papers, file: 'N. McLaren, letters': McLaren's idea for *Neighbours* appears first in a letter to Evelyn Lambart from Germany on 15 May 1951: 'I am having ideas for a[n animated] film which involves using only human beings—live ones, I mean.' Referring to the Ekman case discussed below, he added: 'I am deeply shocked about the latest news about the LMPC titles reshoot.'

30. NAC, RG 146, RCMP files entitled 'NFB—Penetration of—Canada Generally' have been released to the National Archives of Canada as a result of various Access to Information requests. For the years 1947–60, see RG 146, vol. 1975, file 93-A-00053 (3 parts), vol. 1976, files 93-A-00080 (3 parts), 93-A-00081 (3 parts), 93-A-00082 (3 parts).

31. In Beveridge, ed., *John Grierson*, 214, Evelyn Cherry recalled that when Grierson left, the staff 'acted like sheep running for the fold, with no shepherd to guide us [we] bleated around in a strange lost manner, rushed for individual cover, sold out our personal friends for gain—in all, acted as if we should never have been worthy of hire to serve our country.'

32. The next released page in the file, following two removed documents, is an organizational chart containing the names of suspects. Beneath the name of Ross McLean are the names of 47 administrative, technical, and creative personnel.

33. Corporal McLaren reported that this distribution officer for medical films had worked against anti-Communists in the Civil Service Association. 'He was formerly ————— and it is alleged that he still "worships the man." ' As disillusioned employees left at the end of their three-month contracts, investigators learned their destinations and contacted prospective employers. According to Doris Rands in Sher, *Un-Canadians*, 85–7, Mounties attempted to dissuade employers from hiring her husband after they fled to Regina.

34. NFB file, 'Tools of War'. This file contains Legg's scripts, none of which substantiates the informant's claim. Nonetheless, it shows that the RCMP had informants within the NFB as early as 1941.

35. Unknown to Grierson, the Gouzenko espionage inquisitors were unable to determine if Vitali Pavlov had operated a NKVD network in Canada separately from the GRU 'Neighbours' (as the Soviet secret services then referred to each other). For inviting doubt Grierson could not have picked a more damaging Soviet official to acknowledge as a friendly acquaintance. For an excerpt of Grierson's testimony, see Robert Bothwell and J.L. Granatstein, eds, *The Gouzenko Transcripts: The Evidence Presented to*

the Kellock-Taschereau Royal Commission of 1946 (Ottawa: Deneau Publishing, 1982), 341–3; for his full testimony, see NAC, RG 33/62.

36. For Grierson's FBI record, see Kirwan Cox, 'The Grierson Files', *Cinema Canada* 36 (June-July 1979): 16–24.

37. Grierson instructed Frank Badgely to hire Ross McLean and Evelyn Spice to work on *The Peoples of Canada*, paying McLean as 'researcher' twice the amount Spice received as writer. See NFB file, 'Peoples of Canada', J. Grierson to F. Badgely, 20 Nov. 1939.

38. The informant was wrong on this point; Grierson recommended James Beveridge, not Ross McLean.

39. The *Sudbury Daily Star* and the *Kitchener Record* reported on 23 October 1949 that the RCMP were investigating charges that NFB staff enjoyed private screenings of 'Soviet propaganda pictures . . . flown to Ottawa in sealed diplomatic pouches.' Constable Miller noted that Distribution Director Jack Ralph 'regarded it as a "story" with no foundation.'

40. Daniel J. Robinson, 'Falling Into Line: The National Film Board, Foreign Policy, and the Cold War', *National History* 2, 2 (1997): 158–72, believes that senior officials in the Department of External Affairs likely took a hand in leaking information to the *Financial Post* regarding the suspension of Defence contracts to the NFB.

41. This remains unsubstantiated, though some employees believed that McLean's dismissal was partly the consequence of his refusal to fire anyone on security grounds. Crawley's involvement in some manner is consistent with René Bonnière's assessment of him in James A. Forrester, ed., *Budge: F.R. Crawley and Crawley Films* (Lakefield, Ont.: Information Research Services, 1988), 43: 'he is a Maoist in that he creates a crisis and the way to solve these crises is the way that the film happens.' Ibid., 35. In 1949, Ross McLean refused Film Board support for Crawley's *The Loon's Necklace*, which went on to earn more than a million dollars. Crawley claimed that McLean had told him, 'It's a small picture and I don't think it is the sort of film for the Film Board.'

42. Wilfred Eggleston, 'A Free Press and the NFB', *Saturday Night*, 3 Jan. 1950, 3, endorsed Arthur Irwin but cautioned that the NFB is not 'free press' but rather 'government information' and cannot always tell 'the truth, the whole truth and nothing but the truth'. Michael Barkway, 'These Documentary Films', ibid., 17 Jan. 1950, huffed that NFB 'termites' were 'interpreting actuality rather too much in the way a Moscow documentary creator would interpret it. . . . When you are spending the taxpayer's money, might it not be better to confine yourself to instructional films?'

43. Tom Daly, in D.B. Jones, *The Best Butler in the Business: Tom Daly of the National Film Board of Canada* (Toronto: University of Toronto Press, 1996), 53 passim, cites Gurdjieff as a way of explaining his own 'continuity' through the security scare: 'A film is a line of attention that the audience goes through, and if you break that line, you break the connection between the film and the audience. . . . Everyone wants to take this attention from us, but it is the priceless thread that connects us to ourselves. So it matters what we put it on, when it comes to our own choice.' Daly's initial aversion to Arthur Irwin changed when he realized that he was more like the new Commissioner than he originally thought.

44. Mrs D.E. McLaren, interview by author, 15 Feb. 1998. Darrell E. McLaren was born in 1911 (three years before Norman McLaren) in Vancouver. He received a BA in Liberal Arts from the University of British Columbia.

45. Gary Evans, *In the National Interest: A Chronicle of the National Film Board of Canada from 1949 to 1989* (Toronto: University of Toronto Press, 1991), 7, reports that in 1948 the Film Board served nine million viewers in community showings.

46. James Beveridge became the NFB's UK liaison; his wife, filmmaker Jane Marsh, was in New York.
47. 'Forms 215' apparently authorized more intrusive surveillance measures.
48. One couple's 1930s activism was re-examined. Evelyn Cherry resigned in December 1950 and worked for a business college; her husband Lawrence stayed on for several more years. Irwin thought 'Cherry was paranoid' and that she, Nick Balla, and Jack Ralph were in 'a communist cell' of eight persons. She credited Irwin with crushing the idealism of the Grierson period. NAC, MG 31 D, Evelyn Cherry Papers, vol. 14, file 1, 'Resignation from NFB'; NAC, MG 31 E97, vol. 23, Arthur Irwin Papers.
49. Evans, *In the National Interest*, 24–5. Norman McLaren demurely credited the genesis of *Neighbours* to Irwin's visit to his studio to solicit some project 'of international significance'. Through the fall of 1951 McLaren and his two actors—fellow NFB animators Grant Munro and Paul Ladouceur—shot *Neighbours* in Rockliffe Park, not far from the John Street studios, courtesy of funding appropriated to the NFB by the Psychological Warfare Committee.
50. This was Douglas Ross Sinclair. See Cox, 'The Grierson Files', for similar charges Sinclair sent to the FBI.
51. This information was spurious; photograph 'KO-72' (filed in NAC, Acc. 1971–271) is an innocuous shot of a Mountie holding a bugle.
52. NAC, RG 2, vol. 234, file S-100–2-S-1, 'Security Organization—Course at Rockliffe RCMP Barracks, December, 1952'. During a three-day seminar organized by Peter Dwyer, NFB security officer Michael Spencer heard McClung's lecture on 'The theory and history of Communism'. Peter Dwyer spoke on the 'Soviet Secret Intelligence Services', George McClellan on 'The history and development of Communism', and Inspector Terry Guernsey on 'Soviet Intelligence Operations on Canadian Government Departments'. The Englishman Spencer, graduate of Rugby and Oxford, was active in the wartime NFB as well as military film units. He was designated NFB Security Officer in 1950, a fact that became public knowledge in 1953. See NFB Archives historical file, 'Michael Spencer'.
53. Michael Denning, *The Cultural Front: The Laboring of American Culture in the Twentieth Century* (London: Verso, 1996), xviii.
54. Perhaps the RCMP investigators did not differentiate the men from the women, either as suspected subversives or as useful informants, because they gender-coded the entire Film Board as 'feminine'. See *Four Days in May* (Montreal: National Film Board, 1976), for a glimpse of the NFB women's perspectives of the security scare.
55. Broadcast by John Grierson, 21 January 1940, in Beveridge, *John Grierson*, 143.
56. Ibid. (The NFB motto is now rendered monocularly as 'The Eye of Canada.')
57. Grierson interviewed at York University, 1970, ibid., 152, emphasis in original.
58. Ibid.
59. Peter Morris, 'After Grierson: The National Film Board 1945–53', in Seth Feldman, ed., *Take Two* (Toronto: Irwin Publishing, 1984), 187.
60. Ibid. Of particular note is Don Mulholland's 1947 pursuit drama, *File 1365: The Connor's Case*. The chase is seen only from the Mounties' perspective and never from that of the pursued man. Robert Anderson's 'Mental Mechanisms' series similarly adopts the perspective of the medical establishment.
61. The concept of mimetic desire discussed here is that developed by René Girard. For a useful synthesis and development of the Girardian model, see Paisley Livingstone, *Models of Desire: René Girard and the Psychology of Mimesis* (Baltimore: Johns Hopkins University Press, 1992).

62. Maynard Collins, *Norman McLaren* (Ottawa: Canadian Film Institute, 1976), 69.
63. NFB file, 'Neighbours'. That McLaren wanted the film to be poised between both readings is made clear in his doubts about complying with distributors who wanted to censor the baby-bashing sequence. McLaren agreed, but only because he worried that these sensational scenes detracted from the formal balance he sought to achieve.
64. Giorgio Agamben, 'Notes on Gesture', in his *Infancy and History: Essays on the Destruction of Experience* (London: Verso, 1983), 137.
65. NFB file, 'Neighbours'. The *Times Educational Supplement* thought it 'more religious than any explicitly religious film'.
66. After numerous viewings I concluded this is not a special effect but simply the transition of early to late autumn light on McLaren's outdoor set.
67. NFB file, 'Neighbours'. Glover and Mulholland demurred from this and similar requests from other distributors. The entire distribution picture changed when *Neighbours* astonished critics by winning the Oscar for best documentary short of 1953. *Neighbours*, as the NFB's Director of Distribution told his field agents, was suddenly 'the most promotable item you will ever get to work on'. Incidentally, Scellen also was of interest to the RCMP because she was Grierson's first secretary at the time the Film Board was created.
68. Ibid. Norman McLaren, 'Some Notes on Stop-Motion Live-Actor Technique', 12 Aug. 1952.
69. NFB file, 'Neighbours', C.M. Anderson to T. Daly, June 1955.
70. Michel Chion, *Audio-Vision: Sound on Screen* (New York: Columbia University Press, 1990), 114–17.
71. NAC, RG 25, vol. 8060, file 2755-A-40. Irwin's propaganda initiative exceeded the expectations of External Affairs, necessitating Charles Ritchie's carefully drafted letter of 15 July 1952 for Undersecretary L.D. Wilgress (a staunch anti-Communist with a seat on the NFB). Irwin was advised that NFB films were now 'leaning too much in the direction of straight propaganda'.
72. NAC, R3698, Bernard Devlin, interviewed by Kirwan Cox, n.d. (*ca* 1975). At the time of the three public firings in March 1950, Devlin was deputized to bear a protest from NFB cinematographers to Arthur Irwin. Twenty-five years later Cox asked him about his visit to Irwin's office. 'Oh,' he sighed, 'Arthur Irwin.' Irwin informed him tightly that 'they are considered security risks' but 'I can't tell you why.' Devlin left the meeting angry and bewildered: 'I knew all three of them. Maybe they might have been NDP, you know, I just can't see them being Party members.' The scare had 'a terrible impact on the Film Board', he recalled, because it created a climate of self-censorship. 'There was a drastic effect on hiring,' he said, 'good people were refused posts, and there was an influx of mediocre "reliables."' The disappearance of the NFB administrative files from the 1940s and 1950s—they are neither in the National Archives nor with the NFB—in itself raises a question. Who authorized the removal or destruction of this material, and why has the National Archives not investigated it?
73. NFB Archives, personal communication confirming periods of employment for Allan Ackman (15 October 1945 to 1 April 1950), Nathan Clavier (29 December 1944 to 18 April 1950), and David Smith (16 August 1945 to 1 April 1950).
74. NAC, RG 146, ATIP release AH-1999–00121/dg, 33–34. The RCMP had a house program listing 'Nat Clavier' as a chorus member in a satirical review, 'Tabloid Reds', for Montreal's New Theatre Group in April 1936.
75. 'Allan Ackman is alive and well', *Canadian Professional Photography* (June 1969), 24.
76. NAC, Acc. 1983/298, Michael Spencer, interviewed by Kirwan Cox, *ca* 1977.

77. Ibid., reel 3695, John 'Jack' Chisholm, interviewed 6 Dec. 1977: 'Grierson was not going to do us [private film interests] any good . . . a pusher upper. There's a long story to be told . . . but this is politics; plus I don't want to get mixed up in it. It never happened this way or that way. You keep the hell out. I mentioned this at the NFB recently [but] I wouldn't go further on it. . . . Bob Winters was really the one who straightened this thing out. He called me at the house one night, came down from Ottawa. . . . Winters said, 'what are we going to do with McLean?' and I said, 'get rid of him.' Just like that. I said, 'get his assistant [Ralph Foster] and fire him.' They did, and they brought in Irwin, a very good friend of mine. . . . Well, Foster was—he was in my hair, not too openly, but things he did. . . . There were Communists at the Film Board . . . no bombs in their pockets . . . but there was a lot of spreading Communism in this country [and] nothing to control it. The Mounties were too busy cleaning up after a war. That sound sensible to you?'
78. Granatstein and Stafford, *Spy Wars*, 74.
79. NFB file 51–228, 'Square Dance Stereo', Norman McLaren to Donald Mulholland (copied to Arthur Irwin), 5 May 1952.
80. Ibid. Ekman was taken on at the NFB on 16 January 1950 and let go on 22 July 1950.
81. Ibid., n.d., unaddressed memo by Norman McLaren. The cluster of documents related to the issue of Ekman's credit is stapled together and heavily creased, as if McLaren carried them around in his pocket for several days.
82. NAC, MG C243, Lambart Papers, file: 'N. McLaren, letters', N. McLaren to E. Lambart, from New Delhi, 15 Nov. 1952.
83. John Grierson in Beveridge, ed., *John Grierson*, 308.
84. Don McWilliams, interview by author, Feb. 1998.
85. McClung, interview by Littleton, 15 Jan. 1981. NAC, ISN 61911.

Chapter 3

1. Don Wall, Patrick Watson, Ann Young, interviews by author. The Canada Council's Ann Coffin also attended from time to time. NAC, MG 30 E516, Henry Hindley Papers, vol. 5, file 5.8, pp. 10–11. When the Belle Claire was torn down the luncheon group shifted briefly to Sam Kauffman's new premises before settling into the Press Club located above the Connaught Restaurant on Confederation Square, and finally in the National Press Building on Sparks Street.
2. Don Wall and Mark McClung, interviewed by James Littleton, NAC, CAVA 1987–0416, *ca* 1981. Don Wall said that 'dealing with secrecy and suspicion and doubt, is in the long run a soul-destroying business and there's just no escaping that.' McClung stated: 'Security work is predicated on human distrust . . . this means everyone is suspect. And it gets to you. . . . Over the long term it is soul destroying.'
3. Ernest Renan, 'What is a Nation', trans. Martin Thom, in Homi K. Bhabha, ed., *Nation and Narration* (London: Routledge, 1990), 11. See Bhabha's dense but striking essay, 'DissemiNation: time, narrative and the margins of the modern nation', ibid., 291–322.
4. Jonathan Bordo, 'Jack Pine—Wilderness sublime or the erasure of the Aboriginal presence from the landscape', *Journal of Canadian Studies* 27, 1 (Winter 1992–3): 98–128. Of course, Aboriginal people all along have been targets of security intelligence and some files have been partially declassified. Reg Whitaker, 'The Politics of Security Intelligence Policy-making in Canada II, 1984–91', *Intelligence and National Security* 7, 1 (Jan. 1992), 66, cites Native leader George Erasmus's acknowledgement that he was a CSIS target: 'I do not care about CSIS, I am not interested in

formal complaints [to the Security Intelligence Review Committee], about CSIS getting all excited about our looking closer and deeper into their affairs . . . I want to get them out of our lives.'

5. Michael Dorland, 'A Thoroughly Hidden Country: *Ressentiment*, Canadian Nationalism, Canadian Culture', *Canadian Journal of Political and Social Theory* 12, 1–2 (1988): 132; David Stafford, 'The Delicate Balance: Security, Liberty and the Canadian Intelligence Community', Canada House Lecture 55, 3 Mar. 1993, 5; Peter Hennessy, *Whitehall* (London: Fontana, 1990), 346–7.

6. James Eayrs, 'New Weapons in the Cold War: A Study of Recent Techniques in International Propaganda', *International Journal* (1952): 36–47.

7. Benedict Anderson, *Imagined Communities: Reflections on the Origin and Spread of Nationalism* (London: Verso: 1991), ch. 11, 'Memory and Forgetting'.

8. Whitaker, *Double Standard*, 18.

9. R. Gordon Robertson, 'Official Responsibility, Private Conscience, and Public Information', an address to the Royal Society of Canada annual meeting, St John's, 6 June 1972 (Library of Parliament, Ottawa). Robertson's positions here are generally consistent with those developed by Don Rowat, *Administrative Secrecy in Developed Countries* (New York: Columbia University Press, 1979).

10. R.G. Robertson, interview by Tom Earle, *ca* 1980, transcript, Library of Parliament.

11. Robertson, 'Official Responsibility, Private Conscience, and Public Information'.

12. For a critical assessment of Canadian Access to Information, see Alasdair Scott Roberts, *Limited Access: Assessing the Health of Canada's Freedom of Information Laws* (Kingston: School of Policy Studies, Queen's University, 1998). For the limitations placed on parliamentary oversight, see Stuart Farson, 'Parliament and its Servants: Their Role in Scrutinizing Canadian Intelligence', *Intelligence and National Security* 15, 1 (Spring 2000): 225–58.

13. In passing, three observations are relevant here. (1) There are alarming signs of insensitivity to historical relevance. For instance, why destroy the file of Dr W.E.B. Du Bois when more than a thousand pages of material gathered on Paul Robeson were retained and released (albeit expurgated by CSIS, partly at my expense)? Could it be that the name 'Du Bois' simply did not strike the former officers as having significance? (2) The systematic removal of RCMP documents with 'top secret' designations (or higher) in effect limits the releasable records to relatively mundane transactions and case files rather than the policy and administrative records of senior management. (3) There is ample internal evidence in the released files of an enormous collection of surveillance photographs, films, and audio recordings created by the RCMP Security Service over a period of decades. My requests for specific audiovisual items met with a complete blank, and ultimately the CSIS representative at the National Archives advised me that all such audiovisual materials were destroyed prior to the transfer to the Archives.

14. John Bryden, *Best Kept Secret: Canadian Secret Intelligence in the Second World War* (Toronto: Lester Publishing, 1993), 332; Gregory S. Kealey, 'The Royal Canadian Mounted Police, the Canadian Security Intelligence Service, the National Archives, and Access to Information: A Curious Tale', *Labour/Le Travail* (Spring 1988): 227–32.

15. Granatstein, 'The "Hard Obligations" of Citizenship, 36–49.

16. Zuhair Kashmeri, *The Gulf Within: Canadian Arabs, Racism and the Gulf War* (Toronto: Lorimer, 1991), xi.

17. Arjun Appadurai, 'Patriotism and Its Futures', *Public Culture* 3, 5 (1993): 423.

18. Ibid., 427.

19. NAC, RG 37. For example, file 60–5–E1, Public Record Office (England), contains an interesting exchange prompted by Professor Trevor Lloyd of McGill University, a prominent Arctic specialist. Lloyd was conducting research in the Public Record Office in London in 1971 when he learned 'that a large number of files in the Dominion Office, including files related to Canada, were being destroyed for the period of the 1940s.' Lloyd told a Canadian archivist that he was 'concerned that a good deal of source material on Canadian history is being destroyed'. Of course, from the point of view of this book, Dominions Office records of British activities in Canada in the 1940s would be highly interesting. Nonetheless, when the matter was brought to the attention of National Archivist Dr Wilfred Smith (M. Swift to W. Smith, 1 Sept. 1971), Smith merely wrote to his PRO counterpart, Jeffrey Ede, on 7 Sept. 1971: 'I am sure there is a reasonable explanation and it might be useful if I could be armed with it, if that could be arranged without inconvenience. I hope to see you [at the conference] in Bad Godesburg.' It was hardly an inquiry designed to halt the document destruction then underway. Furthermore, from this meticulously kept file containing the entire sequence of Public Archives of Canada/British PRO correspondence over a period of decades, Ede's reply is missing, as is Smith's counter-response dated 4 October, and referred to in the following letter. The gap is unique; the correspondence resumes on 30 October with a letter from Ede about the release of sensitive documents: 'If you have any questions about the physical handling of affected records (e.g. where only parts of files or volumes are closed) I will be glad to give you the benefit of our experience—both happy and unhappy! But I will not depress you with a reminder of problems you may want to forget for the moment. You might, however, be interested to know that to avoid withholding of entire volumes or the undesirable practice of removing from them a few sensitive papers, we have, where possible, made up for search room use duplicate 'photocopy' volumes with the sensitive items omitted.' The question of the document destruction was not pursued, and it is difficult to feel assured that the National Archivist served the Canadian public interest in this case.

20. Graham Carr, 'Harsh Sentences: Appealing the Strange Verdict of Who Killed Canadian History?', *American Review of Canadian Studies* 28, 1–2 (Spring/Summer 1998): 167–76. For further insight into Granatstein's compact with the national security state, see RCMP intelligence reports in NAC, RG 146, file 93-A00039 part 1, 'York University, 22–12–67 to 12–7–68', departmental minute, 30 May 1968. Granatstein was prepared to trade off the freedom to publish his research (by undergoing a security clearance and agreeing to hold 'material under bond in vaults for an agreed period of years') in exchange for insider knowledge. As the writer of the minute put it, Professor Granatstein's 'intention was . . . to supplement [public knowledge] in ways beneficial to us [External Affairs] as well as to historians.'

Chapter 4

1. Mavor Moore, *Reinventing Myself: Memoirs* (Toronto: Stoddart, 1990), 107: 'The IS—what is it about these initials: first Intelligence and Security and now [CBC's] International Service?' See, too, Moore's obituary of gallery director and former intelligence officer Moncrieff Williamson (d. 5 Aug. 1996) in the *Globe and Mail*. Another such figure is Theodore Heinrich (Heinrich Papers, University of Regina Archives), an American art intelligence officer in Germany before becoming director of the Royal Ontario Museum and founder of the visual arts program at the University of Regina.

2. *Report of the Royal Commission on National Development in the Arts, Letters and Sciences 1949–1951* (Ottawa: Printer to the King, 1951); Maria Tippet, *Making Culture: English-Canadian Institutions and the Arts before the Massey Commission* (Toronto: University of Toronto Press, 1990); Paul Litt, *The Muses, the Masses and the Massey Commission* (Toronto: University of Toronto Press, 1991); J.L. Granatstein, *Canada 1957–1967: The Years of Uncertainty and Innovation* (Toronto: McClelland & Stewart, 1986); André Fortier and D. Paul Schafer, *Review of Federal Policies for the Arts in Canada, 1944–88* (Ottawa: Canadian Conference of the Arts, 1989).

3. Gregory Kealey, 'The Early Years of State Surveillance of Labour and the Left in Canada: The Institutional Framework of the Royal Canadian Mounted Police Security and Intelligence Apparatus', *Intelligence and National Security* (July 1993): 129–48; Reginald Whitaker, 'Origins of the Canadian Government's Internal Security System, 1946–52', *Canadian Historical Review* (Spring 1984): 155–83; John Bryden, *Best Kept Secret: Canadian Secret Intelligence in the Second World War* (Toronto: Lester Publishing, 1993); Reg Whitaker and Gary Marcuse, *Cold War Canada: The Making of a National Insecurity State, 1945–1957* (Toronto: University of Toronto Press, 1994).

4. Kealey, 'The Early Years', 143; Wesley Wark, 'Security Intelligence in Canada, 1864–1945: The History of a National Insecurity State', in Keith Neilson and B.J.C. McKercher, eds, *Go Spy the Land: Military Intelligence in History* (Westport, Conn.: Praeger, 1992): 153–78; Denning, *The Cultural Front*, 77. Denning writes: 'Indeed, it was the growing influence of the Cultural Front in the state cultural apparatuses and the major cultural industries that provoked the cultural civil war known as the "Red Scare" or "McCarthyism." '

5. The UK-US Venona Project's decoded Soviet intercepts from August and October 1944, released in 1996 and available on the National Security Agency's Venona Web site <www.nsa.gov>, indicate clearly that Soviet intelligence valued White as a source. Both Bruce Craig, 'Unsealing Federal Grand Jury Records: The Case of the Harry Dexter White Transcript', *The Public Historian* 20, 2 (Spring 1998), and James M. Boughton, 'The Case Against Harry Dexter White: Still Not Proven' (IMF Working Paper, Aug. 2000), after combing newly uncovered sources, remain unconvinced that White knowingly acted as an informant.

6. David Caute, *The Great Fear: The Anti-Communist Purge under Truman and Eisenhower* (New York: Simon and Schuster, 1979), 48–9, attributes Truman's hesitancy to act against White to his deep suspicion of the Republican fear-mongers, and Brownell's attack on Truman he views as merely an attempt to steal some of McCarthy's 'glamour'.

7. 'McCarthy Calls Truman a Liar', *Ottawa Journal*, 11 Nov. 1953; 'Truman Won't Answer Subpoena', ibid., 12 Nov.; 'Truman Lashes back at Brownell's "Mealy-Mouthed, Phony" Attack' and 'The White Case—Truman Defends Action', *Ottawa Evening Citizen*, 17 Nov. 1953.

8. 'Promotion to Monetary Post "Hampered" FBI—Hoover', *Montreal Gazette*, 18 Nov. 1953.

9. J.E. Hoover to H.H. Vaughan, 1 Feb. 1946, NSA Venona Web site: <www.nsa.gov/docs/venona/venona—docs.html>. According to this Web site Hoover sent five memos to the White House concerning Harry Dexter White between November 1945 and July 1946.

10. Ibid.

11. James Minifie, 'Canada Protests Security Breach in Spy Probe', *Ottawa Journal*, 20 Nov. 1953; 'PM Says Hoover's Mention of Canadian a Nasty Surprise', 18 Nov. 1953.

12. NAC, RG 25, vol. 8561, file 50303–40, part 1.1, 'United States Investigations into Subversive Activities in US—Implication of Canadian Officials'. On a dispatch from the Canadian embassy in Washington dated 9 September 1948, Escott Reid highlighted for Pearson's attention Richard Nixon's statement in Congress naming Harry Dexter White as an espionage suspect in addition to Alger Hiss. Nixon also praised the Canadian government's firm handling and swift convictions of espionage suspects named by Gouzenko. The dispatch described the general pattern of developments as 'sensational' and warned that 'no less than seven committees and sub-committees, embracing some 150 of 531 members of both houses, were conducting separate probes involving Communism, and were competing for headline publicity.'

13. Ibid. Seeking to avoid publicity, the Canadians had not conveyed to the HUAC investigators what the FBI had known since 1945, namely that Gouzenko's disclosures pointed to 'an assistant' to Secretary of State Stettinius.

14. NAC, RG 25 vol. 8561, file 50303–40, part 1.1, 'United States Investigations into Subversive Activities in US—Implication of Canadian Officials', R.A. MacKay to L.B. Pearson, 17 Nov. 1953: '[George] Ignatieff has just phoned me to say that he has been informed by Miniffe [presumably journalist James Minifie], who had seen the text of the speech, that Laskey [sic] will say that you transmitted vital information to a Red Spy Ring, that Elizabeth Bentley so testified . . . and that that testimony was suppressed at your request. . . . The speech links the above statement up with our refusal to produce Gouzenko and Herb Norman's "promotion" to New Zealand.'

15. James Littleton, *Target Nation* (Toronto: Lester & Orpen Dennys/CBC, 1986), 31–7, sets out how the McCarran subcommittee extrapolated from Elizabeth Bentley's testimony to cast suspicion on Pearson and other Canadian officials.

16. An anti-Communist propagandist with CIA connections, Victor Lasky (1918–90) edited the *American Legion Reader* in 1953. See his profile on the Namebase Web site: <www.pir.org/namebase> and <archives.ashland.edu/lasky.html>. Apparently Lasky was referring to Bentley's purported conversations with Hazen Sise, NFB liaison in Canada's Washington embassy during the war.

17. *Ottawa Journal*, 20 Nov. 1953.

18. 'Doubt Top Placed Canadian Warned FBI White Soviet Spy', *Ottawa Journal*, 18 Nov. 1953.

19. Solicitor General of Canada, Ottawa ATIP Division, Document 114 117–90–83, file 'Harry Dexter White'.

20. 'Tip Forwarded to President, Senators Told—Officials Doubt Hoover Report Correct', *Globe and Mail*, 18 Nov. 1953.

21. 'Talented Casts To Present Winning Workshop Plays', *Ottawa Journal*, 14 Nov. 1953.

22. Patricia Close, 'Citizenship and Security', Research Paper, Macdonald Commission, partially declassified as NAC, Solicitor General, ATIP file 8400–80, 16. During the probationary period the applicant for naturalization must 'illustrate foremost allegiance to the current democratic processes of the Canadian nation-state.'

23. John Burns, 'The New Chief of Handouts to the Arts', *Globe and Mail*, 17 Jan. 1970.

24. Robert Fulford, 'The Canada Council at Twenty-Five', *Saturday Night* (Mar. 1982): 36.

25. Chris Dwyer, interview by author, 4 Mar. 1996.

26. Kim Philby, *My Silent War* (New York: Grove Press, 1968), on Dwyer: 'I knew him for a brilliant wit, and was to learn that he had a great deal more to him than just wit.' Alan Edmonds, 'Spy and superspy: one man's view of Kim Philby', *Maclean's* (Apr. 1968): 3. Edmonds's overture to Dwyer while preparing his review of *My Silent War* produced nothing: 'Dwyer will not discuss the Fuchs case or his secret service life.'

27. CBC Radio Archives, *Max Ferguson Show*, 3 Jan. 1972. Dwyer could not conceal the bitterness he felt towards Philby, telling Ben Wicks, 'well, it was *treason* of a form, wasn't it.' On the other hand, Dwyer told Naim Kattan (interview by author, 31 Mar. 1996) that 'Philby was so charming and cultured, you would have liked him.'
28. Burns, 'The New Chief'.
29. NAC, RG 32, acc. 85–86/096, box 39, 'Peter Michael Dwyer', personnel file (henceforth NAC, Dwyer personnel file), Copy of Entry of Birth, General Registry Office, London.
30. Ibid.; Dulwich College, historical profile, available at: <www.dulwich.org.uk>. Founded as a school for the poor in 1618 by Shakespeare's rival Edward Alleyne, prominent graduates included P.G. Wodehouse and Sir Edward Shackleton.
31. Keble College Web site: <www.keble.ox.ac.uk/about.html>.
32. NAC, Dwyer personnel file. He graduated a Bachelor of Arts (Honours) in Modern Languages, 3rd class. Several years later, after war broke out, Keble College would house the British security service MI5.
33. For example, Dwyer's weekly diary in *The Cherwell*, 'Samuel Pepys—Undergraduate', 19 Nov. 1934, 144, remarked of the chiding of his 'Tewtor': 'I am ever after writing of my diary and other matters soe I do neglect his pesky essays.'
34. 'O.U.D.S. Smoker', *The Cherwell*, 30 Nov. 1935, 157. In 1951–2 this play, or a version of it, received honourable mention in the Ottawa Little Theatre competition.
35. David Vincent, *The Culture of Secrecy: Britain 1832–1998* (Oxford: Oxford University Press, 1998), 22. Vincent further describes this code of silence as 'a strategy which sought maximum privacy for the civilized, and complete publicity for the unwashed'.
36. Douglas Owram, *The Government Generation: Canadian Intellectuals and the State, 1900–1945* (Toronto: University of Toronto Press, 1986), 144–5.
37. NAC, Dwyer personnel file; Allan Jarvis, *Diplome d'honneur* address, 18 Oct. 1971.
38. Alan Jarvis directed the National Gallery during Dwyer's years of internal security co-ordination in the 1950s. Mischievously, Jarvis drew attention to Dwyer's intimate 'knowledge of workings of public administration' gained through 'services within government, prior to joining the Canada Council'.
39. NAC, 1987–0416, Robert Bryce, interview by James Littleton, *ca* 1981; Naim Kattan, interviewed by author. Reg Whitaker, *Double Standard: The Secret History of Canadian Immigration Policy* (Toronto: Lester & Orpen Dennys, 1987), 19, writes that Peter Dwyer's 'liberalism was sharply circumscribed by an overriding concern with the Communist threat.'
40. Peter Dwyer, 'Shakespeare and the Cinema', *The Cherwell*, 3 Nov. 1934.
41. Peter Dwyer, 'Oxford Party', *The Cherwell*, 8 Dec. 1934. Dwyer responded to a fellow student's play by publishing his own dialogue:
PAT: You fool, you're supposed to have sufficient intelligence up here to put you above the rut of society.
A COMMUNIST: Intelligence! What use is intelligence in this twentieth-century chaos? . . . It's not we who are rotten but the whole state of the world.
A POLITICIAN: We're at a point in history where civilisation is breaking down.
42. Peter Dwyer, 'Is Oxford Degenerate?', *The Cherwell*, 26 Oct. 1935.
43. Max Beloff, John Gwyer, Robert Irving, and Airey Neave are cited in Robin Ramsay, ed., *A Who's Who of the British Secret State* (Hull, UK: Lobster, 1989).
44. H. Montgomery Hyde, *Room 3606* (New York: Dell, 1962), 205.
45. Eric Maschwitz, *No Chip on My Shoulder* (London: Herbert Jenkins, 1957); Nicholas J. Cull, 'Did the Mounties and the NFB fake Nazi Atrocities?', *Globe and Mail*, 3 June 1995.

46. Peter Dwyer, 'Words and People', *The Cherwell*, 19 Oct. 1935.

47. See Isham genealogy at: <www.oblevins.com/Blevins/D0013/G0001340.html>.

48. Peter Dwyer, 'The Bridge in the Parks', *The Cherwell*, 25 May 1935.

49. Peter Dwyer, 'On Sundays', *The Cherwell*, 16 Nov. 1935.

50. Author's interview with Don Wall, Mar. 1996; *The Cherwell*, 1 Feb. 1936. During his final Oxford term, Dwyer glimpsed a distant Canadian horizon when Grey Owl appeared at the Oxford Town Hall. *The Cherwell* reported empty seats, 'owing perhaps to the poster's description of [Grey Owl] as The Modern Hiawatha'. But the audience's initial skepticism evaporated as they were won over by a 'brilliant lecture, illuminated with mordant humour and illustrated by some very fine films'. How mordant, they did not know: 'Grey Owl said in passing he was not sure where he was lecturing.' The reviewer never suspected that the English-born Archie 'Grey Owl' Belaney's bookshelf at Beaver Lodge held a copy of *Round About the Mitre at Oxford*.

51. 'Samuel Pepys—Undergraduate', *The Cherwell*, 3 Nov. 1934.

52. *The Cherwell*, 2, 30 May 1936; Don Wall, interview by author. Dwyer told Wall that he discovered 'deep-voiced' actress Joan Greenwood while working as an assistant editor for Fox.

53. Anne Young, interview by author, 26 June 1998. Dwyer amused associates with the ineptitude of his call-up by MI6 in 1939. 'My name is Dwyer', whispered a voice on the telephone. 'So is mine', Dwyer whispered back, and the caller rang off in embarrassed confusion. Henry Hindley, NAC, MG E 516, vol. 5, file 5.8, 18, recounts the same anecdote, but rather less funnily.

54. Florence Fancott, interview by author, 4 Apr. 1996. Ottawa actress Fancott grew up in Bletchley village and she actually recognized Dwyer when he joined the Ottawa Little Theatre in 1950: 'We knew he was part of some hush-hush group.'

55. NAC, Dwyer personnel file; Chris Dwyer, interview by author. Their Renault's poor steering nearly cost them their freedom. Dwyer fell asleep, exhausted, on the deck of a PT boat, and woke up pummelled by empty brass shell casings from the anti-aircraft gun.

56. Ibid. Donald Brittain's documentary *On Guard For Thee*, Part 2, contains a still photo of Dwyer and his associates in a Panama City bar, *ca* 1942. Dwyer jauntily holds a cocktail, and his cane suitcase rests at his feet.

57. Hyde, *Room 3606*, 19. William Stephenson was dubbed the 'quiet Canadian' by playwright and OSS propaganda specialist Robert Sherwood, who also was a member of Dorothy Parker's circle at the Algonquin Hotel.

58. NAC, Dwyer personnel file.

59. David Stafford, *Camp X* (Toronto: Lester & Orpen Dennys, 1986), 260–3. See Stafford's interview with Jean-Paul Evans about his involvement in the case.

60. Mark McClung, interview by James Littleton, *ca* 1981, NAC, CAVA 1987–0416; Dwyer was again working in connection with his Oxford mentor, Gilbert Highet. Highet later downplayed his security intelligence activities and any possibility that they inspired his wife Helen McInnes's bluntly propagandistic espionage novels. Highet told interviewer Shaun Herron, CBC *Thursday Night*, 'The Two Bills', 1968: 'I thought of myself as a research and analysis man. . . . I set up large card files for personalities, both German and other, throughout Latin America, which would enable our office to predict [their reactions,] the same kind of thing a historian does in studying Greece and Rome. For instance, Sir Ronald Sime at Oxford, who taught me, makes a specialty of this called prosopography. History not seen through big class movements or nations but individuals and their families. [This is the] same as research and analysis of the President of Brazil and his brother, and his acquaintances, aides-de-camp, and so forth. You write

down the facts and make deductions. . . . If you have the cards which indicate weaknesses of that kind, reaching so deep into a man's personality, [you may] play and counter-play.'

61. Chapman Pincher, *Too Secret, Too Long* (New York: St Martin's, 1984), 104–10. Pincher reports that Dwyer's telex in MI6 archives is creased and folded in four as if Philby pocketed it, showed it to his contact, and afterwards replaced it in the file. The habitually suspicious Pincher remarks approvingly of Dwyer that he was 'an able officer, about whom there have never been any official doubts'. According to Svetlana Gouzenko, her husband first saw Peter Dwyer in newspaper photos 'when he took a public post in Canada'. Released Venona decrypts include Moscow's transmission to Philby's NKVD controller ['Bob'] on the evening of 17 September 1945. This message confirms that 'Stenli's [Philby's] information does correspond to the facts'; the Soviets feared for the safety of their networks following the defection.

62. Anthony Cave-Brown, *'C': The Secret Life of Sir Stewart Menzies* (New York: Macmillan, 1987), 696. A less flattering portrait of the British security services in Washington is found in Francis Thompson's *Destination Washington* (London: Robert Hale, 1960). This savagely homophobic account by Thompson, the embassy's security officer (1948–51), jubilantly reports organized gay-bashing sprees with his FBI counterparts. Thompson, too, frequented the men's bar of the Mayflower Hotel and must have known Peter Dwyer, but in his jaundiced eye 'most members of the security services [were] no more than well-meaning amateurs.' Robert Lamphere, interview, at <http://www.pbs.org/redfiles/kgb/deep/kgb—deep—ref—frm.htm> recalls 'Peter Dwier' [*sic*] as 'a suave British gentleman and a good negotiator'. The former FBI official explained that Fuchs had figured in one of the earliest of the decoded Venona intercepts, which Dwyer had obtained permission to read from 'our number three man'. Dwyer told Lamphere in August 1949 he would be leaving to take a job in Canada, but the FBI man was not impressed with Philby, who was 'sloppily-dressed compared to Peter Dwier' [*sic*]. Philby nonetheless inherited Dwyer's Venona reading privileges, thus tipping off the Russians 'to the fact that we were inside their system [and] able to identify people.'

63. Peter Dwyer, interviewed by Ben Wicks, *Max Ferguson Show*, Jan. 1972 (CBC Radio Archives). Dwyer interjected: 'Who says I didn't suspect him? We knew it was Kim Philby. Kim Philby crossed one's mind', but then he added, confusingly, 'he was tied to so many people and so many things . . . one refused to believe it . . . it was surprising, yes.'

64. NAC, Dwyer personnel file.

65. Chris Dwyer, interview with author, reports that in the early 1950s his father taught at a Canadian 'spy college' associated with CBNRC and then operating at or near the Kemptville Agricultural College, south of Ottawa. Not surprisingly, documentary evidence for this is scant. John Starnes's 'Dissemblers' trilogy of spy novels is spiced with his experiences in Canadian security intelligence, and in *Scarab* (Ottawa: Balmuir, 1982), 51, 93, he alludes to 'McClung' and to an 'Agricultural College'. Speaking to Donald Brittain, Arnold Smith mentioned study visits in 1947 to examine British and American espionage techniques for the establishment of such a training centre in Canada (NAC, CFI Collection, ISN 61915).

66. Ibid., F.T. Rosser memo to file, 30 Nov. 1949; Don Wall, interview by author; NRC Archives, C.J. Mackenzie Diary, 2 Nov. 1949: 'Mr. Glazebrook in later in the afternoon to discuss matters in connection with Communications Research—.' Unfortunately the entry cuts off at that point.

67. CBC Radio Archives, *Max Ferguson Show*, 3 Jan. 1972, pre-recorded phone interview with Peter Dwyer; Robert Chadwell Williams, *Klaus Fuchs, Atom Spy* (Cambridge, Mass.: Harvard University Press, 1987), 116–20.

68. NRC Archives, C.J. Mackenzie Diary, 6 Feb. 1950. When the Fuchs story broke, NRC President C.J. Mackenzie was grilled by reporters on the security of Canadian atomic research.

69. Dwyer personnel file, Rosser to Dwyer 21 Apr. 1950, marginal note. The stamp-sized negative of Dwyer's security photograph fell loose from inside the binding of his government personnel file when I unfastened the metal clasps. Normally, such photos are removed during file screening.

70. NAC, RG 37, vol. 48, 'Privy Council Office' file, July 1947, security booklet issued by Arnold Heeney, Chairman of the Security Panel.

71. See John Bryden, *Best Kept Secret*, and Wesley Wark, 'Cryptographic Innocence: The Origins of Signals Intelligence in Canada in the Second World War', *Journal of Contemporary History* 22, 4 (Oct. 1987): 639–65.

72. Don Wall, interview by author. Rosser used this description when he recruited Wall, then an MA candidate at the University of Saskatchewan, in June 1950.

73. Jaffrey Wilkins, interview by author, 13 May 1998.

74. Soeur Marie-Gilbert, interview by author, 26 Mar. 1996. She was a novice at Hurdman Bridge when the military took it over in 1941, and recalls the novices' loss of liberty moving from the open countryside to the stricter environs of the Mother House. DND, RMH 3–6–1-A, 13 Jan. 1941. Lt. Col. H. Buck wrote in English to the Mother Superior on 13 January 1941, appreciating the sisters' 'sacrifice of such serene surroundings', adding rather thoughtlessly that their 'sacrifice was exceptionally small when compared to that of many other communities.'

75. NRC Archives, C.J. Mackenzie Diary, 25 Aug. 1948.

76. DND correspondence file, Soeurs de la charité, Ottawa. One small matter of record is the nuns' financial arrangement with their electronically alert tenants. When Peter Dwyer arrived on the scene in 1950 they collected a quarterly rent of $5,000. NAC, RG 2, vol. 2654, cabinet decision 12 May 1954. By comparison, in 1951 the RCMP paid $370,000 per year to rent the almost adjacent monastery headquarters from the Archdiocese of Ottawa; in 1954 the cabinet approved its outright purchase for $5,250,000.

77. NRC Archives, C.J. Mackenzie Diary, 17 Jan. 1949: 'Mrs. Oliver from the Communications Section came in to see me. She is leaving for England where she will spend a year as liaison officer with the opposite unit in England. She . . . will become technically efficient as well as proficient on the administrative side'; 28 Feb. 1950: 'Mrs. Oliver in at noon to give me a report on her work in England in her very secret field. Apparently the cooperation between our two countries is growing better every day and more confidence is being shown in our group.'

78. Not a word is said about the Communications Branch in Wilfred Eggleston's humdrum accounts of the NRC: *Scientists At War* (Toronto: Oxford University Press, 1950), *Canada's Nuclear Story* (London: Harrap, 1966), and *Research in Canada: The National Research Council, 1961–66* (Toronto: Clarke, Irwin, 1978). On the other hand, there is a beguiling dottiness in C.J. Mackenzie's diary, which records the peculiarity of clandestine electromagnetics during the Cold War: sociable visits from a personal courier delivering top-secret electronic gadgets from England; an associate's 'fantastic theory about all life being electricity' that had brought him personal philosophical equilibrium; and a pesky NRC scientist who merely wanted to invent the Internet. He

accosted his chief with 'another one of his inventions', and Mackenzie fumed that 'he is always on something that is impracticable . . . [T]his time he wishes to set up a central broadcasting facility connected with telephones so that anyone can dial in and get any program on the Continent.'

79. NRC Archives, C.J. Mackenzie Diary, 14 Feb. 1950.

80. Peter Dwyer, *Hoodman-Blind*.

81. Chris Dwyer, interview by author. Chris Dwyer recalls visiting the Nunnery, climbing up to the top floor, and seeing the electronics mounted in wooden cabinets. His father once brought home an early Ampex tape recorder to record his own guitar music.

82. NAC, MG 28 I 30, Ottawa Little Theatre, vol. 10, 1952–3 Annual Competition, file 'Peter Dwyer, *Hoodman-Blind*'.

83. David Bevington, ed., *The Complete Works of William Shakespeare*, 3rd edn (Glenview: Ill.: Scott, Foresman & Co., 1980), 1102.

84. See also Naim Kattan, 'Décès de Peter Dwyer', *Le Devoir*, 3 Jan. 1973: 'Il n'avait pas une conception idéologique ou politique de ce role.' Kattan told Elizabeth Gray on CBC Radio's *Anthology*, 17 Feb. 1973, that Dwyer had a 'personal relationship with Hamlet and with Shakespeare'.

85. Naim Kattan, interview by author.

86. NRC Archives, C.J. Mackenzie Diary, 9 Feb. 1949. '[A] great flap today about a BUP reporter who is making enquiries re communications work. I do not think he is after Drake's show but we will have to be careful.' In 1974, a CBC *Fifth Estate* crew filmed Communications Security Establishment Director Kevin O'Neill woodenly exiting the CSE's Tilley Building and driving off in his car; straining credulity, journalist Jeff Carruthers ('Few in Ottawa know of secret NRC group', *Globe and Mail*, 11 Jan. 1974) reported that the CSE had been kept so secret that even Prime Minister Trudeau learned of its existence only through the CBC item.

87. Don Wall, interview by author. Don Wall does not recall seeing the production.

88. NAC, RG 2, acc. #1990–91/154, box 55, file N-30, 'National Theatre—Official'.

89. Ibid., Peter Dwyer to Robert Bryce, 8 Sept. 1954.

90. Ibid. Although not located at Landsdowne Park, the National Arts Centre is much closer to Whitton's original specifications than either Bryce's or Dwyer's. It occupies almost exactly the eight-acre area (though not the site) foreseen in her proposal. It has three auditoriums, totalling more than 3,650 seats, and the opera house's backstage area is one of the largest in North America.

91. Florence Fancott, interview by author, 4 Apr. 1996.

92. Iris Winston, *Staging a Legend: A History of the Ottawa Little Theatre* (Carp, Ont.: Creative Bound, 1997). Fire destroyed the church in 1970 and in 1972 a fully equipped purpose-designed theatre, with a fly-tower and modern stage systems, took its place.

93. Dwyer perhaps knew Tennyson's 'In Memoriam': 'Again our ancient games had place / The mimic picture's breathing grace / And dance and song and hoodman-blind.'

94. Peter Dwyer, 'Fall', *Saturday Night*, 11 Dec. 1954, and 'Loon', 13 Nov. 1954; Canada Council, Annual Reports, 1958–9 to 1970–1.

95. See Tippet. *Making Culture*, 9: 'They were the preservers and keepers of the established and the familiar, and very much content to be so.'

96. NAC, MG 28 I 30, Ottawa Little Theatre, vol. 10, file '1952–53 Annual Competition', Adjudicator's notes.

97. Don Wall, interview by author.

98. NAC, RG 2, vol. 232, file s-100–1, NA, Robertson to St Laurent, 29 Jan. 1952. Dwyer was granted Canadian citizenship in 1955. Dwyer's initial 'top-secret' memo to

Robertson, 4 Mar. 1952, indicated his surprise at the Security Panel's ignorance of counter-intelligence and its preoccupation with 'trivial matters of physical security'. Reading the minutes and documents, Dwyer concluded that the Panel 'has not so far concerned itself with what seems to me the heart of the matter—the operations and the targets of foreign intelligence services within Canada . . . our main purpose must be to deny intelligence to the agents of foreign powers. . . . We seem to have been throwing up earthworks without very much consideration of the firepower of the real enemy.' He urged upgraded measures, including further penetration of front organizations and 'the acquisition of defectors'.

99. Ibid., Norman Robertson to Deputy Ministers and heads of federal agencies, 22 Apr. 1952. Before taking up his new censorship function, Gaskell went around the circuit of senior officials introducing Peter Dwyer. For Gaskell's writerly activities, see Lyn Harrington, *Syllables of Recorded Time: The Story of the Canadian Authors Association, 1921–81* (Toronto: Simon & Pierre, 1981), 193–4.

100. Solicitor General of Canada, [A]TIP Division, Security Panel Document PS-121, Peter Dwyer, 'The Soviet Secret Intelligence Services: A Guidance for Security Officers', 3 May 1952; also see Chapter 2, note 52.

101. NAC, RG 2, vol. 235, file S-100–6, 'Security Organization—Arctic Security, 1952'; P.M. Dwyer to N.A. Robertson, 5 Apr. 1952. See R.G. Robertson to N.A. Robertson, 4 Apr. 1952: 'Dwyer's memo seems sensible . . . [he] suggests that security restrictions should be related not to latitude or to region . . . but rather to the intrinsic nature of any particular place or thing.'

102. George Bain, 'Low-Priced Peek at Secrets', *Globe and Mail*, 8 Oct. 1952.

103. NAC, RG 2, series 18, file S-100–11–S, P.M. Dwyer to J.W. Pickersgill, 29 Oct. 1952. 'It occurs to me that the significance of this incident is that a Canadian newspaper man gave the Russians what they thought was useful, and what, for all he knew, may have been very valuable information. . . . this story might be given to the press off the record at a convenient press conference . . . since it shows so clearly what damage a senseless disclosure might do.' NAC, RG 25, vol. 4249, file 8531–40, pt. 3. Dwyer wrote with the same suggestion to Glazebrook at External Affairs, where Hume Wrong thought that 'Mr. Pearson might be interested in this curious relationship between the press and—others', and he instructed the Press Office to take note.

104. Howard Margolian, *Unauthorized Entry: The Truth About War Criminals in Canada, 1946–56* (Toronto: University of Toronto Press, 2000), 193–4, repeats Reg Whitaker's hearsay speculation that Dwyer was part of a secret triumvirate that inducted war criminals into Canada. But he adds no new evidence for this. On the other hand, it is perplexing that Margolian blanks out Dwyer's years at CBNRC by dating his arrival in Ottawa in *1952* rather than 1950. This casts some doubt on the independence of Margolian, who, as a War Crimes Unit historian, presumably was sworn to secrecy under the Official Secrets Act and thus cannot mention Dwyer's connection with the CBNRC. He does make a good point, though, in arguing that 'it seems inconceivable that [Dwyer] would not have been made aware of [Kim] Philby's role in Nazi smuggling during the transitional period [in Washington], if he had not already known about it.'

105. NAC, RG 2, 1990–1/154, vol. 15, file C-34, 'Canada Council—Offl.', R.B. Bryce to John Deutsch, 2 May 1957. Bryce cautioned that 'for the reasons indicated' Albert Trueman should not state this priority 'first' in representing the activities of the Council. See also RG 2, file N-14 'National Library—Offl.', 1952–8. For one example of a Soviet specialist receiving a Canada Council grant, see RG 63, vol. 261, file 'John N. Westwood'. Westwood, a former British military intelligence officer, earned a Ph.D. in

Slavic Studies at McGill. His vast knowledge of and passion for Soviet railways is attested to by his several books, and also by his arrest and expulsion from the USSR while travelling on a Canada Council grant. This was the fourth such expulsion, on this occasion for photographing a train bridge. See 'Canadian's Photos Drove Soviets Loco', *Vancouver Sun*, 4 Mar. 1963. Other press stories similarly made light of the case, despite the fact that Westwood was 'not anxious for publicity in this matter'. Access to Information staff withheld Westwood's two-page report of the incident, but not Canada Council Director Albert Trueman's final comment on the case: '!'. NAC, RG 146, [RCMP] file 93-A-00019, Canada Council, part 2, contains a partially released press clipping and a note that the following six pages—presumably the record of the follow-up inquiries—were exempt from release under the Access to Information Act.

106. NAC, RG 2, 1990–1/154, vol. 15, file C-34, P.M. Dwyer to Ross MacDonald, 2 Apr. 1957.

107. Robert Bryce, interview by Littleton, *ca* 1981, NAC; NAC, Dwyer personnel file. During his brief tenure at the PCO Jack Pickersgill completed delicate negotiations initiated by Norman Robertson with the Public Service Commission to raise Dwyer's status without divulging any specifics regarding his work.

108. It seems that the theme of blackmail was in the air. On 16 November the Metropolitan Opera celebrated its seventieth anniversary by opening a new production of Gounod's *Faust*.

109. NAC, RG 2, 1990–1/154, vol. 15, file C-34, R.B. Bryce to P. Pelletier, 30 Aug. 1954.'[R]elating to the Canada Council, Peter Dwyer is very much interested in this and it would be quite satisfactory to have him devote some of his time to these affairs, for which it would seem to me that he is qualified.'

110. NAC, RG 2, vol. 140, C-34 'Canada Council—Offl. Secret, 1951', E. Reid to N.A. Robertson, 28 Sept. 1951; R.G. Robertson to A. Heeney, 1 Oct. 1951. Reid wrote: 'the minority, which has hitherto done in Canada what little has been done for the arts, letters and music (not infrequently at considerable sacrifice), will almost certainly be alienated [if Robertson's suggestions about the Canada Council prevailed]. It should be as independent as possible.'

111. Ibid., vol. 15, file C-34, Peter Dwyer to R.G. Robertson, 16 Oct. 1953, with attachments. Robertson noted for St Laurent that 'Dwyer of this office is very interested in the Canada Council. [His paper] contains some interesting views which you might like to see.' Ibid., 19 Oct. 1953, Robertson replied to Dwyer: 'PM saw this & undoubtedly read it. I don't know what his reaction is, but he will have weighed and considered it.'

112. Ibid.

113. Ibid.

114. *The Rising Tide of Democratic Canadianism and the Fight to Put Canada First*, Cultural Commission, Annual Cultural Conference of the LPP, Toronto, Apr. 1955.

115. Ibid.

116. NAC, RG 2, vol., file C-34, Prime Minister's speech drafted by P.M. Dwyer, 11 Jan. 1957. R. Bryce noted: '? this does not appeal to me as having much point.'

117. Chris Dwyer, interview by author. Maurice Oldfield had taken over Dwyer's old post in Washington following Kim Philby's departure.

118. NAC, RG 63, vol. 1377, file 'Massey, Vincent (Patron)', V. Massey to A. Trueman, 19 Oct. 1959, and attachments.

119. Ibid., vol. 1364, file 'Soundings, 1969'.

120. Ibid.; author's interview with Naim Kattan. Beneath Dwyer's affability Kattan detected an innate concern for security. For example, he once instructed Kattan, who commuted

from Montreal to work in Ottawa, often carrying Council papers, never to lose physical contact with his briefcase, and, whenever possible, to keep it between his knees.

121. NAC, RG 146, file 'Canada Council'. From 1958 the RCMP ran file checks on Council members, executive officers, and every grant recipient named in the annual reports, as well as monitoring press clippings for grants to organizations and other Canada Council prizes. While Toronto's Arts Club Theatre and various individuals and groups were investigated, Inspector McLaren felt the briefs were 'inadequate' and complained that 'the press clippings service has failed to produce reports on the Canada Council grants.'

122. Ibid., William Kelly to O.C. 'A' Div., 6 Jan. 1965. As Assistant DCI in 1962, Kelly inquired: 'What is the full extent of Canada Council grants to communists?' In a marginal note, one investigator wondered: 'Can we work this through ————?' and DSI George B. McClellan concurred. Kelly was to 'please discuss approach with me.' These excisions may or may not refer to Peter Dwyer. In a press clipping filed by the RCMP, Dwyer states that 'people are beginning to learn that culture is not like castor oil—to be taken because it is good for you, they are finding that it is something to entertain civilized people.'

123. George Bain, 'Writer Claims Mackenzie King Tipped FBI on White's Loyalty', *Globe and Mail*, 20 Nov. 1953. The story naming Mackenzie King as the source ('All signs point to that fact') was written by Isaac Don Levine for the Scripps Howard Newspapers. Levine was a Russian-born, anti-Soviet journalist specializing in Soviet intelligence services, ghost writer of memoirs by previous Soviet defectors, and a HUAC informant against Harry Dexter White.

124. NAC, RG 25, vol. 8561, file 50303–40, part 1.1, 'United States Investigations into Subversive Activities in US—Implication of Canadian Officials', G.G. Crean to A. Smith, 19 Nov. 1953. Bruce Muirhead's biography of Rasminsky, *The Public Life and Times of Louis Rasminsky* (Toronto: University of Toronto Press, 1999), 325, n. 90, adds a tantalizing anecdote linking Harry Dexter White to what seems to have been a Soviet attempt at Bretton Woods in 1944 to entrap Rasminsky in a compromising sexual liaison. According to Muirhead, White tenaciously enforced American dominance of the IMF and its Board structure, and, despite the complexity and confusion that marked these negotiations, it is not easy to see how Dwyer's 1946 telegram could be other than a kind of vengeful move against White for his pro-American obstinacy. White had been the focus of British ire for several years and J.M. Keynes as well as others were infuriated by the 'U.S. domineeringness' White represented. (White was the object of anti-Semitic remarks even from Keynes, and he was vilified by right-wing US financial interests.) The British may have rightly sensed that White was vulnerable to a campaign of innuendo.

125. Ibid., A.D.P. Heeney to L.B. Pearson, 19 Nov. 1953.

126. Bruce Craig, 'A Matter of Espionage: Alger Hiss, Harry Dexter White, and Igor Gouzenko—The Canadian Connection Reassessed', *Intelligence and National Security* 15, 1 (Spring 2000): 211–24, concludes that Gouzenko's defection did not yield any specific information concerning Harry Dexter White, as is suggested by James Barros, 'Alger Hiss and Harry Dexter White: The Canadian Connection', *Orbis* (Fall 1977): 598–9.

127. According to Stafford and Granatstein in *Spy Wars*, November 1953 also happened to be the month in which Soviet spy 'Gideon' turned himself over to the RCMP, although the authors provide no indication of how they came to know this.

128. NAC, RG 25, vol. 8561, file 50303–40, part 1.1, G. Ignatieff, Ottawa dispatch, 23 Nov. 1953.

129. Ibid., R.A. MacKay to C. Ritchie, 20 Nov. 1953. Gouzenko's information included a reference to an assistant to Secretary of State Stettinius, suspected to be Alger Hiss. This information was provided to the FBI but not to HUAC.
130. Ibid., A. Smith to G.G. Crean, 24 Nov. 1953. Israel Halperin's notebook became famous in 1951 when it was revealed it had contained Klaus Fuchs's name, a crucial fact apparently overlooked during the Gouzenko inquiries.
131. Neither Crean nor Smith seems to have known that Mackenzie King, as a result of Norman Robertson's briefing on 5 February 1946, entered in his diary that betrayal in the US was now suspected 'right up to the top of the Treasury, naming the person'. As Craig, 'A Matter of Espionage', 216, points out, this is only 'possibly an indirect allusion to Harry Dexter White', but it suggests that King and Robertson may not have processed privy information acquired from Britain or the US as a result of their centrality in the Gouzenko case in such a way as to make it available to senior Canadian officials such as Smith or Crean during the following years.
132. *Ottawa Citizen*, 24 Nov. 1953.
133. Ibid.
134. Ibid., Lester Pearson, Secretary of State for External Affairs, Ottawa, to Norman Robertson, Canadian High Commissioner, London, 25 Nov. 1953. 'Most Immediate', in cipher. In fact, both men were in Ottawa at the time, and Robertson approved the wording of the text, as did Charles Ritchie and G.G. 'Bill' Crean. It was also circulated to Arnold Smith prior to its transmission to London. As head of DL(2), Crean was the appropriate originator for a message to 'C', as the head of British MI6 customarily was known:

Most Immediate. Following for Collins personally from Crean. Would you please pass the following message <u>immediately</u> to 'C'. Begins. For 'C' from Crean. You will no doubt have seen reports of a letter [of 1 February 1946] from Edgar Hoover to General Vaughan at the White House concerning Harry Dexter White (and which was released by Attorney-General Brownell). The letter purports to make it clear that the F.B.I. received a tip-off concerning White from a highly placed Canadian source or sources in the Government. After some research we have found a copy of a telegram which was sent to the F.B.I. on or about January 28, 1946 by Peter Dwyer who, you may recall, was at that time your Liaison Officer in Washington and was, in fact, at the relevant dates in Ottawa assisting in the examination of Gouzenko. Dwyer, you may know, is now a Canadian Government servant and Secretary to our Security Panel. Unfortunately Dwyer cannot recall the precise circumstances in which the telegram was sent, though he believes it may have been inspired by Sir William Stephenson, but it is clear that Hoover's letter is at least in part based upon the information and language contained in that telegram. The telegram was sent to Dwyer's office in Washington with the request that it be <u>shown</u> to Whitson of the F.B.I. on a <u>personal</u> basis. For convenience, in case you are unable to trace the message in your files, the following is the text: Quote. Show following to Lish Whitson personally. Begins.
1. For your most private information only we have learned from an informed diplomatic source something which would seem of great concern.
2. As you will know Harry White's name has been sent to Congress by the President for ratification as one of the two U.S. delegates on the International Bank for Reconstruction and Development under the Bretton Woods agreement. This, of course, is none of our affair.
3. However we now learn that the two British and two Canadian delegates will nominate and support White for the position of President of this Bank. . . . With this

backing we gather that White's nomination to this important post would be a more or less forgone conclusion.

4. This would seem particularly alarming when taken in conjunction with the fact that Russia has not ratified the Bretton Woods Agreement.

5. Situation therefore is this. If we allow Canadian and British delegates to carry out their present plan, we allow them to place a Soviet agent in a position of utmost importance in international relations. On the other hand we should not wish to warn our delegates without your complete agreement.

6. You will perhaps be aware of above and may have already taken steps with regard to it. For this reason we are consulting with you unofficially in this way and would ask whether you see any way out of this dilemma which concerns us all. We would appreciate your earliest advice in this as our delegates arrive on Friday.

7. This message has blessing of RCMP and has been shown to Bethel with whom matter has been discussed in fullest detail. Please keep para. 3 under your hat. I suggest you may like to make use of this channel of reply through Miss Dack.

Ends. Unquote.

2) So far as we can make out here, what in fact happened is that someone, ~~Canadian or otherwise~~ [phrase struck out in original], advised Dwyer that Harry White was about to be nominated to a post either in the International Bank or the International Monetary Fund. Although the telegram doesn't square with either the policy of the Canadian government toward the nomination of White at that time or, indeed, with the constitutional set-up of either the Bank or the Fund, it seems to us to have been quite a normal thing to tip off the F.B.I. in case they did not know that White's name was about to be sent to the Senate for confirmation as the United States member of the Executive Board of Directors of the I.M.F.

3) In the circumstances, my Minister and the Prime Minister feel they are bound to make a statement in the House and it will probably be done this afternoon. My Minister was anxious, however, that you should be aware of the line the Government proposes to take in the House before the statement is actually made. Perhaps the main point at issue for you is that the Government has seen no alternative but to refer to a message having been sent from Ottawa by a Liaison Officer from a third friendly power. I hope that in the circumstances no undue embarrassment will occur for you, though it is not impossible that the Foreign Office will receive press enquiries. There is also the possibility that the author's name may become public since a member of the Press Gallery here was employed in British Security Co-ordination in New York during the war, and if he wishes to publish Dwyer's name, he is probably aware of Dwyer's official position at that time. I am sure you will understand that the necessity for making a statement along these lines arises through the inaccuracies in Hoover's letter to General Vaughan when he chose to attribute, for reasons, unknown to us this particular tip-off to a highly placed Canadian source. I should, of course, add that the only security information Canadian authorities ever possessed on White came from American sources. Ends.

135. This correspondent may have been *Financial Post* writer Michael Barkway. The British-born Barkway was a frequent commentator on security-related issues. For instance, his timely palliative concerning the NFB security scare, 'This Screening Business: The Check-ups Protect Us From Our Own Termites', *Saturday Night*, 3 Jan. 1950, 3, evidently drew upon direct security intelligence experience. His *Who's Who* entry allows that during World War II he was with the Political Warfare Executive and afterwards with some unnamed Washington organization.

136. *Ottawa Journal*, 26 Nov. 1953.

137. Barros, 'Alger Hiss and Harry Dexter White', 598–9.

138. NAC, Dwyer personnel file, Alan Jarvis, 18 Oct. 1971. In fact, this paraphrases Martin Esslin, *Reflections: Essays on Modern Theatre* (New York: Doubleday, 1969), 221.

139. NAC, RG 63, vol. 1364, 'Secretary of state', P.M. Dwyer to M. Pitfield, 12 July 1968. This 'personal and confidential' letter is filed along with an internal memorandum from Undersecretary of State G.G.E. Steele to his minister, Maurice Lamontagne, 13 June 1968. Steele justified their department's independent grant-giving on the basis that the Canada Council had concentrated on the fine arts, 'displaying little interest in film, broadcasting, museums, folk arts and crafts'. Henry Hindley's unpublished memoir, p. 11, does mention that the conversation at Sammy's 'ranged over a vast field of subjects, often of a confidential nature.'

140. Ibid.

141. Department of Foreign Affairs, file PSIR 7–1–6–1, E.R. Rettie to file, 23 Oct. 1970; E.R. Rettie to Marc Lalonde, 23 Oct. 1970.

142. Anthony Cave-Brown, *Treason in the Blood: H. St. John Philby, Kim Philby and the Spy Case of the Century* (Boston: Houghton Mifflin, 1994), 599; NAC, RG 149, vol. 74, file 6.11, 'Correspondence with Peter Dwyer'. Before his death Dwyer acted as consultant to Hamilton Southam and the National Arts Centre, but poor health prevented him from drafting NAC annual reports as foreseen. (Henry Hindley took over that task.) That Dwyer had initially opposed Southam's proposed opera festival made this a generous gesture from one ex-intelligence official to another. Dwyer counselled Southam to survey people's tastes and develop an Ottawa opera audience with a diet of popular favourites before risking esoteric productions. Of Britten's *A Midsummer Night's Dream* (presented lavishly in the summer following his death) he wrote, 'I think it would be a very courageous thing to do in view of the lack of sophistication of your summer audience.'

143. Robert Bryce, interview, 1981. Bryce was touchy about this question:
Interviewer: Does having access to secret information take a human toll?
Bryce: Yes. But you learn to live with it in due course. You, it's . . . um. I can't think of people breaking down owing to the anxieties they had, but . . . ah, it does have some effect . . . Okay?
Interviewer: Okay.

144. Don Wall and Mark McClung, interviews by Brittain and Littleton, NAC, *ca* 1981.

145. NAC, Dwyer personnel file, typed note to Canada Council staff, 19 Nov. 1971.

Chapter 5

1. Edith Elizabeth Harrison was born in London, England, in 1907 and studied painting before moving to Canada in 1933. An active member of the Canadian Federation of Artists, she also served as Supervisor of Art Education in the Kingston public schools.

2. NAC, RG 25, vol. 2936, file 2960–40, 'Appointment of George Glazebrook'. University of Toronto President H.J. Cody wrote to Norman Robertson on 30 December 1941: 'I know you will find Mr. Glazebrook an admirable colleague—intellectually keen, full of knowledge, and conscientious and thorough in all his work. We wish him godspeed in his service with you for our country and for the great cause.'

3. British press officer Milward Rodon Kennedy Burge was Arnold Davidson Dunton's British counterpart at the Quebec Conference; he published an espionage novel titled *Escape to Quebec* (London: Pan Books, 1946).

4. See John Bryden, *Best Kept Secret: Canadian Secret Intelligence in the Second World War* (Toronto: Lester, 1993), 123–4.

5. NAC, RG 25, vol. 5699, file 4–J(s), 'Special Censorship of Telephone Conversations'. This 'most secret' material shows that in 1943 the Department of External Affairs was concerned with the degree of censorship applied to consular communications in general. There were strong indications that the FBI and possibly other US agencies were routinely intercepting all Canadian embassy calls. One such report prompted Pearson in Washington to request of Robertson that he explore formalizing certain reciprocal exemptions with the Americans. This proposal went nowhere, but the problem was still fresh in mind when the question of Canadian interceptions of Soviet communications cropped up.

6. Ibid. Glazebrook must have been on the lookout for such an example since the RCMP identified the communicants by their phone numbers alone. In his neat miniature script Glazebrook wrote 'probably Soviet Consulate' and then crossed out 'probably' after verifying the number. When queried, the RCMP allowed that the conversation was recorded on a cylinder at Halifax and then translated at their Ottawa headquarters.

7. Ibid.

8. Ibid. Glazebrook reported to Robertson on 2 November 1943 his verbal exchanges with the suspicious and homophobic Commissioner Wood. Wood allowed that RCMP censorship monitored embassy phone conversations 'only for cases of espionage or suspected espionage', but 'there is no possibility of it being misused.' Glazebrook then retreated from his idea of restricting RCMP phone censorship. He reported to Norman Robertson that 'there seems every reason to believe the present system is free from abuse. No doubt it would be more satisfactory if all monitoring were under censorship but I suspect that this could not be done without difficulty.' Robertson concurred, luke-warmly: 'I think these arrangements are pretty free from objection.'

9. Ibid. S.T. Wood's capitulation to Robertson on 23 December is carefully phrased: 'The names of the various foreign consular officers in Halifax have been forwarded under secret cover to our Officer Commanding at that point to ensure that all necessary precautions may be taken to ensure that under no circumstances will incoming or outgoing calls respecting these officials be censored by members of this Force.'

10. Igor Gouzenko, *This Was My Choice* (Toronto: J.M. Dent & Sons, 1948), 222–3. Zabotin was the Soviet military attaché in Ottawa and Gouzenko's immediate superior.

11. J.L. Granatstein, *A Man of Influence: Norman A. Robertson and Canadian Statecraft, 1929–68* (Toronto: Deneau, 1981).

12. Wartime employment of artists for camouflage painting had been discussed at the Kingston Artists' Conference held in June 1941. Elizabeth Harrison and André Biéler co-edited the proceedings, republished as *Kingston Conference Proceedings* (Kingston: Agnes Etherington Arts Centre, 1991).

13. Elizabeth Harrison, interview by author, 16 Apr. 1996; Robert Bothwell and J.L. Granatstein, *The Gouzenko Transcripts: The Evidence Presented to the Kellock-Taschereau Royal Commission of 1946* (Ottawa: Deneau, 1982), 168. Kay Willsher had access to secret and top-secret material. On the other hand, she was not privy to operational intelligence matters. She testified to the Royal Commission that documents classified above 'top secret' bypassed the registry altogether. A tantalizing trace of Soviet and British jockeying in wartime Ottawa occurs in the guest book of Hull's Café Henry Burger. Above Colonel Zabotin's expansive signature on the page dated 11 October 1943 is the controlled cursive of Patrick Duff, second secretary of the British mission, apparently dining at a nearby table.

14. Elizabeth Harrison, interview by author; NAC, MG 30 D282, Wilfred Eggleston Papers, file 'Ottawa Civil Liberties Union, 1946'. According to Eggleston's records, Mrs Harrison attended the founding meeting, chaired by the NFB's Stan Rands, at which former Chief Censor Eggleston agreed to accept the chairmanship on a temporary basis.

15. Gouzenko, *This Was My Choice*, 238; NAC, RG 25, vol. 4249, file 8531–40 FP. Anatoli and Alexandra Kirsanov arrived in May 1944 and moved out of 511 Somerset two months prior to Gouzenko's defection; *Ottawa City Directory*, 1944.

16. James Littleton, *Target Nation: Canada and the Western Intelligence Network* (Toronto: Lester & Orpen Dennys/CBC Enterprises, 1986), 17. Granatstein and Stafford, *Spy Wars*, call Gouzenko 'the man who started the Cold War'.

17. Solicitor General—ATIP Division, document 141, file 117–91–99, 'Security Screening in the NRC, 1940–46'. Judge T.C. Davis, Canada's High Commissioner to Australia, sent dispatches to Ottawa on 15 and 17 April 1946 describing a 'hysterical' meeting of the Australian Association of Scientific Workers, which 'charged that the Gouzenko affair was put-up by Western Intelligence to discredit the Soviet Union, and passed resolutions calling for the freeing of Nunn May and [Dr. Raymond] Boyer.'

18. Bothwell and Granatstein, *Gouzenko Transcripts*, 18.

19. H. Montgomery Hyde, *Room 3606* (New York: Dell Publishing, 1964), 19. The nickname was coined by American playwright and OSS propagandist Robert Sherwood.

20. William Stevenson Papers, University of Regina Archives, file 800.1–3, (Sir) W. Stephenson to W. Stevenson, 16 May 1974. Hyde and Ellis were former 'Beescites' who had worked directly under Stephenson during the war; Stevenson's early career was spent running a Far East news bureau. He worked for the CBC in the 1960s and 1970s and continues to write about Intrepid from time to time, including a recent beyond-the-grave dialogue with his old mentor in the *Globe and Mail*, 8 Apr. 2000.

21. For assessments of Stephenson's legacy, see Timothy Naftali, 'Intrepid's Last Deception: Documenting the Career of Sir William Stephenson', *Intelligence and National Security* 8, 3 (July 1993): 72–92; David Stafford, 'Intrepid: Myth and Reality', *Journal of Contemporary History* 22, 2 (Apr. 1987): 303–18. Reg Whitaker, 'The Politics of Security Intelligence Policy-making in Canada: II 1984–91', *Intelligence and National Security* (Jan. 1992): 60, points to secrecy as an 'occupational disability' frequently resulting in publicity for intelligence failures rather than successes.

22. Hyde, *Room 3606*, ch. 8, 'Finalé'.

23. David Stafford, *Camp X* (Toronto: Lester & Orpen Dennys, 1986), 252 passim.

24. Bryden, *Best Kept Secret*, 272.

25. Hyde, *Room 3606*, 257–8.

26. In William Stevenson's widely discredited *Intrepid's Last Case* (New York: Villard, 1983), a Reagan-era rewrite of the Gouzenko affair and the British molehunt, Sir William Stephenson changes his story, hinting not only that he had had prior contact with Gouzenko, but that he had engineered the defection himself. As the Gouzenkos fled from office to office on 6 September, denied sanctuary by Mackenzie King and Norman Robertson, Stevenson reports how Robertson's initial hostility to the 'director of a secret British organization [pulling] strings in the Imperial manner' (p. 53) was overcome by providing him with a foretaste of Gouzenko's list of Canadian traitors. As Reg Whitaker and Gary Marcuse, *Cold War Canada: The Making of a National Insecurity State, 1945–1957* (Toronto: University of Toronto Press, 1994), 60, point out, 'if proven this account would reveal a case of massive deception, duplicity and the manipulation of elected officials by the security agencies.'

27. Bryden, *Best Kept Secret*, 273: 'There seems little doubt that this is the one Stewart Menzies who headed Britain's Secret Intelligence Service.' Since Bryden's visit to the Chateau Montebello to examine Seigniory Club records the Club itself has been wound up and its papers have been transferred to the Canadian Pacific Archives in Montreal. The registry containing Menzies's membership card viewed by Bryden was not included in this transfer and apparently remains in the safekeeping of a former Club member.

28. Stevenson Papers, Regina, cable from Stephenson, 20 Mar. 1974. Stevenson apparently believed this particular cable was intercepted or interfered with—it is marked 'COL RCMP'—and it appears that he complained about this to CNCP Telecommunications; on 20 Apr. 1974, Stephenson added that for 'practically every word, situation, name [provided by] Gouzenko [and] results thereof we provided special rockex circuit all traffic from which [was] exclusively myself for distribution.' He emphasized '[Mackenzie] King's naïveté in matter, particularly [during his] visits to Winston . . . Winston of course having been fully informed from first.'

29. Ibid., 4 June 1974.

30. A CSIS training school at Camp Borden is called the Sir William Stephenson Academy.

31. NAC, MG 30 E350, vol. 2, file 27. On 12 September 1946, in London, Tracy Philipps sent his copy of the Kellock-Taschereau Report to 'My Dear Lord Justice', writing that '[t]here is nothing surprising about the Report, except perhaps that the Canadians are surprised.' He sent a copy to V.J. Kaye in Ottawa, adding, 'Pity yr. street is not BEVIN!' (referring at once to Kaye's former address on Bevan St. and the political wilderness conservatives occupied while Ernest Bevin reigned in the Foreign Office).

32. Paul Virilio, *Open Sky* (London: Verso, 1997), 40, writes that 'another area of research beckons: the area of *ecological pollution*. The pollution not only of air, water and other "substances", but also of the unperceived pollution of "distances" . . . we should be equally anxious to study this pollution . . . triggered by the growth of real-time technologies.'

33. Stevenson Papers, University of Regina, file 801.1–5, 22 Mar. 1975. That Stephenson's one area of real sophistication was telecommunications is documented in the unbroken stream of half-encrypted cablegram patois tapped out by the old man from his Atlantic outpost in Bermuda, formerly the wartime censorship capital: 'The craft of cybernetics includes a great variety of electronic instrumentation which can serve man in a multitude of helpful ways. But the more services it is designed to render, the more the device requires the delicate and accurate human repeat HUMAN control.' Stephenson was acutely conscious of cable censorship and he reminded Stevenson that certain matters were 'inappropriate for this means of communication'. He used nicknames, allusions, multiple spellings, ran words together and broke others apart presumably in order to evade word-sensitive screening equipment. This did not prevent him from broadcasting en clair his dislike of people such as John Le Carré ('minor past bureaucrat F.O. . . . not reached his teens when early complicated preparations were hot on grill . . . immature') or *Maclean's* editor Peter C. Newman ('the fellow we arranged to get out to where he is now just ahead of the gas showers') or various competing writers on intelligence matters ('satiation chokes them into nosediving death crash. Cavebrowns and their like of no consequence') or Lord Halifax ('obtuse . . . holier-than-thou'). On the other hand, he delighted in encouraging journalists like Peter Worthington to attack 'left-wing' organizations such as the CBC: 'here is communist penetration to generate Worthies most ferocious and killing attack.'

34. Stafford, *Camp X*, 251; Hyde, *Room 3606*, 155.

35. John Sawatsky, *Gouzenko: The Untold Story* (Toronto: Macmillan, 1984), 24.

36. NAC, RG 25, vol. 5699, file 4–J(s), L.B. Pearson to N.A. Robertson, 2 Dec. 1943; Robertson to Pearson ('Most Secret'), 9 Nov. 1943.

37. Ibid.

38. NAC, RG 25, vol. 3217, file 5353-AB-40, 'Canadian Liaison', T.A. Stone to C.D. Jackson, 6 Mar. 1944. Jackson (at that time vice-president of Time Inc.) served in London as Eisenhower's deputy for Political Warfare.

39. Don Page, 'Tommy Stone and Psychological Warfare in World War Two: Transforming a POW Liability into an Asset', *Journal of Canadian Studies* 16, 3–4 (Fall-Winter 1981): 110–19.

40. Campbell Moodie was London liaison for the Wartime Information Board.

41. NAC, RG 25, vol. 3217, file 'NFB'. Robertson issued a tepid remonstrance to Grierson requesting he keep External Affairs better advised of his activities.

42. Ibid., vol. 3211, file 5353–Z-40, T. Stone to R. Bruce Lockhart, Nov. 1944.

43. Moore, *Reinventing Myself*, 95–6. Moore may or may not be right about MI5 and Hess, but his perception that Stone, his immediate superior, was running on the outside track in London is reliable enough.

44. NAC, RG 25, vol. 3217, file 5353–V-40, 'Co-operation of National Film Board with PWC', T. Stone to G. Glazebrook, 22 Nov. 1944.

45. Ibid., vol. 3211, file 5353–Z-40, T. Stone to N.A. Robertson, 15 Aug. 1944. 'The Russians are now attending the Central Directive meetings . . . Lockhart handles the Russians, of course, with great ability. . . . He has opened all the possible files of the P.I.D. to the Russians. . . . P.S. I should add that the General [Vassilieff] brought along with him this morning an extremely pretty and capable lady interpreter who introduced a note of sweetness and light into the meeting.'

46. David Stafford, *Churchill and Secret Service* (Toronto: Stoddart, 1997), 344. Churchill was 'exceptionally well-acquainted with . . . intelligence techniques [and] grasped the importance of signals intelligence. Yet, by character excitable and impulsive, he was often mesmerized by the original texts of intercepts, irresistibly drawn into their tactical and operational use.'

47. Ibid., 314–16; Martin Gilbert, *Never Despair: Winston S. Churchill, 1945–1965* (Toronto: Stoddart, 1988).

48. Ibid.; see also Anthony Cave-Brown, *'C': The Secret Life of Stewart Menzies* (New York: Macmillan, 1987); Nigel West, *MI6: British Secret Intelligence Service Operations, 1909–45* (London: Granada, 1985).

49. E.P. Thompson, *Beyond the Frontier: The Politics of a Failed Mission, Bulgaria, 1944* (Stanford, Calif.: Stanford University Press, 1996), 95: Churchill, 6 Apr. 1944, '[We] are weeding out remorselessly every single known Communist from all our secret organizations.' And on 13 Apr. 1944, 'We are purging all our secret establishments of Communists because we know they owe no allegiance to us or our cause and will always betray secrets to the Soviet, even while we are working together.'

50. Venona traffic, 8–13 June 1945: <www.nsa.gov/docs.june45/june45.html>. Ciphered warnings alerted Soviet intelligence sections abroad, including Ottawa and Halifax, that a 'foreign intelligence service has recently begun to show an unusually large amount of interest in Soviet diplomatic post and is setting itself the aim of trying to extract documents.' Larry Black, 'Canada and the Soviet Union in 1945', in Greg Donaghy, ed., *Uncertain Horizons: Canadians and Their World in 1945* (Ottawa: Canadian Committee for the History of the Second World War, 1997), 285–304, argues

that by 1945 Moscow had discounted any chance of achieving a pro-Soviet stance through the Canada-Soviet friendship movement because of Canada's vulnerability to the 'intra-imperialist' influence of Britain and the US.

51. Ibid.; Cave-Brown, '*C*', 452. His only other wartime excursion, according to Cave-Brown, was a short visit to France; as has been seen, Bryden places Menzies in Canada first in 1940 and again in 1945—neither visit is mentioned by Cave-Brown.

52. 'Stalin Honors Beaverbrook', *Globe and Mail*, 6 Oct. 1944.

53. Gilbert, *Never Despair*, 139; Charles McMoran Wilson, *Winston Churchill: The Struggle for Survival, 1940–1965* [Lord Moran diaries] (London: Constable, 1966).

54. This reference, presumably to Gouzenko's previous neighbour and colleague, Kirsanov, was never properly accounted for before the Royal Commission. Harold Main bicycled in person to make the complaint, and evidently he gave police the apartment number but not the name. 'Kirsanoo' is how Kirsanov was listed in the 1944 *Ottawa City Directory*.

55. NAC, CAVA ISN 61904, C. Bayfield, interviewed by D. Brittain, 3 July 197[?]. Disguised as a mail courier, Bayfield sat behind Alan Nunn May in the Lancaster bomber ferrying the scientist from Montreal to England on 5 October 1945. In the crowd at the airport Bayfield spotted British agents whom he already knew. They took over surveillance of Nunn May from that point.

56. Sawatsky, *Gouzenko*, 45–9; NAC, RG 33/62, pp. 470–91. It is significant that neither in his report written at 3 a.m. on the 7th (exhibit 61) nor in his testimony seven months later before the Royal Commission did Constable McCullough mention 'the big lodge' or these unnamed officials. The Commission did not invite him to describe the 'further disturbances' that punctuated that night, or to explain why his written report is so peculiarly wrong on a number of obvious points, including reversing the apartment numbers of the Gouzenkos and the Elliotts. He hinted to Sawatsky that his report was considered highly sensitive and had been carefully kept out of public view.

57. NAC, CAVA ISN 61904, C. Bayfield. The former Mountie supplied an indication of police attitudes towards the media coverage of the case: 'The Press were marvelous . . . breathed not a word about it, it was marvelous, they really maintained the silence.'

58. J.W. Pickersgill, ed., *The Mackenzie King Record*, vol. 3 (Toronto: University of Toronto Press, 1970), 84–6. On 26 October 1945 King wrote: 'A little wine was served, and also some vodka . . . brought from Russia. Mrs. Churchill told the waiter not to use it, but to throw it out. She said brandy was a better substitute. It was clear that the vodka had been brought in with view to discussing Russian conditions.'

59. Ibid.; Whitaker and Marcuse, *Cold War Canada*, 39. Regarding King and security intelligence, see Stafford, *Camp X*, 36: King was 'unaware of the structure being created'; indeed, Charles Vining noted that he and Stephenson 'knew that King would not allow a British operation to operate in Canada.'

60. Whitaker and Marcuse, *Cold War Canada*, 50–4, show that King wanted to dispose of the Gouzenko case quietly and with a minimum of publicity in December 1945, but was dissuaded from doing so by RCMP Commissioner S.T. Wood.

61. Public Record Office, London (PRO), PREM 81908, E. Bevin to C. Attlee, 11 Oct. 1945.

62. Ibid., C. Attlee to E. Bevin, 12 Oct. 1945.

63. As Peter Dwyer wrote in his 1952 paper, 'The Soviet Secret Intelligence Services: A Guidance to Security Officers': 'We know of two Soviet intelligence services which we may expect to find operating in Canada . . . *the GRU* (Glavnoye Razvedivatelnoye Upravlemie—the chief intelligence directorate of the Red Army General Staff) [and] the MGB (Ministerstvo Gosudarstvennoi Beznopasti—the Minister of State Security).' The MGB succeeded the NKVD.

64. Venona traffic, Sept. 1945. Four days prior to Gouzenko's defection Moscow was concerned that the informant 'Dendi', one of their own members, 'is being developed by the greens.' On 16 September the Soviet post in New York reported that 'local intelligence means to achieve complete encirclement of the consulate. We are [subject] to great risk.' An earlier defector, Krivitsky, already had exposed Soviet intelligence-gathering in America before his mysterious death in a New York hotel room. Kravchenko defected in 1944 from the Soviet purchasing mission, AMTORG.
65. Wesley Wark, 'Cryptographic Innocence: The origins of Signals Intelligence in Canada in the Second World War', *Journal of Contemporary History* 22, 4 (Oct. 1987): 639–65; the 'lost innocence' theme is also central to J.L. Granatstein's biography of Norman Robertson, *A Man of Influence*.
66. Bryden, *Best Kept Secret*. From the Soviet side, post-Communist contributions such as Pavel and Anatoli Sudaplatov, with Jerold L. and Leona P. Schecter, *Special Tasks: The Memories of an Unwanted Witness—A Soviet Spymaster* (Boston: Little, Brown, 1994), 215, 217, raise the general level of uncertainty around Gouzenko. Sudaplatov recalls that the case 'had deep repercussions', effectively blocking atomic espionage operations in the US by the end of 1946. He remembers there was suspicion that the FBI, in order to mislead them, had falsified a cable from the Soviet consulate in New York reporting Harry Gold meeting Klaus Fuchs at his sister's house. PRO, HW 15/2, Venona-Bride intercept, 7 Apr. 1946, signed by 'Petrov' [Beriya]: the Russians only advised their own foreign NKVD stations of the full extent of Gouzenko's treachery on 7 Apr. 1946, after it became the focus of worldwide media attention. An intercepted transmission deciphered at Bletchley Park, Britain's secret wartime code-breaking centre, describes various lax precautions that permitted a mere cipher clerk to do such 'great damage . . . and very greatly complicate our work in the American countries'. Assessing all of the evidence, the transmission stated, it appeared that Gouzenko was 'preparing to betray his country long before the day on which he defected.'
67. NAC, RG 25, vol. 4249, file 8531-d-40, part 1, 'Publication of Igor Gouzenko's Autobiography'. Even as the espionage suspects were put to trial, External Affairs was approached by intelligence writer and anti-Soviet provocateur Isaac Don Levine, primed with an introduction from Sir George Sansom, British Far East intelligence expert, seeking world rights on behalf of *Reader's Digest* and Putnams to ghost write Gouzenko's autobiography. Despite the promise of international release and royalties of $20,000–$30,000, External Affairs' Hume Wrong judged the Russian-born Levine an inappropriate choice and thought 'some native Canadian talent might be found.' The RCMP's F.J. Mead preferred Gouzenko be kept in isolation, particularly from Levine, 'for security reasons', but he encouraged External Affairs to pursue a worldwide publishing deal.
68. Very briefly: in 1947 *Cosmopolitan* ran a series of articles and Bernard Newman published *The Red Spider Web: The Story of Russian Spying in Canada* (London: Lattimer, 1947); Gouzenko's autobiography, *This Was My Choice*, appeared in 1948 along with Darryl Zanuck's film, *The Iron Curtain*. Gouzenko's novel, *The Fall of a Titan*, appeared in 1954 and filmgoers heard him narrate the epilogue to Jack Alexander's *Operation Manhunt*. Svetlana Gouzenko's *Life Before Igor* appeared in 1960. In addition, the case was the subject of countless articles and television and radio programs. In the 1950s the CBC was criticized in the press for not developing a television series based on Gouzenko's exploits.
69. Sawatsky, *Gouzenko*, interviews with Andy O'Brien, Lydia Black, and especially Don Fast, 140: 'I would say Black wrote the book'; Igor Gouzenko, *The Fall of a Titan*, trans. Mervyn Black (New York: W.W. Norton, 1954), 140.

70. Gouzenko, *This Was My Choice*, 201 (subsequent page references are as indicated). Chapman Pincher, *Too Secret, Too Long* (New York: St Martin's Press, 1984), 112, reports that British counter-intelligence officers visited Ottawa in late 1944 or early 1945, including Guy Liddell of MI5. Other shadowy visitors in 1944–5 included BSC's Herbert Sichel, Peter Dwyer, and possibly 'C's' cousin and close associate, Rex Benson. Cyril Mills was the MI5 liaison stationed in Ottawa during the period leading up to the defection.

71. Malcolm MacDonald, *People and Places* (London: Collins, 1969). See ch. 15, 'The Gouzenko Affair', 185: 'According to the story I heard, he felt that the moment for his change of loyalty had arrived when an error which he made in the Embassy was discovered and reported to the powers-that-be in the Kremlin. By mistake he once left a secret document lying among various unimportant papers on his desk. . . . He reported the slip-up to his boss, the military Attaché, a certain Colonel Zabotin . . . a capable and genial man [who] held his tongue. . . . Unfortunately . . . the document . . . had been noticed by a certain significant female . . . the charlady . . . an agent of Moscow's Secret Police (the NKVD) . . . under . . . Vitali Pavlov.'

72. Ross Chambers, *Room For Maneuver: Reading the Oppositional in Narrative* (Chicago: University of Chicago Press, 1991). Gouzenko as 'narrator' is a composite of propaganda writers whose ends can only be served by disproportionately accentuating Gouzenko as the object of the narrative rather than as its *narrator*. The character Gouzenko (i.e., the narratee) attains primacy over Gouzenko the 'subjective' narrator who tells the story. This splitting is a feature of any autobiographical text but an obvious imbalance between narratee and narrator can signal the hidden hand of propaganda.

73. Heroes and villains here form an unstable polarity. For example, there is no reason why Emma Woikin, Zabotin's informant in the Department of External Affairs' cipher room, and thus in a sense Gouzenko's opposite number, should not be 'heroic' from the Soviet perspective. See June Callwood, *Emma* (Toronto: Stoddart, 1984).

74. Sawatsky, *Gouzenko*, 150. Propaganda expert James Eayrs (ibid., 17) was impressed by Gouzenko's 'utter lack of self-knowledge'.

75. NAC, WLMK Diary, 31 Oct. 1948, microfiche T-261. There is an explanation for King's confusing Gouzenko's title, *This Was My Choice*, with Victor Kravchenko's *I Chose Freedom: The Personal and Political Life of a Soviet Official* (New York: Charles Scribner's Sons, 1946). WLMK Papers, vol. 446, reel 9176, pp. 372747–8. In fact, King himself in July 1946 proposed the idea of a Gouzenko autobiography to S.J. Reginald Saunders, a Toronto publisher who previously had sent him Kravchenko's opus. King envisioned a similar Gouzenko volume to be entitled, 'I, Too, Chose Freedom'. But 'this is only a suggestion', he told Saunders, 'and I should not wish to be quoted as the one who made it.' King approached Scribner's through his former schoolmate Whitney Darrow, who replied unhelpfully, 'we ought not go in for this project because we do not wish to be partisan . . . and we have taken on a number of anti-communist books in a bunch. I only wish we could find something to counterbalance them.' Ibid., reel 11048, p. 399267, 31 May 1948: King thanked Gouzenko personally upon receipt of the book. 'May I add a word of special thanks for the inscription you have placed in the volume. That a word of mine should have remotely contributed to the writing of the book gives me a feeling of real satisfaction and pride. As for the book itself, [i]t is a fitting sequel to your heroic decision to unmask the treachery that threatened the existence of our free way of life. . . . It must make you very happy to see how your high purpose is finding its fulfillment far beyond anything you had believed possible; and the end is not yet. The

circles of inquiry and influence your example has inspired are constantly widening, and will continue to widen through the years.'

76. NAC, RG 25, vol. 4249, file 8531-D-40, part 1, G. Crean to L. Pearson, 7 Oct. 1946.

77. Vladimir Mikhaelovich and Evdokia Petrov, *Empire of Fear* (London: Andre Deutsch, 1956).

78. At that time the Governor-General's Award for Fiction was administered by the Canadian Authors' Association, shortly to be headed by Watson Kirkconnell. Its former secretary, Eric Gaskell, was the PCO's co-ordinator of a shadow postal, telecom, broadcast, and press censorship organization. Another active member was the RCMP's Ukrainian specialist, Michael Petrowsky. The chairman of the Governor-General's Awards Committee in 1954 was Frank Stiling, University of Western Ontario.

79. According to Granatstein and Stafford, *Spy Wars*, 48, 'Novikov' was also the name of an actual counsellor in the USSR's London embassy who assured George Ignatieff in 1943 that the Comintern truly was defunct and that Soviet diplomats were not its agents; in his testimony to the Royal Commission (p. 73), Gouzenko explained that 'Novikov' was the GRU codeword for intelligence material sent back to Moscow in the diplomatic bag.

80. Gouzenko, *The Fall of a Titan*, 136–7 (subsequent page references are as indicated).

81. Arnold Smith's attitude regarding Gouzenko's propaganda value is noteworthy. A regular at the Dwyer-McClung lunch table in later years, Smith spoke Russian, was connected to British Intelligence during the 1930s, headed the Political Warfare Division at the British embassy in Cairo during the war, and afterwards studied fifth-column activity as third secretary to Dana Wilgress at the Canadian embassy in Moscow. As lead writer of the Kellock-Taschereau Royal Commission Report, he told Donald Brittain (NAC, ISN 6195), 'I wanted to debunk the nihilistic totalitarianism and separate it very clearly from left-wing ideology and socialism. . . . the Report was designed to influence and wake up public opinion about [Communist] conspiracy [but] not against the Russians.'

82. Ibid. *The Fall of a Titan* plays on the rumour that Stalin ordered the poisoning of writer Maxim Gorki.

83. The patchy records of the Canadian Authors' Association provide no insight into the 1954 selection process.

84. Granatstein, *Man of Influence*, 180.

85. The phrase 'purely oral' sits uncomfortably with concessions permitting Granatstein's 'oral history' project to proceed in the first place. See ibid., 172, n. 21.

86. Sawatsky, *Gouzenko*, 46–7. Glazebrook also casually mentioned meeting the two British agents at the train station, although Jean-Paul Evans distinctly recalled to David Stafford that he arrived by air. When Glazebrook reviewed *A Man Called Intrepid* for *International Perspectives* (July-Aug. 1976): 38–40, he did not take the opportunity to set the record straight about Stephenson's involvement. He deemed *AMCI* to be 'good reading, as well as informative', although parts of it 'are dramatic', he warned. Indeed, he chided Stevenson for his 'curious omission' of Sir William Stephenson's 'routine' presence in Ottawa on the night of the defection.

87. Gouzenko, *Fall of a Titan*, 101–2. Mervyn Black's authorial hand may be detected in Alexei's suspension of his own creative writing for personal security reasons. Black's widow Lydia claims, in Sawatsky, *Gouzenko*, that her husband, a would-be writer, wrote parts of the novel as well as translating it. The character Alexei has found a 'private haven' in translation where 'he is required to decide nothing, nor to think for himself: the material . . . is selected, read and approved by a government official.'

88. MacDonald, *People and Places*, 189. MacDonald makes no mention in his memoir of his very sudden and very brief recall to London in August 1945, returning just three weeks prior to the defection. See NAC, King Papers, reel C9876, document 346148, 8 Aug. 1945, MacDonald to King: 'I am leaving Ottawa today for a short visit to the U.K.' Incidentally, a notice on MacDonald's personal papers warns researchers that the material was screened by a government department before deposit. Josef Frolik, *The Frolik Defection* (London: Leo Cooper, 1975), 102, mentions 'a terrible blunder on the part of the RCMP through which the Russians learned that [Gouzenko] wanted to defect.'

89. Charles Rivett-Carnac, *Pursuit in the Wilderness* (London: Jarrold's, 1967), 304. Rivett-Carnac's self-published volumes of poetry (National Library of Canada) are little better, but such literary limitations did not impede his stellar rise through RCMP ranks.

90. Joe Garner, *The Commonwealth Office, 1925–68* (London: Heinemann, 1978), 185.

91. Solicitor General, ATIP, Security Panel document SP-121, Peter Dwyer, 'The Soviet Secret Intelligence Services: A Guidance for Security Officers', 3 May 1952, 10.

92. Callwood, *Emma*, 124, recalls this broadcast. Gouzenko, *This Was My Choice*. Pincher, *Too Secret, Too Long*, 626, quotes a letter from Gouzenko to the RCMP dated 6 May 1952 stating that 'the favorite places for a dubok [dead letter drop] are . . . toilets (inside the water tank).'

93. NAC, RG 25, vol. 8561, file 50302–40.

94. 'Presenting the Seigniory Club in the Province of Quebec', undated booklet *ca* 1935, National Library of Canada.

95. NAC, RG 25, vol. 5758, file 81(s), 'Anti-Semitism Re Reception of Mr. Sol Bloom at Seignory Club [*sic*]'. Club members previously had objected to the visit of Henry Morgenthau and his family.

96. NAC, RG 25, vol. 5220, file 8100-F-4–40, part 5, Report of Conference 8–9 Nov. 1962.

97. Chad Gaffield, *Language, Schooling and Cultural Conflict: The Origins of the French-Language Controversy in Ontario* (Montreal and Kingston: McGill-Queen's University Press, 1987), xiv; Brooke Claxton, 'La Petite Nation and the Papineaus: Background to the Seigniory Club' (mimeographed booklet, 1957, National Library of Canada).

98. According to Michael McLoughlin, *Last Stop Paris: The Assassination of Mario Bachand and the Death of the FLQ* (Toronto: Viking, 1998), 185, and in a personal communication with the author, this was still the case when the CIA's Tom Karramessines stayed at the Chateau Montebello during a two-week visit to Ottawa in August 1970.

99. Bryden, *Best Kept Secret*, 273, reports that Menzies, regular member #145, joined the Seigniory Club on 22 September 1940.

100. NAC, RG 2, acc. 1990–1/154, box 7, file 'Bell Canada'; RG 2, vol. 239, file U-15-USSR-Offl., A.D.P. Heeney to L. St Laurent, 7 Mar. 1952. Soviet embassy staff were restricted to a 25-mile radius of Ottawa in retaliation for similar restrictions on Canadian diplomats in Moscow.

101. Sawatsky, *Gouzenko*, 135–40.

102. M. McClung, interview by J. Sawatsky, *Gouzenko*, 136–7. McClung drafted a speech to be used in case Gouzenko 'disappears . . . I was given access to all the Gouzenko files. It was fascinating . . . so we drafted a speech which exposed him for what he was.'

103. M. McClung, interviewed by James Littleton, *ca* 1981, NAC, CAVA 1987–0416.

104. NAC, RG 25, vol. 8561, file 50302–40; Gouzenko, *This Was My Choice*, 220. Farafontov's presence among the four Soviets who broke into Gouzenko's apartment suggests that they may have worried that Gouzenko did somehow take NKVD as well as GRU material.

105. NAC, RG 25, vol. 2620, file 7–1–5–7, vol. 48, 5280, proceedings of 15–17 May 1946.

106. Bill MacDonald, *The True Intrepid: Sir William Stephenson and the Unknown Agents* (Surrey: Timberholme, 1998), 176. In New York, Jean Peacock was retained by BSC to operate the coding machine after other staff had departed in 1945. She told MacDonald that 'I was the only one left . . . and they apparently got worried that there was a message coming through, and it was about Gouzenko.' She went back 'two or three times and decoded the messages about Gouzenko . . . and that was in *August* or September, I guess it was in September' (emphasis mine).

107. MacDonald, *People and Places*, 183.

108. Bruce Craig, 'A Matter of Espionage: Alger Hiss, Harry Dexter White, and Igor Gouzenko—The Canadian Context Reassessed', *Intelligence and National Security* 15, 1 (Spring 2000): 211–24, argues persuasively that the Canadians in fact fed back to the Americans their own suspicions regarding White that had originated from Bentley and Chambers. Gouzenko apparently added no knowledge of White and he said so again at Montebello in 1953. This does not help explain the source of Dwyer's parallel knowledge regarding White's appointment, which he did not share with his Canadian colleagues in 1946.

109. NAC, RG 25, vol. 4482, file 50026–40, James Stephens to Lester Pearson, 3 May 1950 and two subsequent undated letters.

110. Ibid., 3 May 1950. Spelling and syntax unaltered.

111. Ibid., A.D.P. Heeney to J. Stephens, 16 Feb. 1951.

112. Paul Dufour, ' "Eggheads" and Espionage: The Gouzenko Affair in Canada', *Journal of Canadian Studies* 16, 3–4 (Fall-Winter 1981): 188–98, discusses Israel Halperin's acquittal.

113. Sawatsky, *Gouzenko*, 2–8, 40–9.

114. NAC, King Correspondence, vol. 403, Edwin F. Elliott to King, 25 Mar. 1946, typed copy headed 'Confidential Please', original not entered on the file. Elliott received a degree in mining engineering from Queen's University in 1913. An accident in 1938 left him with limited vision, and in 1945 he was serving as an adviser on mining labour issues for the Unemployment Insurance Commission.

115. Ibid., vol. 403, E.F. Elliott to King, 8 May 1946. Presumably, the 'plan' Gouzenko had in mind was the suicide Mackenzie King had half hoped for.

116. Ibid., reel 11053, p. 406018, copy of letter from Frank Ahearn to J.W. McConnell, 19 Jan. 1949.

117. Ibid., vol. 444, E.F. Elliott to J.W. McConnell, 31 Jan. 1949.

118. For a full account of Darryl Zanuck's commandeering of Gouzenko's story, see Daniel J. Leab, ' "The Iron Curtain" (1948): Hollywood's First Cold War Movie', *Historical Journal of Film, Radio and Television* 8, 2 (1988): 153–88. Leab shows that former OSS chief William 'Wild Bill' Donovan attempted to have Gouzenko sign with literary agent Gertrude Algase. In NAC, RG 25, vol. 5783, file 219–B(s), 'Negotiations With 20th Century Fox for Film Rights, etc., involving Igor Gouzenko', G.G. Crean and L.B. Pearson were reluctant to supply Zanuck with direct assistance or information. Curiously, Crean advised Pearson that the suggestion of Algase as Gouzenko's literary agent came not from Donovan but 'Mr. Stephenson', presumably Sir William Stephenson.

119. NAC, RG 25, vol. 4249, file 8531-d-40, part 1, 'Publication of Igor Gouzenko's Autobiography'.

120. NAC, MG 55/30 #162. The contents of the essay itself are unremarkable: Gouzenko's passion for writing derived from his wish to see the Russian people free of Communism. The National Archives received it from Tatiana Daniell, née Long, widow of Ray Daniell. From 1953 until Ray's death in 1969 the couple were Ottawa correspondents

for the *New York Times*. 'Tania' became music publicist for the National Arts Centre, from whence she mailed the Igor Gouzenko typescript to the Archives. How it came into the Daniells' possession is unknown.

121. Another key participant was NRC President C.J. Mackenzie, who said he only learned of the defection several days afterwards. His diary entries proceed as usual throughout the period, but there is a conspicuous three-week gap in his correspondence file (NAC, MG 30 B 122, vol. 3, file 5–2) beginning on 28 August, a week before the defection. The NRC chief typically generated 30 to 40 pages of correspondence in any three-week span, but these pages are missing. The file resumes on 25 September with a letter to Sir John Cockcroft about vetting all atomic-related press statements. In this light, the exact date of the atomic research director Cockcroft's clandestine night visit to Ottawa from Montreal to be briefed on Alan Nunn May's duplicity would be interesting to know, and Mackenzie may have recorded it. MacDonald, *People and Places*, 192, does not explain why *he* (and not C.J. Mackenzie, as Cockcroft's nominal superior) should have been the one to brief Cockcroft.

122. According to James Barros, 'Alger Hiss and Harry Dexter White', n. 28, this is true of US archives as well: 'I cannot help but note that Gouzenko's file in the State Department's name index file for 1945–50 (National Archives, Washington) may have been tampered with. . . . The initial FBI reports from Washington were indexed—the index cards have now been removed from the file.'

123. NAC, MG 26 J 4, vol. 417. After my request was turned down in 1999, Bruce Craig, 'A Matter of Espionage', attempted unsuccessfully to have these volumes released, although in this case an officer agreed to read the files for any mention of Harry Dexter White, and evidently there was none.

124. NAC, AH-1999–00219/dg. In response to my request, 76 severed pages were released and 11 were withheld in their entirety.

125. NAC, AH-1999–00280/dg, RG 146, vol. 4944, 'Missing Mackenzie King Diary', M. Pitfield memorandum, 1981.

126. The Edmonton-born Haythorne earned a Harvard Ph.D. in economics in 1949 and was Deputy Minister, Department of Labour (1961–9). By 1972 he had left Ottawa to teach at the University of Botswana in Lesotho.

127. Ibid., memorandum for file, 26 Aug. 1969. The writer of this memo points out that in 1945 Roger Hollis of MI5 pressed King for immediate arrests of the suspects, whereas the American view was that they should be 'delayed as long as possible'. Ominously for Hollis, suspected in post-Philby Britain of being another Soviet mole, the writer added that Hollis's attitude 'may be pertinent in another regard'.

128. Ibid, memorandum for file, 'Re: Featherbed', 14 Aug. 1968.

129. J.W. Pickersgill, interviewed by Kirwan Cox, 12 Dec. 1977. NAC, acc. 1983–298.

130. PRO, PREM 8/908. Once the case was in the public domain, King gradually came to understand its propaganda value. In London, Churchill, as Leader of the Opposition, immediately and repeatedly pressured a reluctant Clement Attlee to publicize the Canadian Royal Commission Report as widely as possible. He wanted every MP to receive a copy, and his intent to bring such a motion before the House prompted lively exchanges between senior civil servants regarding how to use Gouzenko to the fullest propaganda advantage. For example, Hector McNeil to Herbert Morrison, 20 November 1946, reported on the distribution of 4,000 copies of the Report (including earmarked copies for the Labour Party and the Trades Union Congress), the plan for an inspired parliamentary question to coincide with a BBC talk stressing Zabotin's instructions regarding Soviet post-war strategic aims, and plans to produce popular versions

of the Report 'on an informal, unofficial basis'. Lord Addison wanted the publicity emphasis be kept on Canada and the source of information was to be 'through private channels. . . . If we identify ourselves too much in public with reproaches to the Russians for espionage activities, we may find ourselves vulnerable to a somewhat similar charge on the ground of our own activities.'

131. This film footage was included in a television documentary broadcast on CBC in 1998.

132. Ontario Public Archives, Michael Petrowsky Papers, 1919–77, reel 1. Eric Gaskell, wrote to Petrowsky on Canadian Authors' Association business on 15 October 1941. The letter is addressed to Petrowsky at 535 Somerset Street West. Several other letters (from the censor Eggleston and CPR's J.M. Gibbon) refer directly to intelligence work and they also were sent to the same address. This is both startling and puzzling. Startling, because it situates the Petrowskys not even 100 metres west of Gouzenko's front door at 511 Somerset. Puzzling, because so far as one can tell Russian legation staff did not live there until 1944. Petrowsky gave a false address (331 Richmond Road never existed) in the 1944 and 1945 city directories and no address at all in 1946, when he seems to have been on the move with the Gouzenkos.

133. NAC, RG 33/62, reel T-1368, p. 378.

134. Yvanna Petrowska, interview by author, 27 Mar. 2000. Taken aback, I asked her about the RCMP's chief translator in 1945, Moïse Arnoni. She had not known him personally, she said, but her husband knew him well. He had ended up in 'some trouble with a bank, money missing'. I was convinced that although elderly she not only remembered events from the 1940s, but has nurtured their recollection as central aspects of her life story.

135. Ibid. The opportunity was a post vacated by RCMP translator Mary Babuka, who married a senior officer and retired with him to British Columbia.

136. In 1941 or 1942 Yvanna Petrowska recalls being taken to lunch at the Chateau Laurier by a charming if somewhat eccentric English 'Lord', Tracy Philipps. He merely wanted to advise her, off the record, that his wife might possibly be a German spy. Yvanna and Michael must be most cautious in their dealings with her, Philipps warned, and also with her protector, the foreign-language press censor Ladislaus Biberovich.

137. Gordon Lunan, *The Making of a Spy: A Political Odyssey* (Montreal: Robert Davis, 1995). For Judith Alexander's sympathetic biographical sketch of the economist Agatha Chapman, see <www.yorku.ca/research/cwen/liveswom.htm>.

138. W.E.C. Harrison, introduction to Charles Comfort, *Artist at War* (Toronto: Ryerson, 1956), x.

Chapter 6

1. In Martin Duberman, *Paul Robeson* (New York: New Press, 1989), for example, the concert surfaces as the high point of a dismal year of harassment by the FBI and neo-Fascist elements bent on extinguishing his career. In Reg Whitaker's *Double Standard*, the event is evidence of the anti-Communist imperative in immigration policy. In Mine-Mill histories, the 1952 concert and the three annual concerts that followed it are cited as cultural achievements of the union. See Mike Solski and John Smaller, *Mine-Mill: The History of the Mine Mill and Smelter Workers in Canada since 1985* (Ottawa: Steel Rail, 1985); Al King with Kate Braid, *Red Bait! Struggles of a Mine Mill Local* (Vancouver: Kingbird, 1998); Mercedes Stedman et al., eds, *Hard Lessons: Mine Mill Union in the Canadian Labour Movement* (Toronto: Dundurn, 1995).

2. Lee Siegel, 'The Red and the Black', *The New Republic* (Jan. 1999): 18–26, criticizes a recent Robeson travelling exhibition for downplaying his political activities. Also see Barry Finger, 'Paul Robeson: Flawed Martyr', *New Politics* 7, 1 (Summer 1998): 132.

3. Michael Denning, *The Cultural Front: The Laboring of American Culture in the Twentieth Century* (London: Verso, 1996), 115–16, recuperates Robeson into a cultural nationalist narrative, singing Earl Robinson's 'unofficial anthem of the Popular Front' during his triumphant 1940 national tour. Capacious as it is, Denning's 'laboring of American culture' cannot circumscribe Robeson's range.

4. 'Seeking spy under every bed Robeson says of Toronto ban', *Toronto Daily Star*, 17 May 1947.

5. 'U.S. City Bars Paul Robeson', *Montreal Gazette*, 19 Apr. 1947.

6. *The Daily Tribune* published a United Press wire story dated 13 August 1947 reporting the revocation of the Negro Branch of the Peoria Legion's charter 'after the visit of Paul Robeson . . . last April'.

7. 'Toronto may ban Robeson: Ponders whether concert would breach peace', *Montreal Star*, 17 May 1947.

8. 'Will Robeson be allowed to spout Communism? Police Board to decide', *Globe and Mail*, 17 May 1947.

9. 'Seeking spy under every bed Robeson says of Toronto ban', *Toronto Daily Star*, May 17th, 1947; NAC, RG 33/62, reel T-1370, p. 4565. Robeson had no idea that Norman Veall had told the Kellock-Taschereau Royal Commission a year earlier that he first met Fred Rose 'when Paul Robeson, the actor was playing in Othello in Montreal, and there was a party given at Dr. Boyer's house, a sort of reception for Mr. Robeson.' Ibid., p. 1952, David Shugar explained that he first met Matt Nightingale among 'a large number of people going down to Halifax or the United States to hear this fellow Paul Robeson.'

10. NAC, RG 146, ATI 96-A-00053, vol. 4272, 'Paul Robeson' (henceforth RCMP, Robeson file), G.B. McClellan to A.S. Cooper, 16 Oct. 1940.

11. Ibid., unidentified press clipping, 30 June 1937.

12. Ibid., A.H. Owen-Jones, CIB Intelligence Section, Vancouver, 24 Nov. 1941; Mark Leier, *Rebel Life: The Life and Times of Robert Gosden, Revolutionary, Mystic, Labour Spy* (Vancouver: New Star Books, 1999), 120–1: 'William Bennett, often called "Ol' Bill", was an organizer and writer for the Communist Party of Canada.'

13. Ibid., J.E.M. Barrette, Intelligence Branch, Montreal, 20 May 1942. The RCMP already kept a file on Boyer as an organizer of the Canadian Association of Scientific Workers.

14. Ibid., Constable Norman O. Jones, Toronto Intelligence Branch report, 27 June 1942.

15. Ibid.

16. 'Negroes in Toronto Greet Paul Robeson', *Toronto Daily Star*, 8 Feb. 1943.

17. RCMP, Robeson file, Reid W. Foresee to S.T. Wood, 11 Feb. 1943.

18. British-born vocalist Goss was called the 'Canadian Robeson' as a result of his political activism (he ran as an LPP candidate in Vancouver). His light baritone lacked Robeson's sheer force, but he was, like Robeson, a serious scholar of folk music. In 1952 he was interrogated and ejected from the United States with writer Margaret Fairley after being paraded by FBI agents out of the Peace Congress banquet in New York. NAC, RG 25, vol. 5787, file 228–BP(s) part 1, L. Pearson to H. Wrong: 'This matter seems to have been dealt with by the FBI in a way to ensure maximum publicity and inflict the maximum of humiliation on those concerned. . . . If these Canadians were legally in the United States, it is difficult to understand why they should have been molested at a banquet.' Yet Pearson did not intervene on their behalf; Goss returned to England and died soon after.

19. Ibid., reports of 17 Sept. 1943, 8 Feb., 1 Mar. 1944; *La Victoire*, 30 Sept. 1944.
20. Duberman, *Paul Robeson*, 263–79. Robeson's Broadway Othello was a breakthrough for black American actors.
21. RCMP, Robeson file, Windsor Detachment, report, 2 Nov. 1944.
22. Ibid., 28 Nov. 1944. The RCMP supplied names of Canadians whom Robeson had met, including Fred Rose and Stanley Ryerson, both of whom were already subjects of files. Also see Duberman, *Paul Robeson*, 253. In January 1943, Hoover recommended custodial detention for Robeson, and such a card was issued on 30 April 1943.
23. RCMP, Robeson file, Windsor Detachment, reports, 11, 19 Nov. 1945. This address formerly was owned by industrialist George Weston before being converted to apartments. It became known to the Toronto Special Branch when Saul Kolchin invited members of the Mackenzie-Papineau Battalion to rest over there upon their return from Spain.
24. The singer returned to Toronto briefly in May 1946, but he seems to have been careful not to attract attention to friends and associates.
25. RCMP, Robeson file, reports of 18 July, 3, 8 Aug. 1946.
26. 'Paul Robeson Impenitent', Quebec *Chronicle Telegraph*, 5 Nov. 1946.
27. Ibid.
28. Louis-Philippe Roy, 'Robeson Chante Faux', *L'Action Catholique*, 5 Nov. 1946. 'Si jamais l'ARTISTE revient à Québec pour alimenter sa caisse et faciliter "son combat" il se rendra compte que les Québécois n'ont pas oublié le POLITICIEN. Des notes fausses pourraient bien alors troubler l'harmonie de sa publicité. Les Québécois sont des gens qui souviennent. Tenez-vous le pour dit, M. Robeson.'
29. RCMP, Robeson file, Constable J.H.F. Chénier, 8 Nov. 1946.
30. Ibid.
31. Ibid., Toronto Special Section reports of 19, 22 Nov. 1948.
32. 'Women Liberals Compare Paul Robeson to Tim Buck', *Globe and Mail*, 28 Feb. 1947.
33. 'College Campuses in U.S. Stalked by Red Spectre', *Globe and Mail*, 16 Apr. 1947; *Ottawa Journal*, 16 Apr. 1947.
34. RCMP, Robeson file, Vancouver Special Branch, Constable D.E. MacLaren, 17 Feb. 1947; Winnipeg Special Branch, C.S. Hogg, 18 Feb. 1947.
35. Wessely Hicks, 'Robeson Needles Police', *Toronto Daily Star*, 19 May 1947. RCMP, Robeson file, Constable J.J. Cranney, report, 22 May 1947, estimated 5,000 attendees.
36. 'Paul Robeson Skips Speech But Songs Were Significant', *Ottawa Journal*, 19 May 1947; Arthur Walker, 'Robeson Speaks', *Daily Tribune*, 19 May 1947: 'he succeeded in making this concert a social, musical, and political document'; Joseph Pach, interview by author, Mar. 1997.
37. RCMP, Robeson file, Constable Cranney's report.
38. Hicks, 'Robeson Needles Police'.
39. RCMP, Robeson file, Constable Cranney's report; *Ottawa Journal*, 19 May 1947: 'police officials stood by with notebooks.'
40. Editorial, *Globe and Mail*, 20 May 1947. The writer linked Parliament's debate on a bill of rights with the Robeson incident, defending his right to speak, and pointing out that 'police are only concerned in what they say after they have said it, not before.'
41. 'Robeson Concert Police Privately Hired', *Toronto Evening Telegram*, 20 May 1947; 'This Mare's Nest Was Elaborately Constructed', *Toronto Evening Telegram*, 23 May 1947: 'it was falsely represented that the police were there with notebooks.'
42. 'No Discrimination . . . , Mayor Declares', *Globe and Mail*, 27 May 1947.

43. 'Mob Rule or Law Rule', *Toronto Saturday Night*, 4 June 1947; 'Coercion by Indirection', *Prince Albert Herald*, 16 June 1947.
44. 'Ask Police Commission to Apologize', *Toronto Daily Star*, 21 May 1947.
45. 'Inspector Told Me We'd Need Police', *Toronto Daily Star*, 22 May 1947. For reminiscences of Annie Buller's activism, see Louise Watson, *She Never Was Afraid: The Biography of Annie Buller* (Toronto: Progress Books, 1976).
46. Mary Lowrey Ross, 'Left, Right, Left', *Toronto Saturday Night*, 4 June 1947.
47. RCMP, Robeson file, C.C. Winmill to J. Leopold, 27 May 1947; L.H. Nicholson to J. Leopold, 4 June 1947.
48. NAC, RG 25, vol. 5787, file 228-AX(s), 'Paul Robeson—Activities of', G.G. Crean to E. Reid, 20 Dec. 1948, with Leopold's brief attached.
49. Ibid., E. Reid, marginal note to G.G. Crean.
50. RCMP, Robeson file, E.W.T. Gill to Superintendent Wood, 2 Dec. 1948.
51. 'A Phony "Peace Conference"', *Globe and Mail*, 6 Dec. 1948; Alex Barris's flippant 'Accused of being "Red"—Singer's Feelings Hurt' appeared the next day.
52. 'Robeson Lauds Negro Advance Under Britain', *Toronto Evening Telegram*, 7 Dec. 1947. The headline ridiculed Robeson's positive reference to Jamaica and Trinidad in light of his 'anti-British' stance, but the article itself is sympathetic. In the southern US, he said, someone might 'blow my brains out' just for asking for a hotel room. 'One can hardly say one lives in dignity.' He praised the Toronto Jewish Choir's invitation to him as 'a symbol of the unity between Jew and Negro as victims of oppression. . . . If there is ever anything I can do in the struggle to live decently, call upon me.'
53. Gilles Fauconnier, *Mappings in Thought and Language* (Cambridge: Cambridge University Press, 1997), 37–41.
54. Paul Robeson, *Here I Stand* (New York: Othello, 1958), 43: 'There was a cultural logic to this cultural struggle . . . and the powers-that-be realized it before I did.'
55. The adoption of the word 'Progressive' by the Conservative Party of Canada under John Bracken in 1942 indicates the political significance it had acquired in the socially restive war years. This also prepared the way for its recuperation into conventional national political discourse in the post-war years.
56. NAC, King Papers, vol. 417, files 8 and 9. It is worth comparing Granatstein and Bothwell's *Gouzenko Transcripts* with the full proceedings. For example, the published version underplays the severity of Commissioner Kellock's verbal bullying of Willsher. She was in a shattered state, intimidated to the point of believing she would face execution, and her replies to these questions were barely audible.
57. Ibid. Unlike Willsher, Chapman had not breached an oath of office or secrecy. Criminal prosecution for hosting a study group in her home was dubious, to say the least, yet she was tried. Acquittal could not undo the discrediting of her 'progressivism', and within a few years she fled Canada.
58. C.W. Harvison, *The Horsemen* (London: Macmillan, 1967), 158–9; NAC, ISN 6195, Arnold C. Smith, interview by Donald Brittain; also see Chapter 5, n. 81.
59. NAC, ISN 61911, Mark McClung, interview by James Littleton, 15 Jan. 1981.
60. See Michael J. Hostetler, 'The Enigmatic Ends of Rhetoric: Churchill's Fulton Address as Great Art and Failed Persuasion', *Quarterly Journal of Speech* 83 (1997): 416–28.
61. Spencer Warren, 'Churchill's Realism', *The National Interest* (Winter 1995–6): 38–49.
62. Duberman, *Paul Robeson*, 303–4.
63. Paul Robeson Jr, CBC *As it Happens*, Jan. 1996; Duberman, *Paul Robeson*, 352–4. For a Canadian angle, see 'Robeson applauded when he appears on Moscow stage', *Ottawa Journal*, 9 June 1949. It reported that tickets were completely 'sold in a few hours', that

most Soviet leaders were in attendance, and that it was 'one of the highlights of Moscow's musical season'. The controversial encore is not mentioned, but it claims that 'Scandalize my Name' was dedicated by Robeson to the 'so-called free Western press'.

64. Fred Rose, *Spying on Labour* (Toronto: New Era Publishers, 1938), 36; emphasis in original.

65. For a sympathetic portrait of Rose, see Merrily Weisbord, *The Strangest Dream: Canadian Communists, the Spy Trials, and the Cold War*, 2nd edn (Montreal: Véhicule, 1994), 168–9. The electrician-turned-politician was a Polish-Canadian Montrealer for 25 years, she asserts, and not an 'alien' who fled 'back home' to Poland. Gerald Tulchinsky, *Branching Out: The Transformation of the Canadian Jewish Community* (Toronto: Stoddart, 1998), is more critical: 'Although popular in the Cartier riding, Rose was in serious trouble with the law. He had been arrested in September 1942 on charges of subversive activities as a member of the CPC (The CPC was outlawed in 1940 and renamed itself the Labour Progressive Party in 1942). He confessed to all the charges, promised not to participate in party activities and was released.... Rose was soon engaged in serious espionage activities on behalf of the Soviet Union.... Like Rose, [Sam] Carr also worked for Soviet Intelligence. Both men, in fact, were agents of the NKVD (the precursor of the KGB) for years, reporting on the CPC, various political matters, and, on rare occasions, ... Canadian political, military, and diplomatic matters.'

66. RCMP, Robeson file, report of two sold-out concerts in Montreal dated 17 Jan. 1948. Although Robeson 'refrained from making any political comments', he dedicated 'Joe Hill' to Fred Rose, with Tim Buck present in the audience. Commissioner Wood thought this 'very interesting'. Within the Special Branch, Norman Jones wrote to Len Higgit, 'You may come to see this from ———— angle.' Higgit replied, '————, I guess should be advised.' These deletions likely refer to Glen Bethel, who 'noted with thanks' a letter sent to FBI headquarters containing these facts, along with names and descriptions of Canadians attending the concert, the concert's printed program, and information concerning the 'assisting artist, Aube TZERKO'. On 20 December 1948, the *Montreal Star* called Robeson 'irritating' after he remarked to Jewish schoolchildren that Rose was 'a fighter for the poor' and that 'they won't kill his spirit', thus keeping alive an issue that the *Star* believed 'the LPP would much rather allow to be forgotten.'

67. For example, Stephen J. Whitfield, *The Culture of the Cold War* (Baltimore: Johns Hopkins University Press, 1991), dismisses Robeson out of hand.

68. William Glenesk, 'Art, Music, Drama: Paul Robeson', *Varsity*, 5 Dec. 1949.

69. Weisbord, *Strangest Dream*, 86. She is referring to Raymond Boyer, Fred Rose, and Irene Kon.

70. Irene Kon, 'A Reminiscence of Paul Robeson', *Black Voice*, 30 Apr. 1973.

71. At a time when the Soviet ally bore the brunt of the war, Boyer broke the rules and passed on his research on RDX, a high explosive. See his unsentimental but sensitive portrait of the Bordeaux prison, *Barreaux de fer, hommes de chair* (Montreal: Éditions du jour, 1972), for an indication of the remarkable person lost to Canadian society as a result of the spy hysteria.

72. Michael Horn, 'Leopold Infeld and the University of Toronto', *Dalhousie Review* 79, 3 (Autumn 1999): 319–34, traces the university's failure to support Infeld at the critical moment.

73. NAC, RG 25, vol. 8561, file 50224–40, vol. 3, 'Passport Security Measures Taken by Canada—General', A.D.P. Heeney to G.B. McClellan, 25 Oct. 1950.

74. RCMP, Robeson file, 'The Case of Paul Robeson's Passport: A Fact Sheet', 29 Feb. 1952. The FBI seized his passport on 28 July 1950. 'Among those similarly deprived are two

outstanding Negro women leaders: Mrs. Charlotta Bass . . . Mrs. Therese Robinson', and Dr Du Bois.

75. Paul Fussell, *Abroad: British Literary Traveling Between the Wars* (New York: Oxford University Press, 1980), ch. 4, 'The Passport Nuisance', esp. 30–4. Fussell traces literary allusions to the rise of the passport system after World War I. Increasing inconvenience at border crossings through the 1930s (when Robert Byron could still observe 'there is something absurd about a land frontier') by World War II became a 'ritual occasion for anxiety'. Fussell cites poet Basil Bunting ('The Passport Officer') without mentioning that Bunting was with MI6 for many years.

76. Daniel C. Turack, *The Passport in International Law* (Lexington, Mass.: Lexington Books, 1972), 251.

77. Nigel West, *MI6: British Secret Intelligence Service Operations, 1909–45* (London: Granada, 1985). In 1999 the RCMP's on-line bulletin featured J.E.M. Barrette's reminiscences of his years as a passport control officer. Barrette was one of the intelligence officers who monitored Paul Robeson in 1942 (see note 13 above).

78. Fussell, *Abroad*, 30.

79. NAC, RG 25, vol. 8561, file 50224–40, vol. 3, 'Passport Security Measures Taken by Canada—General', US State Department, press release, 24 May 1952.

80. Ibid., E. Reid to L. Pearson, 23 Apr. 1952. Reid's views did not impress Pearson: 'Notwithstanding the position which you put so forcibly you would withdraw a passport from a Canadian who owes the government a hundred dollars.' The difference, Reid countered, was that revoking consular privileges on the basis of a person's political views left them no route of appeal.

81. NAC, RG 2, vol. 235, file s-100–11. Within the Privy Council Office, Peter Dwyer and his colleagues circulated a reprint of F.R. Scott's 'Publishing False News', *Canadian Bar Review* (January 1952), as a ready-made legal opinion on the Endicott case. By Scott's reasoning, Endicott might successfully have been prosecuted for 'seditious libel'. But this required the US to admit that bacteriological weapons were used, for as Scott points out, 'the greater the truth, the greater libel'. The contemplated litigation proceeded no further.

82. NAC, RG 25, vol. 8561, file 50224–40, vol. 3, E. Reid to L. Pearson, 20 May 1952.

83. Ibid., L. Wilgress to L. Pearson, 27 Sept. 1952: '*Off the record*, it has been pointed out that passport controls without exit controls cannot prevent Canadians from traveling to Iron Curtain countries.'

84. Ibid., G. Glazebrook to Consular Division, 5 Nov. 1952.

85. Ibid. In an exchange between Canadian visa control, Paris, and William Kelly, Security Section at Canada House, London, P.J. Vaucher requested clearance to exchange information with the Sureté National (DST). His DST counterpart sought data concerning Soviet diplomatic representatives and Canadian Communists visiting France, 'so that they could keep them under surveillance.' George McClellan raised this with External Affairs only because an earlier overture for such an arrangement with the French had been rebuffed. Glazebrook had no objection to sharing data concerning Soviet diplomats, but he expressed caution to McClellan about routinely informing the French on Canadian citizens. McClellan then assured him that 'reopening negotiations . . . could produce the converse effect of what is desired', implying that the matter could be settled between the two police agencies themselves.

86. Ibid., dispatch, 18 Sept. 1951.

87. Wilgress's career of anti-Communism began with a secret denunciation of Louis Kon during the 1919 Canadian Trade Commission to Siberia. L.D. Wilgress, *Memoirs*

(Toronto: Ryerson Press, 1967), 53, writes: 'I got on well with Kon.' Cf. Solicitor General ATIP, RCMP file 'Louis Kon', Wilgress to Deputy Minister Trade and Commerce, secret letter, 7 May 1919: 'I consider it my duty . . . to call to the attention of the proper authorities the necessity of watching [Kon] on his return to Canada. . . . He is regarded as a Jew . . . holds socialist views [which] might possibly prove to be a menace.'

88. NAC, RG 25, vol. 8561, file 50224–40, vol. 3, D.Wilgress to L. Pearson, 7 July 1952.

89. Ibid., Oslo dispatch, 31 Dec. 1952.

90. Ibid., George Glazebrook to J. Thomson, 19 Dec. 1952. Notification of Boyer's visit was sent through Canada House to the Treaty Division of the Foreign Office on 6 December 1950.

91. Turack, *The Passport in International Law*, 9–10.

92. Canadian papers carried stories such as, 'U.S. Negroes Won't Fight Soviet Robeson Tells Red Paris Parley', *Montreal Gazette*, 21 Apr. 1949. A related AP wire story two days later reported that a 'disturbed and ashamed' official in Robeson's home state of Connecticut had proposed that the state attorney general 'keep this man out' of the state.

93. 'Robeson Wants to Become "The Black Stalin"', *Ottawa Journal*, 15 July 1949.

94. King, *Red Bait*, 116, reproduces an internal FBI document dated 17 January 1952. Acting on this Canadian tip, the investigator checked and reported that Robeson's file contained nothing about a visit to Vancouver. The State Department then issued fresh advisories to all border posts.

95. RCMP, Robeson file, J. Leopold to C. Harvison, 29 Jan. 1952.

96. 'Robeson Halted at U.S. Border', *Vancouver Daily Sun*, 14 Feb. 1952.

97. 'Paul Robeson Under "Domestic Arrest"', *Vancouver Daily Sun,* 1 Feb. 1952.

98. RCMP, Robeson file, Vancouver Special Branch report, 14 Feb. 1952; 'Robeson Heard by 2000 in Concert Over Telephone', *Vancouver Daily Sun*, 14 Feb. 1952. The article reported that 'B.C. telephone company officials said they were "not concerned" about Robeson having used a long distance line. . . . The Royal Canadian Mounted Police had "no comment" to make.' See also King, *Red Bait*, 115.

99. NAC, RG 146, vol. 1191, file 93-A-00087, 'Harvey Murphy and aliases'.

100. RCMP, Robeson file, report, 14 Feb. 1952; 'Singer Set for Border Concert', *Vancouver News Herald*, 14 Feb. 1952.

101. RCMP, Robeson file, report on Civil Rights Congress, New York, 29 Feb. 1952.

102. Ibid., transcripts of Mine-Mill broadcasts, Feb. 1952, by E.L. Walker, Percy Berry, and Al King, discussing the exit ban and playing a recording of Robeson's phone concert.

103. Ibid., 'E' Division report on League for Democratic Rights, 14 Mar. 1952. G.J. Archer pointed out to Harvison that Ukrainian attendance at the meeting was 'a further example that these language groups are the backbone of such Communist controlled organizations'. For Du Bois's refused admission, see Frank Park's letter in NAC, RG 146, file 92-A-000047, IUMMSW—Canada, 643: 'They waved to us as they got off the plane but that was the last we saw of them.' Regarding the upcoming concert: '10,000 progressive citizens are expected to be on hand to greet him', *Pacific Tribune*, 11 Apr. 1952.

104. Jolee Edmondson, 'Hazards of the Game', *Audubon* (Nov. 1987): 28. This golf course was part of 470,000 acres of golf courses in the US in 1950.

105. 'Peace Arch Provincial Park', BC Ministry of Lands, Parks and Housing, brochure, *ca* 1980, National Library of Canada.

106. King, *Red Bait*, 115.

107. Paul Robeson, *I Came To Sing* (IUMMSW/Othello Records, 1953), sound recording.

108. Paul Gilroy, *The Black Atlantic: Modernity and Double Consciousness* (London: Verso, 1994), 57: 'The expressive cultures developed in slavery continue to preserve in

artistic form needs and desires which go far beyond the mere satisfaction of material wants. In contradistinction to the Enlightenment assumption of a fundamental separation between art and life, these expressive forms reiterate the continuity of art and life. They celebrate the grounding of the aesthetic with other dimensions of social life. The particular aesthetic which the continuity of expressive culture preserves derives not from dispassionate and rational evaluation of the artistic object but from an inescapably subjective contemplation of the mimetic functions of artistic performance in the processes of struggle towards emancipation, citizenship and eventual autonomy. Subjectivity is here connected with rationality in a contingent manner.'

109. Ibid., 69.
110. Sterling Stuckey, *Slave Culture: Nationalist Theory and the Foundations of Black America* (Oxford: Oxford University Press, 1987), 321–8; emphasis added.
111. John Berger, *About Looking* (New York: Vintage, 1991), 66–7: 'There is never a single approach to something remembered. Numerous approaches or stimuli converge upon it and lead to it. Words, comparisons, signs need to create a context for a printed photograph in a comparable way. . . . A radial system has to be constructed . . . simultaneously personal, political, economic, dramatic, everyday and historic.'
112. Marion Gerry, 'The International Peace Arch (and a piece of the Mayflower)', *The Mayflower Quarterly* 56, 4 (Nov. 1990): 316–18.
113. Recent geodesic surveys using 'global positioning systems' locate the Peace Arch several hundred feet south of the 'true' forty-ninth parallel.
114. West, *MI6*, 54–5. Thompson is suspected of forging Sir Roger Casement's lurid diaries; eventually Thompson himself was imprisoned on charges of gross indecency.
115. Duberman, *Robeson*, 400, 706 n. 46: '[John Gray], field representative for the United Freedom Fund, who accompanied PR on much of the tour, reports: "Mobilization on this side of the border was non-existent, although 1000 or so were there thru no special effort. Concert was tops. Response *grand*."'
116. Whitaker, *Double Standard*, 170 passim.
117. 'Three-Mile Car Jam at Robeson Concert', *Daily Province*, 19 May 1952: 'Murphy said . . . 40,000 persons. . . . Customs officials set the figure at 15,000.' 'Robeson Barred', *Canadian Tribune*, 26 May 1952: 'Upwards of 25,000 Canadians and over 2,000 Americans . . . 4,000 cars . . . 22 buses and 3,000 police.'
118. RCMP, Robeson file, DEA Dispatch 545, R.A.D. Ford, Moscow, 'Canada in the Soviet Press', Tass, 20 May: 'the trade union organized a meeting on the Canadian-American border which was attended by 4,500 people. Paul Robeson appeared on a tribune constructed on the other side of the border. His performance was given over a loud-speaker'; RCMP, Robeson file, Constable Thomas, 20 May 1952: 'approximately 5,000 people'.
119. Ibid. The action itself is excised, but Thomas added, 'Further reports on this phase of activity may be anticipated.' To be thorough, the RCMP also kept their eye on 'Sid and Jean Brown's . . . 75¢ chicken plate supper', held at their White Rock home after the concert.
120. Ibid., Robeson file, 5 Apr. 1956.
121. Bruce Mickleburgh, 'An exclusive interview with Paul Robeson', *Horizons* (Apr. 1956): 29.
122. Ibid., 39
123. E.W. Carver, CSIS, to author, 23 Apr. 1996. The card released to me bears the heading 'Pual [*sic*] Robeson, A black American Singer' but its contents have been blanked out.
124. RCMP, Robeson file, C. Rivett-Carnac to Commissioner, 22 Jan. 1958; N.O. Jones to —————————, 23 Jan. 1958.

125. Duberman, *Robeson*, 493–4.
126. National Archives, Washington, RG 57, CDF 1960–63, O32 Paul Robeson, box 40. The American representatives had by no means idly waited for Robeson to arrive. In September, the Wellington legation cabled Washington requesting: '[d]etails [of] Robeson'[s] background which might lessen [his] impact if fed carefully [to a] chosen list [of] editorial writers. . . . Useful quotes by leading Negroes re Robeson. . . . Number of Negros owning cars in US compared with total cars in USSR. . . . Similar comparative figures re Negro students attending universities.' They received from the United States Information Agency and State Department a wide range of anti-Robeson material. Even his theorizing regarding folk music was noted as a possible weakness. An article Robeson 'hoped' would be published in the Soviet *Literary Gazette* 'has not appeared to date.' To the Americans' dismay, Australian and New Zealand media did not seize the prepared material and Washington heard afterwards from Adelaide that 'the recent visit by Paul Robeson must be accounted a complete propaganda success. He was accepted [with] naive critical welcome.'
127. Duberman, *Robeson*, ch. 24, 'Broken Health', 498–521.
128. RCMP, Robeson file. An 11-page report concerning Robeson received on 8 May 1961 by the RCMP (likely from British or American counterparts) is removed from the released file. Apparently it did not inform the RCMP of the extent of Robeson's health breakdown. Surprisingly, an attached transit slip notes that Robeson 'may soon be a visitor to Canada. Should steps be taken to bar his entry?' The RCMP somehow knew that 'the Party' did not expect that the singer would be allowed to enter, but 'we should no doubt write Imm[igration]' and see if 'some of the Divs. come up with infor[mation] on this.'
129. Paul Robeson, interview by Elaine Grand, CBC TV, *Close-up*, aired 29 Aug. 1961, video cassette. NAC, RG 41, vol. 197, file 11–18–36, 'Close-Up', H.G. Walker to J.D. Nixon, 6 Feb. 1961: 'the Paul Robeson interview is scheduled for Close Up. Pls. do not let this become a commitment.' (Note that this was not the same Ross McLean who worked under Grierson at the NFB.)
130. Duberman, *Robeson*, chs 24–6.
131. Tzvetan Todorov, *Mikhail Bakhtin: The Dialogical Principle*, trans. Wlad Godzich (Minneapolis: University of Minnesota Press, 1984), 96.
132. Terry Eagleton, 'Nationalism, Irony, Commitment', in Eagleton, Fredric Jameson, and Edward W. Said, *Nationalism, Colonialism and Literature* (Minneapolis: University of Minnesota Press, 1990), 23–5, wants to recover a Utopian possibility by prying open this uneasiness about the nation and tracing 'within the present that secret lack of identity with itself . . . where a feasible future might germinate'.

Conclusion

1. Giorgio Agamben, *The Coming Community*, trans. Michael Hardt (Minneapolis: University of Minnesota Press, 1993), 65.
2. Will Kymlicka, *Liberalism, Community, and Culture* (Oxford: Clarendon Press, 1991), 95.
3. Michel Foucault, *The Order of Things: An Archaeology of the Human Sciences* (New York: Vintage, 1973), 371: 'History constitutes . . . for the social sciences . . . a fixed ground, and, as it were, a homeland; it determines the cultural area—the chronological and geographical boundaries.'

4. Surface tensions are measured in 'dynes', whose root is the Greek *dunamis*, i.e., force or power.

5. Ernst and Young, 'CSIS, Report on the Use of Polygraph Examinations in the Candidate Selection Process', Solicitor General, ATIP Division, n.d., 8.

6. Ibid. Emphasis added.

7. William Baltruweit, *Down and Out in Canada's Intelligence Service* (Ottawa: author, 2000), VII, 80–1. Baltruweit is a former CSIS intelligence officer who claims he was 'willingly and deliberately coerced by intimidation' at the hands of CSIS management. They 'gained submission by inducing fear', he explains, and apparently were unable to respond appropriately to his clinical depression. Baltruweit sought to support his allegations of harassment with a polygraph test; but he suspected the in-house polygraph expert, psychologist Linda Dodd-Kelly, of secretly evaluating his mental state. Perhaps the 'right degree of tension' was obtained when a senior manager answered Baltruweit's greeting, 'How are you?' with 'Fine. (Pause) I think I'll take a polygraph on that.'

8. Malcolm Ross, 'Faith or Fear', Commencement Address to the Kingston Collegiate and Vocational Institute, 19 November 1960. (National Library of Canada.)

9. In this regard, one cannot help recalling critic Robert Fulford's uneasiness about Margaret Atwood's intuition that he may have had some connection to the CIA. Robert Fulford, *Best Seat in the House: Memories of a Lucky Man* (Don Mills, Ont.: Collins, 1988), 185–6: 'Given the climate [of the mid-1970s] it wasn't preposterous that someone would identify me as a CIA man.' Fulford was part of the Chalmers/*Maclean's* constellation that could have had some relation to the CIA's Cold War information project. In 1950 Chalmers released *Maclean's* editor Arthur Irwin to go and 'clean up' the National Film Board. In his memoirs, *Both Sides of the Street: One Man's Life in Business and the Arts in Canada* (Toronto: Macmillan, 1983), 204, Chalmers chuckles that when he personally guaranteed the $650,000 in loans necessary to get the Stratford Festival off the ground his personal fortune 'wasn't worth anything like that.'

10. Frances Stonor Saunders, *Who Paid the Piper: The CIA and the Cultural Cold War* (London: Granta, 1999), 5: 'Were reputations secured or enhanced by membership of the CIA's cultural consortium? How many of those writers and thinkers who acquired an international audience for their ideas were really second-raters, ephemeral publicists, whose works were doomed to the basements of second-hand bookstores?' Also see Giles Scott-Smith, ' "The Masterpieces of the Twentieth Century" Festival and the Congress for Cultural Freedom: Origins and Consolidation, 1947–52', *Intelligence and National Security* 15, 1 (Spring 2000): 121–43. This account is sensitive to the problem that such 'white' propaganda presents: 'It is not the actual covert history of the [Congress for Cultural Freedom] that makes it so intriguing; rather, it is the blend of covert and overt influences' (138).

11. Canada Council, *Twelfth Annual Report*, 7. If Massey-era policy is now to be revisited, recall that the commissioners were, as biographer Claude Bissell writes in *The Imperial Canadian: Vincent Massey in Office* (Toronto: University of Toronto Press, 1986), 10, ' "clerisy", concerned with the exposition and defence of traditional values. . . . The absence of an artist—a poet, a painter, sculptor, or dramatist—was a typical act of Canadian caution. Massey was well-disposed towards artists . . . but he thought their activities should be circumscribed by more sober citizens.' Indeed, the Commission report (377) firmly rejects any possibility of artists having statutory representation on the proposed arts council: 'With this view we are unable to agree. . . . [The Council] should be free to consider all problems before them . . . without restraints.'

Index

Access to Information, 141–2, 171; Act, 90, 91, 93; as cultural policy, 88–9; and removal of names, 74–5; and secrets, 178
Ackman, Allan, 81
L'Action Catholique, 189
Adams, Eric, 140
Agamben, Giorgio, 78, 228
agendas, hidden, 165–70
Aitken, Max, 151
'alliance politics', 183
Anderson, Benedict, 90
Anderson, Celia M., 79–80
Anderson, Robert, 72
anglophilia, 148–9
Anthony, M.E., 200
anti-colonialism, 16
anti-Semitism: and Chateau Montebello, 162; and Philipps, 47; in *The Man Who Knew*, 10–11
anti-Sovietism, 150, 154–61
Appadurai, Arjun, 93
Arroyo, José, 53
artists: and Canada Council, 124–6; Grierson's view, 50
Atlee, Clement, 153
'audio-visual': citizenship, 49–51, 75–8; narrative, 51
Australia: and passports, 207; and Petrov case, 157–8
Aylen, Peter, 21, 24

Bain, George, 119, 126, 131
Barr, Robert Mackenzie, 106
Barros, James, 132
Barwick, Jack, 138
base space, supernational, 199–200
Beaverbrook, Lord, 151
Bedell Smith, Walter, 128–9
Bentley, Elizabeth, 96–7, 210
Bernstein, Sydney, 148
Bethel, Glen, 128

Beveridge, James, 63, 70, 76, 81–2
Bevin, Ernest, 153
Biberovich, Ladislaus, 4, 21, 27, 33–5, 39
Biggar, O.M., 31, 139
Black, Mervyn, 48, 155, 165
Boetzelaer, Baron von, 208–9
Bothwell, Robert, 142, 170
Boyer, Robert, 204, 209
Bretton Woods, 96
Brewin, Andrew, 194
Briggs, W.E.S., 226
British Empire, Robeson's view of, 188–9
British High Commission, 140
British Intelligence Service (MI6), 146; Canada's reliance on, 209; and Dwyer, 104–6; and Gouzenko, 163–4, 165, 179; *see also* MI6
British Security Co-ordination, 105, 143
Brittain, Donald, 58, 136
Browder, Earl, 185
Brown, Lawrence, 189, 218
Brownell, Herbert, 97–8
Bryce, Robert, 112, 120–2, 129, 136
Bryden, John, 92, 144, 146, 154
Buchanan, Donald W., 27, 29, 30, 50–1
Buck, Tim, 203
Buller, Annie, 184, 192, 193–4
Burge, M.R.K., 138
Burianyk, Bill, 9
Burns, John, 100, 104

'C', 153, 166; *see also* Menzies, Sir Stewart
Cadieux, Marcel, 162
Camp X, 144, 146, 147
Canada Council for the Arts, ix, 96, 120–1, 122, 124–6; 132; and FLQ, 134; and national culture, 89; records of, 92
Canada-Soviet friendship, 141, 150
Canadian Broadcasting Corporation (CBC), xvi–xviii; and censorship, 23–4; and foreign-language broadcasts, 21; and national culture, 89; records of, 92; and Robeson, 187, 225

Canadian Information Abroad, 162
Canadian Tribune, 65, 66, 184, 186, 192
Canadian Unity Council, 30
Canadians All, 24–5
Carr, Mrs Sam, 188
censorship: and Access to Information, 74; and
    des Graz, 31–2; and history, 54–5; and NFB
    purge, 59; Robertson's plan for, 139;
    telephone, 139; women as censors, 32
Chalk River nuclear research station, 109
Chambers, Whittaker, 96–7, 210
Chapman, Agatha, 200
Chénier, J.H.F., 190, 191
Chicago Tribune, 98, 99
Chisholm, Jack, 82
Chronicle Telegraph, 189
Churchill, Winston, 141, 150, 151, 153–4, 175;
    'Iron Curtain' speech, 141, 201–2; and
    security metaphors, 201–2
citizenship: 'audio-visual', 49–51, 75–8; and
    cultural and security agencies, 84–5
Clare, John, 162
Clavier, Nathan, 81
Claxton, Brooke, 131
Cliveden Set, 13
Coetzee, J.M., 11, 55
colonialism, 11
'Coloured Persons' Index', 224
Committee on Co-operation in Canadian
    Citizenship, 21–2
Communications Branch of the National
    Research Council (CBNRC), 105–6, 107,
    109–10, 141, 221; 'Nunnery', 108, 109–10
Communications Security Establishment,
    records of, 92
communication technologies, xii–xiii, 146, 147,
    2221, 222
Communist(s): Canadian, 208, 214; Party, 203;
    purged from NFB, 55, 60–73; *see also*
    Robeson; Soviet
conscience, national, 123
consular policies and practices, 205–11
contagion, 39–42
Corby Case, 145, 200
cosmopolitanism, 122
Cox, Kirwan, 81–2, 173–4
Crawley, F.R. 'Budge', 65
Crean, G.G. 'Bill', 63, 105–6, 107; and Dwyer,
    128, 129; and Gouzenko,157, 163–5, 171;
    and Robeson, 195–6
Croll, David A., 65–6
Crompton, Maurice, 78
Cronjé, Geoffrey, 11
Cross, James, 133
Canadian Security Intelligence Service (CSIS):
    and Access to Information, 142, 171; and
    National Archives, 92; and tension, 228–9
Cullingham, Gordon, 86
cultural and security agencies, 95–136; and
    citizenship, 84–5

culture: as collective sensing system, xii–xiv;
    national, 87, 89, 95; and official secrecy,
    88–94; polarization of, 89; professionalized,
    123; and security, 86–7, 141, 180, 232–3

Dack, Geraldine, 128
Dahl, Roald, 144
Daly, Tom, 77, 82
Dark Princess, 16, 41
Darlan, Admiral, 151
Daviault, Jean, 174
Davis, T.C., 3, 7, 9, 20–1, 27, 28, 29, 139
Deleuze, Gilles, 228
Denning, Michael, 74, 96
des Graz, Charles, 31–2
Deutsch, John, 120
Devlin, Bernard, 232
Diefenbaker, John G., 207
disinformation, 156–7
Dorland, Michael, 88
Doughty, Arthur, xiv
Drake, Edward M., 105–6, 107, 108, 109
Dreisziger, N.F., 6–10
Drew, George, 65
Drew-Brook, Thomas, 106
Du Bois, W.E.B., 15–20, 41–2, 202, 214
Duberman, Martin, 218, 219, 221–2, 226
Dunton, Arnold Davidson, xvi–xviii, 27–8, 39,
    226, 229
Duplessis, Maurice, 190–1
Dwyer, Peter, ix, xiii, xix, 63, 71, 86, 89,
    95–136; and Canada Council, 120–6, 132–4;
    early life, 100–4; and Gouzenko, 146, 161,
    165–71, 173, 178; as 'Janus', 96, 100, 116,
    232; and PCO, 106–9, 118–24

Eggleston, Wilfred, 21, 34–5, 109, 139
Ekman, Gretta, 82–3, 85
Elliott, Frances and Edwin, 168–70, 178, 179
Endicott, James, 196, 206–7
England, Robert, 4, 7, 23, 42–5
ethnic organizations, 67
Evans, Jean-Paul, 105, 146
External Affairs: and anglophilia, 148–9;
    documents of, 141–2, 166; and Gouzenko,
    152; and White, 165
'Eye of Canada, The', 49–54, 75–6

Fall of a Titan, The, 158–61, 180, 232
Fauconnier, Gilles, 197–8
Fauteux, Gerard, 198–200
Federal Bureau of Investigation (FBI), 148; and
    Gouzenko, 99, 165; and Robeson, 187, 188,
    205, 210, 214, 216, 226; and White, 96–7,
    126–32
Ferron, Jacques, 133
film: distribution, 50–1, 67–8, 70–1;
    documentary, 50, 53; *see also* National Film
    Board
Financial Post, 63, 65

Ford, R.A.D., 208
Foresee, Reid, 187
'forgetting' and national culture, 88–90
Fortier, Laval, 212
Foster, Ralph, 66, 67
Foucault, Michel, 228
Foulds, Frank, 44–5
Fraser, G.J., 62
Front de Libération du Québec (FLQ), 133–4
Fuchs, Klaus, 106, 135, 166, 168
Fulford, Robert, 100, 136
Fussell, Paul, 205
Fyfe, David Maxwell, 206

Gaffield, Chad, 162
Gardner, Raymond Arthur, 208
Garner, Joe, 138, 140, 161, 164
Gaskell, Eric, 71, 105, 118
Gibson, E.L., 66
Gill, Eric, 196
Gilroy, Paul, 16, 218
Glazebrook, George, 204, 207, 209; and Dwyer,
    105–6, 109, 119, 129, 137–40; and
    Gouzenko, 165, 166, 167–8, 171, 172, 178; as
    historical actor, 159–61; and Philipps, 22, 28,
    29–30, 31, 33–5
Glenesk, William, 203
Globe and Mail, 66, 100, 119, 191, 196
Goss, John, 187
Gouzenko, Igor, xvi, xix–xx, 35–7, 87, 95, 98,
    99, 105, 107, 126–32, 134, 232;
    autobiography, 154–8; British intelligence
    operation, 149–54; as a 'character', 156–8;
    missing information in case, 170–1; and
    progressive movement, 141–20;
Granatstein, J.L., 82, 93, 142, 159, 164, 170, 172
Grand, Elaine, 226
Grierson, John, xv, xvi, 4, 7, 23, 27, 30, 39,
    41–2, 49–54, 59, 148, 231; and NFB, 75–8;
    and McLaren, 80; RCMP investigation of,
    63–4, 70; statist outlook of, 53
GRU (Soviet military intelligence), 139–40, 141,
    145, 154
Guattari, Félix, 228
Guernsey, Terry, 119

Haida, xii–xiii
Halifax, Lord, 12–13, 15
Halperin, Israel, 168
Halpin, James, 190
Halward, J.T., 65
Hamlet, 110–11
Harrison, Elizabeth, 137–9, 140, 148, 180
Harrison, Eric, 180
Harvison, C.W. 'Cliff', 136, 146, 200–1, 212,
    225
Heeney, Arnold, 31, 98, 101–2, 128–9, 207
Hennessy, Peter, 88
Hicks, Wessely, 192–3
Highet, Gilbert, 102, 103, 144

Hill, Samuel, 220
Hindley, Henry, 86–7, 95, 133
Hiss, Alger, 96–7
historians: and censorship, 54; and objectivity,
    159–61; and official secrecy, 92–4
Hitler, Adolf, 19
Hoare, John, 117
Hoodman-Blind, 99, 109, 110, 111–18
Hoover, J. Edgar, 97, 99, 126, 128–9, 132, 148,
    165
Hour, The, 24–30
Hughes, Elwood, 184, 194
Huxley, Michael, 22–3
Hyde, H. Montgomery, 143, 144–7, 161

Ignatieff, George, 129
immigration, 51–2
imperialism: and Hitler, 19; and Philipps, 9–15,
    17
information gathering: and consular practices,
    207; *see also* Access to Information
Innes, John, 184, 193
International Monetary Fund, 97
international relations, and secrecy, 91
International Union of Mine, Mill, and Smelter
    Workers, 181, 211
internment, wartime, 25
'Intrepid', *see* Stephenson, Sir William
Irwin, Arthur, 67, 68, 69, 70, 71–2, 81–3
Isber, P., 69–70, 71
Isham, Gyles, 102–3

Jackson, C.D., 148
Jameson, Fredric, xviii
Janowski, Trudy, 138
'Janus', *see* Dwyer, Peter
Japanese Canadians, resettlement of, 7–8
Jarvis, Alan, 101, 132
Jenner, William E., 97–8, 163
Johnson, Manning, 210
Jones, Norman O., 186, 225

Kash, Eugene, 68–9
Kashmeri, Zuhair, 93
Kattan, Naim, 86, 110, 124, 132
'Kaye', *see* Kysilewsky
Kealey, George, 96
Kellock-Taschereau Commission, 128, 154,
    163–4, 176, 198–201
Kelly, William H., 126
King, Al, 216–17
King, Mackenzie, 144, 146, 153–4, 157, 169,
    171, 179; diaries of, 172–5
Kirkconnell, Watson, 34, 35, 51, 177;
    Humanities in Canada report, 24
Kolessa, Lubka, 3–4
Korntoff, J.H., 66–7, 69
Kysilewsky, Vladimir, 3, 4, 26–7, 28, 31, 33,
    43, 45

labour organizations, 67–8
Labour Progressive Party, 65, 66, 72, 122, 188, 202
LaFlèche, Léo R., 3, 27, 29, 33, 44
Lalonde, Marc, 134
Lamb, W. Kaye, 120, 173–4
Lambart, Evelyn, 83–4, 85
Lapointe, Ernest, 8
Larivière, O., 61, 66, 70
Lasky, Victor, 98–9, 129
Laval University, 190
Lawrence, T.E., 14, 17
Left, Canadian: and Gouzenko, 141–2
Legg, Stuart, 52, 63
Leopold, John, 38–9, 47–8, 62, 63, 65, 177–8, 195, 196, 212
liberties, civil: and secrecy, 92
Littleton, James, 85, 141
Love Your Neighbours, see Neighbours

McCann, James J., 60, 61
McCarthy, Joseph, 97
McClellan, George B., 56, 57–8, 60, 69, 70, 72–3, 85, 185, 204
McClung, Mark, 56–9, 71–2, 75, 84–5, 86–7, 89, 105, 133, 136, 163, 201
McCombe, J.D., 71
McConnell, J.W., 170
Macdonald, Grant, 138
MacDonald, Malcolm, 22, 146, 155, 161, 164–5
McDonell, D.N., 211–12
McEwen, Tom, 223
McInnes, Helen, 102, 103
MacKay, R.A., 129
McKechnie, Leslie, 157
MacKenzie, C.J., 108, 109
Mackenzie King Record, 172
Mackenzie-Papineau Battalion, 191
McLaren, D.E., 61, 63–73, 76
McLaren, Norman, xvi, 49, 53–4, 56, 59, 66, 69, 75–8, 84, 231; and Ekman, 82–4; and Grierson, 80
McLean, Ross, 60, 63, 64, 65, 66, 67, 82, 226
MacMillan, Sir Ernest, 182
MacNeil, R.A.S., 62, 65, 67, 68, 71
McRuer, James C., 163
Man Called Intrepid, A, 143–4
Man Who Knew, The, 10–12, 14, 15, 39–40, 231
Manning, Preston, 177
Marcuse, Gary, 182
Marston, William N., 228
Maschwitz, Eric, 103
Massey Royal Commission on the Arts, Letters and Sciences, 87–8, 95, 96, 120
Massey, Vincent, 116, 124, 148–9
Maynard, Léon, 44
Mead, F.J., 37–9
Meinertzhagen, Richard, 14–15, 43, 47
Menzies, Sir Stewart, 146, 150–1, 152, 154, 163, 173, 178; see also 'C'

MI6, 104–6; see also British Intelligence Service
Mickleburgh, Bruce, 224
Minifie, James, 97–8
minorities, ethnic: and Tracy Philipps, 4
Montebello, Chateau, 162–3
Montreal Gazette, 68–9
Moodie, Campbell, 148
Moore, Mavor, 96, 149
Morris, Peter, 76
Morris, Robert, 129, 163
multiculturalism, 89; origins of, xv, 6, 7–8; 'multicultural neutrality', 93; and state security, 4
Mundell, David, 163
Murphy, Harvey, 211–14, 216–17, 223, 224
music: in Neighbours, 80; and Robeson, 218–19

Narodna Wolya, 33
National Archives, xiv–xv, 92, 141; civic memory, 94; and national culture, 89; Review Unit, 92
National Arts Centre, 96, 111; and national culture, 89; records of, 92
National Defence records, 92
National Film Board, xv–xvi, 21; allegations of homosexuality in, 71; and ethnic organizations, 67; and Gouzenko, 141; and immigration, 51–2; and King diaries, 173, 174; and national culture, 75–6, 89; and 'norm enforcement', 81–4; purge of, 59–85; and RCMP, 49–85; see also film; Neighbours
National Film Society, 50
National Library, xiv–xv; and national culture, 89
nationalism, xix; cultural, 182–4, 229; and 'forgetting', 88; and nationality, 183, 199, 216
Nationalities Branch, 2, 3, 6–10, 30–1, 33, 42–5
nationality, xviii–xix; and nationalism, 183, 199, 216; and Communism, 201
Neighbours, 54, 59, 72–3, 77–80, 82, 231; and 'imitative violence', 79–80; 'neighbours' metaphor, 55–6; palindromic reading, 77–8; pixillation in, 78–9
Nicholson, L.H. 'Nick', 165, 195
NKVD (Soviet political intelligence directorate), 154
'norm enforcement', 81–4
Norman, Herbert, 123
Nunn May, Alan, 105, 145, 155, 161
'Nunnery' (CBNRC), 108, 109–10

O'Brien, A.W. 'Andy', 155
October Crisis (1970), 133
Oldfield, Maurice, 123
Oliver, Mary, 32, 108
Orders-in-Council, 91–2
Ottawa: as 'Cloud-Cuckoo-Town', 3–6; Little Theatre, 112, 116
Ottawa Citizen, 66, 67, 69, 70, 116
Ottawa Journal, 63–4, 73, 99, 126, 128, 191, 193; and Gouzenko, 145, 147, 153

Pacific Tribune, 214, 223
Pal, Leslie, 4–6
passports, 204–11
Pavlov, Vitali, 145, 152, 163, 164–5
Payne, Chester, 3, 4
Peace Arch: Park, 181, 214–5; cache within, 220–1; concert, 182, 211–24
Pearson, Drew, 145, 175
Pearson, Lester, 98–9, 126, 130, 131, 146, 147, 157, 165, 166, 207, 208, 209
Pelletier, Monsignor, 190
Peoples of Canada, 21, 51–3
Petegorsky, David, 41
Peterborough Examiner, 193
Petrov, Vladimir and Evdokia, 157–8
Petrowska, Yvanna, 175–8, 179, 232
Petrowsky, Michael, 36–7, 48, 175–8, 179
Philby, Kim, 100, 105, 106, 134–5, 142–3
Philipps, Tracy, xv, 1–48, 139, 147, 231
Phylon, 18–19, 41–2; Conference, 18, 20
Pickersgill, Jack, 81–2, 112, 121, 137–8, 140, 166, 203; and King diaries, 172–5
Pincher, Chapman, 105
Pitfield, Michael, 132–3, 172
'postnational belonging', 93
'presuppositional float', 197–8
privacy: personal, 90; Cabinet, 90–1
Privy Council Office (PCO), 105; and Dwyer, 106–9, 118–24
progressivism: and Gouzenko, 141–2, 157; as 'presuppositional float', 197–8, 200
propaganda: Canadian, during World War II, 148; and disinformation, 156; and Gouzenko, 154–61; and Grierson, 75; and Kirkconnell, 24–5; and minorities, 20–4; and *Peoples of Canada*, 53
Public Information Commissioner, 94

race, 11–13, 15–20, 218, 220
Rae, Saul, 28
Ralph, Jack, 61, 67, 82
records, primary: and Gouzenko, 161–71
Reid, Escott, 121, 195–6, 206–7, 208
Renan, Ernest, 86, 88
Reuther, Walter, 125
right to know, 90–3
Ritchie, Charles, 120
Rivett-Carnac, Charles, 146, 161, 171, 224–5
Robertson, Norman: and Dwyer, 105, 106, 118, 129; and Gouzenko, 137–40, 145, 146, 147–8, 149, 159, 165–6, 171–4, 200; and Philipps, 4, 7, 9, 21, 27, 30, 31, 33, 43–4
Robertson, R. Gordon, 90–3, 121
Robeson, Paul, xx, 181–227, 232; criticism of British Empire, 188–9; and Communist party, 202–4; at Peekskill, NY, 210; Peace Arch Concert, 211–24; in Quebec, 188–92; speech ban, 184–5, 192–6
Robeson, Paul, Jr, 202, 225
Robinson, Judith, 126–7

Roe, Sydney, 33, 34
Rose, Fred, 140, 202–3
Ross, Malcolm, 27, 29, 30, 229–30
Ross, Mary Lowery, 195
Rosser, Fred T., 106, 107
Roy, Louis-Philippe, 189
Royal Canadian Mounted Police (RCMP), xiv–xv, xvi; and Canada Council, 126; and consular practices, 207–8; and counter-intelligence, 139; and Gouzenko, 144, 145; and King diaries, 173; and FBI, 209–10; and Mine-Mill union, 213–14; and NFB, 49–85; and Petroswky, 177; and Philipps, 4, 20, 36–9; and Robeson, 185–8, 190, 192, 195–6, 202, 211–14, 216, 220, 224, 226; and rumours, 2; and telephone censorship, 139; and White, 165
Rumour Summary, 1–2
Russian-language programs, 120

St Laurent, Louis, 65, 71, 98, 118, 126, 166, 195, 212
Saturday Night, 116
Sawatsky, John, 152, 155, 159
Scellen, Janet, 78–9
secrecy, 88–94, 132; and effective government, 90–1; and international relations, 91; and Orders-in-Council, 91–2; and sovereignty, 91
security: and borders, 226; and citizenship, 84–5; and civil liberties, 92; and cultural administration, 95–136; and culture, 86–7, 89, 228–9, 232; after 11 September 2001, 230–1; and Gouzenko, 141–2; national, 90–1, 132; polarization of, 89; 'scare' at NFB, 59–85
Security Panel, 141
Sedgewick, Eve, 78
Shakespeare, Ken, 65
Ship, Reuben, 226
Silcox, David, 86
Simpson, George W., 6, 7, 30–1, 37
Sinclair, John, 129
Smith, Arnold, 86, 128, 130, 163, 165
Smith, David A., 81, 85
Solomon, Starr, 86
'soundings', 124–6
Southam, G. Hamilton, 96, 111, 225
Soviet: friendship with Canada, 141, 150; intelligence gathering, 139; military intelligence (GRU), 139–40, 141, 145; studies, 120
Sparling, Gordon, 51–2
Spencer, Herbert, xiv
Spencer, Michael, 73, 81–2
Spice, Evelyn, 51–2
Spry, Graham, 101–2
Stafford, David, 88, 150
Stalin, Joseph, 150, 151, 155, 158–9, 161; and Robeson, 202
Star Weekly, 162
Starnes, Courtland, xiv
Starnes, John, 86

Stephens, James 166–8
Stephenson, Sir William, 105, 130, 142–8, 150, 159, 161, 165, 173, 174, 178
Stevenson, William, 143–4, 156
Stewart, Allistair, 69
Stokes, Anson Phelps, 18
Stone, T.A., 'Tommy', 22, 137, 145, 159, 171, 208–9; and Gouzenko, 146, 148–9
Strapp, Everet J., 212–3
Stuckey, Sterling, 219
Sullivan, William, 210

Taylor, Bill, 86
Thompson, E.P., 92
Thompson, Sir Basil, 220–1
Thomson, J.S., 23, 24
tolerance, 52
Toronto Star, 63–4, 186, 192, 194
Toronto Telegram, 193, 196
Toronto: Police Commission, 184, 192–4; and speech ban on Robeson, 184–5, 192–6
Tovel, Freeman, 133
'Tracey, Phillip', 10–11, 231
Trudeau, Pierre Elliot, 208
Trueman, Albert, 120, 123
Truman, Harry, 96–7, 153
truth, historical, 6–10
Tuan, Yi-Fu, xii
Turack, Daniel, 210

Ukrainian: Canadian Committee, 9, 29, 33–4; Canadians, 8–9, and censorship, 21; and Philipps, 26–7, 30; 'Question', 29
United Nations Resettlement and Rehabilitation Administration, 43–4, 45

Vincent, David, 101
violence, imitative, 79–80
Virilio, Paul, 147
Vlastos, Gregory, 187

Walker, Arthur, 192
Wall, Don, 86, 87, 89, 104, 111, 136
War Services, Department of, 2, 3
Wark, Wesley, 96, 154
Wartime Information Board, 4, 174
Watson, Patrick, 86, 87
Webster, F.A.M., 10–11, 14, 16, 39–40
Whitaker, Reg, 89, 182, 222–3
White, Harry Dexter, 96–99, 126–7, 129–32, 165–6
Whitson, Lish, 128, 129, 168, 171
Whitton, Charlotte, 111–12
Wicks, Ben, 134–5
Wilgress, Dana, 208
Williams, Raymond, xi, 226
Willsher, Kathleen 'Kay', 140, 164, 198–200
Winters, Robert, 65, 82
women: as censors, 32
Wonnacotte, R.W., 65
Wood, Edward, 12–13
Wood, S.T., 15, 20, 36, 60, 61, 139, 165, 187, 196
Wrong, Hume, 44

Yuill, L.S., 139

Zabotin, Nikolai, 139–40, 155

THE CANADIAN SOCIAL HISTORY SERIES

Terry Copp,
The Anatomy of Poverty:
The Condition of the Working Class
in Montreal, 1897–1929, 1974.
ISBN 0–7710–2252–2

Alison Prentice,
The School Promoters:
Education and Social Class in
Mid-Nineteenth Century
Upper Canada, 1977.
ISBN 0–7710–7181–7

John Herd Thompson,
The Harvests of War:
The Prairie West, 1914–1918, 1978.
ISBN 0–19–541402–0

Joy Parr, Editor,
Childhood and Family in Canadian History, 1982.
ISBN 0–7710–6938–3

Alison Prentice and
Susan Mann Trofimenkoff, Editors,
The Neglected Majority:
Essays in Canadian Women's History, Volume 2,
1985.
ISBN 0–7710–8583–4

Ruth Roach Pierson,
'They're Still Women After All':
The Second World War and
Canadian Womanhood, 1986.
ISBN 0–7710–6958–8

Bryan D. Palmer, Editor
The Character of Class Struggle:
Essays in Canadian Working-Class History,
1850–1985, 1986.
ISBN 0–7710–6946–4

Alan Metcalfe,
Canada Learns to Play:
The Emergence of Organized Sport, 1807–1914,
1987.
ISBN 0–19–541304–0

Marta Danylewycz,
Taking the Veil:
An Alternative to Marriage, Motherhood, and
Spinsterhood in
Quebec, 1840–1920, 1987.
ISBN 0–19–541472–1

Craig Heron,
Working in Steel: The Early Years in Canada,
1883–1935, 1988.
ISBN 0–7710–4086–5

Wendy Mitchinson and
Janice Dickin McGinnis, Editors,
Essays in the History of
Canadian Medicine, 1988.
ISBN 0–7710–6063–7

Joan Sangster,
Dreams of Equality: Women on the Canadian
Left, 1920–1950, 1989.
ISBN 0–7710–7946–X

Angus McLaren,
Our Own Master Race: Eugenics in Canada,
1885–1945, 1990.
ISBN 0–19–541365–2

Bruno Ramirez,
On the Move:
French-Canadian and Italian Migrants in the
North Atlantic Economy, 1860–1914, 1991.
ISBN 0–19–541419–5

Mariana Valverde,
The Age of Light, Soap, and Water:
Moral Reform in English Canada, 1885–1925,
1991.
ISBN 0–7710–8689–X

Bettina Bradbury,
Working Families:
Age, Gender, and Daily Survival in
Industrializing Montreal, 1993.
ISBN 0–19–541211–7

Andrée Lévesque,
Making and Breaking the Rules:
Women in Quebec, 1919–1939, 1994.
ISBN 0–7710–5283–9

Cecilia Danysk,
Hired Hands: Labour and the Development of
Prairie Agriculture, 1880–1930, 1995.
ISBN 0–7710–2552–1

Kathryn McPherson,
Bedside Matters: The Transformation
of Canadian Nursing, 1900–1990, 1996.
ISBN 0–19–541219–2

Edith Burley,
Servants of the Honourable Company: Work,
Discipline, and Conflict in the Hudson's Bay
Company, 1770–1870, 1997.
ISBN 0–19–541296–6

Mercedes Steedman,
Angels of the Workplace: Women and the
Construction of Gender Relations in the
Canadian Clothing Industry, 1890–1940, 1997.
ISBN 0–19–541308–3

Angus McLaren and
Arlene Tigar McLaren,
The Bedroom and the State: The Changing
Practices and Politics of Contraception and
Abortion in Canada, 1880–1997, 1997.
ISBN 0–19–541318–0

Kathryn McPherson, Cecilia Morgan, and
Nancy M. Forestell, Editors,
Gendered Pasts: Historical Essays in Femininity
and Masculinity in Canada, 1999.
ISBN 0–19–541449–7

Gillian Creese,
Contracting Masculinity: Gender, Class, and
Race in a White-Collar Union, 1944–1994, 1999.
ISBN 0–19–541454–3

Geoffrey Reaume,
Remembrance of Patients Past: Patient Life at
the Toronto Hospital for the Insane, 1870–1940,
2000.
ISBN 0–19–541538–8

Miriam Wright,
A Fishery for Modern Times: The State and the
Industrialization of the Newfoundland Fishery,
1934–1968, 2001.
ISBN 0–19–541620–1

Judy Fudge and Eric Tucker,
Labour Before the Law: The Regulation of
Workers' Collective Action in Canada,
1900–1948, 2001.
ISBN 0–19–541633–3

Mark Moss,
Manliness and Militarism: Educating Young
Boys in Ontario for War, 2001.
ISBN 0–19–541594–9

Joan Sangster,
Regulating Girls and Women: Sexuality, Family,
and the Law in Ontario 1920–1960, 2001.
ISBN 0–19–541663–5

Reinhold Kramer and Tom Mitchell,
Walk Towards the Gallows: The Tragedy of
Hilda Blake, Hanged 1899, 2002.
ISBN 0–19–541686–4

Mark Kristmanson,
Plateaus of Freedom: Nationality, Culture, and
State Security in Canada, 1940–1960, 2002.
ISBN 0–19–541866–2